Economics of Professional Sports

Brad R. HUMPHREYS
West Virginia University, Department of Economics

BRH Publishing, Morgantown WV
2015

ISBN: 978-0615909356

Contents

Foreward

I started writing this textbook when I was on the faculty at the University of Alberta, where I taught an undergraduate class on the economics of professional sports for many years. After using other textbooks, I couldn't seem to find one that included all the topics I was interested in covering. I developed so much supplemental material that I ultimately decided to bite the bullet and put together my own book. I have been a working sports economist since about 2000, and have taught sports economics at the undergraduate and graduate level for years. This book contains what I think are the important elements of sports economics presented at the advanced undergraduate level. The book contains no fancy pictures or "boxed" material. I hope you, the reader, will forgive me for the lack of color graphics and pictures, and engaging stories about sports economists of yore like Gerry Scully or characters from the sports industry like Bill Veeck.

This book reflects the areas of sports economics I find interesting, with a focus on professional sports in North America and Europe, in keeping with the title of my undergraduate economics courses at West Virginia University and the University of Alberta "The Economics of Professional Sports." I do not address several important topics in sports economics like the economics of intercollegiate athletics and labor relations. The book is intended as a one semester third or fourth year undergraduate course in sports economics, and I simply cannot cover all of sports economics in a single semester.

This book is intended for an audience of upper level undergraduates who have had principles of microeconomics and a basic statistics class. It is a work in progress, and comments from readers are always welcome.

I want to thank my former colleagues in the Department of Economics at the University of Alberta, and my current colleagues at West Virginia University, who tolerated and supported a colleague who spent his time and effort working in an area considered by many to fall well outside the mainstream of economic research. I thank in particular those who I have managed to drag into my ongoing research agenda in the economics of sport: Jane Ruseski, Haifang Huang, Henry van Egteren, Adam Nowak, and especially Li Zhou. I am especially indebted to Rachidi Kotchoni who read the entire text in Fall 2011 and provided me with an extensive set of comments and suggestions for improving the book and to Brian Soebbing who used the book at LSU in the Summer of 2013 and provided me with valuable comments.

Morgantown, West Virginia
Spring 2015

Part I

Introduction: Sports and Economics

Chapter 1

An Economic Approach to Sport

Chapter Objectives

- Explain how economists work

- Understand the role models play in economics

- Understand why the professional sports industry is a unique and interesting setting for learning about the interaction between economic models and economic evidence

1.1   Introduction

Economics is the study of human decisions about scarcity. All economic agents, consumers, firms, the government, non-governmental agencies, and others, face fundamental decisions about how to allocate scarce things to meet unlimited wants. Scarcity exists in the professional sports industry. A limited number of elite athletes exist at any time; sustained success at the highest level, in the form of "dynasties" in professional sports league occur very infrequently; teams face capacity constraints in the number of tickets they can sell to games; leagues play a limited number of games during the regular and post-season; sports fans have limited income and time to spend on following professional sport. Economists study decisions about scarcity using models. Models are both tools and compact, concise messages communicating complicated ideas about human behavior. This book focuses on economic models applied to specific conditions in the professional sports industry, and the interaction between economic models and empirical evidence about economic outcomes and decisions. The general approach taken here is to emphasize the interplay between economic models, institutional characteristics of the markets in the professional sports industry, and empirical evidence about economic outcomes in these markets.

1.2   Models and Markets

Economists use models to organize their thoughts about how agents make economic decisions. Economic models are generally composed of equations - mathematical expressions that show the relationships between the important economic variables in each situation being studied. Sometimes, economic models are represented by graphs that summarize key features of economic models. By developing formal models, economists clearly spell out how they think the world works by explicitly writing down their assumptions, clearly defining the relationship between different key elements, and generating predictions that can be compared to real-world outcomes and possibly provide explanations for why some outcomes occur. Economic models are stylized representations of the behavior of the important economic agents in markets and capture relevant aspects of behavior.

Economic model building is as much art as science. A useful economic model strikes a balance between accurately reflecting real world economic behavior and generating predictions. A useful economic model does not explain every decision made by an agent, but instead explains the important decisions and abstracts from the unimportant ones. A useful economic model captures the essence of the behavior of economic agents, generates predictions that match the decisions made by these agents, and omits unrelated or unimportant factors. A useful economic model is a powerful tool for understanding economic behavior that allows the user of the model to gain insight into observed outcomes in the economy. For these reasons, the text emphasizes the role of economic models and their use as tools for understanding economic thinking.

Economic theory tells us that most economic activity takes place in markets. A market does not have to be a physical location, but it can be; a market can also operate in a medium like the internet. A market contains three key components: sellers, buyers, and a well-defined good or service being bought and sold. The buyers and sellers are economic agents - individuals, organizations like firms or sports teams - who either have some particular good or service to sell or want to buy some of that good or service. Markets match sellers and buyers who agree on a price for a specific quantity of the good or service being exchanged. Markets allocate goods and services, and the allocation mechanism is the mutually agreeable price set in the market.

People participate in markets all the time. Consider, for example, the purchase of a cup of coffee. A buyer (or consumer) wants to purchase a specific quantity of a good - in this case a cup of coffee. This cup of coffee could be purchased from many different sellers - coffee shops, restaurants, convenience stores, vending machines, etc. - at various prices. Note that all three elements are present in this market: a buyer, sellers, and a well-defined good. Buyers will take into account the location of the seller, the perceived quality of the coffee, and most importantly the price of the cup of coffee when deciding to make a purchase. The sellers will decide on the amount of coffee sold at various prices based on things like cost and other factors. The outcomes of the interaction between coffee buyers and coffee sellers is a price for a cup of coffee in this market and some specific number of cups of coffee bought and sold.

Markets determine the price of many goods and services in an economy. One such service is labor. Economists define labor as the service provided to firms by workers. The price of labor (called a wage or a salary) is determined in labor markets. This wage determines who will work and for how long - wages allocate labor services in the economy. Individual workers supply (or sell) labor in labor markets; firms demand (or buy) labor in labor markets. The labor services bought and sold in labor markets are composed of a temporal element – so many hours, days, or weeks of time working – and in some cases a quality element as well. For example, Major League Baseball (MLB) teams hire workers (purchase labor services) in the labor market for a season, but not all workers have the characteristics that MLB teams desire. Few people can throw a baseball 90 miles per hour, hit a slider, or cover center field; baseball teams want to hire only individuals who can provide these specialized skills.

1.3 Economic Models and Economic Evidence

Economic theorists develop and solve models; empiricists use models to guide their research, informing data collection and development and key decisions about issues like model specification. Since economics is primarily a non-experimental field, we cannot often rely on carefully designed experiments with random assignment to sort out the difference between correlation and causality. Instead, economic models provide a description of causal relationships.

A useful economic model evolves. Careful and compelling empirical research can either confirm or refute the predictions made by economic models, and sometimes shed light on the veracity of the assumptions made by economic models to generate these predictions. A good economic theorist is an informed consumer of empirical research, understanding the nuances of economic data and the pitfalls inherent in empirical research. A good empirical researcher is an informed consumer of economic theory, using economic models as a guidebook to provide important information about where to look for interesting economic decisions and how to go about identifying and collecting the right data to test theoretical predictions.

The professional sport industry is a particularly rich source of information about economic outcomes. Inputs and outcomes can be readily measured, and with more precision, in the sports industry compared to many other settings. For example, the effort and output of specific employees can be observed and measured in sport. Important evidence about how individuals respond to incentives, and about how workers' compensation varies with productivity has been generated using data from professional sport. Bets on sporting events like horse races and football games can be viewed as simple financial instruments with clear payoffs at specific points in time. Important evidence about the informational efficiency of markets has been generated using data on sports betting.

Because of these unique characteristics, the professional sports industry is an excellent setting for examining the interaction between economic models and economic evidence. The institutional characteristics and outcomes in the professional sports industry are unusually clear and familiar, compared to, for example, the insurance industry. A number of economic theories in diverse fields like industrial organization, labor economics, consumer choice, and agency theory apply directly to key aspects of the professional sports industry. Throughout this book, I emphasize the fruitful interaction that takes place between economic models and economic evidence in the setting of the professional sports industry.

Chapter 2

The Sports Industry

Chapter Objectives

- Discuss the difficulties associated with defining sport in economic terms

- Understand the dimensions of the sports market in North America

- Understand how professional teams earn revenues

- Understand professional team's costs

- Describe the functioning of advertising and the market for sports programming rights

- Understand why market power lies with the leagues in these markets

- Explain why advertising rights can be large but variable across teams and leagues

- Understand how rising ad revenues increases compensation to athletes but can negatively affect fan's perceptions

- Understand basic facts about professional sports teams and leagues in North America and Europe

2.1 Introduction

Sport is a complex activity encompassing events like the Olympic games and informal pick-up hockey games in recreational rinks; a recreational skier, a skier competing in the Downhill at the Vancouver Olympics – a competition with elite participants – and people watching the Olympic Games on television all participate in sport in some way. Academic research on sports can be found in many disciplines, spanning the humanities, social sciences, laboratory sciences, law and business. What is sport, and how can sport be defined, from an economic perspective?

Relatively little attention has been paid to defining sport in economic terms or to estimating the value of economic activity in the sports market, perhaps because of difficulties formulating an economic definition of sport. A thorough accounting of the dimensions of the sports industry is an important undertaking for several reasons. First, an estimate of the dimensions of the sports industry provides general context for the academic study of sport in economics and finance. Second, the sport industry receives significant subsides from federal, provincial, and local governments. These subsidies take many forms, including facility construction and operation, training for elite athletes, promotion of participation in sport for health benefits, among others. Any full cost-benefit analysis of sports subsidies should take into account the relative importance of the sport industry in the economy. Finally, unlike other industries, the sport industry has a cultural significance extending well beyond its economic boundaries. An economic definition sport and the sport industry must begin with a discussion of economic dimensions of the industry.

How can we define sport? Several definitions have been proposed. Sociologist Jay Coakley (2003) characterized sports as activities involving gross motor skills, competition, and an organized set of rules. Economist Rodney Fort (2006) qualifies Coakley's competition criteria to include only competition based on objective scoring and further restricts sports to activities only using simple devices, like bats and balls, or no devices at all. These definitions, and others, like the criteria that some participants must receive a financial reward for success, suffer from the limitation that many sport-like activities exist. For example, hot dog eating and bass fishing would both appear to qualify as a sport under both these definitions.

One key issue in defining sport involves identifying criteria that separate sport from games of skill like chess or poker and from recreational activities like dancing, hiking, fishing, and gardening. A secondary issue involves identifying criteria that appropriately define competition in a way to distinguish sport from exercise. For example, running has a competitive dimension but jogging does not. Weightlifting is an Olympic sport, bodybuilding is a professional sport, and competitions based on athlete's performance on fitness equipment like stationary rowing machines, elliptical trainers and stationary bicycles exist, blurring the already murky distinction between exercise and sport.

Defining sport in a way that allows estimation of the value of economic activity in the sports industry in a straightforward manner is very difficult. One must proceed by making arbitrary, but defensible decisions about which activities constitute sport, exercise, recreation, and games of skill.

2.2 An Economic Definition Sport

In economic terms, sporting events are entertainment goods that are produced by teams, leagues, and other sports organizations and purchased by households and businesses. A number of working definitions of sport exist in the literature. The most comprehensive was proposed by Borland and Macdonald (2003), who define the product produced by sports teams as games or contests between two teams and the product produced by leagues as the annual regular season and post season competitions for the league championship. This definition leads to two types of demand for sport: direct demand based on live attendance at sporting events and derived demand based on mediated viewing of sports and the purchase of related goods like merchandise bearing team names or logos.

Given this definition, four different factors affecting demand for sporting events can be identified: consumer preferences, economic factors, quality of viewing, and the nature of the contest or event. Consumer preferences affect demand for all goods and services in a fundamental way. Consumer preferences for sporting events, however, are in many ways more complex than preferences for other goods or services, because, unlike preferences about consumer necessities like housing or food, consumers' preferences for sporting events depend on phenomena like habit formation, when the marginal utility of current consumption depends on past consumption, conspicuous consumption, defined as consumption engaged in to display income, and bandwagon effects, which take place when individuals consume a good simply because they observe others consuming that good, may alter preferences over time. The economic factors affecting demand for sport are similar to those affecting demand for other goods and services. The price of attending or watching a sporting event, the price of substitute activities, the opportunity cost of time, income, and macroeconomic factors like the unemployment rate all affect direct and indirect demand for sporting events in much the same way that they affect demand for television sets or mp3 files. The quality of viewing sports depends on environmental factors like weather, temporal factors like the day and time of the sporting event, as well as the facility and the amenities at the facility (sight lines, concession stands, scoreboards, etc.). The nature of the contest or event depends on the relative quality of the two teams involved and uncertainty about the outcome of the event as perceived by buyers. Generally, contests with greater uncertainty of outcome will generate greater direct and induced demand than contests with a lesser degree of uncertainty of outcome, at both the match and season level.

Many of the factors that affect direct and induced demand for sporting events will not be affected much by macroeconomic and financial conditions in the economy. For example, the relative quality of teams, environmental factors like the weather, and temporal factors related to day and time of games played should all be relatively insensitive to the economic and financial climate in the general economy. In addition, uncertainty about the outcome of games or seasons, identified as an important component of direct and induced demand for sporting events, should be entirely unaffected by general economic and financial conditions in the economy. Much of the core of the sports product, and many of the factors that affect direct and induced demand for sports events, should lie outside the influence of the business cycle and any turmoil in financial markets.

However, macroeconomic and financial conditions can significantly affected consumers' employment and income, and businesses' revenues. Both consumers and businesses purchase tickets to sporting events, and consumers watch sporting events on television, generating important revenue streams for professional sports teams. Thus the macroeconomic and financial environment may have a significant impact on the revenues earned by professional sports teams. The next section describes the institutional characteristics of the professional sports industry in North America to explain how the financial condition of teams depend on revenues from consumers and businesses.

In addition to defining the product, an economic analysis of sport also requires defining the scope of the sport market in economic terms. Gratton (1998) discussed a general method for identifying the economic dimensions of the sports industry from national income and product accounts, and points out that economic interest in sport extends well beyond the boundaries of professional sports. While a national income and product accounting approach has some appeal, because of the well-developed methodology and the existence of rich set of frequently updated national income and product accounts for many developed economies, it also has a number of weaknesses. First, on the national product side, we are at the mercy of the existing production classification system. As a prime example, consider that the North American Industrial Classification System (NAICS) does not identify the sports industry as a separate entity in that taxonomy. The sports industry makes up only a fraction of the activity in any existing industry classification, leading to difficulty identifying the sports industry in national income and product accounts and over estimates of the size of the sports industry from this data source. Second, on the national income side, the published spending data are not detailed enough to identify the size of consumer spending on sports, no matter how broadly defined. Third, in North America all levels of government are involved in the provision of sports facilities and other important activities on the supply side of the sports market, and national income and product accounts do not contain detailed estimates of government spending. Fourth, much of the activity in the sports market involves non-traded goods and labor inputs not valued at market prices. For example, the labor inputs provided by intercollegiate athletes are not valued at market prices. Fifth, sports markets feature both significant consumer surplus and non-market consumption benefits that are not reflected in national income and product accounts.

Given these problems, an alternative is to draw on data from a wide number of sources and use these data to develop estimates of the economic value of sports from different perspectives. The sports market can be defined based on three primary components:

1. Activities involving participation in sport

2. Activities involving attendance at spectator sporting events

3. Activities involving following spectator sporting events through some media.

While some sport-related activities are not included in this list, all three items can be thought of as part of sport and are also easily defined and measured. Each component contains elements that could be defined as recreation, exercise, or games of skill. For example, including participation in sports means that some activities that could be defined as exercise, like aerobics or walking, will be included. Including spectator sports means that auto racing, figure skating, and other such activities fall into this definition of the sports industry. The most difficult choice we face is the inclusion or exclusion of activities like hunting, fishing, kayaking, horseback riding, sailing, and hiking. These popular activities attract many participants, and require both considerable time and expensive equipment. Many are recognized Olympic sports. However, we exclude these activities from our definition of the sports market because we believe that they fall under recreation, not sports.

2.3   Participation in the Sport Market

Individuals can participate in the sport market in three ways: by participating in some type of physical activity, by attending a sporting event, or by watching or listening to a sporting event on television, radio, or the internet. Each generates direct and indirect economic activity. Participating in sport requires equipment, fees, and potentially travel, all of which generate economic activity. Attending a sporting event involves purchasing tickets, travel and perhaps other purchases like food and souvenirs. Watching or listening to sporting events requires equipment, in the form of televisions, radios or computers, as well as subscriptions to broadcast services. Since all of these economic activities increase with the number of participants, documenting the number of participants is an important indicator of the size of the sports market.

More importantly, individuals' participation in the sports market generates significant economic benefits beyond direct and indirect economic activity. Individuals derive satisfaction, or utility, from participation in the sports market, which has economic value. In the jargon of economics, individuals' participation in the sports market produces consumption benefits. These consumption benefits are not bought and sold like tickets, but they are important when assessing the overall size of the sports market. Although placing a dollar value on sport related consumption benefits is beyond the scope of this chapter, it is safe to say that the value of these consumption benefits rises with the number of participants in the sports market.

2.3.1   Active Participation in Sport and Physical Activity

From an economic perspective, participating in sport or physical activity is a time allocation decision resembling the decision to participate in other leisure time activities like watching a movie or reading a book. Since time is scarce, individuals must trade off participation in sport or physical activity with time spent working, traveling to work, sleeping, engaging in household production like coking and cleaning, and other leisure time activities. In addition to this temporal dimension, participating in sport or exercise involves direct costs for equipment and fees, and also indirect costs, in terms of hours that could have been spent working and earning income. Unlike other leisure time activities, participation in sport or exercise provides health benefits for the participant, which may accrue over the life cycle and can affect other factors like productivity in work and reduce health care costs. The decision to participate in sport or physical activity can be motivated by a standard consumer choice model of the labor-leisure tradeoff. The time spent participating in sport or physical activity will depend on the usual economic factors: own price, the price of substitute activities, income, preferences, and the opportunity cost of time, typically proxied by the hourly wage. Research on the economic determinants of participation in sport and exercise suggest that participation increases with household income and declines with age and the opportunity cost of time. Although many people report participating in sport and physical activity, the frequency and intensity of participation appears to be low; most people participate in sport and exercise irregularly for less than 30 minutes per spell of activity. This lack of participation in sport and exercise has been linked to health problems like obesity and the incidence of chronic health conditions like diabetes and high blood pressure, making an understanding of the economic factors that affect participation in sport and exercise an important economic policy issue.

There are a number of sources of data on participation in sport and physical activity in the United States and Canada. The National Sporting Goods Association (NSGA) periodically produces estimates of the number of participants in sport in the United States. The NSGA participation estimates are based on a mail survey sent to about 300,000 households. Table 2.1 shows NSGA's estimates of the reported number of participants for a selected group of sports in the United States for the most recent year available, 2011.

Walking is by far the most popular sport, in terms of total participation. This is to be expected, because walking is not a costly activity. Participating in walking requires relatively little equipment, few fees, and does not have to involve much travel, since many people can walk simply by stepping outside their home or workplace. Because of the low participation costs, walking also generates relatively little economic activity. The other sports on Table 2.1 generate more economic activity per participant than walking because they require more equipment, membership fees, and travel costs.

Aggregating the number of participants reported on Table 1 points out an important limitation of these estimates as an indicator of economic activity. Table 2.1 suggests that over 500 million individuals participated in sport in 2011 Since the US population was about 311 million, the methodology that generated these estimates involves counting of some individuals multiple times. The survey question asks the respondents to list each sport participated in more than once in the past year, and to list all the sports that every member of the household over the age of seven participated in more than once during the past year.

Clearly, any individual can easily participate in both bowling and golf, so in one sense this accounting method is appropriate for assessing the dimensions of the sports market. The economic activity associated with participation in any sport also depends on the intensity of participation. For example, the participation count for golf on Table 2.1 may include a person who borrows a set of clubs and plays a single round and a person with a country club membership who plays three rounds of golf a week and takes a vacation to play golf every year. The total value of economic activity, in terms of the direct economic activity and consumption benefits generated by these two golfers differs significantly. Because of this heterogeneity in the intensity of participation and expenditure on the activity, the participation figures on Table 2.1 provides imprecise information about the dimensions of sport participation in the US.

A measure of participation in the sports market that accounts for intensity of use will help overcome this problem. The Behavioral Risk Factor Surveillance System (BRFSS) contains data on sport participation that accounts for intensity of use. The main element of the BRFSS is the Behavioral Risk Factor Surveillance (BRFS) survey, a nationally representative survey of the adult

Table 2.1: Estimated Participants in Sport in the United States, 2011

Sport or Activity	Number of Participants
Walking	97,100,000
Exercising with equipment	55,500,000
Swimming	46,000,000
Bicycling	39,100,000
Running/Jogging	38,700,000
Bowling	34,900,000
Health Club Membership	34,500,000
Weightlifting	29,100,000
Basketball	26,100,000
Golf	20,900,000
Soccer	13,900,000
Tennis	13,100,000
Baseball	12,300,000
Downhill Skiing	6,900,000
Mountain Biking	6,000,000
Ice Hockey	3,000,000
Cross Country Skiing	2,300,000

population of the United States conducted by the Centers for Disease Control and Prevention (CDC). The BRFS collects uniform state specific data on health prevention activities, including physical activity. The BRFS employs a telephone survey, meaning that individuals must live in a household with a telephone to be eligible for the survey.

The 2000 BRFS contained detailed questions about sport participation. This included questions that ask respondents to list the sport that they spent the most time participating in, given that they reported participating in any sport; unfortunately, later surveys did not include a question about participation in specific sports. The specific BRFS question was: *"What type of physical activity or exercise did you spend the most time doing during the past month?"* Individuals who answered this question are not just casual, once or twice a year, participants in sport. So the sport participants identified by this survey question probably generate significant economic activity while participating.

Since the BRFS is a nationally representative sample, the survey can generate estimates of the total number of participants in various sports. Table 2.2 shows the estimated number of participants for a group of sports from the 2000 BRFS. Many other types of physical activities, including gardening and housework, were reported as physical activities in the 2000 BRFS, but Table 2.2 contains activities that most people would consider sport, in terms of the definition of sport discussed above.

The totals on Table 2.2 reflecting frequent participants in these sports and the totals on Table 2.1 as reflecting both frequent and infrequent participants. The participation totals on Table 2.1 and 2.2 show some consistency. Walking has the most participants on both tables. About 70 million people, or 25% of the population, reported walking frequently for exercise the BRFS in 2000. About 90 million people, or 35% of the population, reported walking for exercise either frequently or infrequently in 2011. The biggest difference between these two tables is the smaller

Table 2.2: Estimated Sport Participants from BRFSS, 2000

Sport	Estimated Number of Participants		
	Lower bound	Mean	Upper Bound
Walking	68,600,000	69,301,784	70,000,000
Running/Jogging	12,500,000	12,901,119	13,300,000
Weightlifting	7,118,775	7,396,304	7,673,832
Golf	4,787,312	4,982,688	5,178,063
Bicycling	4,588,754	4,791,467	4,994,179
Aerobics	4,189,563	4,355,448	4,521,333
Basketball	3,276,901	3,461,372	3,645,844
Health Club Workout	2,375,871	2,510,246	2,644,621
Swimming	2,216,229	2,356,134	2,496,039
Calistenics	2,054,979	2,208,816	2,362,652
Bike or Rowing Machine Exercise	1,493,113	1,622,729	1,752,346
Tennis	1,072,147	1,171,802	1,271,457
Soccer	878,774	1,010,848	1,142,922
Martial Arts	570,918	649,406	727,895
Skating (Ice and Roller)	544,010	633,485	722,960
Bowling	543,637	611,725	679,813
Volleyball	456,615	531,830	607,045
Snowskiing	315,119	373,660	432,201
Raquetball	298,842	359,900	420,958
Boxing	167,959	208,423	248,887
Touch Football	133,717	179,878	226,039
Waterskiing	120,486	158,624	196,761
Squash	57,243	101,219	145,194
Surfing	57,243	101,219	145,194
Badmiton	29,427	50,090	70,752
Table Tennis	20,818	38,056	55,295
Handball	8,264	18,249	28,234
Softball	4,339	8,203	12,067
Total	118,481,056	122,094,722	125,702,581

number of frequent participants in all the sports except walking. For example, while only 2.3 million people reported swimming frequently for exercise, 46 million people reported swimming in the NSGA survey on Table 1 that includes infrequent participants. This pattern can be seen in the participation counts for all the other sports.

These participation data suggest that in any year over 50% of the US population participate in some sport or exercise regularly, and a larger number participate in sport occasionally. By either measure, individual participation in sport in the US is significant, and generates a considerable amount of economic activity.

2.3.2 Attendance at Spectator Sporting Events

Table 2.3 contains estimates of total attendance for selected sports leagues in 2010-2011. Total attendance reflects the relative popularity of a sport as well as indicating economic importance, as attendance proxies for spending on tickets, concessions, licensed merchandize and other related goods and services. Major League Baseball draws the most spectators of any North American sport, over 73 million people in 2011. An additional 41 million fans attended minor league baseball games in one of the 15 minor leagues in North America (International League 6,504,586, Pacific Coast League 6,796,157, Mexican League 3,814,348, Eastern League 3,791,241, Southern League 2,152,852, Texas League 2,834,864, California League 1,582,174, Carolina League 1,876,081, Florida State League 1,215,020, Midwest League 4,084,343, South Atlantic League 3,056,097, New York-Penn League 1,701,001, Northwest League 896,781, Appalachian League 278,785 and Pioneer League 695,052). This attendance level reflects the large number of professional baseball teams at the major and minor league level, the relatively long baseball season that provides consumers with many opportunities to attend games in these leagues, and the relatively large North American market for professional sports.

Table 2.3: Estimated Total Annual Attendance, 2010-2011

Sport	Total Attendance
Major League Baseball	73,451,522
Minor League Baseball	41,279,382
NCAA Football	37,411,795
NCAA Men's Basketball	27,691,051
Nippon Professional Baseball	21,679,956
National Hockey League	21,470,155
National Football League	17,124,389
National Basketball Association	17,100,861
Bundesliga (Germany)	13,805,496
English Premier League	13,148,465
La Liga (Spain)	11,504,567
Liga MX (Mexico)	7,905,999
Serie A (Italy)	7,765,082
Ligue 1 (France)	7,170,333
Korean Professional Baseball	6,809,965
Australian Football League	6,778,824
Campeonato Brasileiro Serie A (Brazil)	5,660,987
Chinese Super League	4,497,578
NASCAR Sprint Cup Series	3,600,000
Canadian Football League	2,454,723

The next two most popular sports in terms of total annual attendance are US college football and men's college basketball. These totals reflect college attendance at the Division I and FBS levels. Hundreds of colleges and universities have football and men's basketball teams, so this large total is expected, given the ample opportunities to attend these games. Some might be surprised to see that National Football League (NFL) total attendance is smaller than the other major professional sports leagues - including hockey - and smaller than NCAA football and basketball. However, the NFL plays a relatively short 16 game regular season schedule and, as we will soon see, focuses on television viewing as its primary means of public exposure. NASCAR attendance has dropped significantly in the last 10 years; in the early 2000s NASCAR regularly drew more than 10 million fans.

Professional sport is a popular spectator activity around the world. From an international perspective, total attendance at professional baseball in Japan draws large crowds, exceeding attendance at NHL, NFL and NBA games in North America. Attendance is also large at professional football matches in Germany, England, Spain, and Italy. The total attendance at professional football matches in Brazil and China is somewhat surprising; both are large markets with densely populated cities and soccer is very popular in both. Of course income is relatively low in these countries. Of course the populations of the countries listed on Table 2.3 differ, and total attendance depends on the size of the market, which is closely related to population. Another way to compare total attendance across countries is to scale total attendance by the size of the market, proxied by population. Figure 2.1 contains a scatter plot of total attendance and population for professional sports leagues in a number of developed countries around the world. Attendance is shown in terms of the number of attendees per 100,000 in population in each country. The populations of the US and Canada have been added together for the NBA, NHL and MLB, since teams in those leagues play in both countries. Figure 2.1 also contains the results of a simple linear regression where attendance is the dependent variable and population is the explanatory variable. This regression model provides a simple prediction about the level of attendance at sporting events given the population of a country. The regression results are labeled "fitted values" on Figure 2.1. Points above the line indicate leagues where attendance is larger than population would predict and points below the line indicate leagues where attendance is lower than population would predict.

Figure 2.1 shows that one reason total attendance is so much higher in the NFL, NBA, NHL and MLB than other leagues is that the US market is much larger than other markets. These four points lie well to the right of the others on Figure 2.1, highlighting the relatively large size of the combined US-Canadian market for professional sport. MLB and the Chinese Super League are clear outliers on Figure 2.1; attendance at professional baseball games in North America is large and also well above what would be predicted by population alone; attendance at professional soccer matches in China is well below what would be expected given the large population of hat country. In part, this can be explained by the much longer regular season in baseball (which can also be seen from the location of the Nissan Professional League in Japan), and the fact that only baseball is played outdoors in the summer when the weather is nice, but other economic factors must also drive the popularity of baseball. The CFL does not draw large crowds relative to the population of Canada.

Note that only North American leagues and professional baseball in Japan draw better than predicted from the regression model. The outliers, MLB and the Super League, frive the position of the regression line in Figure 2.1 and removing them changes the position of the regression line significantly. Among the professional football (soccer) leagues, La Liga, the Bundesliga and the Premiership draw better than the population of their respective countries would predict when removing China, while Serie A, Ligue 1, the Brazilian top league, and the Mexican Liga MX draw fewer fans. Mexico and Brazil are less developed than the other countries in this group, which may explain why attendance lags there. In general, the relatively wide dispersion in points around the regression line in Figure 2.1 suggests heterogeneity in the other factors that drive attendance at professional sports. Later chapters will develop an economic model of attendance to help explain this heterogeneity.

Total attendance at MLB, NFL, NBA, NHL, minor league baseball and Division I college sports

Figure 2.1: League Wide Attendance per 100,000 in Population

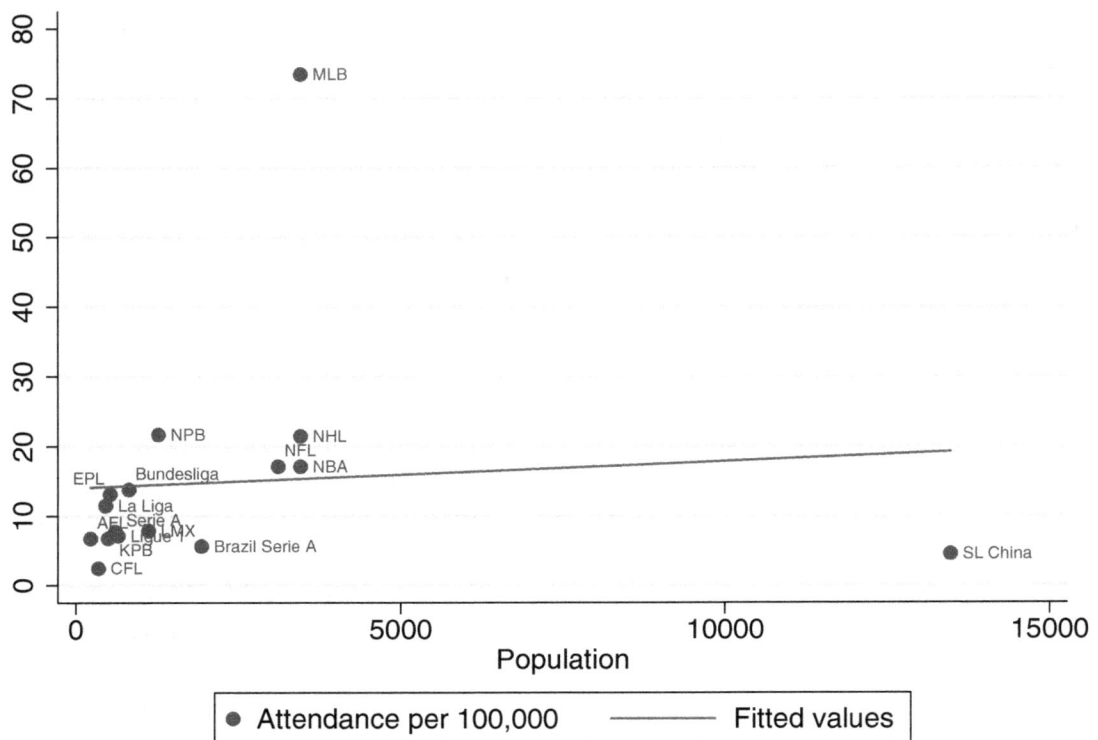

is about 250 million per season, a significant fraction of the population of the US and Canada. This total includes many individuals who bought tickets to multiple games, including season ticket holders who go to many games in one sport every year and people who attend many different sporting events every year. Still, 250 million tickets sold in 2010 is a large number compared to the total US and Canadian population of 346 million. This represents a significant amount of economic activity, both in terms of spending on tickets, spending on other related goods and services like travel, and the opportunity cost of the time spent attending sporting events.

The 250 million people who attended pro and college sporting events in 2010-11 generated a substantial amount of direct and indirect economic activity. Tickets were purchased for each of these events, along with parking, concessions, and souvenirs. For those spectators who traveled long distances to attend a sporting event, attending the event also generated travel spending, including hotels and meals.

2.3.3 Viewing and Listening to Mediated Sport

Spectator sports play an important role in print and broadcast media. Almost every daily newspaper has a sports section and sports broadcasts appear on many local and national television and radio stations. According to the 2010 *Vital Statistics of the United States*, the total multimedia audience in the United States was 228,112,000. This implies that, of the 308,745,000 people counted as the resident population of the US in 2010, 74% of them had access to some form of media, including newspapers, television, radio and internet. Table 2.4 shows the estimated television audiences, in terms of average number of viewers per broadcast, in 2011-2012.

The National Football League has the largest television viewing audience of any US professional sports league. For the three networks that televise NFL games on Sunday afternoons and evenings, NBC, CBS and Fox, the average number of viewers for each game was roughly 20 million. Following the NFL in average TV viewing audience are NASCAR and the National Basketball Association. College football broadcasts on CBS and ABC drew more average viewers than Major League Baseball or the National Hockey League.

Table 2.4: Average TV Viewing Audience per Game

Season	Sport	Network	Audience (mil)
2012	NASCAR	FOX	7.9
2011-12	NBA	ABC	5.4
2012	MLB	FOX	2.5
2011-12	NHL	NBC	1.6
2012	NFL	NBC	21.4
2012	NFL	Fox	19.7
2012	NFL	CBS	17.7
2012	NFL	ESPN	12.8
2011	NCAAFB	CBS	6.9
2011	NCAAFB	ABC	5.5
2011-12	EPL	–	12.3
2011-12	La Liga	–	3.6
2011-12	Bundesliga	–	2.0
2011-12	Serie A	–	4.5

The average television audience per match televised for the four top European professional football leagues (the English Premier League, the Bundesliga in Germany, La Liga in Spain, and Serie A in Italy) were equivalent to non-NFL audiences in North America; the EPL has a larger TV viewing audience than all non-NFL audiences in North America. Note that in many European countries, football matches are only shown on subscription-based satellite television, and not on free over the air broadcasts like in North America.

Aggregate estimates of the number of people who listen to sporting events on the radio in the US are difficult to find. According to the *Statistical Abstract of the United States*, the estimated radio listening audience in 2010 was about 83% of the US population over the age of 18 (228 million people in 2010), a total that is not much smaller than the estimated television viewing audience (93%). Anecdotal evidence suggests that quite a bit of sports programming is available on radio, perhaps as much as is available on television for the NFL, MLB and the NBA.

Determining the amount of sports viewing done over the internet is also difficult to estimate. The *Statistical Abstract of the United States* reports that about 133 million people had access to fixed or mobile broadband internet in 2010. In one recent survey, the fraction of surveyed internet users who reported "checking sports scores or information" was larger than those reporting downloading music, although smaller than those using the internet for email. In any case, the amount of time spent following sports on the internet is proportionate to overall internet use, which is growing rapidly. Furthermore, much of the sport related internet use may take place at work, where many people have internet access, unlike sports viewing on television which takes place primarily at home or in bars and restaurants.

2.4 Overview of the Professional Sports Industry

Almost all modern professional team sports are organized into one or more leagues. Sports leagues have different organizational forms, operating methods, goals, and institutional characteristics than firms in other sectors of the economy. North American professional sports leagues also feature a number of idiosyncratic features that require an understanding of in order to grasp the economics of professional sports. This chapter contains a discussion of the economic characteristics of professional sport in North America. European professional sports leagues have different, equally idiosyncratic characteristics.

2.4.1 Professional Sports Leagues

2.4.2 North American Professional Sports Leagues

North American professional sports leagues have a number of unique features that distinguish them from firms in other industries. Many of these features stem from the joint production that takes place in sports leagues. Although teams in North American professional sports leagues compete on the field, court, or ice, they also produce an inter-related product: the full slate of league games played each season and a post-season championship. One team cannot exist without the other teams in the league to provide a full schedule of regular season and postseason games. In addition, understanding the institutional context provides a basis for the economic analysis of professional sports throughout the rest of the course.

League Structure

There are four major professional sports leagues in North America: Major League Baseball (MLB), the National Football League (NFL), the National Basketball Association (NBA), the National Hockey League (NHL).[1] There are also a large number of minor professional leagues in North America in each of these sports, as well as in other sports like lacrosse. I restrict this discussion to only these four professional leagues because of a lack of financial and economic data from other leagues and because of the prominence of the NFL, MLB, NHL, and NBA in North America.

Professional sports leagues in North America are closed, static leagues. No system of promotion and relegation exists in these leagues, so the composition of each league does not change from season to season. The only change in the composition of the four major professional sports leagues occurs when the leagues periodically expand their membership. The NBA expanded to 30 teams in 1995, adding two teams in Canada, the Toronto Raptors and the Vancouver Grizzlies. The NFL expanded to 32 teams in 1999, adding one team, the Cleveland Browns. An NFL franchise had been in Cleveland for many years, but that franchise, now called the Ravens, moved to Baltimore in 1995. The NHL expanded to 30 teams in 2000, adding two teams, the Columbus Blue Jackets and the Minnesota Wild. MLB expanded to 30 teams in 1998, adding two teams, the Tampa Bay Devil Rays and the Arizona Diamondbacks. League expansion has both costs and benefits, and also must be periodically undertaken to deter the formation of rival leagues as population growth makes more cities viable hosts for a team. Chapter 5 discusses league expansion in detail.

---

[1]A case could be made for Major League Soccer (MLS), and the Canaidan Football League (CFL) as "major" professional sports, although I do not treat them as major sports here.

All professional sports leagues in North America feature exclusive territorial agreements that divide all of the US, and Canada in the case of the NBA, MLB and NHL which have Canadian teams, into distinct geographic areas where each team enjoys monopoly power, except in a few cases where two teams play in the same large metropolitan area like New York City, Chicago, Los Angeles and the San Francisco Bay area. This system exists because leagues have implicit or explicit exemptions from anti-trust law and can operate as monopolies, completely controlling the number of teams in each league and the location of each team.

Leagues also preform important organizational functions that enable play to take place, such as setting the schedule, maintaining the rules of play, overseeing officiating, enforcing rules, and bargaining collectively with players' unions, television networks, and licensed merchandize producers. These functions will be addressed in detail in Chapter 5.

Governance and Team Ownership

Although each professional league in North America has a commissioner with nominal power to make league policy, the true power resides with the owners of the teams in each league. The league commissioners primarily handle day-to-day operations leagues, enforce existing rules governing play, and act as figureheads and spokesmen. No multinational governing body like the Union of European Football Associations (UEFA), which governs football in Europe, exists in North America. Under the North American system, individual teams have much more economic power than their European counterparts. This stems primarily from the static nature of North American leagues.

With very few exceptions, professional sports teams in North America are privately held businesses that do not issue shares on stock exchanges. None are operated by clubs or formal organizations of supporters, as is common in Europe. Because of this ownership structure, information about the financial condition of professional sports teams in North America is almost nonexistent. Professional sports teams in North America are not obligated to release any audited financial data to the public, and seldom open their books for inspection by outside parties. This lack of information about finances makes it very difficult to assess the financial condition of these teams.

On the player side, professional athletes in team sports in North America are unionized. The National Football League Players' Association, the National Basketball Players' Association, the Major League Baseball Players Association, and the National Hockey League Players' Association represent players in the four main professional leagues in North America. In all these leagues, a collective bargaining agreement (CBA) between the players' union and the league governs all aspects of the economic interaction between players and teams. CBAs typically last for five years and the re-negotiation of a CBA often leads to significant work stoppages in North American professional sports leagues. For example, the NHL lost the entire 2004-2005 season to a work stoppage, teams in the NBA played only 50 games, instead of the usual 82, in the 1998-1999 season because of a work stoppage, and MLB canceled the last two months of the regular season and the entire post-season, including the World Series, in 1994 because of a work stoppage. All these work stoppages were related to the renegotiation of the CBA between the players' union and the league.

Revenues

Teams in North American sports leagues earn revenues from five broad sources:

- Game day revenues: Gate revenues from ticket sales, facility-based revenues from concessions and other game-related activities like parking, luxury box leases, and other ticket-related revenues like Personal Seat Licenses

- Postseason appearances: This includes some game day revenues associated with play of the games, media revenues from additional games, and bonuses paid from league revenues

- Local broadcast rights fees: this includes revenues from radio and television broadcasts in the team's market. Negotiated separately by each team. The value of these revenues depend on the size of the market, substitutes in the market and local preferences.

- Shared revenues: Nationally broadcast radio and television rights fees are typically negotiated collectively by the league and shared equally in North American sports leagues. Also, sales of licensed merchandize like caps and jerseys are typically shared equally. Also, some leagues engage in revenue sharing, where large attendance teams subsidize small attendance teams.

- Sponsorship and advertising: Includes revenues from signage in the facility, contracts with businesses to be the "official X of the team," facility naming rights, and other similar revenues. These are typically negotiated separately.

For most of the economic history of professional sports in North America, sales of tickets to individual fans, either in the form of "season ticket" packages to all home games, or tickets to individual games, represented the single largest source of revenues to professional sports teams. Beginning in the 1980s, revenues from media rights, in the form of radio and television broadcast contracts, became an important source of revenues. The advent of big media rights fees radically changed professional sports, as we will soon see. Beginning in the 1990s, teams began to generate significant revenues from premium seating, including luxury boxes and other "club seats" located in special sections of sports facilities separated from general admission seats. A new stadium or arena in North America typically contains between 70 and 140 luxury suites and several thousand premium seats. Tickets for seats in these premium locations typically cost two to four times more than other tickets and come with enhanced concessions and other amenities like personal television screens. Luxury suites must be leased for an entire season at an average price often exceeding $100,000, not including mandatory purchases of food and beverages at each game. The primary customers for premium seats and luxury suites are not individual fans; these seats are primarily sold to corporations and other businesses.

Another important source of revenues in professional sports in North America is sponsorship. In North American leagues, sponsorship revenue comes from facility naming rights fees, revenues from signage in sports facilities, and rights fees associated with product endorsements. Facility naming rights deals can be quite lucrative in North America. For example Reliant Energy paid $10 million per year for the naming rights to the stadium where the Houston Texans play football and Royal Phillips Electronics paid $9.3 million dollars per year for the naming rights to the arena where the Atlanta Thrashers NHL franchise and the Hawks NBA franchises play. Stadium signage rights fees are typically smaller. Product endorsement revenues come from sponsorship deals that make certain products the "official" product of some sports team or league. There are no uniform sponsorship deals in the NFL, NBA, MLB or NHL. Corporate advertising on jerseys is forbidden in these leagues at this time, unlike the current practice in Europe.

Figure 2.2 shows the sources of revenue for a professional sports team in the NFL, MLB, NBA and NHL. The revenue data for the Mariners (MLB) and Chargers (NFL) are from 1998. The data for the Nets (NBA) are from 2004. The NFL, NBA and MLB data are from various media leaks. The data for the Coyotes (NHL) is for the 2009 season, and comes from the team's bankruptcy filing. While a bankrupt franchise in a bad hockey market may not be representative of NHL teams, this is the only detailed NHL revenue and expenditure data available. All revenues have been converted to 2009 dollars using the CPI for ease of comparison.

Figure 2.2: Revenue for Selected North American Professional Sports Teams

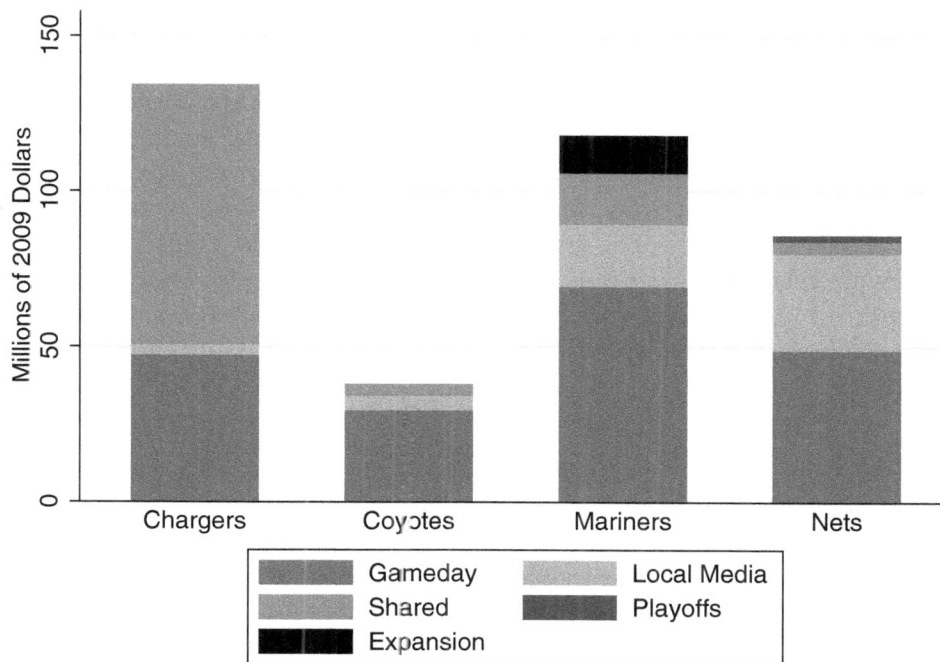

Several important features can be seen on Figure 2.2. First, game day revenues are important for all four teams. Attendance is an important factor determining the revenues earned by all professional sports teams, and local market conditions have a huge impact on the revenues earned by professional sports teams. Note that sponsorship revenues have been included in the game day revenues on this figure. Second, the composition of revenues in the NFL differs from the other three leagues in an important way: NFL teams derive most of their revenues from national media contracts and these revenues are shared equally among all NFL teams. NFL teams operate on a vastly different business model than teams in other professional sports leagues. The huge revenue stream from national media contracts equalizes total revenues across NFL teams to a greater extent than in other leagues, and reduces the importance of local market conditions. A MLB, NHL or NBA team could not survive in a market as small as Green Bay, Wisconsin, (the Designated Market Area – a common media market definition – for Green Bay had 900,000 people in 2009, the 69th largest media market in the US) without the huge revenues generated by the NFL's TV contracts.

Shared revenues, mainly national media rights fees are less important in the NBA and MLB, and of relatively little importance in the NHL, which has limited national television presence. Local media rights fees play an even smaller role in revenue generation in professional sports leagues. Note that postseason revenues only appear for the Nets, as the Mariners, Coyotes and Chargers did not make a postseason appearance in the seasons shown. The Nets lost their first round series with the Bulls 3-0, and only played a single home game in that series. Still, the fact that the revenues from a single postseason game can be seen on the graph indicates that postseason revenues can be important. In most leagues, long postseason runs can generate significant revenues from additional games and related revenue streams like concessions.

Major League Baseball expanded in 1998, adding the Tampa Bay Rays and Arizona Diamondbacks. From Figure 2.2, the Mariners earned a significant amount of revenues in 1998 in the form of a lump-sum expansion payment. These funds came from the owners of the new expansion teams, and offset losses in shared revenues which were divided among two more teams after expansion. Chapter 5 discusses the economic role of leagues and the importance of expansion of leagues.

The Chargers earned the most revenues among these four teams, and economists generally agree that NFL teams earn more than other North American professional sports teams. The Coyotes had relatively low revenues in the season shown, which is not surprising, given that they declared bankruptcy in that season. The Nets and Mariners earned more revenues primarily because of larger game day and local media revenues. The distribution of revenues shown on Figure 2.2 indicates that game day revenues are relatively important, and that understanding the determinants of attendance is an important part of understanding the economics of professional sports. Chapter 3 develops a model of attendance in professional sports based on team profit maximizing decisions.

Costs

Like professional sports teams all over the world, player compensation accounts for the largest operating expense incurred by teams in North American sports leagues. One unique feature of the payroll costs of North American sports leagues is the presence of salary caps that limit the total compensation paid to players in the league. Another is limits on the number of players each team can employ. The current collective bargaining agreements between players' unions and the NFL, NBA, and NHL include salary caps or other restrictions on player salaries. Only MLB does not have a formal salary cap in place at this time. Salary caps in North American sports leagues limit total payroll on each team to a specific fraction of total revenues earned by teams in each season. New players are acquired either through amateur entry drafts that assign rights of new players to specific teams and limit salaries paid to these new players, through trades, or through free agent signings. There are almost no transfer fees in North American professional sports leagues. Players change teams through trades or free agency. The only exceptions are that professional baseball players moving from Japan to North America sometimes require the payment of a transfer fee to a Japanese team, and professional hockey players moving from European teams to NHL teams must require a $200,000 transfer fee be paid to the European club.

Professional athletes in North American leagues have limited free agency. In general, new players in leagues are assigned to teams through amateur entry drafts and the teams assigned the rights to these players can keep them under contract for a number of seasons before players can become free agents and sell their services to the highest bidder on the open market. MLB players can become free agents after playing 6 seasons, NBA players can become free agents after playing 3 or 4 seasons, NFL players can become free agents after playing 3 seasons, and NHL players can become free agents after playing seven seasons or turning 27 years of age. In addition, long term contracts, contracts of duration 3 or more years, are relatively common in North American Sports Leagues.

In general, the costs incurred by professional sports teams can be divided into six broad categories:

- Salaries: salaries for players and signing bonuses

- Player development costs: the operation of minor league teams in MLB and the NHL, and, recently, the Developmental League in the NBA

- Team operation costs; travel, practice facilities, scouting, training, and other costs required as part of playing games

- General and Administrative costs: Front office salaries, marketing and media costs, insurance, and other general costs of operating a business

- Facility Operation and Maintenance: Costs of operating the stadium or arena

- Depreciation: Professional sports teams in North America can take advantage of a special type of depreciation expense - they can depreciate their payroll, under the theory that players are depreciating assets. Since this is not an actual economic expense in that teams do not pay anything out as part of this, the ability to depreciate salary increases the accounting costs of sports teams but has no effect on the actual economic cost of operating a team.

Figure 2.3 shows the costs for the same four professional sports teams shown in Figure 2.2: the Chargers, Coyotes, mariners and Nets. Salary, which includes only player salaries, makes up the largest single category of cost for all four teams. Team operation costs, which include travel, the salaries of coaches and scouts, and the operation of minor leagues to develop players, are the second largest category of costs. Note that, in relative terms, the team operation costs are the highest for the Chargers. NFL teams have the largest roster size, and most of the team operation costs are associated with roster size. NFL teams have a 53 player roster limit, MLB teams have a 25 player roster limit, NHL teams have a 32 player roster limit, and NBA teams have a 15 player roster limit. Even though NFL teams play the fewest games, and thus travel less than teams in other leagues, travel is only one component of team operation costs, and the larger roster size in the NFL drives up team operation costs.

General and administrative costs also contribute significantly to the costs incurred by professional sports teams. Note that teams often inflate their general and administrative costs by paying large "management fees" to the owners of teams or their family members in order to appear to lose money. For example, the Coyotes listed $5.3 million in "other management expenses" in their bankruptcy filing that probably represents a direct payment to owner Gerry Moyes or his wife, the legal owners of the Coyotes.

Depreciation expense is an important part of the expenses the Mariners and Nets. This comes from the "roster depreciation allowance" (RDA) legally granted to all professional sports teams in North America. In 1946, entrepreneur Bill Veeck bought the Cleveland Indians. Veeck convinced the United States Congress that the roster of players employed by the Indians was a depreciable asset, and that he should be able to claim depreciation on this asset as a legitimate expense, just like other firms depreciate the value of their physical capital. Congress agreed, and the RAD was passed into black letter law. Subsequent Congresses expanded on the RDA, and it in it's most recent version, the purchaser of a professional sports team can depreciate 100% of the purchase price of the team for a period of no more than 15 years. Under this so-called 100/15 rule, 100% of the value of a sports team is assumed to be represented by the depreciable salary component of the team. Using straight line depreciation, the 100/15 rule means that, for each $100 million in cost of a franchise, the team owner may claim $6.6 million in depreciation expense in each of the first 15 years of ownership. The RDA is not an economic cost, because it does not represent the use of any scarce resource. The RDA simply increases accounting costs, and decreases accounting profits.

The existence of salary caps, limited free agency, and long-term contracts mean that payroll expenses are relatively stable in North American professional sports leagues. Salary caps place limits on the number of new players that can be acquired in any season, and the limited nature of free agency means that players with relatively little experience are paid low salaries. It also means

Figure 2.3: Costs for Selected North American Professional Sports Teams

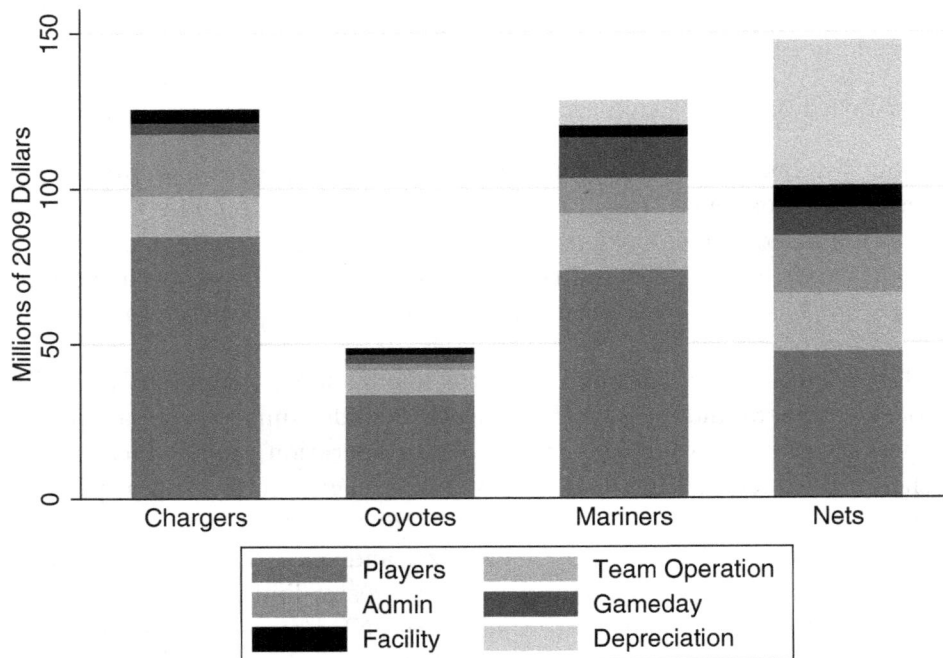

that teams in financial difficulty cannot raise large sums of money quickly through transfer fees earned by selling off star players. The RDA also leads to stability in costs in professional sports teams.

Note that with the inclusion of depreciation, the Nets look like they lost a significant amount of money. including depreciation their costs were almost $150 million, while revenues were under $100 million. However, depreciation is not a real expense, in that it does not involve payment of any money to anyone; depreciation exists only on paper to increase the expenses of professional sports teams (and no other business in North America can claim this expense). Absent depreciation and administrative expenses, which are also quite large for the Nets, the team would roughly break even. Keep this in mind the next time you read that a professional sports team loses money.

None of the teams pay any significant facility operation and maintenance costs. This is because most professional sports teams in North America have been able to extract significant subsidies from local governments for the constriction and operation of facilities over the past thirty years. The effect of these subsidies on costs incurred by professional sports teams is significant. Unlike other businesses, professional sports teams pay little or nothing for their fixed capital, and are also able to use these facilities virtually rent free. This significantly reduces the costs of operating a professional sports team. Chapter 8 discusses this topic in detail.

2.4.3   European Professional Sports Leagues

Major professional sports leagues exist all over the world. High profile professional baseball leagues exist in Japan and South Korea; high profile professional soccer leagues exist in Argentina, Brazil, Mexico, China, and other countries; a major Australian Rules Football league exists in Australia;

scores of other professional sports leagues exist in rugby, basketball, handball, ice hockey, and other sports. However, outside the major professional sports leagues in North America, the most visible professional sports leagues in the world are the professional football leagues in Europe.[2] Although other professional sports leagues exist in Europe, the discussion here will focus only on football in the interest of brevity.

European professional football leagues differ in many ways from North American leagues. In part, this difference stems from that fact that sport in Europe is organized around a club system that differs from the school-based system in place in North America. Few schools at any level sponsor sports teams in Europe. Even universities do not, in general, operate athletic programs. Instead, youth sport in Europe is organized around clubs, private organizations that offer facilities and training to athletes, often in many different sports. These sports clubs charge members (athletes and fans) annual fees and also sell tickets to events. They often sponsor teams in multiple sports, as well as multiple teams at different levels in specific sports. Many of the well known football clubs in Europe, except in the UK, are multi-sport clubs that sponsor teams in many different sports. For example, *Futebol Clube do Porto*, or F. C. Porto, a prominent sports club in Portugal, fields football, basketball, handball, and ice hockey teams. In the UK, the major football clubs like Manchester United, operate only football teams, although many operate both men's and women's teams.

League Structure

The league structures used in European professional football leagues differ markedly from North American leagues. Each country operates a series of domestic professional leagues, often called "divisions." In the UK, this includes the Premier League (the top UK league), the Football League, (which operates the second, third and fourth UK leagues), and the National League System, which operates the next tier of professional teams. The Premier League was only founded in 1992, when a group of clubs broke away from the Football League in order to increase their revenues at the expense of lower profile clubs. The Football League, the oldest professional football league in the world, was formed in 1888. The Football League currently operates the Football Championship, League One and League Two. Teams in all these leagues are professional, and all are linked in a ladder, or hierarchical system.

These professional football leagues are linked in a promotion and relegation system. Under this system, the most successful teams in each league in each season are "promoted" up to the next highest league and the worst teams in the higher league are "relegated" down to the next lowest league. For example the Premier League, the top football league in the UK, contains 20 teams. At the end of the season, the three teams at the bottom of the league standings (called the "table" in Europe) are relegated down to the Football Championship, the next league down the ladder. After the 2010 season, Birmingham, Blackpool, and West Ham, the bottom three teams in the EPL, were relegated from the Premier League to The Football Championship, and Queens Park Rangers, Norwich City and Swansea City, the top three teams in the Football Championship, were promoted to the Premier League. This takes place at every level in the ladder. The bottom three teams in the Football Championship are demoted to League one and the top three teams in League one are promoted to the Football Championship, and so on down the ladder. Sports economists refer to this as an "open" league system, since stronger teams continuously replace weaker teams at all levels. Unlike closed North American leagues, these open leagues have, in economic terms,

---

[2]Throughout the book I will use the European convention of referring to the sport called "soccer" in North America as "football." A strong case could be made that the Indian Premier League, a professional cricket league using the new Twenty20 format of play, is as popular as professional football in Europe.

freedom of entry into the market. Also, European leagues do not expand by adding new teams very often. Expansion through adding new teams is primarily a North American phenomenon.

Each country in Europe operates a similar ladder of professional football teams. The Bundesliga I and II in Germany, Serie A and B in Italy, and so on. The number of teams promoted and relegated differs, and some details of how the promotion and relegation takes place differs. For example, in Germany, a two match home-and-home series takes place between the third to last team in the Bundesliga I and the third from the top team in the Bundesliga II to determine that promotion and relegation spot; the bottom two teams in the Bundesliga I are automatically relegated. In each country, the key feature of promotion and relegation remains. The revenues earned by teams drops significantly in lower ranked leagues, as will be shown later.

In addition, two pan-European football club competitions, the Champions League (CL) and the Europa League (EL), take place at the same time as the domestic league competitions in each country. These competitions are somewhat analogous to the postseason tournaments held by North American leagues in that they identify a "champion" and generate significant revenues. The CL is the top pan-European competition and the EL the second. Club teams qualify for these competitions by finishing at the top of the table in their respective domestic league competitions as well as by participating in qualifying tournaments. The number of teams from each domestic league that qualify for the CL and EL depends on past performance by domestic teams. For example, in the 2011-2012 season the top four teams in three domestic leagues (The English Premier League, the Bundesliga and La Liga) will automatically qualify for the CL.

The promotion and relegation system and the season long pan-European competitions generate a completely different set of economic incentives than in closed North American leagues. The primary difference between static leagues (SLs) like those in North America and promotion and relegation leagues (PRLs) like those in Europe come from the effect of promotion and relegation incentives on team revenues, costs, and the choice of playing talent. The effect of promotion and relegation on revenues and costs cannot be determined from a theoretical model, because promotion and relegation generates many different effects. For example, the threat of relegation may increase fan interest in matches played at the end of the season, increasing ticket sales and revenues, and the prospect of promotion to a higher league might also increase fan interest and revenues. One clear prediction emerges from economic models of league behavior: teams in PRLs will choose a higher average level of quality, in terms of the quality of players hired, relative to teams in SLs, holding constant factors that affect revenues like the size of the market and the income of fans. Football teams in Major League Soccer in North America will never hire as talented a group of players as football teams in European leagues.

Governance and Team Ownership

Professional football in Europe, and football around the world for that matter, has a different governance structure than professional sports in North America. North American professional sports leagues operate independently with no international oversight or international structure of any kind. Professional football is governed by a hierarchical international system. At the top of worldwide football governance is FIFA (The Federation Internationale de Football Association or in English the International Federation of Association Football). FIFA, a federation of international associations, is the international governing body for association football; FIFA organizes the World Cup, and has some influence of the official rules of football.[3] FIFA contains 208 national

---

[3]Technically, the rules of football are decided by the International Football Association Board (IFAB), which consists of four FIFA representatives and representatives from the football associations in the United Kingdom: England, Scotland, Wales and Northern Ireland.

football associations and six football confederations. One of these, the Union of European Football Associations (UEFA), regulates professional and national football in Europe. UEFA organizes and operates national football competitions like the UEFA Cup and pan-European club competitions like the CL and EL. It also controls the media revenues generated by the CL and EL, and the prize money paid out to participants in these competitions.

Individual team ownership of European football clubs takes a wider variety of forms than the ownership of North American professional sports teams. European football clubs are owned by individuals (Russian billionaire Roman Abramovich owns Chelsea Football Club in the English Premier League), owned by stockholders as publicly traded companies (for example Borussia Dortmund of the German Bundesliga and Aston Villa of the English Premier League), and owned by member associations or clubs (Real Madrid of Spain's La Liga is owned by 60,000 individuals, or *socios*, who pay member dues and form an assembly that has ultimate authority over the club). The most common forms of team ownership in European professional football are formal not-for profit organizations of fans, called 'Supporters' Trusts" in the UK, and individuals. In 2008, 42% of the clubs in UEFA were owned by member associations, 38% were privately owned by individuals or groups of individuals, and 4% were listed on stock exchanges.

Revenues

In general, European professional football teams earn revenues from the same sources as North American professional sports teams: match day revenues from ticket sales, concessions, and other similar goods and services; broadcast rights fees; appearances in pan-European competitions like the Champions League and Europa League; and sponsorship, advertising, naming rights, licensed merchandize and other commercial activities. Detailed revenue data for individual European football clubs is relatively difficult to obtain. The most prominent source of revenue data come from consulting firm Deloitte, who publish an annual ranking of the revenues earned by European football teams called *Deloitte Football Money League* (FML). [4]

The FML reports revenues from three aggregated sources: match day revenues, broadcast revenues, and commercial revenues. Match day revenues are primarily ticket sales and membership fees, but can also contain concessions, parking and other revenues generated from team play. Broadcast revenues include local, national, and pan-European terrestrial and satellite broadcast rights fees and radio broadcast rights fees. Commercial revenues include sponsorship, advertising, and other non-match day revenues. European professional football teams earn significant commercial revenues from "kit" or uniform sponsorship deals involving advertising on the team's uniform; this differs significantly from the practice in North America, where teams are prohibited from placing any advertising, other than the logo of the jersey manufacturer. Currently, FC Barcelona receives 30 million euros per year from the Quatar foundation to advertise on their team jersey, Bayern Munich receives 25 million euros per year from Deutsche Telekom, and Manchester United receives 24.8 million Euros per year from Aon. Clubs often have secondary short sponsorship deals as well.

Figure 2.4 shows the total revenues in millions of euros, and the composition of total revenues, for the four highest revenue generating teams in the 2010-2011 FML for the four largest domestic European football leagues. Real Madrid of La Liga topped the list, earning just under 500 million euros and Manchester United of the English Premier League was second, earning more than 350 million euros. Both these clubs had balanced earnings, as about one third of their total revenues came from the three revenue sources. The top revenue team in the Bundesliga, Bayern Munich, and in Italy's Serie A, AC Milan, earned far less from match day revenue sources. Bayern's largest

---

[4]Prior to 2001 this was called the Deloitte "Rich List."

Figure 2.4: Revenues for Selected European Professional Sports Teams

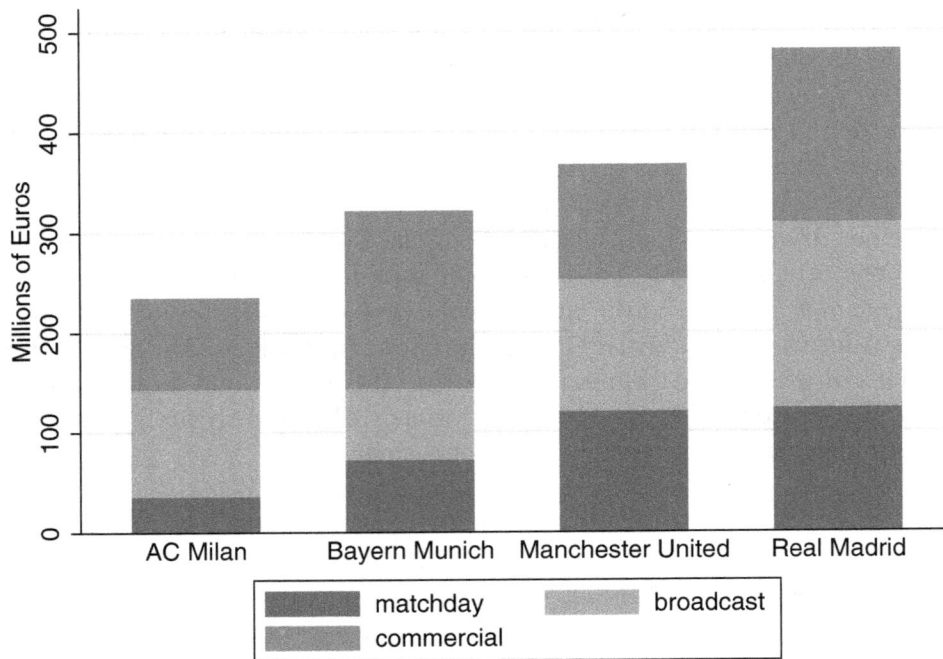

revenue source was commercial revenues, and AC Milan's was broadcast revenues. Bayern's commercial revenues were 177.7 million euros in 2011. In 2011, AC Milan's broadcast revenues were 107.7 million euros. Much of this broadcast revenue came from the 1.149 billion euro, two year Serie A domestic broadcasting rights deal that was in place for the 2010-2011 and 2011-2012 seasons. This broadcast rights deal was collectively negotiated by the league.

Costs

Data on the costs incurred by European professional football leagues are difficult to find. This can be partially attributed to the fact that, unlike in North America, player salaries in European professional football are not made public. In addition, the roster size of European professional football teams are not fixed. Each team can hire as many players as it wants. Finally, unlike North American leagues, no salary caps exist in European football leagues. One reason salaries are public and closely monitored in North American leagues is that teams must comply with salary caps, which requires detailed information about player salaries. The lack of salary caps in European leagues places less emphasis on monitoring salaries, leading to less public information about salaries and team payrolls.

In addition, teams in PRLs must try to win enough matches in each season to avoid relegation, leading to a team objective of win maximization rather than profit maximization. Under win maximization, teams will spend an amount up to their total revenues on player and coaching talent in an attempt to avoid relegation in each season. This also places a premium on measuring revenues instead of costs, because attendance, broadcast rights fees, and sponsorship deals are public information that can be easily collected.

One readily available indicator of the costs incurred by European professional sports teams is the ratio of total payroll to total revenues. UEFA publishes annual estimates of the ratio of total payroll to total revenues for the top domestic league in each country that is a UEFA member. Figure 2.5 shows the ratio of total payroll to total revenues in the top domestic leagues in England, Spain, Germany, Italy and France over the period 1998-2010.

Figure 2.5: Ratio of Payroll to Total Revenues, Selected European Leagues

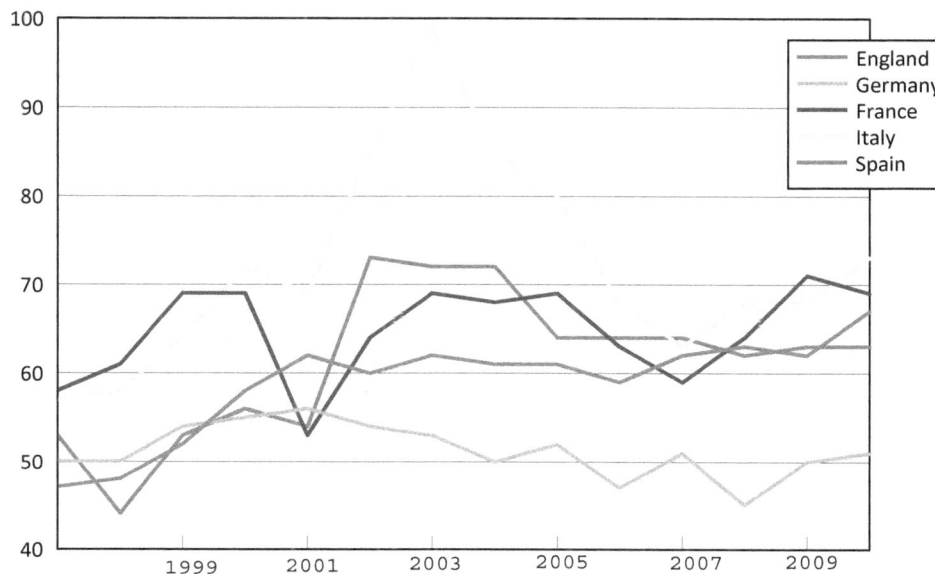

Player salaries are not the only costs incurred by professional football teams. As we saw in Section 2.4.2 above, sports teams also incur player development costs generated by training young players, operations costs associated with travel, administrative costs, and facility operation costs. European professional football teams probably face higher development costs since most operate training academies and field second teams composed of young players already under contract at young ages. Travel costs in Europe may be lower, since teams do not travel as far as in North America. So the ratio of payroll to total revenues shown on Figure 2.5 cannot be used to infer anything about the relative profitability of football teams. We can conclude that the lower the ratio of payroll to total revenues, the more likely are teams in that league to make a positive operating profit.

From Figure 2.5, teams in the Bundesliga have the lowest ratio of payroll to total revenues, and teams in Serie A the highest. Salaries in Serie A appear to have gotten quite high in the period 2003-2005, but declined after that time. A number of Italian football teams were reported to be in serious financial trouble in the mid part of the 2000s. Payroll as a fraction of total revenues have risen steadily in the English Premier League over this period, and the actual increase in salaries in that league was probably much larger, since revenues rose significantly during the period. Put another way, EPL teams were increasing player compensation at a faster rate than revenues were increasing over the past 10 years. The ratio of payroll to revenues League 1 and, more interestingly in La Liga, were relatively sable over the period. The relative quality of La Liga probably increased over this period, as indicated by the success of Spanish teams in pan-European competitions. But the numbers on Figure 2.5 reflect average league payrolls compared to average league revenues, and not the payroll of top La Liga teams like Real Madrid and FC Barcelona.

2.5   Sports and the Media

From Figure 2.2, media rights fees are an important component of the revenues earned by professional sports teams in North America. Media rights fees consist of national media rights fees that are paid by television networks, cable sports networks like ESPN and TSN, satellite providers like DirectTV and Bell, nationwide radio syndicates like the CBC, and satellite radio operators like XM/Sirius and local media rights fees that are paid by radio and television stations in each team's local media market. In North America, sports leagues collectively bargain with media outlets for the rights to broadcast sporting events nationally, pool the revenue from the sale of these rights, and distribute them to teams equally. From Figure 2.2, television rights fees make up the largest source of revenues in the NFL and the second largest source of revenues in the NHL, NBA and MLB.

Table 2.5 summarizes the current state of national broadcast rights fees contracts in the big four leagues. Note that most broadcast rights contracts are for multiple years and are not indexed to inflation. The standard broadcast rights fee contract is for a fixed amount per year over a specified number of years for the rights to broadcast certain games. Note that this structure forces all the risk onto the network, and they must pay the league the specified rights fees no matter what size the tv audience turns out to be.

The NFL followed a policy of differentiation when selling national broadcast rights fees, selling separate rights fee deals for the National Football Conference Sunday afternoon games (Fox), the American Football Conference Sunday afternoon games (CBS), Sunday night football (NBC) and Monday night football (ESPN). The NFL also has a broadcast rights contract with satellite TV provider DirectTV for the NFL Sunday Ticket package (which DirectTV resells to other satellite TV providers like Bell in Canada). Finally, the NFL operates the NFL Network that shows some NFL games and generates additional national television rights revenues. All this money is shared equally by NFL teams.

Table 2.5: Current National Broadcast Rights Fees in North American Sports Leagues

League	Rights Holder	Annual Broadcast Fee	Contract Period
NFL	ESPN	$1.1 billion	2006-2012
NFL	ESPN	$1.9 billion	2013-2021
NFL	Fox	$725 million	2006-2013
NFL	Fox	$1.1 billion	2014-2021
NFL	CBS	$622 million	2006-2012
NFL	CBS	$1.0 billion	2013-2021
NFL	NBC	$650 million	2006-2012
NFL	NBC	$950 billion	2014-2021
NFL	DirecTV	$700 million	2006-2013
MLB	Fox/TBS	$670 million	2006-2013
NBA	ABC/ESPN/TNT	$930 million	2008-2016
NHL	NBC/Versus	$200 million	2011-2021

MLB has a single national television rights contract with Fox and the Turner Broadcasting System/Superstation (TBS) for Saturday afternoon games and the MLB postseason. The NBA has a contract with ABC/ESPN and a contract with TNT for regular season and postseason games. The NHL has a contract with Versus and NBC.

This has not always been the case in North American professional sports leagues. The NFL signed the first national broadcast rights fee contract in 1960 with CBS for $300,000 ($2.2 million in 2010 dollars). MLB signed its first national broadcast rights fee contract in 1962 ($400,000), the NBA in 1964 ($1.5 million) and the NHL in 1981 ($2 million).

Figure 2.6: Real Annual National TV Revenues, 000s of 2012 Dollars

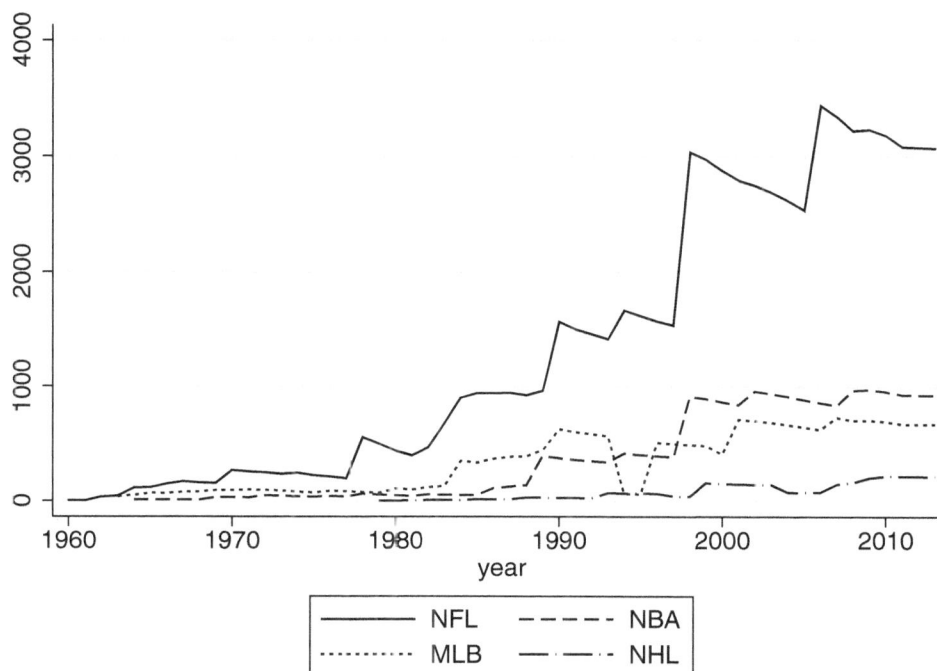

Figure 2.6 shows the annual real value of national broadcast rights fee contracts in each league since the 1960s. The "sawtooth" shape of these time series plots comes from the fact that the contracts are for multiple years in nominal terms, and inflation erodes away at the real value of the contract over the period. From 2.6, national broadcast rights fees did not increase much until the late 1980s. However, these revenues exploded in the 1990s, especially in the NFL. Also note the huge difference between national broadcast fees revenues in the NFL compared to the other three leagues. Bear in mind that local broadcast rights fees are much more important in the NBA, MLB and NHL. While it is difficult to find data on the local broadcast rights fees for individual teams in the NBA, NHL, and MLB, local broadcast rights fees also increased significantly in the late 1980s. Local broadcast rights fees are available for MLB over the period 1962 to 1994. The sum of national and all local broadcast fees for MLB over this period is roughly equal to the value of the NFL's national broadcast fee revenues. However, it is unlikely that local broadcast fees increased as rapidly as the national broadcast rights fees in the NFL, which, from Figure 2.6, took a huge jump in the late 1990s.

Note that the increase in broadcast rights fees roughly coincides with the increase in access to cable and satellite television. These new media played an important role in the increase in broadcast rights fees, as they earned revenues from subscription fees, unlike broadcast networks that earned revenues only through advertising.

2.5.1   The Structure of the Sports Broadcast Market

In order to understand why broadcast fee revenues increased rapidly beginning in the late 1980s, it is important to understand the structure of the sports Broadcasting market. Figure 2.7 summarizes the structure of the sports broadcast rights market. There are three different groups of firms participating in this market: Sports leagues and teams who produce games and sell the rights to broadcast these games to media providers; media providers (television networks, cable/satellite stations like ESPN and TSN, and other providers) who purchase the rights to broadcast sporting events from leagues and teams in exchange for rights fees and sell ad slots (commercials, promotional sports, etc.) to advertisers; and advertisers (firms of all types) who buy ad slots from media providers in exchange for advertising slot fees. Sports leagues and teams sell the rights to broadcast sporting events to media providers. Media providers produce and distribute sports broadcasts that sports fans are interested in watching, generating large relatively homogenous audiences that advertisers want to reach with ads, or perhaps targeted audiences that fit advertisers desired market.

Figure 2.7: The Sports Broadcasting Rights Market

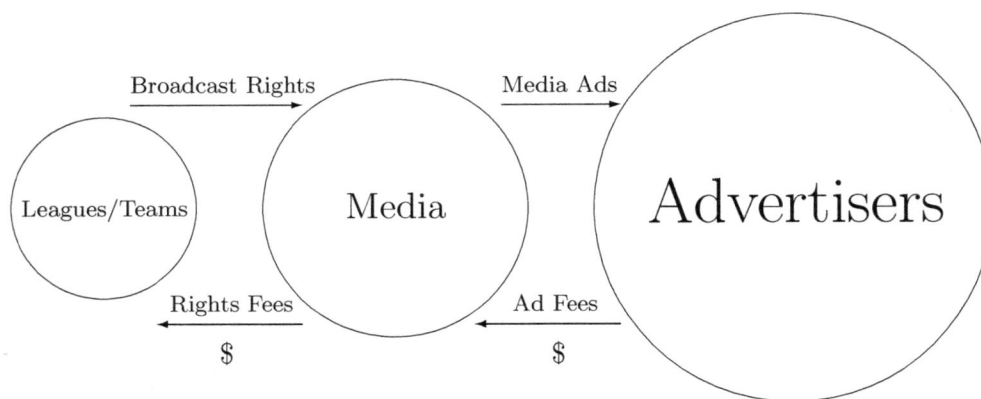

The size of the circles represents the number of firms in each group; the amount of competition increases as we move from left to right on Figure 2.7. At the left, professional sports leagues and teams are monopolies, either in the national market, or in the case of teams, in each local market. For example, the Oilers are the only supplier of NHL games in Edmonton, and the NHL is the only supplier of top-level professional ice hockey in North America. This gives leagues and teams considerable market power.

Moving to the right, in the larger circle, are the numerous media providers. Decades ago, in the age of over-the-air broadcasting, there were only the traditional television networks. But the last 20 years has seen many new entrants in this part of the market, along with the rise of cable television, satellite television, and now streamed audio and video content over the internet. Currently, traditional networks, national cable sports channels like TSN, The Score, and ESPN, regional sports networks, national "super stations" like TBS and WGN, cable channels, and streamed internet video content providers all compete to purchase broadcast rights to professional sporting events. In the last few years the leagues themselves have formed cable/satellite broadcast stations like the NFL Network and the NHL Network to broadcast games and other league related content. Moving further to the right to the advertisers, competition increases even more; the larger circle indicates even more firms competing at this end of the market. There are thousands of firms producing consumer goods and services at the national and local level who are interested in purchasing advertising spots on sports broadcasts. Since the market power lies primarily with the professional sports leagues and teams, they are able to generate substantial rents from this market power.

Media providers pay rights fees for the rights to specific sports programming. These rights are bought and sold in auction markets with a single seller, the sports league or team, and multiple buyers. These auctions only take place periodically. From Table 2.5, the typical broadcast rights fee contract lasts 5 years. Leagues space out the contracts to increase demand for the rights, knowing that at any point in time there will be few alternatives to be bid on. Also, leagues sometimes sell rights to temporally differentiated events, like the regular season and the post season, or in the case of the NFL, to games on different days of the week.

From Table 2.5, media providers are willing to pay relatively large, and increasing sums to purchase the rights fees to sporting events. Much of the media attention to paid to this market focuses on the profitability of these contracts for media providers; in particular, the question of overpayment by media providers gets substantial attention. This question is deceptively difficult to answer, because the overall impact of sports broadcasts on the bottom line of media providers extends well beyond the value of ad spots sold during the broadcasts. The Marginal revenue product of a sports broadcast extends beyond the sports programming division of media providers. Networks advertise their own programs on sports broadcasts, which may make the audience for those other programs larger, generating additional ad slot revenue. And there is sequencing value for sports broadcasts. Many networks debut new programs following high profile sporting events like the Super Bowl; on a smaller scale, media providers schedule programming immediately following sports broadcasts that will appeal to viewers of that sports broadcast, increasing the viewing audience for the following show, also generating additional ad slot revenues. For these reasons, an assessment of the profitability of broadcast rights fee contracts cannot simply compare the value of the rights fees to the ad slot revenues generated during the broadcasts.

Money flows leftward on Figure 2.7, from advertisers to media providers to sports leagues and teams. The most important source of revenues in this market is the advertising fees paid from advertisers to media providers and then on to teams and leagues. Clearly, understanding the economics of advertising is the key to understanding the workings of this market. Also note that sports fans play no substantial role in this market, except that sports fans who watch or listen sports broadcasts are potential customers for the firms who advertise on sports broadcasts.

2.6 Media Providers and Advertising

2.6.1 Ads and Preference Formation

Advertising revenues are generated when firms pay media providers money for ad slots. Why do firms advertise? Economics contains three competing models of advertising:

- *Models of persuasive advertising*: In these models, advertising alters consumers' tastes and creates spurious product differentiation and brand loyalty. The implications are that advertising makes demand for specific products more inelastic, and allows firms to charge higher prices. Persuasive advertising also creates an entry barrier, especially if scale economies exist. Under this model, advertising has important non-competitive effects, and no value to consumers. The model characterizes markets with heavy advertising as having high prices, concentrated production, and large profits.

- *Models of informative advertising*: These models assume that markets contain imperfect information arising from search costs. Because search costs are important, many consumers may not know a product exists. This model emerged from the Chicago school of economics. In this model, advertising is a way to overcome information asymmetries. The implications are that advertising makes demand more elastic, and encourages entry into the market. In this model, advertising has pro-competitive effects and produces benefits for consumers.

- *Models of complementarities between advertising and the advertised product*: These models assume no change in preferences and no changes in information. Consumers value "social prestige" and the consumption of a product generates more social prestige when the consumed product is advertised than when it is not.

These three models of advertising have very different assumptions and implications. Note the important role that market characteristics play in these models, including the heterogeneity of products bought and sold in the markets. If products are homogenous, as economic models of perfectly competitive markets always assume, then only the informative model can explain advertising. In fact, the homogenous product and perfect information assumptions made in neoclassical models of perfectly competitive markets may have led economists to pay little attention to advertising until relatively recently, despite the obvious importance of advertising in modern economies. Another implication from the *persuasive*, *informative* and *complementary* models is that advertising is combative. Producers of similar products will suffer when faced with effective advertising by a competitor under all three models. Thus advertising may affect not only the advertising firms' sales, but the sales of competitors. From this discussion of models of advertising, the importance of why firms advertise, and the related question of why consumers respond to advertising becomes apparent.

A substantial body of empirical research about the effectiveness of advertising exists. The empirical evidence does not consistently support any single model of advertising. Still, a number of clear implications emerge from the empirical research. Not much evidence exists that that advertising generates new or *start-up consumption*, since bans on advertising appear ineffective. Advertising affects current sales, but the effect on sales is very short lived. The reason for this short lived effect is the combative nature of advertising. When one firm increases advertising, it gains sales at the expense of competitors, who respond by increasing their advertising. The effect of advertising on sales appears to vary widely across industries, reinforcing the point that heterogeneity in products plays an important role in advertising. Evidence also exists that advertising informs viewers about a product or service that they did not know about, thus generating new consumers in some settings.

One important finding from the empirical literature on advertising is that advertising informs both "brand choice" and "brand loyalty." Once a consumer has decided to purchase some type of good or service, there are still many choices to be made. Consider what happens when a consumer decides to take up downhill skiing as a hobby. This consumer still must decide what type of ski equipment to purchase, and where to ski. Advertising can influence the decision about what type of equipment to purchase, affecting brand choice. Once a consumer has decided to purchase a particular brand, advertising also appears to generate brand loyalty, convincing consumers to continue to purchase a particular good or service and not to switch to a competing product. Note that these results suggest that advertising is most effective in situations where a consumer has already decided to purchase a specific good, but not in attracting new consumers to a specific product.

A second important finding from the empirical literature is that scale economies may exist in television advertising, but only for consumer goods. Most importantly for the sports broadcast market, the evidence suggests that scale economies in television advertising play an important role in industry concentration in consumer product industries. The scale economies arise because the cost per commercial "message" falls as more commercial "messages" are sent, coupled with the presence of quantity discounts offered to heavy advertisers by media providers.

The presence of scale economies in television advertising for consumer products, combined with the combative nature of advertising and the market power exercised appears to have created a "perfect storm" in this market, leading to the rapid increase in television rights fees in the late 1990s shown on Figure 2.6. The advertisers in this market know that scale economies exist in television advertising, and that their competitors will respond to an increase in advertising with their own increase, in order to hold or increase market share. The monopoly leagues exploit their market power to extract rents from media providers, and advertisers in competitive consumer product markets with a few large competitors (recall the relationship between advertising and industry concentration) must pay increasing fees for ad slots or lose market share.

The main implication of the empirical research on advertising is that, to be effective, advertising must be aimed at groups of consumers who have already decided to purchase some good. In addition, the good being advertised must be a frequently purchased consumer good. The segment of the population that is likely to purchase some good or service is called the *target demographic group*. Advertising on sports broadcasts will be attractive to firms who sell consumer products to a target demographic group that matches sports fans.

What are the demographic characteristics of sports fans? A 2008 Survey (CBS News Poll 2008) asked a representative sample of 1,200 US residents questions on a number of topics. One of the questions was "How interested are you in watching or following professional football?" The three possible responses were "very interested," "somewhat interested," and "not at all interested." Since this was a representative sample of US residents, the characteristics of the people who responded to this question provide information about the average NFL fan.

Table 2.6: Characteristics of NFL Fans, 2008

| Characteristic | Interest in Watching or Following the NFL | | |
	Very Interested	Somewhat Interested	Not at All Interested
Answering each	37%	34%	29%
Male	76%	33%	45%
Average Age	41.2	42.1	50.6
Average Income	$58,877	$50,144	$46,899

From Table 2.6, slightly more than one person in three reported being "very interested" in watching or following the NFL. Those who reported being very interested in the NFL were predominately male and younger than those who where not very interested in watching or following the NFL. Most importantly, the young males who reported being very interested in following the NFL had a higher income than the other groups in the poll. The typical sports television viewer is a male between 18 and 34 years of age. Young relatively affluent males have a lot of disposable income and tend to buy a lot of consumer goods. Advertisers who are interested in reaching young, high income males will clearly be interested in purchasing advertising on sports broadcasts, as sports fans have those characteristics.

2.7   Summary

Defining sport and estimating the size of the sports sector in an economy is a difficult exercise. Defining sport is problematic, because many activities that would not be considered sport, including fishing and eating, have become competitive professionalized contests and share characteristics with sport. National accounts data for economic activity are not well suited to estimating production and expenditure on sport because the sport industry does not fit easily into standard classifications of economic activity. Instead, this chapter discusses the size of the sports industry by examining participation in sport, attendance at sporting events, and viewing sport through media. All three dimensions have significant numbers of participants, suggesting that a large amount of economic activity is associated with the sport market.

Professional sports leagues in North America and Europe have distinct structures and organizations, that the structure and organization of these leagues affects the economics of the league and economic decisions made by teams in these leagues. North American leagues are closed, containing the same teams in each season. European leagues are open, and feature the promotion and relegation system where the membership of leagues changes from season to season. This introduces more competition in European leagues. Game day activities like buying tickets and concessions and media rights are the primary sources of revenues for teams and leagues. Media rights fees have grown significantly over time because of the explosion of media outlets and the monopoly power of leagues. Player salaries represent the largest cost incurred by professional sports teams around the world. Leagues have long struggled to reduce player salaries by imposing restrictions like salary caps and limiting competition for playing talent.

Readings and References

Borland, J. & Macdonald, R. (2003). Demand for Sport, *Oxford Review of Economic Policy*, 19(4), pp. 478-502.

CBS News Poll: 2008 Presidential Election/War in Iraq [computer file]. Roper Center for Public Opinion Research Study USCBS2007-08A Version 2. CBS News [producer], 2007. Storrs, CT: The Roper Center for Public Opinion Research, University of Connecticut [distributor], 2007.

Coakley, J. (2003). *Sport in Society: Issues and Controversies*, 9th edition, Boston: McGraw Hill.

Fort, R. (2006). *Sports Economics*, 3rd edition, New York, NY: Prentice Hall.

Gratton, C. (1988). The economic importance of modern sport, *Culture, Sport and Society*, 1(1), 101-117.

Review Questions

1. *True, False or Uncertain*[5]: Hot dog eating is a professional sport.

2. *True, False or Uncertain*: National broadcast rights fees make up the largest source of revenues in the NHL, NBA, and MLB.

3. *True, False or Uncertain*: Models of persuasive advertising assume the presence of information asymmetries in the market for the good being advertised.

---

[5]To answer this question, explain why the following statement is either true or false, or explain why it could be either true of false, depending on the circumstances. Simply answering "true" or "false" will not receive credit.

Part II

Models of Team, League, and Fan Behavior

Chapter 3

A Short Run Model of Team Decisions

Chapter Objectives

- Explain how teams make short run decisions on ticket pricing and attendance

- Explain short run demand for sports

- Understand demand functions in sport

- Understand the relationship between demand, elasticity, total revenue, marginal revenue

- Understand why sports goods are price inelastic

- Understand the factors that affect team's ticket pricing decisions and secondary ticket markets

3.1 A Tale of Two (NHL) Cities

Selling tickets to games is a core business function of all professional sports teams. In the context of economic theory, a sports team is a monopolist in its own market: the sole supplier of a particular good in certain area. In a few cases, teams are duopolists. For example the Chicago Cubs and White Sox both produce and sell Major League Baseball games in the Chicago metropolitan area. Professional sports teams in many leagues set ticket prices before the season starts. As a monopolist, a team decides on ticket prices and then fans decide how many tickets they want to purchase, given ticket prices and other factors like the quality of the team and facility; this affects total revenues and total profits. This chapter explores these economics decisions.

Consider the following data on ticket prices and attendance from the National Hockey League. Figure 3.1 shows the real average ticket price and total attendance for two NHL franchises, the Anaheim Ducks ("ANA" on the graph) and the Los Angeles Kings ("LA" on the graph) over the 2000-2001 to 2009-2010 seasons. Neither team plays in a "traditional" hockey market; both are located in the greater Los Angeles area, far from the traditional hockey hot beds of Canada and the northeast and upper midwest in the US. Their arenas, the Staples Center in Los Angeles and the Honda Center in Anaheim are only 30 miles apart. Despite this proximity, it is difficult to determine if these two teams play in the same market, or in different markets, due to the size and population density of the Los Angeles metropolitan area.

Figure 3.1: Real Average Ticket Prices and Attendance, Ducks and Kings

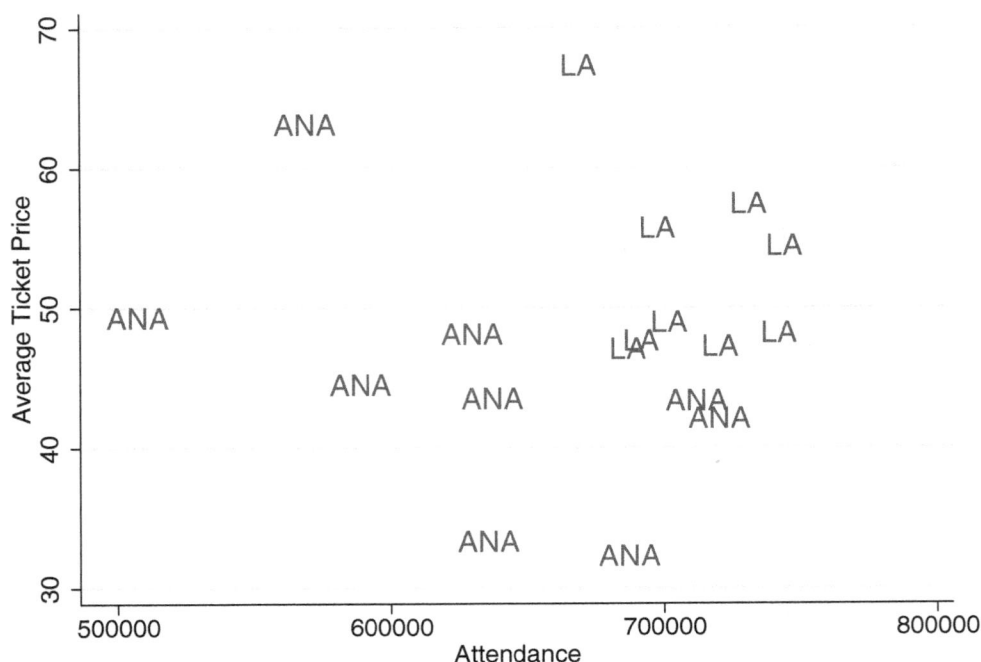

Figure 3.1 provides an imperfect, but informative view of the relationship between the price of the good supplied by NHL teams and the number of tickets sold. It is an imperfect view because the "average" ticket price does not fully reflect the actual prices faced by consumers; travel and time costs also affect the cost of attending a hockey game, and the average price may not reflect the price of tickets available. Despite these limitations, Figure 3.1 reveals several interesting features about the relationship between price and quantity demanded in these two markets.

First, the predicted downward sloping relationship between price and quantity demanded can be seen on Figure 3.1, if the observed price-quantity pairs on the figure are interpreted as reflecting a relatively stable demand curve and variation in the total price of tickets over the period. For both the Ducks and the Kings, lower average real ticket prices appear associated with a higher quantity of tickets sold. Second, the two markets appear to have different relationships between price and quantity demanded. At an average real price of about $50 per ticket, the Kings sell considerably more tickets in a season than the Ducks. In order to sell as many tickets as the Kings, the Ducks appear to have to cut their average real ticket price to about $40 per ticket. Third, consumers of Ducks tickets appear to be more sensitive to price changes than consumers of tickets to the Kings. The price-quantity pairs for the Ducks exhibit more spread than the price-quantity pairs for the Kings. The Kings sold about the same number of tickets at an average price under $50 per ticket as they did at an average price well over $50 per ticket.

Figure 3.1 provides some informal evidence supporting the economic model of market outcomes of a good produced by a monopolist. A systematic relationship between price and quantity can be seen on Figure 3.1, and the difference between the price-quantity relationship for the Kings and Ducks suggests that factors other than price affects demand in sports markets. This chapter develops a model that explains the basic relationship between price and quantity demanded shown

Figure 3.2: A (Linear) Demand Curve

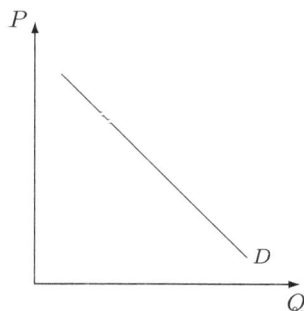

on Figure 3.1. This model assumes that sports teams are profit maximizing firms with market power, and that prices are set to maximize profits given demand in the market.

3.2 Demand for Professional Sport

3.2.1 Demand Defined

Demand quantifies consumers' willingness to pay for some good or service. Consumer demand can be represented by a relationship between price and quantity demanded holding other factors constant. Assume that live attendance is a reasonable measure of demand for professional sport. The variable Q represents the number of people attending specific professional sporting event and a single price, P, represents the total price of attending that professional sports event. A *demand curve* graphically represents the relationship between the price and quantity demanded for a sporting event.

Recall from micro principals that a demand curve can be derived from the standard consumer choice model of utility maximization given a budget constraint. The key point of such a derivation, which can be found in any microeconomics textbook, is that the demand curve for any good or service shows the relationship between the price of the good and the quantity of that good demanded, holding other factors constant. Factors held constant along any demand curve include income, the presence of substitutes for the good, preferences, and all other important economic factors other than the price of the good in question. In sports markets, factors like team quality and on field success are held constant along a demand curve in the short run.

This raises the key distinction between a "change in quantity demanded" and a "change in demand" when using demand curves to analyze the relationship between price and quantity purchased. Figure 3.3 illustrates the difference between a change in quantity demanded and a change in demand. A decrease in price from P_1 to P_2, and the corresponding change in quantity demanded from A_1 to A_2 along demand curve D_1 on Figure 3.3 is a *change in quantity demanded* that holds all other factors constant.

When a factor held constant along a demand curve changes, the entire demand curve shifts. A shift in the entire demand curve is called a *change in demand* and implies that a firm can sell a different quantity of output at a given price. On Figure 3.3, the shift from demand curve D_1 to D_2 is a *change in demand*. Note that after the increase in demand, the firm can sell A_2 units of output at a higher price, P_2' than it could based on demand curve D_1.

What factors determine the position of the demand curve in sports markets? The most important factors include consumers' preferences, including the quality of the team in question and

Figure 3.3: Change in Quantity Demanded vs. Change in Demand

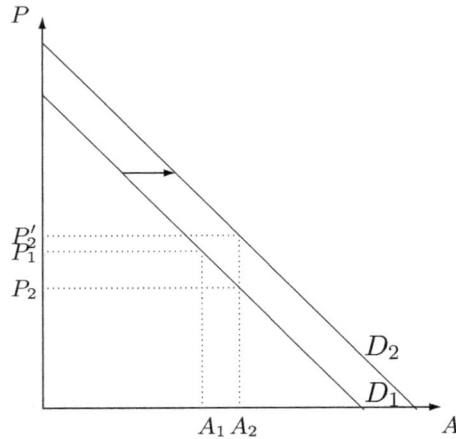

Figure 3.4: Potential Shapes for Sport Demand Curve

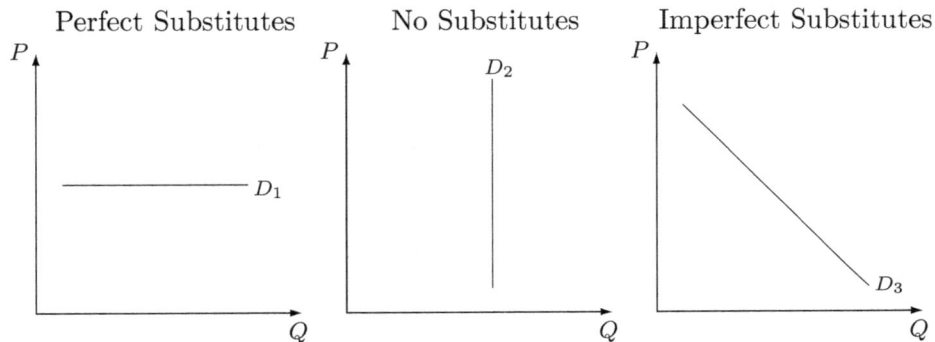

fans' interest in the sport; fans' income and the issue of whether or not sport is a normal good; the price of substitutes for sport, which raises the issue of sport as an entertainment good (if it can be considered an entertainment good like movies and concert, then any other entertainment good could be a substitute for sport.); fans' expectations about the team; and the population in the local market.

What slope does the demand curve for attendance at sporting events have? Recall that the slope of a demand curve depends in part on the presence of substitutes in the market, and the closeness of these goods as substitutes. Figure 3.4 shows the slope of three demand curves along with the nature of the substitute goods that correspond to each demand curve.

If one or more perfect substitutes for a good exist in a market, then the demand curve for that good will be horizontal. At the equilibrium price, the firm can sell all the product it wants, but increases in the price reduce the quantity demanded to zero as consumers switch to the perfect substitute. If no substitutes for a good exist in a market, then the demand curve for that good is vertical. The firm can charge any price and still sell some positive quantity of that good. The intermediate case between these two extremes occurs when some imperfect substitutes exist in the market. In this case, the demand curve for the good slopes down. In order to sell additional units of this good, the firm must lower the price.

Demand curves for sports attendance likely slope down, as imperfect substitutes exist in sports markets. These substitutes include watching the game or match on TV, listening on radio, or attending other entertainment activities. Also, the presence of additional professional sports teams in other leagues can be thought of as an imperfect substitute for a given professional sport.

The slope of sports demand curves may depend on the number of other professional sports teams in a market. A few cities are large enough to support more than one team in a sports league (like New York, Chicago and Los Angeles), this is the exception and nearly all cities have a single team in each professional sports league. In addition, recall that all North American sports leagues define *exclusive geographic territories* for their teams. These exclusive territories reduce the number of substitutes in any market. Territorial agreements also generate *market power* for teams in professional sports leagues at all levels of professional sport.

Another important topic related to demand for professional sports in markets is the existence of so-called "large" and "small" markets. Media commentators, bloggers, and TV talking heads often refer to large and small markets in professional sports leagues. Most major cities in North America are capable of supporting one or more professional sports teams. While disparities in market size exist, this phenomena may be better defined in terms of "high demand" and "low demand" markets. In this sense, differences in local markets can be attributed to differences in population, preferences, local income, and franchise success.

It is also important to bear in mind that a demand curve conveys quite a bit of information about the good or service in question. In addition to showing the quantity of a good demanded at any price, a demand curve also shows consumers' *willingness to pay* for that good or service.

Figure 3.5: Demand, Willingness to Pay, and Consumer Surplus

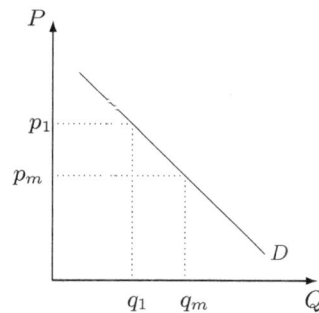

On Figure 3.5, interpret q_1 as a particular ticket to a sporting event that customer 1 wants to purchase. From this demand curve, customer 1 places a value of p_1 on that ticket, and would be willing to pay any price up to p_1 for that ticket. So p_1 can be interpreted as the value that customer 1 places on that ticket, thus a measure of customer 1s willingness to pay for that ticket. p_1 is the maximum amount that customer 1 would pay for the ticket.

A demand curve can also be used to show *Consumer Surplus*. Consumer surplus is the difference between willingness to pay and the market price paid for all units. If a customer places a value of p_1, but only has to pay p_m for a ticket, then consumer surplus for that customer is the vertical distance between p_m and p_1.

More generally, if the overall willingness to pay for tickets in a market is shown by the demand curve, and all tickets are priced at p_m, then consumer surplus is the area above the horizontal dotted line at p_m and the demand curve. As the price of a good falls, consumer surplus rises.

Finally, recall that price elasticity is an important concept related to the slope of a demand curve. Let A represent attendance at a sporting event and P represent the price of tickets to this sporting event. Assume that all consumers are charged the same price for attending. The *Price Elasticity of demand* describes the relationship between changes in price and changes in quantity

Figure 3.6: Price Elasticity of Demand Along a Linear Demand Curve

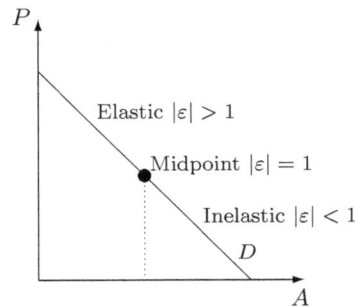

demanded. Formally

$$\varepsilon = \frac{\%\Delta A}{\%\Delta P} = \frac{\Delta A}{\Delta P} \cdot \frac{P}{A}.$$

Since $\frac{\Delta A}{\Delta P} > 0$, the price elasticity is always negative; note that the price elasticity of demand is sometimes expressed as an absolute value, not as a negative number. The price elasticity of demand changes systematically when moving from left to right down a linear demand curve. As shown on Figure 3.6, the price elasticity of demand is greater than 1 in absolute value and declining at all points above the midpoint of the demand curve. In this range, the change in the quantity demanded is more than proportionate to a 1% change in price. The price elasticity of demand is equal to 1 at the midpoint, so the change in quantity demanded is proportionate to a 1% change in price. Below the midpoint, the price elasticity of demand is less than one and falling in absolute value, so the change in demand is less than proportionate to a 1'% change in price.

3.3   Attendance and Revenue Maximization

This section develops a model of demand for tickets at a sporting event. Again, let A represent attendance at a sporting event and P represent the price of tickets to this sporting event. Assume that all consumers are charged the same price for attending. Define total revenue generated by any level of attendance as

$$R(A) = P(A) \cdot A$$

where $R(A)$ is total revenue and $P(A)$ is the price that generates a given level of attendance. This "inverse demand function" is just the P that goes along with any A on a market demand curve.

Assume a linear demand curve

$$P(A) = a - bA$$

where a is the intercept of the demand curve and b the slope of the linear (inverse) demand curve. Figure 3.7 shows the slope and intercept of a linear demand curve. The intercept, a is the price at which the quantity demanded is zero. The slope (rise over run) shows how quantity demanded changes as price changes, holding other factors constant. The slope of a linear demand curve is constant, so the rate of change of price and quantity demanded are the same at all points on a linear demand curve.

Figure 3.7: A Linear Demand Curve

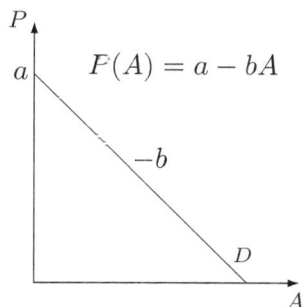

Figure 3.8: Linear Demand and Total Revenue

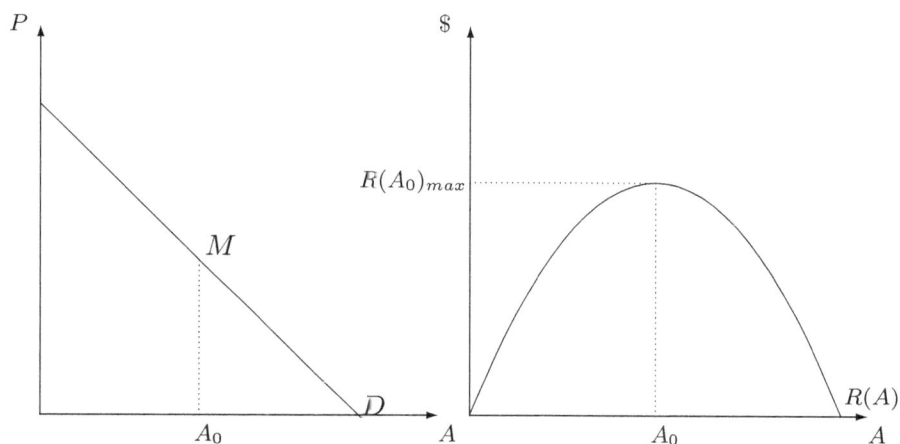

Given a linear demand curve, we can easily derive the relationship between total revenue, marginal revenue, price, and attendance. Total Revenue can be expressed as

$$R(A) = P(A) \cdot A = (a - bA) \cdot A = aA - bA^2 \qquad (3.1)$$

Note that this is a quadratic function – a parabola – in A. The parameters a and b are again the slope and intercept of the demand curve. When A is small, the first term dominates and increases in attendance increase revenues. However. the team must reduce the price to sell more tickets, and, as A gets larger P must get smaller. Eventually, the second term in Equation 3.1 dominates and total revenues fall.

This total revenue function can easily be graphed. Figure 3.8 shows the demand and total revenue curves for Equation (3.1). Notice that total revenue rises with attendance until it reaches a maximum at the midpoint of the demand function and then falls. Again, this reflects the fact that the team must reduce prices to see more tickets (moving along the demand curve from left to right.) Also notice from Figure 3.8 that total revenues are maximized where $|\varepsilon| = 1$, at the midpoint of the demand curve.

Figure 3.9: Linear Demand, Marginal Revenue and Total Revenue

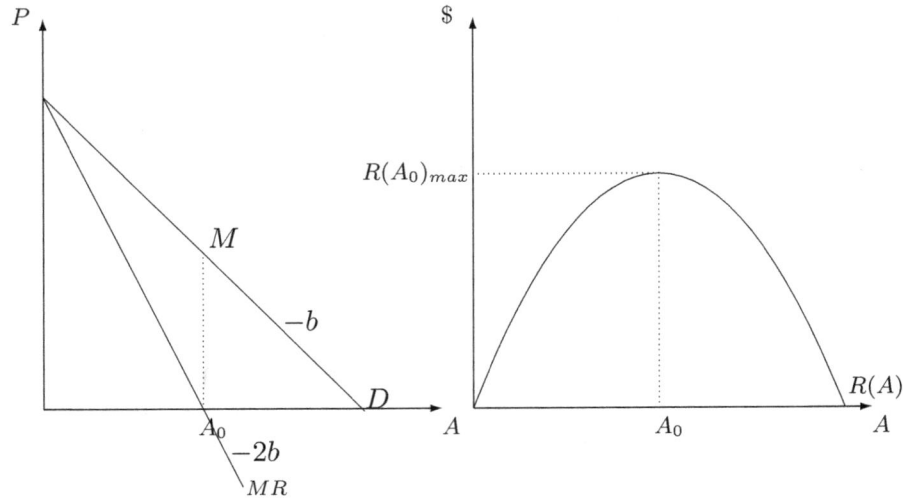

Marginal Revenue can be calculated from the total revenue function, Equation (3.8) simply by taking the first derivative of the revenue function with respect to changes in A

$$MR(A) = \frac{\partial R(A)}{\partial A} = \frac{\partial}{\partial A} aA - bA^2 = a - 2bA.$$

Note the marginal revenue function is also a linear function that has the same intercept as the demand curve and twice the slope of the demand function. Graphed in $(P \times A)$ space, the marginal revenue curve starts at the same intercept as the demand curve and lies below the demand curve, cutting the horizontal axis exactly below the midpoint of the demand curve. Graphically, marginal revenue is just the slope of a line drawn tangent to the total revenue curve at any point. These tangent lines are steep and positive at small values of A and get flatter moving from left to right along the total revenue curve. At the top of the total revenue curve, marginal revenue is zero. This occurs at an easy to derive value for A which depends on the parameters of the demand curve (A_0)

$$A_0 = \tfrac{1}{2}\tfrac{a}{b} \tag{3.2}$$

Notice that three things occur at A_0, the revenue maximizing level of attendance given the demand curve, which is graphed on Figure 3.9

1. Total revenue $R(A)$ is maximized (A_0 is below the highest point on $R(A)$)

2. Marginal revenue $MR(A) = 0$

3. $|\varepsilon| = 1$ when $A = A_0$ (Demand is unitary elastic at the point of revenue maximization)

The revenue maximization model predicts that a revenue maximizing sports team will set ticket prices at the point on the demand curve where the price elasticity of demand is unitary.

Marginal Revenue, Price, and Elasticity An additional interesting relationship between price, revenue, and elasticity can be derived from this model. Begin with the revenue function

$$R(A) = P(A) \cdot A$$

and apply the chain rule to this expression to find the total differential

$$
\begin{aligned}
MR(A) = \tfrac{d}{dA}P(A) \cdot A &= \tfrac{d}{dA}P(A) \cdot A + P(A)\tfrac{d}{dA} \\
&= \tfrac{\Delta P}{\Delta A} \cdot A + P \cdot 1 \\
MR(A) &= \tfrac{\Delta P}{\Delta A} \cdot A + P
\end{aligned}
$$

Factor out P

$$MR(A) = P\left(\tfrac{\Delta P}{\Delta A}\left(\tfrac{A}{P}\right) + 1\right)$$

Recall that $\varepsilon = -\tfrac{\%\Delta A}{\%\Delta P} = -\tfrac{\Delta A}{\Delta P} \cdot \tfrac{P}{A}$

So $\tfrac{1}{\varepsilon} = -\tfrac{\Delta P}{\Delta A} \cdot \tfrac{A}{P}$

$$
\begin{aligned}
MR(A) &= P\left(-\tfrac{1}{\varepsilon} + 1\right) \\
MR(A) &= P\left(1 - \tfrac{1}{|\varepsilon|}\right)
\end{aligned}
$$

The final expression shows that marginal revenue at any level of attendance A is a function of the ticket price, P, and the price elasticity of demand. At the left end of the demand curve, P is large and ε is large, so $1 - \tfrac{1}{\varepsilon}$ is close to one. Moving to the right, P gets smaller, and ε gets smaller, so that $1 - \tfrac{1}{\varepsilon}$ eventually becomes negative.

As an example, consider what happens to total revenues when demand shifts in this model. Suppose that some factor that shifts the demand curve like local population increases. An increase in population shifts the demand curve to the right. At any price, the team can sell more tickets. Figure 3.10 shows the effect of a rightward shift in the demand curve on the total revenue curve. From Figure 3.10, the demand curve shifts right, which leads the right end of the total revenue curve to shift to the right, and the total revenue curve to shift up. The revenue maximizing level of attendance has increased, and the total revenues that can be earned at the maximum level of has also increased. This example shows that teams have two different ways of increasing attendance:

1. Cut prices, move along a given demand curve. This increases revenues only if the team is operating to the left of the midpoint of the demand curve (in the elastic region of the demand curve).

2. Increase demand, shifting the demand curve to the right This unambiguously increases revenues, since more tickets can be sold at any price.

Can teams shift their demand curve? They can increase quality of the team, which may lead to more wins and an increase in demand. Alternatively, advertising or other promotions may also increase demand. Teams should be able to increase demand for tickets to their games, but shifting the demand curve can be very costly, and the cost of shifting the demand curve may outweigh the revenues generated by an increase in demand. To understand this relationship, we need to model the determination of profits.

Figure 3.10: An Increase in Demand

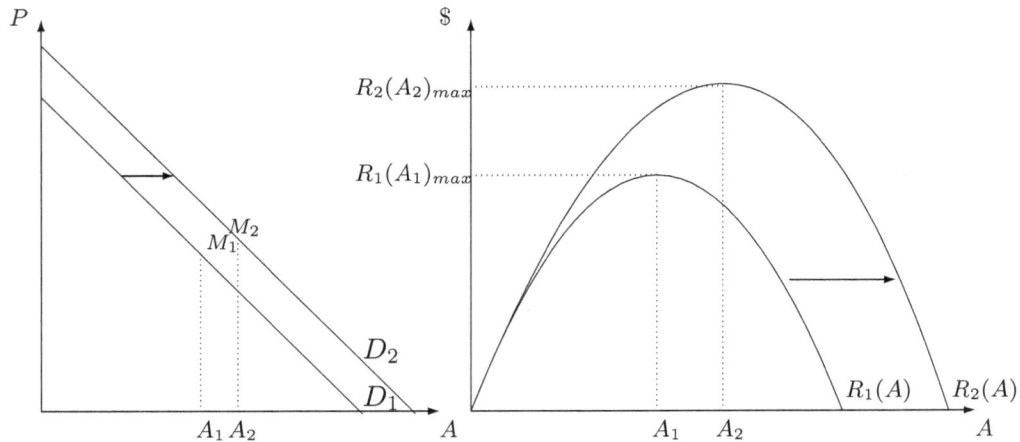

3.4 Profit Maximization

A short run analysis of decisions made by professional sports teams identifies the profit maximizing number of tickets that will be sold by the team given fixed and variable costs and the exogenous factors associated with the team's market that affect the relationship between attendance and total revenues. In this model, teams take the demand curve and marginal production costs as given and set a price to draw the profit maximizing number of fans to games. This model can be used to explain why specific short run outcomes occur in professional sports leagues.

For example, consider Figure 3.11, which shows a scatter plot of total attendance and total gate revenues in the National Hockey League (NHL) in the 2008-2009 season (all revenues have been converted to current US dollars at the annual average exchange rate). Figure 3.11 shows quite a bit of variation in both gate attendance and total revenues, although there is a clear positive association between these two variables. A number of teams drew about the same number of fans and earned widely different amounts in terms of gate revenues, and a number of teams also earned similar gate revenues off of widely varying total attendance.

For example the New York Rangers (NYR on the graph) and the Washington Capitals (WAS on the graph) both drew about 750,000 fans in 2008-2009, but the gate revenues earned by these two teams varied significantly; the Rangers earned about $20 million more in gate revenues than the Capitals from the same number of tickets sold. A short run model of attendance and revenues is a useful tool for explaining why these differences in attendance and gate revenues would be observed. The basic idea is that each point shown on Figure 3.11 is a profit maximizing outcome for each team, given fixed and variable costs and local market conditions. The short run model of profit maximization will identify the specific factors that lead to the different profit maximizing outcomes shown on Figure 3.11.

In order to undertake an economic analysis of the short run decisions made by professional sports teams, it is first necessary to define the output produced by teams, and then to identify the key inputs to the production function and the costs associated with these inputs. Assume that profit maximization is the objective of professional sports teams, and that attendance (A), or

Figure 3.11: NHL Attendance and Gate Revenue 2008

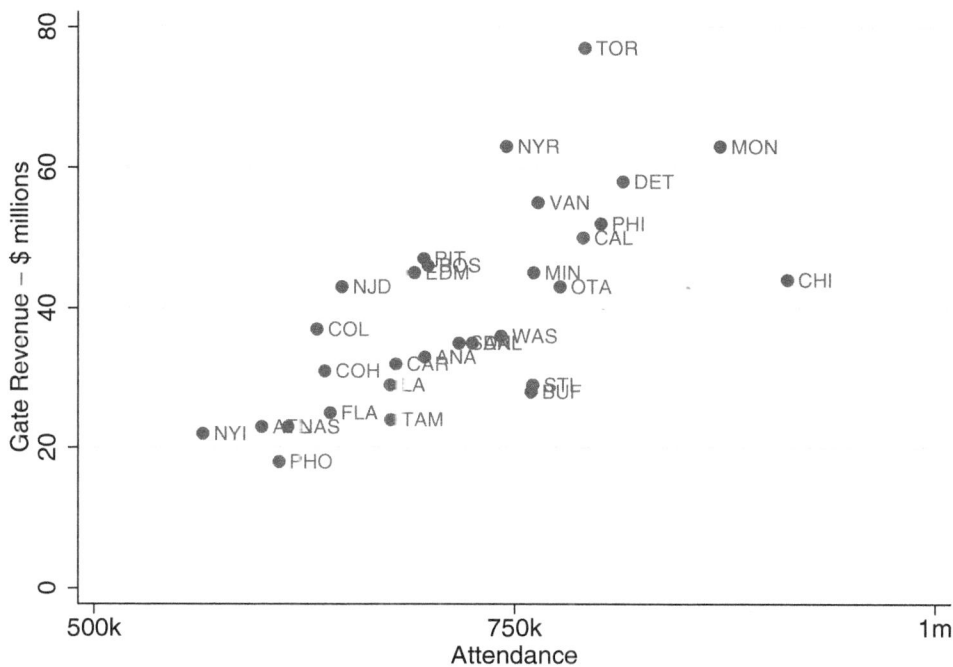

tickets sold, is the short run output of professional sports teams. A general production function for attendance is

$$A = f(I_1, I_2, \ldots, I_N). \tag{3.3}$$

Where A is attendance and I_1, ..., I_N are the inputs to production. An economic analysis of production must identify specific inputs to production and determine which inputs are fixed in the short run and which are variable. Recall that the short run is defined as a period of time short enough that some inputs to production cannot be changed, and the long run is defined as a period long enough that all inputs to production are variable. A large number of inputs are required to produce professional sporting events, including players, coaches, trainers, scouts, front office personnel, facilities, game day labor inputs, travel, and advertising and marketing. The key point is that in the short run there are some inputs to production that are fixed, and other inputs to production that are variable. In this short run analysis, assume that the fixed factors of production are the players, coaching staff, front office staff, and the facility. The roster and coaches are determined prior to the start of the season. This assumption abstracts from in-season trades, injuries, and managerial changes. While these events occur in professional sport, assume that they do not affect short-run demand for tickets to the team's games. The variable factors of production are assumed to be advertising and marketing, scouting and player development, game day operations, travel and other team operations. Team operations include factors like the jerseys and equipment, practice costs, and other items related to practice and play. These factors, primarily advertising, marketing and promotions, are the variable inputs that can be changed in the short run in order to affect attendance. This short run model assumes that players, coaches and the facility cannot be varied by the team in the short run, while advertising, marketing, team travel, scouting, and game day operations like the number of vendors and concessionaires can be changed.

3.4.1 Costs

In general, short run total costs ($SRTC$) can be decomposed into short run fixed costs ($SRFC$) and short run variable costs ($SRVC$)

$$SRTC = SRFC + SRVC.$$

The key feature in this model is that short run fixed costs do not vary with the number of tickets sold but short run variable costs increase with the number of tickets sold. Graphically, $SRFC$ is a horizontal line when graphed against the level of attendance (A) on the horizontal axis. Figure 3.12 shows the short run fixed costs curve.

Figure 3.12: Short Run Fixed Costs

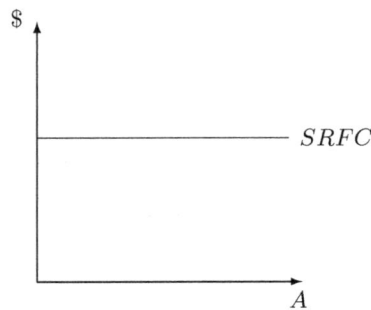

Short run fixed costs are associated with inputs to the production process that cannot be changed in the short run - primarily salaries of players and facility expenses for professional sports teams. The idea that short run fixed costs cannot be changed is simply an assumption that allows us to differentiate between different types of costs faced by professional sports teams.

Short run variable costs are associated with the variable inputs in the production function. These costs rise with attendance. Short run variable costs come from marketing and promotions, team operation, and travel expenses. By assumption, marginal costs are increasing, which makes the short run variable cost curve non-linear. Figure 3.13 shows the short run variable cost curve.

Figure 3.13: Short Run Variable Costs

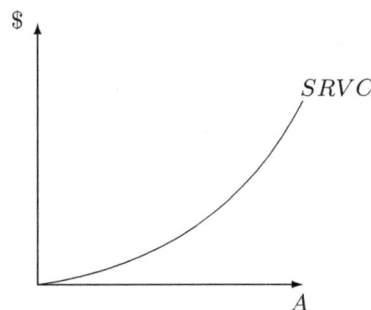

Short-Run Total Costs ($SRTC(A)$) are the sum of total fixed costs and total variable costs. The Short-Run Total Cost curve is just the total variable cost curve shifted up by total fixed costs, as can be seen on Figure 3.14, which shows the short run fixed cost, short run variable and short run total cost curves.

Figure 3.14: Short Run Total Costs

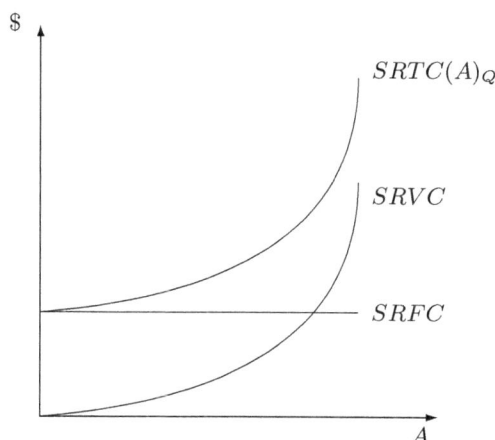

The Short Run Total Cost curve holds team quality constant. Short Run Total Costs rise with attendance, because in order to attract larger crowds to games played by a team with fixed quality, the team must spend increasing amounts on marketing, promotions, etc. in order to sell more tickets.

3.4.2 Revenues

The graphical analysis of short run revenues was discussed in Section 3.3. Recall that each team is assumed to be a monopolist in its own market, and faces a downward sloping demand curve for gate attendance. Given this downward sloping demand curve, a total revenue curve can be derived that has a parabolic shape, shown in the right panel below, on Figure 3.15.

Given a linear demand curve, which implies a linear inverse demand curve of the form

$$P = a - bA$$

with intercept a and slope b, a revenue function $R(A)$ can be derived. Again, the maximum revenues are earned at $A = A_0$, which is at the midpoint of the demand curve M, as shown on Figure 3.9.

3.4.3 Profits

The graphical analysis of short run profits involves combining the short run cost curve and the short run revenue curves developed above on the same graph. Simply graph the $SRTC$ and total revenue functions together. The Figure 3.16 shows both revenues and costs on the same axes. Combining these two graphs gives us enough information to analyze the short run profit maximizing decisions made by professional sports teams. For any level of attendance a team might realize, the graph shows how much profit is earned. For example, pick some level of attendance, say A_1. Go up vertically from A_1 to the revenue curve and read horizontally across to the the vertical axis.

Figure 3.15: Demand and Total Revenue

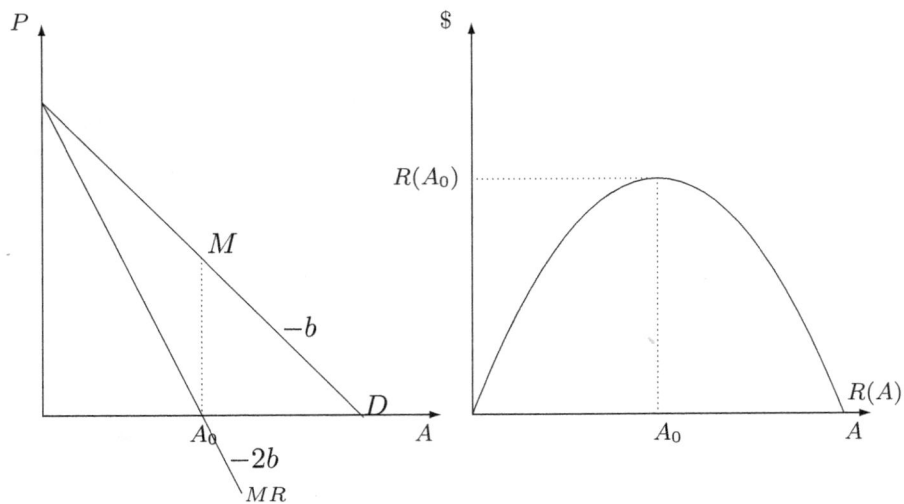

Figure 3.16: Total Revenues and Costs

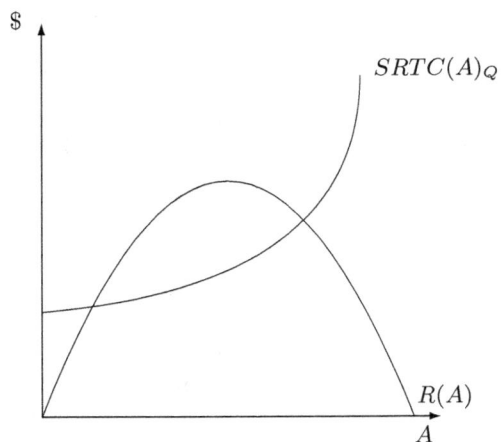

Figure 3.17: Revenues for a Specific Level of Attendance

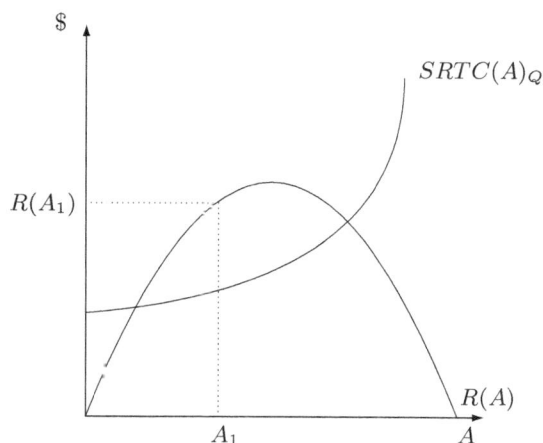

This value shows how much total revenues are earned at level of attendance A_1. In Figure 3.17, A_1 tickets sold generates $R(A_1)$ in total revenues.

In a similar fashion, the total cost of drawing A_1 fans to the arena can be found from the $SRTC$. From A_1, go up vertically to the $SRTC$ curve and read across horizontally to the vertical axis to show the total costs of that level of attendance. As can be seen on Figure 3.18, drawing A_1 fans to the arena leads to $C(A_1)$ in short run costs.

Profit (π) is the difference between total revenues and total costs. Formally

$$\pi_A = R(A) - C(A) \tag{3.4}$$

In this graphical analysis, profit is the vertical distance between the short run revenue curve and the short run total cost curve at any level of attendance. For example, at attendance A_1 the difference between costs and revenues, the vertical distance between $R(A_1)$ and $C(A_1)$, is the profit earned by the team at that level of ticket sales

or algebraically

$$\pi_{A1} = R(A_1) - C(A_1).$$

This exercise can be repeated for every possible level of attendance shown on the graph. When costs exceed revenues, profits are negative (the team earns losses). Note that the profit earned at each level of attendance first increases and then decreases.

3.4.4   Solving the Model

By assumption, teams make decisions to attract the number of fans required to maximize profits by setting ticket prices at the profit maximizing level. We need to come up with a method to determine the level of attendance where profit is maximized - where the vertical distance between the short run total cost curve and the revenue curve is largest. On Figure 3.19 there are two levels of attendance where total revenues equal total costs, labeled $A_{\pi=0}$ below. These are the "break even" points in the model.

Figure 3.18: Costs and Attendance

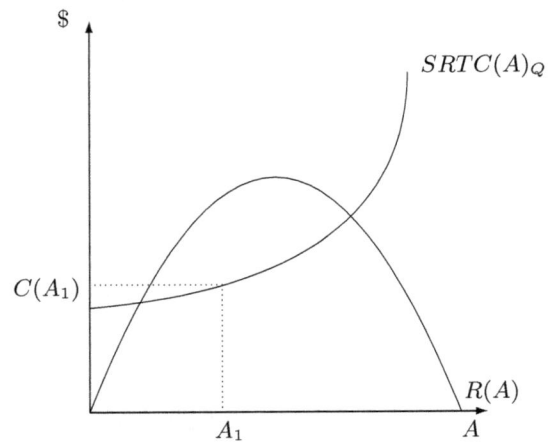

Figure 3.19: Revenues, Costs and Profit

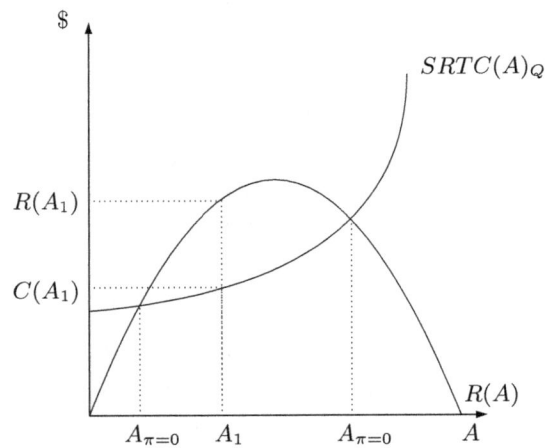

Figure 3.20: Marginal Revenue

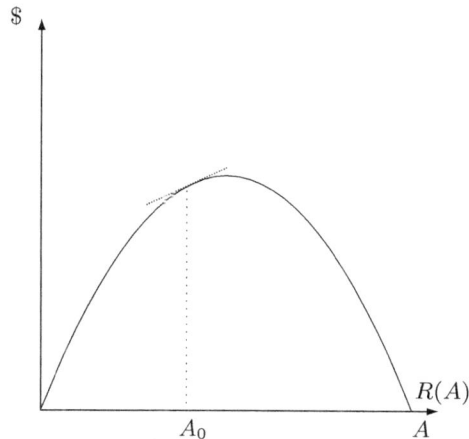

For all levels of attendance lower than the smallest break even A, where profit is zero, revenues exceed costs and the team earns negative profits. For all levels of attendance above the large A, where profit is zero, the also team earns negative profits. For all As between these two points, revenues exceed costs and the team makes a positive profit.

If the level of profits for every possible attendance level (A) were calculated from the revenue and cost functions shown on Figure 3.19, profits would reach a maximum at some A between the two break even points. Because the revenue and cost functions are smooth curves, there must exist a unique level of attendance $A_{\pi*}$ where the vertical distance between the revenue function and the cost function is maximized. This is the profit maximizing level of attendance for this team.

There is an easier way to solve this model. Recall that profit is maximized where marginal cost is equal to marginal revenue ($MC = MR$). If we can find graphical representations of marginal cost and marginal revenue, then the solution to the model becomes easier. The slope of a line tangent to the revenue function $R(A)_Q$ at any point is marginal revenue. For example, to find the marginal revenue generated by selling ticket A_0, go up to the point on the revenue curve above A_0 and draw a line tangent to the revenue curve at that point. The slope of that line is the marginal revenue generated by that fan attending the game.

Figure 3.20 shows a total revenue function and a graphical representation of marginal revenue at a specific point on the total revenue curve. From the origin, where $A = 0$ until the maximum point on the total revenue curve, marginal revenue is positive and decreasing. At these points, the slope of lines drawn tangent to the total revenue curve have a positive slope, and the tangent lines get flatter as attendance gets closer to the level where revenues are maximized. At the point where revenues are maximized, the slope of a line drawn tangent to the total revenue function has a slope of zero; that tangent line is horizontal. At all points to the right of the maximum point on the total revenue curve, marginal revenue is negative. At all these levels of attendance, the sole of a line drawn tangent to the total revenue function has a negative slope, and the slope of these lines gets steeper.

Again, the graphical representation of marginal revenue is reflected in the slope of a line drawn tangent to the total revenue curve at any point. Moving from left to right along the total revenue

Figure 3.21: Marginal Cost

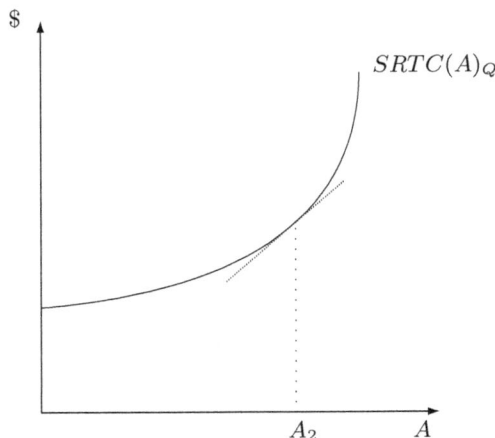

curve shown on Figure 3.20, the slope of these tangent lines change systematically. The slope of these tangent lines are first positive and steep, indicating large, positive marginal revenue. The slope of the tangent lines become flatter (marginal revenue is decreasing) and becomes zero at the point where the total revenue function is largest. Beyond the point where revenues are maximized, the slope of the lines tangent to the total revenue curve are negative and become steeper. Marginal revenue is negative and increasing in this range.

Similarly, at level of attendance A_2, the marginal cost can be found by going up to the short run total cost curve above A_2 and drawing a line tangent to the cost curve at that point. The slope of a line tangent to the $SRTC(A)_Q$ curve at that point is the marginal cost at that level of generating that level of attendance. Figure 3.21 shows a graphical representation of marginal cost. Marginal cost increases as A increases. This is because the team must spend increasing amounts on promotions, advertising, and other factors to get people to buy tickets to games as total attendance increases. Residents of the local market have different preferences for professional sport. Residents with strong preferences will respond to little in the way of advertising and promotions, because they are fans of the team. However, other residents with not so strong preferences for professional sport will require additional advertising, promotions, and other marketing efforts before purchasing a ticket. This increases the marginal cost.

Profit is maximized at the level of attendance where marginal revenue is equal to marginal cost. This occurs at the value of A where the slope of a line tangent to the total revenue curve is equal to the slope of a line tangent to the total cost curve. Point A^* is the profit maximizing level of attendance for this particular total revenue and total cost curve. At A^* marginal revenue is equal to marginal cost. In terms of the graphical solution to the model, a line tangent to the revenue curve above A^* has the same slope as a line tangent to the total short run cost curve above A^*.

Figure 3.22: Graphical Solution

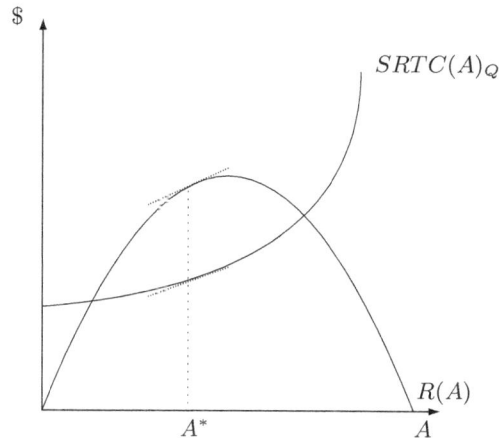

3.5 Application: Revenues and Attendance

The short run models of revenue and profit maximization can be used to explain observed variation in attendance and revenues in professional sports leagues. This section contains several examples of outcomes in professional sport that can be explained by the models developed in this chapter.

Lack of data is clearly a problem when trying to assess the usefulness of the short run models developed in this chapter. Data on the financial performance of professional sports teams are relatively hard to come by, because pro sports teams are privately held companies and are not required to release audited financial data. *Forbes* magazine is one source of data on team revenues and expenses, but because these data are estimated from observable factors like attendance and media rights contracts, and not reported by the teams, they may not be accurate. Teams have incentives to be less than truthful when reporting revenues, because they often seek substantial public subsidies for the construction and operation of their facilities, a topic discussed in Chapter 8. Still, this is the best consistently available data source for team financial information. Look back at Figure 3.11, which shows league wide gate revenue and attendance in the NHL in the 2008-2009 season. From Figure 3.11 Montreal drew more fans, and earned more gate revenues, than Vancouver in the 2008-2009 season. The short run model of profit maximization can be used to explain the difference between the Canucks and the Habs in this season.

Based on the model, the difference between Montreal and Vancouver lies in the market that the two teams play in. For a moment, assume that all costs are fixed, and that the two teams behave as revenue maximizers. Figure 3.23 shows the demand curves for the two teams, Montreal (D_M) and Vancouver (D_V), as well as the total revenue curves for each team. From Figure 3.23, the key difference between the two teams is that Montreal can sell more tickets at an given price level than Vancouver. This could be due to differences in preferences, the population of the local markets, income in the local markets, or the presence of substitutes in the local markets. Because of this difference in the markets, the total revenue curve for Montreal lies above the total revenue curve for Vancouver. The ability to charge a higher price for any ticket in Montreal gives the Habs the ability to generate more revenues at any level of attendance. Also, not that the revenue maximizing

Figure 3.23: Differences in Demand, Price and Total Revenue

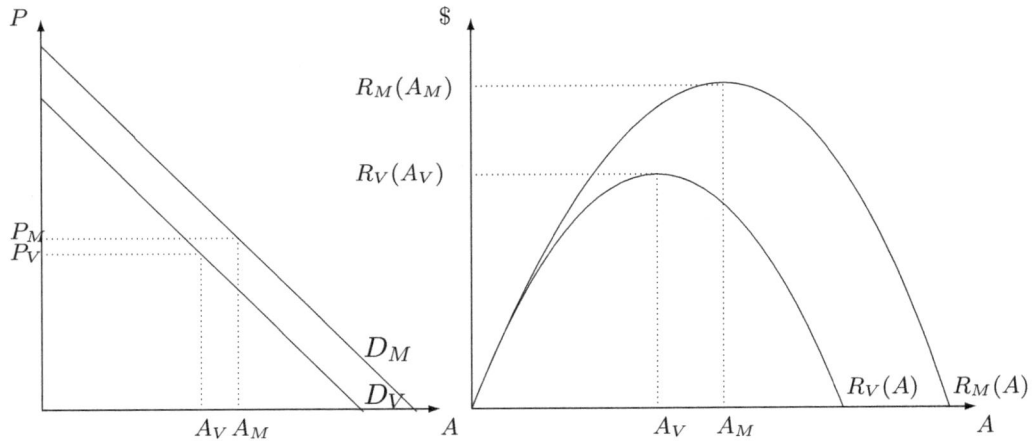

level of attendance in Montreal is higher than in Vancouver, and that Montreal earns more total revenues than Vancouver. All of these predictions are consistent with Figure 3.23.

Finally, note that the model predicts that ticket prices will be higher in Montreal than in Vancouver. The average ticket price to an NHL game in Montreal in the 2008-2009 season was $64.26, and the average price to an NHL game in Vancouver was $62.05. Note that the model does not predict that attendance was different in the two cities because of differences in the quality of the team. The model predicts that the difference in attendance, prices, and gate revenues comes from differences in the characteristics of the markets that the teams play in.

3.5.1 Attendance, Ticket Prices, and Profits

The model also explains observed differences between ticket prices and attendance. Look back at Figure 3.1, which shows average ticket prices and attendance for the Ducks and the Kings. If you interpret this graph as roughly identifying demand curves for the Ducks and Kings, with some variation due to random factors, the demand curve for the Kings appears to lie above the demand curve for the Ducks. The demand curve for the Kings also appears to be steeper than for the Ducks, suggesting that Kings fans are less sensitive to price changes than Ducks fans. The short run model of profit maximization can be used to interpret these outcomes.

Figure 3.24 shows the equilibrium outcomes in the short run model of profit maximization for the Ducks and Kings. D subscripts identify outcomes for the Ducks and K subscripts identify outcomes for the Kings. Based on Figure 3.1, the demand curve for the Kings lies to to right of the demand curve for the Ducks. In addition, the total revenue curve for the Kings is higher than the total revenue curve for the Ducks, demonstrating that the Kings can earn higher revenues than the Ducks at any level of attendance. Figure 3.24 assumes that the Ducks and Kings face the same short run total cost curves.

On Figure 3.24, the pairs of outcomes $(A_D, R_D(A_D), P_D)$ for the Ducks and $(A_K, R_K(A_K), P_K)$ for the Kings are the revenue maximizing level of attendance, revenues, and price. Now that the model has been extended to include profits and cost, the revenue maximizing outcome is different

Figure 3.24: Differences in Demand, Price and Total Revenue

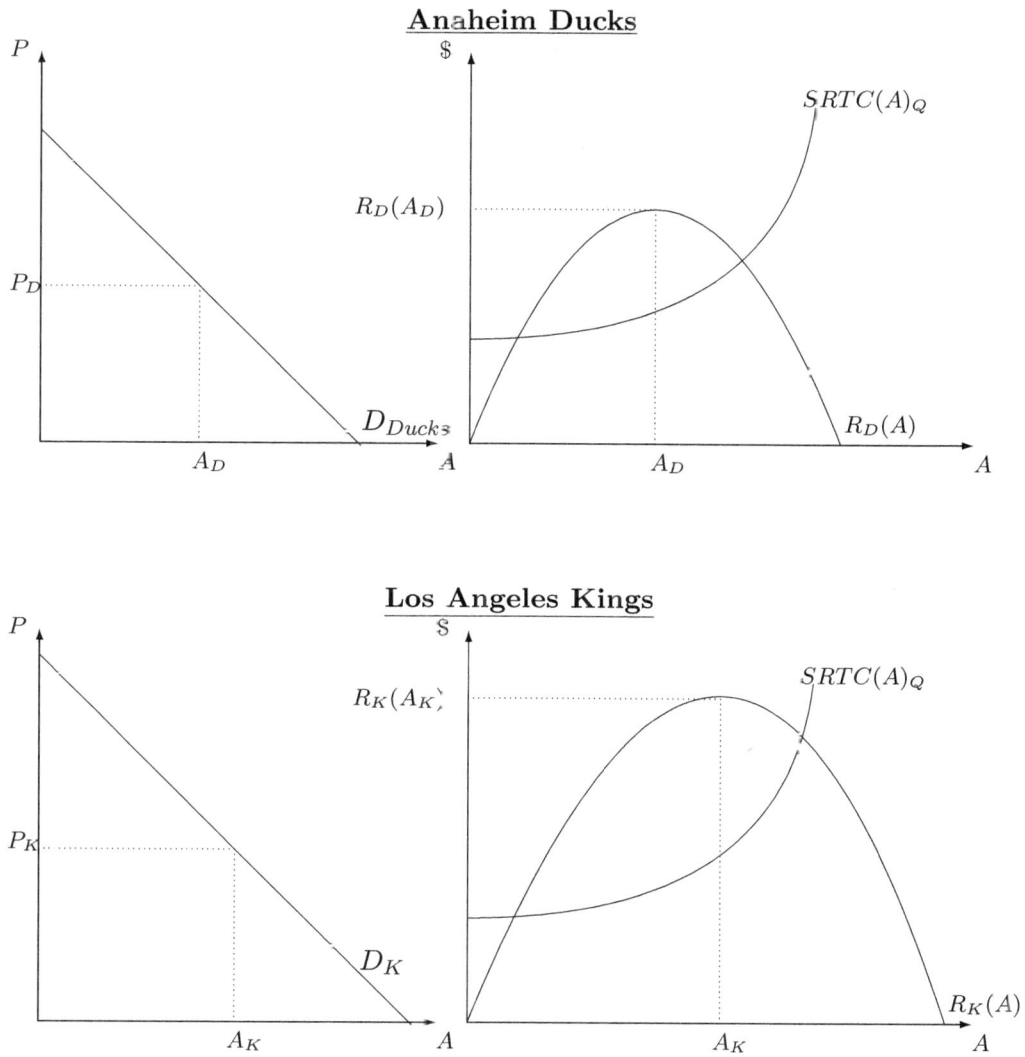

Anaheim Ducks

Los Angeles Kings

from the profit maximizing outcome. Note that at A_D, marginal revenue is zero but marginal cost is positive; marginal revenue is not equal to marginal cost at A_D, so A_D is not a profit maximizing level of attendance. The same is true of the Kings. For both teams, the profit maximizing level of attendance lies to the left of the revenue maximizing level of attendance, where marginal revenue is equal to marginal cost. These profit maximizing points can be found in the same way described above: by identifying a line tangent to the total cost curve (marginal cost) and shifting this up to find a line tangent to the total revenu curve (marginal revenue) that has the same slope. Note that the comparison of the revenue maximizing and profit maximizing points also implies that the ticket price at which profits are maximized is higher than the ticket price at which revenues are maximized, because the teams must raise ticket prices to reduce attendance below the revenue maximizing level.

Figure 3.24 also predicts that gate revenues for the Kings should be higher than gate revenue for the Ducks. The *Forbes* estimates for the period 2005-2006 through 2008-2009 suggest that the Ducks earned higher gate revenues than the Kings over this period. There are three possible reasons why the *Forbes* estimates may differ from the predictions of the model shown on Figure 3.24:

1. The *Forbes* estimates systematically understate the gate revenues earned by the Kings and overstate the gate revenues earned by the Ducks

2. The average price data shown on Figure 3.1 do not reflect the actual price of tickets for these two teams. This could happen if the price distribution for one of the two teams is skewed and the composition of total attendance is also skewed

3. Some factor which is held constant in the short run model is not constant over these four seasons. For example, the model holds team quality constant. The Kings had 68, 71, 79 and 101 points in these four seasons; the Ducks had 110, 102, 91 and 89. The Kings steadily improved while the Ducks got steadily worse over the period. Team quality may not have been constant over the period, and the short run model cannot explain this, because it holds team quality constant. The long run model developed in Chapter 3 will address team quality as a choice variable in an economic model of team behavior.

3.6 Pricing in Sports Markets

The model developed above generates predictions about the relationship between prices and demand based on some simplifying assumptions. Some of these predictions match outcomes in sports markets, providing support for the model. But the model makes one prediction that is not supported by empirical evidence, and the assumption that teams operate as a single price monopolist, charging only one price for tickets, flies in the face of readily observable evidence. Clearly the model needs to be reconciled with this evidence.

3.6.1 Pricing in the Inelastic Region of Demand

Sports economists devote significant attention to the estimation of ticket price elasticities, and the estimates from this literature consistently find price elasticity estimates in the inelastic region of the demand curve using data from professional team sports. From the model developed above, marginal revenue is negative in the inelastic region of the demand curve. Raising ticket prices and reducing the quantity of tickets demanded should raise revenues. Why would sports teams set ticket prices in the inelastic region of their demand curve? Two answers immediately jump to mind:

1. Teams do not care about maximizing profits, so the objective function assumption assumed for this model (profit maximization) is incorrect

2. Teams make more profit off of complementary goods to tickets like concessions and parking. They set prices in the inelastic portion of the demand curve in order to attract more fans and earn higher profits from sales of these complementary goods

Both explanations have appeal. Professional sports teams continually refer to winning as an important organizational goal, but almost never talk about their profits. If professional sports teams want to win, and if having more fans in the stands increases winning, then teams might price in the inelastic portion of the demand curve to improve the chances of winning a game. Concessions and parking typically have large markups inside professional sports venues. Beer, hot dogs, popcorn, and parking all cost more inside stadiums and arenas than in other places. The significant markup on these complementary goods inside sports venues suggests that teams could earn significant profits from their sale on game day.

Rosen and Rosenfeld ("Ticket Pricing," *Journal of Law and Economics* 1997) develop a model that explains the large markups charged by teams for concessions. In this model, teams offer two categories of seats (think of them as box seats and bleacher seats) and give consumers the option to purchase complementary goods (food and beverages) after entering the venue. Since consumers are a captive audience during the game, the seller must determine how to price the complementary goods. The model predicts that if all consumers have identical preferences for the complementary goods, then the seller prices at marginal cost; if consumers have heterogenous preferences, then the seller marks up the complementary goods above marginal cost and extracts monopoly profits from the consumers who choose to purchase the complementary goods. The large markup on food and beverages observed in stadiums and arenas suggests that fan preferences for these goods must be quite heterogenous.

3.6.2 Offering Tickets at Multiple Prices

Most professional sports teams do not charge a single price for tickets. In some cases, teams offer tickets to games at as many as 20 different price points. Why do teams offer tickets to the same game at many different prices, and how does this affect their profits?

Consider the admission policies available to sports teams. A team does not have to sell tickets to a game; selling offering tickets for a specific seat in advance of a sporting event is a choice made by teams. Collecting an admission fee in cash upon entry to a sporting event is a viable alternative admission policy to offering tickets to a game. Many amateur sporting events, and even professional or semi-professional sporting events played at lower levels of competition, operate by collecting a cash fee upon entry to the event. Collecting an admission fee at the gate on entry involves minimal costs to the team, as it requires only hiring workers to collect the admission fee. However, collecting a fee on entry creates two types of uncertainty about attending the game among fans: uncertainty about obtaining a seat at the game and uncertainty about where that seat will be located. Attending a game involves travel costs. If a fee is collected on admission, a fan might not be able to get into the game even after traveling to the game, if all available viewing space is full when the fan arrives at the venue. Recall that the price of a ticket reflects fans' willingness to pay to watch a game. Fans will pay a premium to eliminate uncertainty about gaining admission to a game, and printing tickets for sale in advance of a game eliminates this form of uncertainty. This also increases costs to the team, as tickets that cannot be easily forged must be printed in advance, and the team must operate a box office where these tickets can be purchased. The problem of deterring forged tickets exists under any non- fee on entry admission process.

Advance tickets do not have to be linked to a specific seat. Under "festival" seating, fans purchase tickets at the game or prior to the game that grant admission, and fans choose a seat on entry based on availability and preferences. Clearly, different seats in sports venues offer different experiences in terms of viewing and proximity to the action. Festival seating still generates fan uncertainty about where they will sit during the game, and some fans may be willing to pay a premium for a specific seat to a sporting event, due to differences in the viewing experience and proximity to the action associated with different seat locations.

Uncertainty about the viewing experience and proximity to the action can be eliminated by associating tickets with specific seats in a venue. Like entry uncertainty, fans should be willing to pay to eliminate this form of uncertainty, permitting a team to charge more for tickets for a specific seat. However, associating tickets with seats generates additional costs to the team, in terms of employing ushers to help fans find seats and to enforce the seating agreement. This can be costly, depending on the size of the venue. The pricing policy used by teams that assign tickets to specific seats can be described by to extreme cases: charging the same price for every ticket when each ticket is associated with a specific seat, and charging a different price for every ticket based on the characteristics of the view and proximity of each seat. In practice, actual pricing policies used by teams falls somewhere in between, where ticket prices vary by section and area in the facility.

Scaling the House

"Scaling the house" refers to the practice of charging more for tickets close to the action and with better sight lines and less for tickets farther from the action and with worse sight lines. Charging a different price for different seats in a sports venue is an application of hedonic pricing theory. Hedonic pricing begins from the idea that a good or service can be represented by its fundamental characteristics. For example the characteristics of a particular seat in a sports venue include distance to the action, quality of the view, proximity to concessions and rest rooms, how many steps must be climbed to get there, the width of the seat and legroom, and other characteristics. Each of these characteristics has an associated price, the hedonic price, and the overall price of a good or service can be decomposed into the component hedonic prices.

In practice, professional sports teams do not charge a different price for each seat in a stadium or arena. Instead, seats are grouped into categories, and all seats in each category carry the same price. A great deal of variation exists in the number of seat categories and the prices charged for each category in professional sport. For example, in Major League Baseball in the 2008 season, the New York Mets sold tickets at only six different price categories, the highest being $57 while the Montreal Expos sold tickets at 18 different price categories, the highest being $325. Almost no attention has been paid to analyzing the optimal number of price categories and the optimal price for each category in economic theory.

Scaling the house creates some economic problems for teams. One problem is the cost associated with printing the tickets, numbering the seats, managing the inventory of tickets, and ensuring that fans can find their assigned seats. These costs may explain why teams offer different numbers of ticket categories. A second problem is the enforcement of seat rights. When a team scales the house, it creates an incentive for fans to pay for a low priced ticket and them move to an open seat in a higher priced section during the game. Enforcing seat rights requires more ushers, and perhaps security to escort fans unwilling to move from seats they do not have tickets for, increasing costs even more.

Scaling the house and the associated incentive for fans to "upgrade" from low priced seats creates an additional problem for teams: they may not be able to sell premium seats close to the ice or playing field if fans expect that those seats will not sell out. The intuition behind this result is that if a fan expects that not all of the premium seats will be sold, and that she can costlessly move to one of those open seats, then the optimal decision is to not buy a premium seat. If all fans follow this decision rule, then demand for premium seats will be low. The optimal response to by teams to this sort of fan decision rule is to deliberately underprice premium seats so that they sell out. So those $325 premium seat prices at Expos games were actually underpriced, according to this approach to understanding ticket pricing when teams scale the house.

Price Discrimination

Price discrimination occurs when a producer charges different customers different prices for the same product. Price discrimination takes place in many markets. For example, airlines, car rental companies, and restaurants all price discriminate to some extent. However, not all observed price variation is price discrimination. Differing prices may reflect differing costs of providing a good or service to different consumers, or quality variation in the good. In professional sport, a seat by the ice is better than a seat in the last row of the arena because the seat by the ice offers a better view of the game and close proximity to the athletes and the play. Part of the difference in the price of seats near the ice compared to seats in the upper deck can be attributed to differences in the quality of the experience, as discussed above.

Walk-up customers are more expensive to service than season ticket holders, as the team has to staff the box office for walk-up sales and maintain a database of tickets still available. Teams typically save some seats for walk up fans, and they may mis-forecast the number of seats need for walk up fans. So walk-up fans are charged a ticket price plus the implicit cost of saving a seat for them. This is an example of different costs (and prices charged) for the same good, so it represents price discrimination.

To identify true price discrimination, one must identify a case where fans are being charged different prices for identical tickets. One example of this is student discounts. When a sports team offers discounts to students, fans who buy tickets at the student discount price are sitting beside fans who paid full price for their tickets. Why do sports teams offer student discounts?

Recall that the factors that determine price elasticity are pretty much the same as the factors that determine willingness to pay: income, closeness of the contest, availability of substitutes, expectations, adjustment time. Students have less disposable income than working adults, so they have a higher price elasticity of demand.

Suppose that a team has two types of fans: Students (S) and the general public (G). Students have a higher price elasticity of demand for tickets, so $\varepsilon_S > \varepsilon_G$. Also, recall that the relationship between marginal revenue and price elasticity is

$$MR(A) = P\left(1 - \frac{1}{\varepsilon}\right)$$

Since the price elasticity of demand differs for the two groups, so will the marginal revenues. The owner maximizes revenues by setting prices such that the marginal revenues from each group are the same

$$MR_S(A) = P_S\left(1 - \frac{1}{\varepsilon_S}\right) = MR_G(A) = P_G\left(1 - \frac{1}{\varepsilon_G}\right)$$

Clearly, if $\varepsilon_S = \varepsilon_G$, then the revenue maximizing pricing scheme is $P_S = P_G$. But since $\varepsilon_S > \varepsilon_G$, in order to equalize the marginal revenues, the appropriate pricing scheme is $P_S < P_G$

Demand Uncertainty

Teams face considerable uncertainty about the number of tickets they will sell to any particular game. Two types of demand uncertainty exist in this setting: aggregate demand uncertainty and individual demand uncertainty. Aggregate demand uncertainty stems from factors that affect demand for all tickets to a sporting event. For example, demand for tickets to professional sports events held outdoors can be affected by the weather, generating aggregate demand uncertainty. In general, economic models that explain pricing decisions under demand uncertainty are called *peak load pricing* models. Individual demand uncertainty arises because some individuals cannot plan ahead to attend a sporting event; they only learn shortly before an event if they can attend or not.

The presence of demand uncertainty has important implications for pricing decisions and revenues earned from live attendance. Most economic models of demand uncertainty predict that it leads firms to underprice tickets. Firms in other markets also face demand uncertainty, but demand uncertainty in professional sports differs from, say, demand uncertainty in the sale of automobiles because live game attendance in professional sports is a perishable good; a ticket to a particular game loses all value after the game is played. In other settings, firms deal with demand uncertainty by holding stocks of the good, called inventory, that build up during periods of low demand and get drawn down during periods of high demand. Because of the perishability of tickets to live sporting events, teams cannot manage demand uncertainty through holding inventories of unsold tickets.

The perishability of tickets, coupled with demand uncertainty, leads teams to choose seating capacities for their venues that are smaller than the largest audience they could potentially draw under ideal circumstances. The larger the seating capacity of a venue, the larger the number of potentially perishable tickets that could go unsold; the number of perishable tickets declines with venue size. This means capacity constraints sometimes bind in periods of high demand; sellouts are sometimes observed in professional sports. Of course a team could easily sell out every game by pricing tickets sufficiently low to increase the quantity of tickets demanded to the venue capacity. However, this might not be a profit maximizing choice, based on the model developed above.

Variable and uncertain demand may lead teams to offer tickets at multiple levels to maximize profits. A number of models of monopoly pricing under uncertain and variable demand show that offering a menu of prices to consumers leads to higher profits than offering a single price. Note that this phenomenon is called "price dispersion" and it differs from price discrimination in that consumers are paying different prices for different related goods, and not different prices for the same good.

Sports teams offer a portfolio of live events against different opponents on different days and at different times over the course of a season. One common practice in professional sports is to bundle tickets to specific games, in the form of mini-season ticket plans, or bundle tickets to the entire season as *season tickets*. Since teams sell both season ticket packages and single-game tickets, this ticket selling practice is called "mixed bundling" in the pricing literature. Mixed bundling has been shown to be a profit-maximizing strategy under very general market conditions in terms of costs and demand. Season tickets are typically priced lower than single game tickets. Again, one reason for this outcome is that season ticket sales are easier to service than walk-up single-game ticket sales. Another is that season ticket sales reduce demand uncertainty for teams, and they are willing to pay for this reduction in demand by offering season tickets at a lower price.

3.6.3 Secondary Ticket Markets and Resale

Tickets to professional sporting events are available in two markets, a primary market where the team sells tickets to fans either in advance as season tickets or advance sales to specific games or on game day at the ticket office, and a secondary market where individuals who purchased tickets in advance from the team sell tickets to other individuals. The sellers in the secondary ticket market are either *ticket brokers* or *scalpers*. There is no economic distinction, as from an economic perspective both are suppliers in secondary ticket markets, but *ticket brokers* like StubHub or Ticket Master, eBay, or smaller local firms, operate large-scale ticket resale operations while *scalpers* are more informal and sometimes viewed as less legitimate than *ticket brokers*. The economics of secondary ticket markets are interesting.

Ticket brokers and scalpers sell a large number of tickets to sporting events. Some estimates suggest that secondary market ticket sales account for as much as 10% of the market, and perhaps a much higher percentage of high-end seats are sold on the secondary market. Since secondary ticket prices typically exceed the face value of tickets, outcomes in secondary ticket markets provide additional evidence that teams underprice tickets in the primary market. The fact that secondary ticket prices typically exceed the face value of tickets set in primary markets drives much of the research on secondary ticket markets, as well as policy interventions.

Models of ticket resale incorporate the key elements of ticket pricing discussed above (primary markets where prices are set by teams, advance purchase, demand uncertainty, variation in seat quality by section) and also introduce consumer heterogeneity. The standard ticket resale model assumes that two types of consumers exist in the market: "diehard fans" who plan to attend games well in advance no matter what conditions might exist on game day (the team's record, the opponent's record, weather, etc.) and "busy professionals" who only decide to attend a game at the last minute. The utility that both types of consumer get from attending a game is identical; they only differ in terms of when they decide to attend a game. In this sense, the model is quite general, in that it only relies on assumptions about *when* a fan decides to attend a game.

Diehard fans make commitments to attend games well in advance and these decisions involve costs associated with travel, accommodations, and perhaps time off work to attend. If diehard fans do not commit in advance to attend a game, they are willing to pay zero for a ticket; if they commit to attending, they are willing to pay p_d. Busy professionals do not find out if they want to attend a game until the last minute, and they are willing to pay p_b when they learn that they want to attend. By assumption, there are many more diehard fans than busy professionals in the ticket market. In the standard ticket resale model, busy professionals are willing to pay more for tickets than diehard fans after they learn that they want to attend a game, so $p_b > p_d$.

The model includes teams who decide on the capacity of the venue and offer tickets for sale in the primary market at a specific price, p_0, the face value of the ticket. The buyers in the primary market are both diehard fans and ticket brokers; the difference between diehard fans and ticket brokers is that ticket brokers buy tickets in the primary market for resale, while diehard fans buy ticket in the primary market with the intention to attend games. The profit maximizing decision for the team in this model is to offer tickets in the primary market at $p_0 = p_d$. Both diehard fans and ticket brokers buy these tickets. Then the ticket brokers sell their tickets to the busy professionals in the secondary ticket market at a price p_1 to the busy professionals. Clearly, since only busy professionals buy tickets in the secondary market, $p_1 = p_b > p_0$. Secondary market ticket prices exceed primary market ticket prices.

The interesting feature of the standard ticket resale model is that the team cannot devise any way to keep the ticket broker from buying tickets in the primary market at p_0 and selling them in the secondary market at an arbitrage profit of $p_1 > p_0$. In particular, the team cannot vary either the face value of the ticket or the number of tickets offered in the primary market in a way to drive out the brokers and capture their profits. Because there are more diehard fans than busy professionals, the team cannot hold back most of the tickets to sell to busy professionals in the secondary market, because they will lose revenues by not selling tickets to diehard fans (who must plan in advance to attend). The only equilibrium in the model is where the team sells tickets early to diehard fans at p_0 and sets venue size in a way that accommodates both diehard fans and busy professionals attending games. Any outcome where the team maximizes profits must leave an arbitrage profit opportunity for brokers. So the model predicts that teams want to deter ticket brokers from operating in order to reduce this profit.

How do teams deter ticket brokers? By convincing local government officials that ticket resale should be illegal. The resale of goods exists all over the world. Craigslist, eBay, classified ads, and flea markets are filled with examples of the resale of goods, and little legal attention is paid to this activity. But a number of US states and Canadian provinces have passed laws explicitly forbidding the resale of tickets to sporting events and concerts in the secondary market, and these laws are typically enforced with vigor. In Ontario, reselling of tickets is prohibited by the Ticket Speculation Act and anyone caught doing this is punishable by a $5,000 fine (or a $50,000 fine if the perpetrator is a corporation). Quebec passed a law in 2012 making the sale of tickets above face value illegal and punishable by a $1,000 fine. In Australia, teams have tried to eliminate resale by selling tickets with a picture of the purchaser on it, and by prohibiting people without tickets from going near stadiums and arenas. In the United States, 27 states have laws making ticket scalping illegal, and two states (Ohio and Virginia) allow local governments to pass ant-ticket scalping laws. Imagine if states regulated the resale of something like textbooks or real estate. Of course the standard model of ticket resale shows that these laws simply reflect the fact that teams cannot capture the profits made by ticket brokers, so they try to outlaw all ticket resale.

The most recent attempt by teams to capture the profits made by brokers is "dynamic pricing" of tickets. In 2012 three MLB teams (St. Louis, San Francisco and Oakland) instituted a dynamic pricing procedure for walk-up ticket sales and teams in other leagues have followed. Under this system, somewhere between several dozen and several thousand walk-up tickets to games are sold at a variable price depending on day of week, opponent, game conditions, and other factors. Before dynamic pricing was adopted, these teams sold walk-up tickets at the same face value as advance sale prices. Clearly, dynamic pricing is an attempt to potentially charge a higher price to busy professionals in the primary ticket market. However, under dynamic pricing walk-up tickets could also be sold at a lower price than advance sale tickets.

3.7 Summary

Gate revenues are an important component of the revenues earned by professional sports teams. Professional sports teams are monopolists. Like all monopolists, teams take the total demand for tickets to their games as given and set prices on tickets to maximize profits. In the short-run model of team's decisions developed here, talent, and team quality, are assumed to be fixed in the short run and teams make pricing decisions to sell the profit maximizing number of tickets given consumer preferences, income, the price of substitutes (i.e. the position and slope of the demand curve) facility capacity and marginal costs. The model makes specific predictions about what will happen to attendance and ticket prices when exogenous factors like local income and population change, and also about how different teams will charge different prices for tickets.

The model assumes that teams are a single price monopolist. However, actual ticket pricing decisions in professional sports leagues differ significantly from single price monopoly. Because tickets are perishable goods and consumer demand is variable and uncertain, teams engage in price dispersion, price discrimination, and other pricing policies to maximize profits under these conditions. Also, the sale of complementary goods like concessions in sports venues complicates team's pricing decisions. Finally, heterogenous fans with different willingness to pay who decide to attend games at different times leads to both primary and secondary ticket markets, which further complicate team's pricing decisions.

Review Questions

1. Suppose that the Oilers face a demand curve for tickets shown in the graph below. Based on this demand curve, answer the questions below on the axes provided.

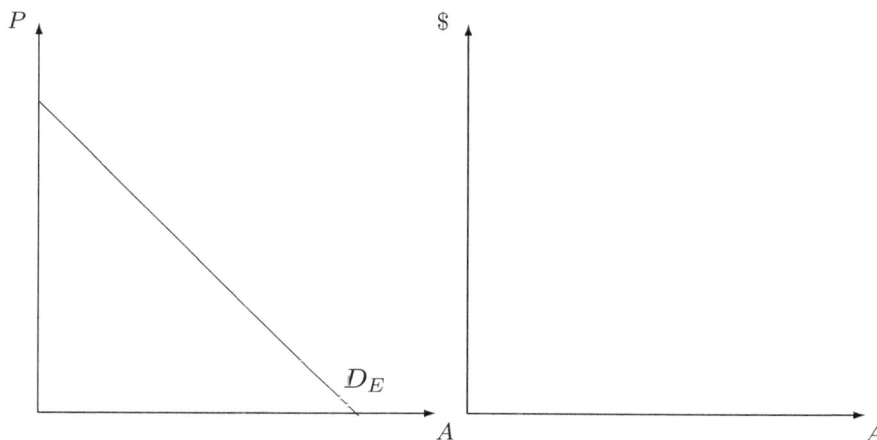

   (a) Draw the marginal revenue curve for the Oilers based on this demand curve and label it MR_E

   (b) Draw the total revenue curve for the Oilers based on this demand curve and label it $R_E(A)$

   (c) Locate the level of attendance that maximizes the Oilers' revenues on both the total revenue curve *and* the marginal revenue curve. Label this level of attendance A^*.

   (d) Pick some level of attendance $A_1 > A^*$ and graph this point, and the total revenues that the Oilers will earn if they draw A_1 fans in a season on the total revenue graph.

   (e) On the demand curve, show the ticket price that the Oilers would have to charge to draw A_1 fans.

   (f) Would the Oilers charge this price for tickets? Explain your answer.

2. *True, False or Uncertain*: (Using the axes below, explain why the following statement is either true or false, or explain why it could be either true of false, depending on the circumstances). An decrease in demand for tickets leads to a decrease in the profit maximizing level of attendance and an increase in the profit maximizing price of tickets.

P ↑ $ ↑

                                   A   A

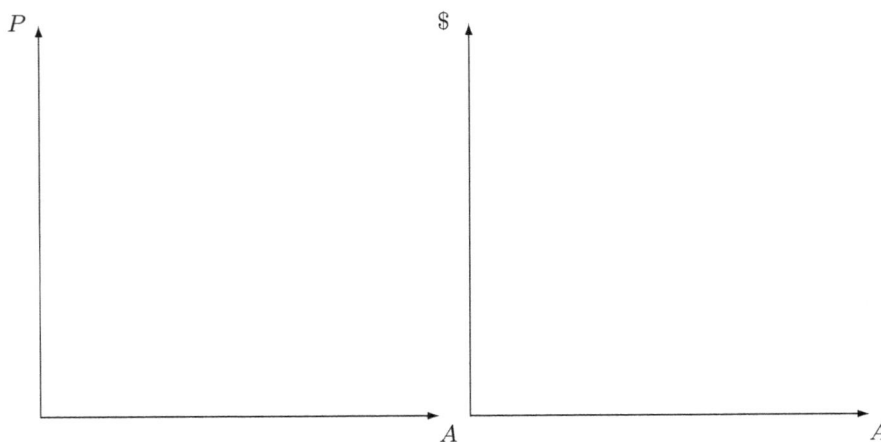

3. Although the model developed in Chapter 2 predicts that sports teams should price tickets where the price elasticity of demand is equal to one, empirical estimates of the price elasticity of demand indicate that teams actually price in the inelastic portion of the demand curve. Give one reason why teams might price their tickets like this.

Chapter 4

A Long Run Model of Team Decisions

Chapter Objectives

- Understand the tradeoff between success and profits that professional sports teams face

- Understand the long run production of wins, and the long run cost of wins faced by professional sports teams

- Understand how unsuccessful teams can be profitable and how successful teams can be unprofitable

- Understand how promotion and relegation systems affect team decisions about hiring talent

- Understand how win maximizing teams operate relative to profit maximizing teams

Chapter 3 developed a short run model of team decision making. In that model, team quality was held fixed and teams facing a downward sloping demand curve chose a ticket price and level of attendance to maximize short run profits. A long run analysis of the profitability of professional sports teams must focus on an analysis of the relationship between winning, payroll, and profits because in the long run, sporting success depends largely on the quality of the team that each team chooses to field and fielding higher quality teams requires larger payrolls. A fundamental tension exists between winning and costs on professional sports teams: fielding a winning team requires spending money on talent, and spending money on talent drives up costs, which may reduce profits.

To illustrate this point, consider two Major League Baseball teams, the New York Yankees and the Detroit Tigers, over the 12 year period 1993-2004. Over this period the Yankees had an average winning percentage of 0.598, while the Tigers had an average winning percentage of 0.419. Why were the Yankees so good, and the Tigers so bad, over this long period? The long run model developed here provides an economic answer to this question.

In brief, the economic explanation is that it was profit maximizing for the Yankees to field a very good baseball team over the period 1993-2004 and it was also profit maximizing for the Tigers to field a bad baseball team over the period. The quality of the team chosen is a long-run choice made by team owners, not the result of good or bad luck. Luck evens out over seasons. The best indicator of team quality in Major League Baseball, where there are no salary caps, is total team payroll. The average total team payroll for the Yankees over this period, in real 2004 dollars, was $97.4 million; the average total team payroll for the Tigers was $44.2 million. This chapter develops a long run profit maximizing model to explain these outcomes.

4.1   Teams' Long Run Decisions

The model assumes that the relevant decision maker for a sports team is the owner of the team. This assumption abstracts from the real world operation of sports teams in that few sports team owners direct the day to day operation of their team. Instead, owners hire general managers and other front office personnel to run the team on a day to day basis. Still, the owner of a sports team has a powerful influence on the behavior of these organizations, and the model implicitly assumes that observed outcomes on the field are causally related to the decisions made by the team owner in an important sense.

The model also assumes that the goal of a team owner is to maximize profits. This assumption may or may not reflect the motivations of the owners of professional sports teams. The sports economics literature contains many different objectives for sports teams, including maximizing on-field success, maximizing the utility of the owner, and other objectives. Developing a profit maximizing model of sports team behavior does not lock the analysis into this particular goal. It simply develops a benchmark model that generates predictions that can be compared to the predictions generated by models with other assumptions about the goal of a sports team.

The model assumes that the team owner maximizes profits by choosing the level of on-field success of the team. In other words, the winning percentage of the team is assumed to be a choice variable - an owner can choose to field a team that wins a large fraction of its games, about half of its games, or a small fraction of its games. In this model, the choice of a winning percentage for a team is the factor that the team owner manipulates to achieve the goal of maximizing profits. For some teams, profits may be maximized by fielding a team that wins very few games; for other teams, profits may be maximized by fielding a team that wins many games.

At first glance, the assumption that team owners maximize the profits by choosing a level of on-field success may seem inappropriate. A perusal of the sports pages, and listening to the radio and television announcers on pro sports broadcasts, suggests that the goal of all sports teams is to win as many games as possible each year. The fans of most sports teams invest a considerable amount of attention and energy in their team based on such an assumption. Again, the model can be expanded to include different team objectives, including win maximizing, but profit maximization by choosing a level of on-field success is a common assumption in the sports economics literature, and models based on this assumption generate predications that strongly resemble outcomes in sports leagues. So this approach can provide insight into the behavior of agents in sports leagues.

The assumption that team owners choose a level of winning percentage to maximize profits also has some support in observed outcomes in sports leagues. Consider the case of two teams in the National Basketball Association, the Los Angeles Lakers and the Los Angeles Clippers. Both teams play in the same market, Los Angeles, and since 1999 both have played in the same facility, the Staples Center. Over the period 1999-2005, the Clippers had a winning percentage of 0.334; the Clippers won about one third of the games they played. Over the same period, the Lakers had a winning percentage of 0.648; the Lakers won almost two thirds of the games they played. According to *Forbes* magazine, the Lakers made $35.8 million in operating profits in 2004, and had a winning percentage of 0.683 and the Clippers made $22.4 million dollars in operating profits in 2004 and had a winning percentage of 0.341. How can these two outcomes be reconciled? One possibility is that both teams were trying to maximize winning percentage and the Lakers did a better job at it than the Clippers. Another possibility is that both were trying to maximize their profits, and that the Clippers maximize profits by winning about a third of their games while the Lakers maximize their profits by winning about two thirds of their games. Note that the first explanation implies that the Clippers were doing a terrible job at maximizing winning percentage over a seven year period, while the second implies that the Clippers were following a successful business strategy over this period.

The model assumes that teams make decisions to maximize profits. Recall that profit, π, is defined as total revenues (R) minus total costs (C)

$$\pi = R - C.$$

We first address revenues and then costs. Then revenues and costs are compared to generate predications about how a team owner will decide on a profit maximizing level of talent, which maps into on-field success. In Chapter 5 decisions of one owner will be examined in the context of a league, where other team owners are also making profit maximizing decisions about their on-field success. For now, the analysis is confined to the decisions made by a single team.

4.1.1 Team Revenues

Assume that teams earn revenue only from selling tickets, and that the only determinant of ticket sales is on-field success. Under these conditions, the team's total revenue can be described by a revenue function

$$R_i = R_i(W_i, A_i)$$

where R_i is total revenue for team i, $R_i(\cdot)$ is a concave function, W_i is the level of on-field success of team i, and A_i is a parameter capturing the "market potential" of the city that team i plays in. A_i reflects the population of the city, as well as other factors like the preferences of local residents for attending sporting events. W_i can be interpreted as the winning percentage of team i. Assume that the revenue function is concave in winning percentage, so $R_i' > 0$ and $R_i'' < 0$ (the first derivative of the revenue function with respect to winning percentage is positive and the second derivative of the revenue function is negative).

Note that this revenue function differs from the revenue function developed in Chapter 3, even though the function looks similar. Playing talent was assumed constant in Chapter 3, and the team faced a downward sloping demand function for tickets and set prices to maximize profits. In this case, talent is assumed to be variable and demand for tickets depends only on team success and the characteristics of the market.

Graphically, the revenue function can be represented as a concave curve. On figure 4.1, total revenues ($) are graphed on the vertical axis and winning percentage (W_i) is graphed on the horizontal axis.

The revenue function shows the value of revenues that will be generated for any possible winning percentage, given a value of the "market potential" variable A_i. So, for example, given a market potential parameter A_1, from Figure 4.2, a team with winning percentage W_1 generates R_1 in total revenues. One key feature of the revenue function is that revenues initially rise with winning percentage, but after some point, winning percentage W_{RM} on Figure 4.2, revenues decline.

Technically, this pattern in the relationship between on-field success and revenues is a consequence of the assumption of concavity of the revenue function. Intuitively, this pattern reflects the idea that fans respond to better on-field performance, but only up to some point. Beyond some level of success, fans no longer respond to improvements in on-field success. This convex total revenue function can be motivated by the *uncertainty of outcome hypothesis* (UOH), an important concept in sports economics. The UOH refers to the idea that fans prefer sports contests with relatively uncertain outcomes to those with certain outcomes, other things equal. Demand will be higher for games with relatively uncertain outcomes than for games with less uncertain outcomes. If this

Figure 4.1: The Revenue Function

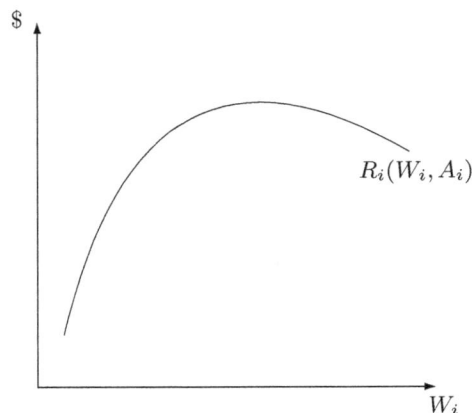

Figure 4.2: Revenues and Winning Percentage

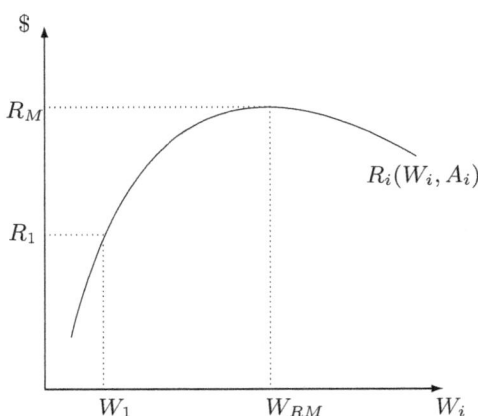

describes fan's preferences, then revenues begin to decline at some winning percentage because outcome uncertainty declines as team quality increases.

The key property of this revenue function is that revenues rise and then fall as winning percentage increases. The amount by which revenues rise and fall is not important to the model, only that the revenue function is convex (has no irregular dips or bumps) and rises and eventually falls. The decline in revenues could be large or small. For convenience, I have drawn the curve with quite a bit of increase and decrease, but the revenue curve could be drawn much flatter with no loss of explanatory power in the model.

Marginal Revenue

In order to solve the model and generate predictions about the behavior of teams, we will need to characterize the relationship between winning percentage and revenues in more detail. In particular, we will need to understand exactly how much revenues change when winning percentage changes. The relationship between changes in winning percentage and changes in revenues can be described by *marginal revenue*. Marginal revenue is simply the change in revenues when winning percentage increases by one unit

$$\text{Marginal Revenue} = \frac{\Delta R}{\Delta W}.$$

If you have had a calculus class, you will recognize that marginal revenue can be interpreted as the partial derivative of the revenue function with respect to a change in winning percentage

$$\text{Marginal Revenue} = \frac{\partial R}{\partial W}$$

Graphically, marginal revenue is represented by the slope of a line tangent to the revenue curve at any point. For example, from Figure 4.3 , the marginal revenue at winning percentage W_2 is the slope of a line tangent to the revenue curve at that point.

Figure 4.3: Marginal Revenue

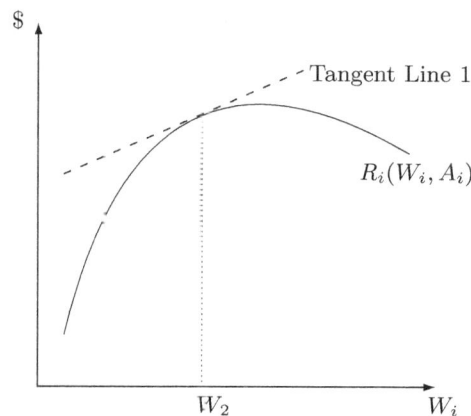

Tangent Line 1 has a positive slope, so marginal revenue is positive at W_2. The flatter the slope of the tangent line at any point on the revenue curve, the smaller is marginal revenue (and the smaller the change in revenues for a one unit increase in winning percentage.

Note that moving from left to right along the revenue curve, marginal revenue starts out large and positive and gets smaller and smaller as W increases. At W_{RM} on Figure 4.2, marginal revenue is zero, because the line tangent to the revenue curve at that point is horizontal, and the slope of a horizontal line is zero. When winning percentage increases beyond W_{RM}, marginal revenue becomes negative. Increases in winning percentage beyond this point decrease total revenues.

The parameter A reflects the revenue generating potential of the city that is host to a sports team in this model. Assume that $\bar{R}'_A > 0$. This means that an increase in A at any given level of W increases revenues.

Figure 4.4 shows the effect of a change in A on the revenue function. Suppose that Team 1 plays in city one that has $A = A_1$ and Team 2 plays in city two that has $A = A_2$. Note that $A_2 > A_1$ could be due to city 2 having a larger population than city 1, but it could also be interpreted as city 1 and city 2 having the same population, but city 2 having more loyal, or more interested, fans than city 1. Alternatively, a change in A could be interpreted as due to a change in ownership. An inept owner might only be able to generate R_1 in revenues out of a winning percentage of W_1, while a successful owner could earn higher revenues ($R_2 > R_1$) out of the same level of on-field success. Note that at the same winning percentage, W_1, team 2 earns more revenues than team 1, because $A_2 > A_1$. Also note that the marginal revenue is higher at W_1 on revenue curve $R_1(W_i, A_2)$,

Figure 4.4: The Effect of Changing A on Revenues

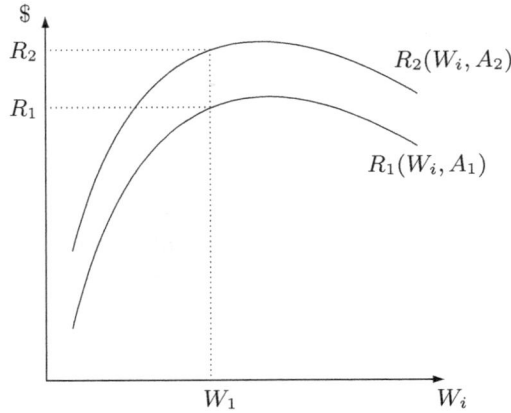

because the slope of a line tangent to revenue curve at W_1 is steeper on revenue curve $R_1(W_i, A_2)$ than on revenue curve $R_2(W_i, A_1)$.

4.1.2 The Production and Cost of Wins

Consider writing down a production function for wins in the long run for a professional sports team. Suppose that T is a variable reflecting the amount of playing talent hired by a sports team and M a variable reflecting managerial talent hired by the team. These are the inputs to the win production function. Given these inputs, the production function is

$$W\% = F(T, M) \tag{4.1}$$

where $W\%$ is the team's winning percentage, the output of the production function. Holding managerial talent constant, the relationship between talent and winning percentage is non-linear, at first increasing at a slow rate and then increasing quickly for an interval of talent hired. This relationship simply reflects changes in the marginal product of playing talent. Recall, from standard producer theory, that the marginal product of an input is the amount by which output changes when an input increases by one unit. In this case, the marginal product of talent, MP_T, is

$$MP_T = \frac{\partial F(T, M)}{\partial T}. \tag{4.2}$$

MP_T is represented by the slope of a line tangent to the long run production function at any point. Figure 4.5 shows a general example of this production function. From Figure 4.5, MP_T falls as T increases along the production function. This is the familiar assumption of diminishing marginal product of inputs from producer theory. Marginal product begins to diminish in any economic model of production as a more of a variable input (playing talent in this case) becomes spread over a fixed input (managerial talent). In addition, on sports teams, there are a fixed number of plater-minutes in each game, so no matter how much talent a team acquires, all those players cannot be on the ice or field at the same time. Eventually, the labor inputs get in each other's way, and the marginal product of talent declines. In this case, there are only so many roster spots on any team. This pattern of change in MP_T leads to a production function that has the shape of the curve shown on Figure 4.5.

Figure 4.5: The Long Run Production Function for Wins

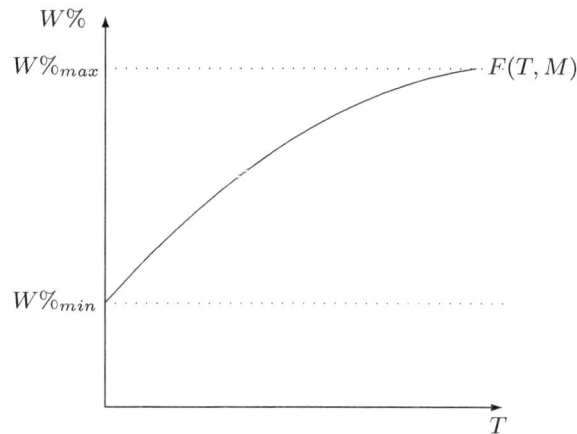

To get from the production of wins to the cost of producing wins, simply flip the axes on this graph around so that winning percent is on the horizontal axis. After flipping the production function graph, each unit of talent purchased by a team needs to be multiplied by the unit cost of talent in order to get a long run team salary cost curve.

This production function can be motivated in terms of hiring "star players" and the salary of star players. The idea is that a team can choose to hire either regular "journeyman" players or star players at each position on the team. Star players cost more than regular players. The payroll of a team with no stars is relatively low; the first few stars come at a price higher then the existing journeyman players, and the last few superstar players hired are very expensive in terms of of salary. However, a simpler assumption can justify increasing marginal cost of talent. Suppose that most playing talent is available at an equilibrium salary W^* in the labor market for players. Only exceptional players (the "superstars" alluded to above), command extremely high salaries. Under this assumption, the unit cost of talent is constant for much of the relevant range of T for teams. This unit cost only rises toward the far end of the production function, where it increases sharply.

If unit costs work this way in sports labor markets, them the long run relationship between winning and costs, the Total Team Salary Cost Curve, shown on Figure 4.6 is an upward sloping curve as shown below. The cost curve on the graph below, $C(W\%)$, shows the payroll required for any franchise to field a team that, in the long run, has a winning percentage of $W\%$.

Constant Marginal Costs

Many models of talent choice by sports teams in the sports economics literature simplify the cost function by assuming that the team faces a linear cost function

$$C_i = FC_i + p_i W_i$$

where C_i is the total cost of producing any given level of on-field success, FC_i is the "fixed cost" of putting a team on the field, W_i is the level of on-field success, and p_i is the "price" of increasing

Figure 4.6: The Total Team Salary Cost Curve

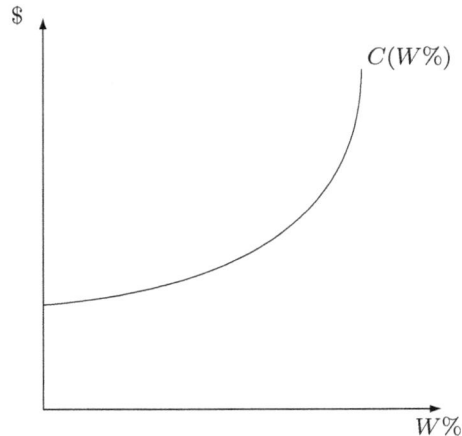

on-field success by one unit. A linear cost function is analytically easier to work with than a non-linear cost function. This linear cost function decomposes operating costs into two components: a component that does not change with the level of on-field success, and a component that rises with the level of on-field success.

The fixed cost component reflects factors like travel expenses, facility operations and maintenance, front-office salaries, uniforms, and so forth. No matter how successful or unsuccessful a team is on the field, these costs do not change (although they might vary across teams, which is accounted for by the i subscript on this variable.

The second term in the cost function, $p_i W_i$ is variable cost. This term reflects the fact that if a team wants to improve on the field and have a higher winning percentage, it must hire better, or more talented players. More talented players are more expensive, so the total cost of increasing W_i rises. In the sports economics literature, changes in on-field performance are related to hiring better players. Implicitly each team has some level of talent t_i, and on-field success is a function of the level of talent

$$W_i = F(T_i)$$

where $f_t > 0$ so hiring more talent leads to more on-field success. Under the simplifying assumption that

$$\frac{\partial W}{\partial T} = 1$$

increasing winning percentage by one requires hiring one additional "unit" of talent. In this case, p_i is the price of one additional unit of talent in the player's labor market, and should be related to prevailing player's salaries in the sport.

In this analysis, we will focus on the team owner's choice of W_i, and p_i will be interpreted as the marginal cost of increasing W_i, but keep in mind that underlying this change is a corresponding change in the level of talent of the team, and that p_i reflects players salaries.

Figure 4.7: The Linear Cost Function

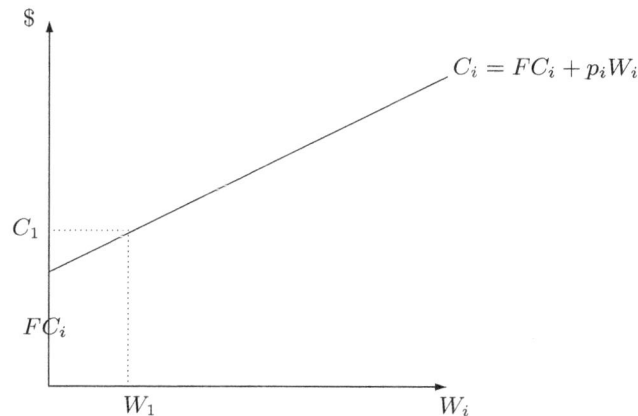

Graphically, the cost function is simply a straight line with slope p_i and intercept FC_i. Figure 4.7 shows the cost function for given fixed costs (FC_i) and price of talent (p_i). From this figure, the cost of putting a team on the field that has a winning percentage of W_1 is C_1, given fixed costs of FC_i and a marginal cost of talent of p_i. Increasing the team's winning percentage requires hiring more talented players, and this drives up variable costs. Note that this approach to modeling costs abstracts from the fact that teams in North American sports leagues have a limit to the number of players they can employ on their roster. An increase in talent in this model can be interpreted as getting rid of a less talented player in exchange for a more talented player that plays the same position.

The most important factor that shifts the cost function is changes in the price of an additional unit of winning percentage, p_i. Recall that changes in p_i reflect changes in the price of talent in the sports leagues. So an increase in the average salaries of players in the league will increase the price of talent in the league, and also increase the cost of achieving any particular level of on-field success.

Figure 4.8: A Change in p_i

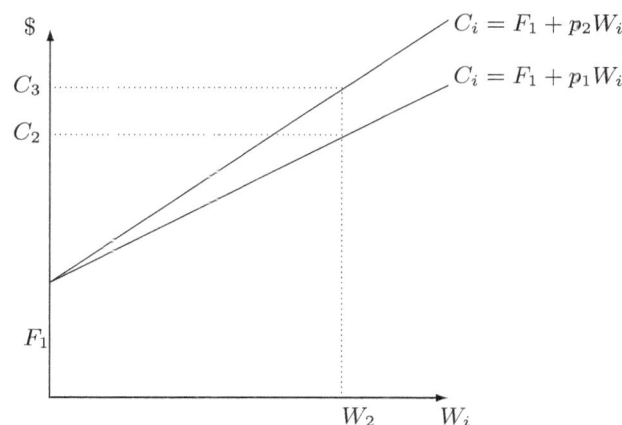

Figure 4.8 shows the effect on cost of an increase in the marginal cost of talent. Initially, fixed costs are F_1 and the price of an additional unit of talent is p_1. For these parameters, the cost of

putting a team on the field that has a winning percentage of W_2 is C_2. If the cost of an additional unit of talent rises to p_2, the cost of fielding a team with a winning percentage of W_2 rises to C_3.

4.1.3 Profit Maximizing Decisions

Owners choose a level of on-field success to maximize their profits. Formally, this decision can be written

$$\max_{W_i} \ \pi = R_i(W_i, A_i) - C_i \tag{4.3}$$

which means in words "team owners choose a level of winning percentage (W_i) to maximize profits (π), defined as revenues less costs." This maximization problem can easily be solved using calculus. To solve the model analytically, simply take the derivative of the objective function with respect to changes in W_i, set this equal to zero, and solve the expression for W_i. To do this, first note that the profit function can be expressed

$$\max_{W_i} \ \pi = R_i(W_i, A_i) - FC_i - p_i W_i.$$

Next, take the derivative with respect to changes in W_i and set equal to zero (economists call this term the "first order conditions" for the profit maximization problem)

$$\frac{\partial \pi}{\partial W_i} = R_i'(W_i, A_i) - p_i = 0.$$

$R'(\cdot)$ is marginal revenue - the amount by which revenue increases when winning percentage increases - and p_i is the marginal cost of increasing winning percentage by one. This expression can be rearranged to

$$R_i'(W_i, A_i) = p_i \tag{4.4}$$

which shows that the profit maximizing level of winning percentage, given FC_i and p_i, is where marginal revenue is equal to marginal cost. At this winning percentage, the last dollar earned by increasing the team's winning percentage is exactly equal to the cost of increasing the team's winning percentage. Any further increases in winning percentage will increase costs more than revenues, and decrease profits.

Graphical Solution

In this case, additional insight into the workings of the model can be gained by solving the model graphically. Note that this graphical solution is identical to the analytical solution above in all respects. The graphical solution is just a different way of reaching the same conclusion. To graphically solve the model, include both the revenue function and the cost function on the same graph. In particular, suppose that team i plays in a market with revenue potential A_1 and faces fixed costs F_1 and a marginal cost of talent of p_1. Figure 4.9 shows the cost and revenue functions for this team.

Figure 4.9 illustrates the relationship between costs and revenues at each possible level of winning percentage. Recall that moving from left to right along the horizontal axis means that the team is increasing its winning percentage, and this increase takes place because the owner is buying more talent in the market for players. For all winning percentages less than W_1, revenues are lower than costs, and the team earns an operating loss. For all winning percentages between

Figure 4.9: Revenues and Costs

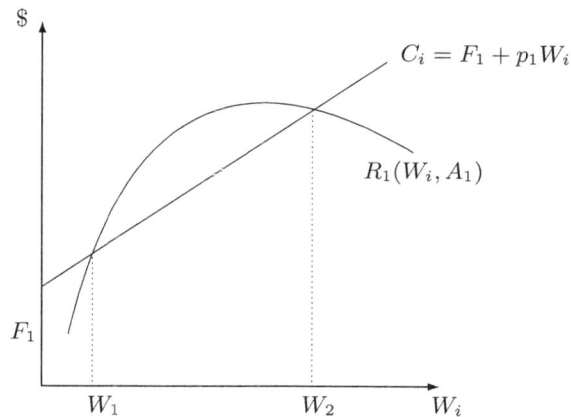

W_1 and W_2, revenues are greater than costs, and the team earns an operating profit. But if the owner decides to increase the team's winning percentage above W_2, by buying even more talented players, this increases costs by more than the corresponding increase in revenues, and the team makes an operating loss.

Profit is the vertical distance between the revenue curve and the cost curve. The larger the distance, the greater the profit. The team earns zero profit at two winning percentages, W_1 and W_2. To graphically solve the model, we need to determine the winning percentage where the vertical distance between revenues and costs is the greatest. One way to do this would be to measure the distance for each W_i. But the expression for profit maximization in the previous section, Equation (4.4), provides an easier method. Recall that this expression shows that profits are maximized where marginal revenue is equal to marginal cost. Graphically, marginal cost is the slope of the cost function, p_1. Recall that marginal revenue is graphically represented by the slope of a line tangent to the revenue function at any point.

Figure 4.10: Maximum Profits

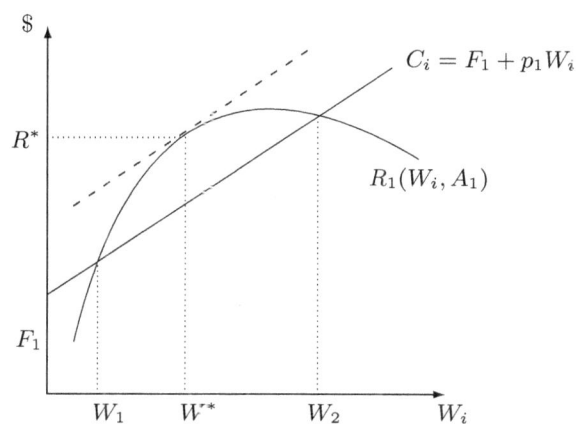

Figure 4.10 shows how to find the profit maximizing level of winning percentage for this team. According to the analytical solution, the profit maximizing W is the one directly below the point where the slope of the cost function is equal to the slope of a line tangent to the revenue curve.

This can be found by shifting the cost function up until it's tangent to the revenue curve. Line T has the same slope as the cost function; lines T and C_i are parallel. In terms of the model, at W^*, the winning percentage directly below this point, the slope of the revenue curve (R') is equal to the slope of the cost function (p_1). This is exactly the profit maximizing condition shown in Equation (4.4). In other words, given that team i faces (A_1, F_1, p_1), the profit maximizing winning percentage for this team is W^*, and the amount of revenue associated with this level of winning percentage is R^*. Note that this amount of revenue is lower than the maximum amount of revenue that the team could earn. Revenue maximization is not the same as profit maximization.

4.1.4   Team Level Comparative Static Analysis

Graphically or analytically characterizing the solution to the profit maximization problem given by Equation (4.3) is an important step, but not particularly interesting. In general, the interesting predictions that emerge from economic models like this one are in the form of comparative static results. A comparative static analysis shows how the equilibrium outcomes (the *endogenous variables* in a model change in response to a change in an *exogenous variable*. Endogenous variables are determine within a model. In this case, there are three endogenous variables (W, R and C) and three exogenous variables (F, A and p). Note that while F may be largely under the control of the team owner, because the team owner can exert control over the level of spending on travel, facilities, etc., the value that this variable takes is not determined in the model, so F is exogenous.

The general format of comparative static analysis is:

1. Start at an equilibrium in a model

2. Change an exogenous variable

3. Show the effect of this change on the equilibrium values

This procedure can be applied to a change in any exogenous variable in a static model.

Example: Changes in A

Suppose that Team X faces exogenous variables F_{X1}, A_{X1} and p_{X1}. That is there is some known level of fixed costs (F_{X1}), known market revenue potential (A_{X1}), and known price of talent (p_{X1}). In this case, the model predicts that the team's owner will select a profit maximizing winning percentage of W_1^*, and the team will earn profits of π_1^* on revenues R_1^* and costs C_1^*. Figure 4.11 shows the equilibrium outcome [$W_1^*, \pi_1^*, R_1^*, C_1^*$] in the model. Call this vector of values Equilibrium 1.

Now, suppose that the market's revenue generating potential increases; the exogenous variable A_{X1} increases to $A_{X2} > A_{X1}$. This could be due to an increase in the population in the market, or some other factor. How does this increase in A affect the profit maximizing level of winning percentage selected by the team owner? To see this, simply increase A and find the new equilibrium in the model. Figure 4.12 shows the new equilibrium. From Figure 4.12, in response to the increase in A, the team owner increases the talent level on the team by enough to increase winning percentage to W_2^* from W_1^*. This increase in talent increases costs to C_2^* from C_1^*. And finally, the increase in talent increases both the revenues and the profits earned by the team. Revenues increase to R_2^* and profits increase to π_2^*.

The comparative static analysis of a change in the team's market revenue potential shows that an increase in A leads to an increase in W, R, C and π.

Figure 4.11: Equilibrium 1

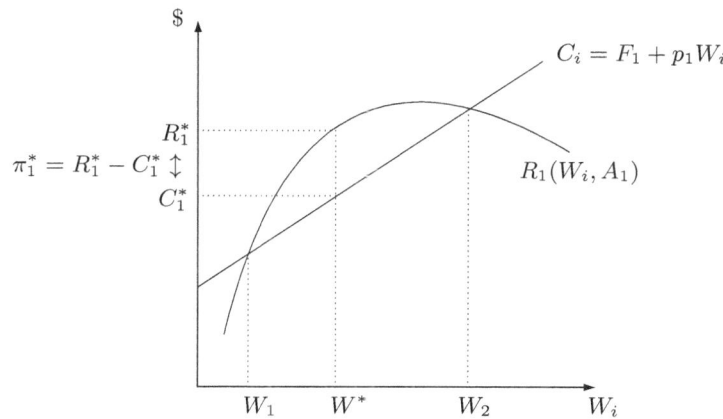

Figure 4.12: Equilibrium 2

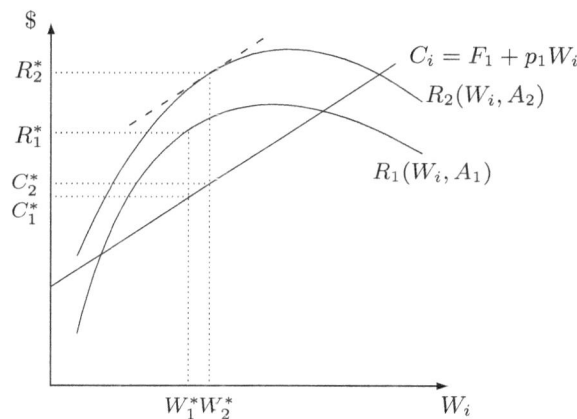

4.1.5 Example: Explaining the Difference Between Detroit and New York

This chapter was motivated by the observation that the New York Yankees played considerably better than the Detroit Tigers over the period 1993-2004. We have now developed a model that generates predictions about the on-field success of teams operated by profit maximizing owners. Let's use this model to explain why the Yankees would be better than the Tigers over a long period of time.

In the following graphs, the Tigers will be identified by a D subscript and the Yankees by an N subscript. For simplicity, assume that both teams face the same cost functions, so $C_D(W) = C_N(W) = C(W)$. The difference between the two teams in this case is that the Yankees, playing in a larger and more lucrative market have a higher marginal revenue from winning than the Tigers. In the context of this long run model of profits and winning percents, this means that the revenue line for the Yankees is steeper than the revenue line for the Tigers, and $MR_N > MR_D$, and that $A_N > A_D$. In the graph below, the revenue line $R_N(W\%)$ is steeper than $R_D(W\%)$.

To see why the Yankees would field a better team than the Tigers, just find the profit maximizing winning percent for each team. Recall that to do this, shift the revenue line over until it is tangent to the cost curve. At this point, marginal revenue will equal marginal cost, and profit will be

Figure 4.13: The Yankees and the Tigers

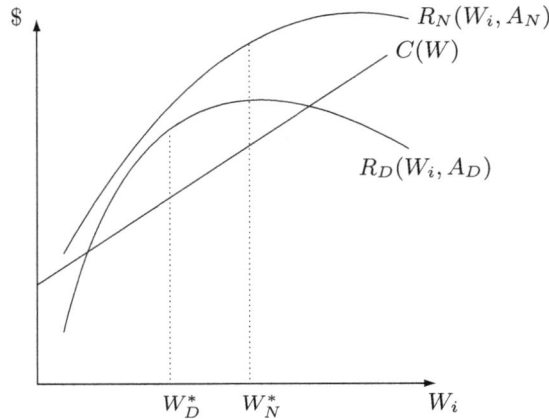

maximized at that winning percent.

Figure 4.13 shows the profit maximizing winning percent for both the Tigers (W_D) and the Yankees (W_N) given these assumptions about costs and revenues for the two teams. The profit maximizing winning percent for the Yankees is greater than the profit maximizing winning percent for the Tigers [$W_D < W_N$]. Note that both teams maximize profits at this outcome. The Tigers could not earn more profits by putting a better team on the field, and the Yankees would earn lower profits by fielding a less talented team. Also note that the model predicts that the Yankees earn more profits (the vertical distance between the cost and revenue functions at W_N^* is larger than the distance at W_D^*) and have a higher payroll than the Tigers; both these predictions are consistent with the observed profitability and payrolls of the two teams over this period.

4.1.6   Profit Maximizing Decisions Under Promotion and Relegation

The model developed in this chapter can be used to understand the decisions made by teams in promotion and relegation leagues relative to teams in closed leagues. Begin with the objective function for a team in a closed league, Equation 4.3

$$\max_{W_i} \pi = R(W_i) - cW_i$$

Assume that total revenues depend only on winning percent (or talent), W_i, as before $R' > 0$ and $R'' < 0$. Also assume that costs depend only on winning percent/talent and the marginal cost of talent is c. Teams choose W_i to maximize profits.

Suppose that there are only two leagues in the promotion and relegation ladder, League 1, the top league and League 2, the second league. For teams in the top league, the probability of remaining in League 1, or avoiding relegation, p^{ar}, is a function of the quality of the team

$$p^{ar} = ar(W_i) = ar \times W_i \qquad 0 < ar < 1$$

the probability of relegation decreases as team quality increases, and ar is the marginal increase in the probability a team is not relegated when team quality increases. For teams in the second league, the probability of promotion, p^p, is a function of team quality

$$p^p = p(W_i) = p \times W_i \qquad 0 < p < 1$$

the probability that a team gets promoted from the second league to the first league increases with team quality and p is the marginal increase in the probability a team is promoted when team quality increases.

Teams in the Top League

Assume that teams in the top league earn revenues $R_1(W_i)$ and face a marginal cost of c_1. The objective function for teams in League 1 include both revenues and costs for this period and expected revenues and costs in the next period, when the team could be in either League 1 or League 2. Suppose that d is some appropriate rate of return for teams, so that costs and revenues next period are discounted back to this period by $\frac{1}{1+d}$. The objective function for a team in League 1 can be written

$$\max_{W_i} \ \pi = R_1(W_i) - c_1 W_i + \frac{1}{1+d}\left[ar \cdot W_i \left(R_1(W_1^e) - c_1 W_1^e\right) + \left(1 - ar \cdot W_i\right)\left(R_2(W_2^e) - c_2 W_2^e\right)\right]$$
$$(4.5)$$

where W_2^e is the profit maximizing level of talent that the team expects it would choose next period if it plays in League 2 and W_1^e is the profit maximizing level of talent that the team expects it would choose next period if it plays in League 1. The final term on the right hand side of Equation 4.5 is the expected value today of the teams's profits next period taking into account the probability of relegation and the time value of money. Again, teams in League 1 choose W_i to maximize profits. When profits are maximized

$$\frac{\partial \pi}{\partial W_i} = R_1'(W_i) - c_1 + \frac{ar}{1+d}\left(R_1(W_1^e) - c_1 W_1^e\right) - \frac{(ar)}{1+d}\left(R_2(W_2^e) - c_2 W_2^e\right) = 0.$$

where again $R_1'(\cdot)$ is marginal revenue - the amount by which revenue increases when winning percentage increases - and c_1 is the marginal cost of increasing winning percentage.

Assume that teams in League 1 and League 2 compete for the same playing talent, so that $c_1 = c_2 = c$. Also, assume that at any given level of success, teams in League 1 earn greater revenues than teams in League 2, because they can charge higher ticket prices and fans will pay this to see a higher level of competition. Then $R_1(W_i) > R_2(W_i)$. The first order condition becomes

$$\frac{\partial \pi}{\partial W_i} = R_1'(W_i) - c + \frac{ar}{1+d}\left(R_1(W_1^e) - c W_1^e\right) - \frac{(ar)}{1+d}\left(R_2(W_2^e) - c W_2^e\right) = 0.$$

Since $R_1(W_i) > R_2(W_i)$, Then $(R_1(W_1^e) - c W_1^e) > (R_2(W_2^e) - c W_2^e)$ and teams in League 1 earn higher profits than teams in League 1. Since $0 < ar < 1$ both the last two terms in this equation are positive. This means that the W_i that solves the objective function for a profit maximizing team in a closed league is smaller than the W_i that solves the profit maximizing objective function for a team in the top league of an open promotion and relegation league. To see this, rearrange the equation to

$$R_1'(W_i) + \frac{ar}{1+d}\left(R_1(W_1^e) - c W_1^e\right) + \frac{(1-ar)}{1+d}\left(R_2(W_2^e) - c W_2^e\right) = c. \qquad (4.6)$$

The left hand side is marginal revenue plus some amount which depends on ar, the discount rate, and the difference in expected profits in League 1 and League 2. In a closed league, $R_1'(W_i) = c$, but in this league the left hand side is bigger than c. To reduce the left hand side, a team acquires more talent, increasing W_i. This reduces marginal revenue, reducing the left hand side of the equation.

Graphically, the difference between an team in an open league and team in a closed league can be seen on Figure 4.14. Under the assumption of equal marginal cost, both teams face the same total cost curve. The revenue function for the closed league is R_{closed} and the revenue function for the open league R_{open} is above the one for the closed league because of the additional incentive provided by the promotion and relegation system.

Figure 4.14: W^* in Open and Closed Leagues

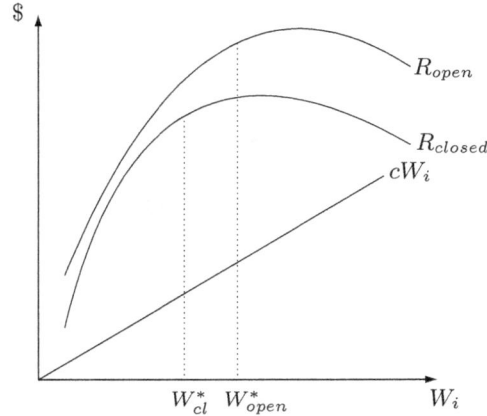

Given marginal costs, c, a team in the closed league chooses W_{cl}^* to maximize profits while a team in an open league chooses to hire more talent and get to W_{open}^*. Promotion and relegation systems induce teams in the top league to acquire more talent than they would in a closed league.

Teams in the Bottom League

Teams in the bottom top league of a promotion and relegation ladder earn revenues $R_2(W_i)$ and face a marginal cost of c_2. The objective function for teams in League 2 include both revenues and costs for this period and expected revenues and costs in the next period, when the team could be in either League 1 or League 2. Under the assumption that $c_1 = c_2 = c$ the objective function for a team in League 2 can be written

$$\max_{W_i} \ \pi = R_2(W_i) - cW_i + \frac{1}{1+d}\left[p \cdot W_i\left(R_1(W_1^e) - cW_1^e\right) + (1 - p \cdot W_i)\left(R_2(W_2^e) - cW_2^e\right)\right] \quad (4.7)$$

where again W_2^e is the profit maximizing level of talent that the team expects it would choose next period if it plays in League 2 and W_1^e is the profit maximizing level of talent that the team expects it would choose next period if it plays in League 1. The final term on the right hand side of Equation 4.7 is the expected value today of the teams's profits next period taking into account the probability of promotion, p and the time value of money. Teams in League 2 choose W_i to maximize profits. When profits are maximized

$$\frac{\partial \pi}{\partial W_i} = R_2'(W_i) - c + \frac{p}{1+d}\left(R_1(W_1^e) - c_1 W_1^e\right) - \frac{(p)}{1+d}\left(R_2(W_2^e) - c_2 W_2^e\right) = 0.$$

where again $R_2'(\cdot)$ is marginal revenue - the amount by which revenue increases when winning percentage increases - and c is the marginal cost of increasing winning percentage. Again, $R_1(W_i) > R_2(W_i)$. We can again rearrange this equation to

$$R_2'(W_i) + \frac{p}{1+d}\left(R_1(W_1^e) - cW_1^e\right) - \frac{(p)}{1+d}\left(R_2(W_2^e) - cW_2^e\right) = c.$$

The left hand side is marginal revenue plus some amount which depends on p, the discount rate, and the difference in expected profits in League 1 and League 2. With no possibility of promotion $R_1'(W_i) = c$, but in this league the left hand side is larger than c. To reduce the left hand side, a team acquires more talent, increasing W_i. This reduces marginal revenue, reducing the left hand side of the equation. Even in the lower league, the promotion and relegation system induces teams to acquire more talent.

All teams face these incentives in promotion and relegation leagues. It remains to be seen what happens to overall outcomes in the league under these conditions. That topic is examined in Chapter 5.

4.2 Win Maximizing Teams

Using the model of talent determination developed in the previous section, it is straightforward to develop predictions about the behavior of win maximizing teams like those in European professional football leagues, or potentially teams in North American leagues that do not car about profits. These teams still have revenue functions and cost functions that depend on winning percentages, just like those for profit maximizing teams shown above. The difference is that a win maximizing team faces a break even constraint, where total revenues must equal total costs

$$R(W) = C(W).$$

and chooses a level of talent to maximize W given the revenue and cost functions and this break even constraint. Figure 4.15 shows the talent decision for a profit maximizing team relative to the talent decision made by a win maximizing team under the assumption that both teams have identical cost functions ($C_i = F_1 + p_1W_i$) and revenue functions ($R(W_i, A)$).

Figure 4.15: Profit Maximization and Win Maximization

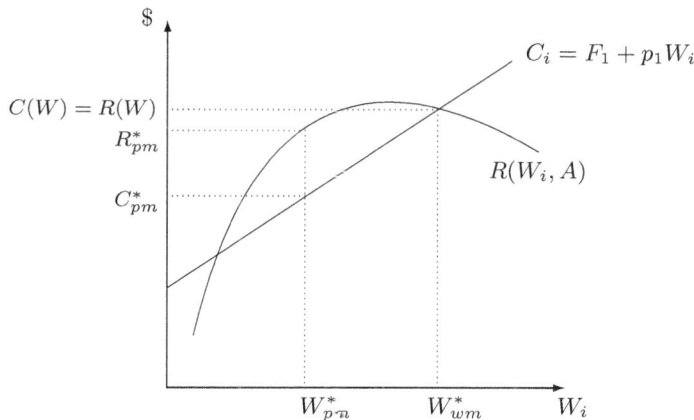

The profit maximizing team chooses a level of talent that maximizes profits – that is the W_i where marginal revenue is equal to marginal cost – at W_{pm}^* on Figure 4.15. The win maximizing team wants to hire more talent to increase the number of wins with no regard to profits. This implies that a win maximizing team will continue to hire talent beyond the point where marginal revenue is equal to marginal cost, driving up total cost. A win maximizing team only stops hiring talent when total cost has increased to the point where it equals total revenues, at W_{wm}^* on Figure 4.15. At this point, the break even constraint binds: total revenues are equal to total costs, and total profits are zero. Clearly, at W_{wm}^*, marginal cost exceeds marginal revenue. A win maximizing team will field a higher quality roster than a profit maximizing team, other things equal.

For the profit maximizing team, at W_{pm}^* marginal cost is equal to marginal revenue $[R' = p_1]$. But this is not true for the win maximizing team. At W_{wm}^* total cost is equal to total revenue $[R(W_{wm}^*) = F_1 + p_1 W_{wm}^*]$. This expression can be rearranged

$$\frac{R(W_{wm}^*) - F_1}{W_{wm}^*} = p_1 \tag{4.8}$$

to show that for a win maximizing team the marginal cost of talent is equal to average revenue net of fixed costs. The left had side of this expression is equal to the slope of a straight line drawn from the intercept of the cost function to any point on the total revenue curve. There are two points on Figure 4.15 where Equation 4.8 holds: at the winning percentages where the total revenue curve and total cost curve cross. We know that a win maximizing team does not choose the first of these points, because wins are not maximized there subject to the break even constraint. This condition will be useful in Chapter 5, when we examine the inter-related nature of decisions made by teams in sports leagues.

Some win maximizing teams may exist in leagues with profit maximizing teams. The win maximizing teams will finish at or near the top of the league standings every season, and will earn relatively low profits. The profit maximizing teams will, on average, finish lower in the league standings and earn, on average, higher profits. Since North American professional sports teams do not release audited financial data, and accounting practices allow teams to over or under state revenues and costs according to their preferences and goals, it is difficult to determine if any specific team is following an organizational goal of profit maximization or win maximization. But most economists agree that teams in North American professional sports leagues are profit maximizers. The case in European professional sports leagues may be quite different. The promotion and relegation system generates very different incentives in these leagues, as teams must try to win as many games or matches as possible in each season to avoid relegation.

Put another way, a traditionally poor performing team like the Pittsburgh Pirates of MLB, who experienced 18 consecutive losing seasons (1993-present) and finished last in their division seven times during this streak would have been relegated to the nether regions of a PRL ladder long ago. But in a closed static league like MLB, the Pirates can follow a profit maximizing strategy of fielding weak teams for decades, claiming poor luck and bad breaks, and continuing to maximize profits. In 2010 a number of confidential financial documents for the Pirates and other MLB teams were made public. These documents showed that the Pirates were making profits in the 2007 and 2008 seasons, when the team won only 41% of the games it played and finished in last place.

4.3 Summary

This chapter develops a long run model of team's decisions about the choice of talent to hire, including costs, revenues, and profits. The model explains why some teams choose to hire many talented players and win many games or matches and others choose to hire less talent and win fewer games. The central observation is that talent choice and team quality reflect the returns to winning relative to the marginal cost of winning more games. Teams like the Los Angeles Clippers, Toronto Maple Leafs and Chicago Cubs win a relatively small number of games every season over long periods of time because it is profit maximizing for them to field relatively poor teams. They play in markets where the marginal revenue from an additional win is relatively small. If these teams hired more talent, and won more games, their profits would be lower. They have no economic incentive to increase their quality.

Of course the owners of teams like the Clippers, Leafs and Cubs do not publicly say "we are a bad team because it makes me richer." Fans would not be happy with such statements, and demand for the team's core product, tickets to professional sporting events, might be reduced. Instead, team owners, managers and coaches, and players all uniformly express a desire to win games and championships. But the long-run lack of success by such teams is easily explained by the profit maximization motive, and the ultimate goal of all professional sports teams in closed, static North American teams to maximize profits above all else.

In the next chapter, the implications of the profit maximizing decisions made by individual teams will be investigated in the context of sports leagues, where teams interact and compete. Introducing the presence of other teams competing for both players and wins will have additional implications for the economic decisions made by professional sports teams.

Review Questions

1. Consider two professional basketball franchises, S and L. Franchise S faces higher long run costs of winning than franchise L, and also has a higher marginal revenue from winning than franchise L. This question is about the relative quality of the teams that each franchise chooses to field in the long run. Use the axes below to depict the choices made by franchise S and L.

   (a) On the axes below, graph the long run cost function $[C(W)]$ and the long run revenue function $[R(W\%)]$ for each team. Also, label the winning percentage that each team will select in the long run to maximize profits.

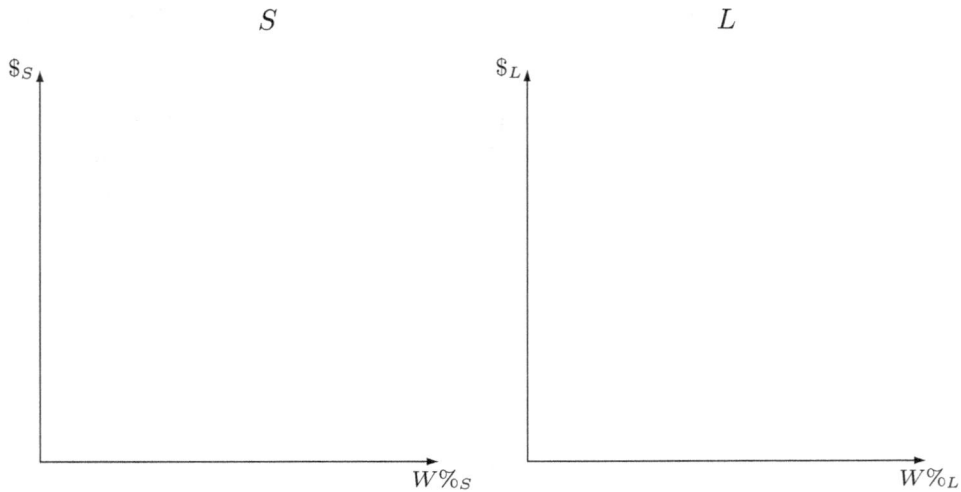

   (b) Based on your graph, which team will be more successful in the long run? Explain your answer.

   (c) Based on your graph, which team will make more profit in the long run? Explain your answer.

2. This question is about the past success of the Edmonton Oilers. Between the 1981-1982 season and the 1987-1988 season, the Oilers averaged 112 points per season and won four Stanley Cups. Between the 1992-1993 season and the 1998-1999 season, the Oilers averaged 67 points per season and appeared in the postseason only three times. Assume that these two six year periods are long enough to be considered the "long run" in economic terms.

   (a) In the long run, what is the output produced by the Oilers? Describe the relevant factors of production that are inputs to the Oilers production function.

   (b) The Oilers face long run costs of production in order to generate the output described in the previous section. In the profit analysis model of Chapter 3, long run costs are described by a long run total cost curve. On the axes below, graph the Oilers long run total cost curve and explain the key features of this curve. Be sure to define marginal cost and discuss how to find marginal cost on your graph.

(c) The Oilers also earn revenues based on the amount of output produced. On the axes below, show the Oiler's total revenue curve and describe the relationship between output and revenues. Define marginal revenue and show how to find marginal revenue on your graph.

(d) In the 1980s, the Oilers put extremely successful teams on the ice each season. According to the long run profit analysis model, this is the result of an economic choice made by team ownership. On the axes below, graph the Oiler's cost and revenue curves for this period. Label the profit maximizing level of output, the total costs and total revenues earned by the Oilers as predicted by this model.

(e) In the 1990s, the Oilers put a less successful team on the ice in every season. On the axes below, compare the Oilers of the 1980s to the Oilers of the 1990s. Your graph should show the total cost and total revenue curves for each era, as well as the profit maximizing level of output, costs and revenues, and profit for each era. Your graph should match the relative levels of success described above.

1980s   1990s

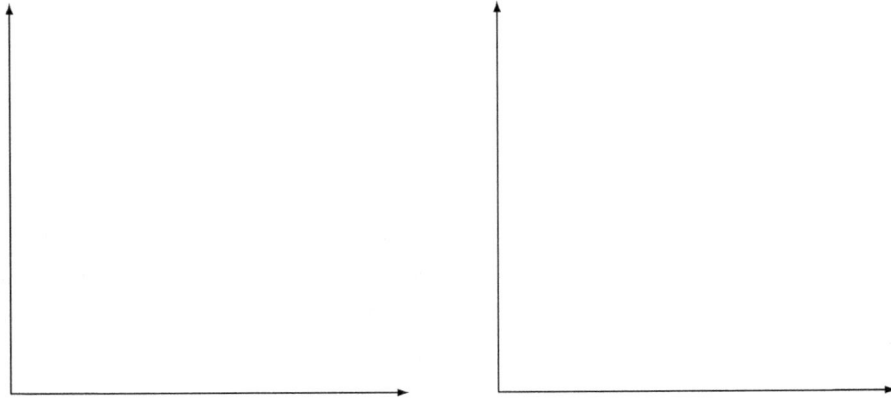

(f) During which era did the Oilers earn larger profits? Explain your answer.

Chapter 5

Sports Leagues

Chapter Objectives

- Understand that leagues facilitate play and maintain the business structure

- Understand the factors that drive league expansion and relocation

- Understand rival leagues

- Understand the nature and implications of the joint venture nature of sports leagues

- Understand the two team model of sports league outcomes and the nature of competitive imbalance in leagues

- Understand how league policies aimed at improving competitive balance work in the two team model

5.1   Introduction

Professional team sports have not always been organized in leagues, and not all professional team sports are organized into leagues. The most prominent example of a professional team sport that is not organized into a league is international test cricket. This form of cricket takes place between the national teams of a small number of nations where cricket is popular, including the UK, Australia, India, Pakistan, and a few other former commonwealth nations. While some regularly occurring test cricket matches exist, like The Ashes, a biennial match between the UK and Australia, most test cricket competitions consist of irregularly scheduled matches between countries. Another example of a professional team sport not organized into a league was the National Association of Base Ball Players (NABBP), a baseball organization that proceeded the National League. Despite its name, the NABBP membership was baseball *clubs*, not baseball players, making this an early example of a sports league. Although the NABPP upheld the ideal of amateurism for much of its existence (1857-1875), it permitted professionalism in the 1869 and 1870 seasons. The NABBP only set rules of play and scoring. It did not organize a regular season schedule, award a championship, or restrict membership of clubs. Individual clubs were responsible for arranging a schedule of games in the NABPP. The NABBP shows that a team sport can exist without the standard league organization present in modern North American leagues, but given that the NABBP was replaced by the National Association of Professional Base Ball Players in 1871, the limitations of the NABBP from an economic perspective are apparent.

Another alternative to leagues can be found in the history of the Negro Leagues, a succession of professional baseball leagues that operated in the United States from the mid 1880s until the early 1960s. These leagues did not have a formal regular season scheduled, although teams would play each other regularly during the summer "regular season" and postseason championships were held at the end of each season. The Negro leagues also generated revenues by "barnstorming" the practice of traveling to different towns and cities to play exhibition games against local all-star teams. The Negro leagues were professional baseball leagues and flourished for decades with little formal league organization. However, they were successful primarily because Major League Baseball prohibited blacks from playing on MLB teams until the 1940s, providing the Negro leagues with a large pool of talented baseball players with no other viable labor market; after MLB integrated in 1947, the Negro leagues remained viable for another 15 years.

Although leagues are not necessary for a team sport to succeed, leagues clearly perform a valuable economic function. In this chapter, we examine the economic role played by sports leagues, and develop a model that helps to explain the fundamental tension that exists in all sports league: the tradeoff between success and profits at the league level.

5.2   Sports League Functions

Sports leagues perform two types of economic activities:

1. <u>Single-entity functions</u>: Cooperative actions that must occur for play to take place.

2. <u>Joint Venture functions</u>: All cooperative actions not related to making play happen; these include primarily functions aimed at increasing profits above what could be earned acting individually

5.2.1   Single-entity Functions

Single-entity functions involve anything required to make play happen in sports leagues. Obviously, making play happen is an important function of sports leagues. Without single-entity cooperation, play would not take place and teams would not earn revenues. One important type of single-entity cooperation is the setting of a schedule. The league schedule must include all teams in the league and establish the length of the season. It must also ensure that each team plays the same number of games and the same number of home games. Teams would have trouble setting schedules individually, as each team would want more home games, more games on weekends, and so on. Also, teams would prefer to play more games against opponents who draw bigger crowds. Setting the schedule also provides fans with information about when and where games will take place. Finally, setting the schedule allows leagues to exercise monopoly power. The length of the regular season is set to maximize profits, and economic theory predicts that monopolists reduce output to maximize profits. Contests are one of the outputs of sports leagues, and the implication of economic models of monopoly is that monopoly leagues would set a season length lower than would be set under competition.

Table 5.1 shows the number of games in each season and the number of teams in the NHL. Note that the number of games in each season has expanded over time, although the current 82 game season is shorter than was in place in the 1990s. This expansion of the number of regular season games has also taken place in other North American professional sports leagues. The NFL is currently debating expanding its regular season to 18 games, for example. In setting the season length, leagues must balance the exercise of monopoly power (restrict quantity to maximize profits)

Table 5.1: NHL Season Length and Number of Teams

Seasons	Games	Teams	Seasons	Games	Teams
'17-'18	22	4	'70-'72	78	14
'18-'19	18	3	'72-'74	78	16
'19-'24	24	4	'74-'78	80	18
'24-'25	30	6	'78-'79	80	17
'25-'26	36	7	'79-'91	80	21
'26-'31	44	10	'91-'92	80	22
'31-'32	48	8	'92-'93	84	24
'32-'35	48	9	'93-'94	84	26
'35-'38	48	8	'94-'95	48	26
'38-'42	48	7	'95-'98	82	26
'42-'46	50	6	'98-'00	82	28
'46-'49	60	6	'00-'04	82	30
'49-'67	70	6	'04-'05	0	30
'67-'68	74	12	'05-'10	82	30
'68-'70	76	12			

against the fact that each additional game played in the regular season will generate additional revenues. For this reason, the length of the regular season has expanded slowly in most North American professional sports leagues. The number of teams has also expanded. The size of the league falls under joint-venture cooperation, which will be discussed in detail in the next section.

A second important single-entity function is setting the rules of play. Leagues set and enforce rules like the designated hitter rule, definition of the strike zone, and so on in MLB; the NHL sets and enforces rules on icing, penalties, and so on. Teams might have trouble agreeing to rules individually, as individual teams might want to alter the rules to suit their particular personnel or style of play. In addition, rules can have economic impacts. For example, a relatively small strike zone in MLB would favor offense and increase scoring, which might be attractive to fans, potentially increasing attendance.

A third important single-entity function is the determination of the structure of the league championship. This includes factors like how many teams make the playoffs, how long each series lasts, and how ties will be broken during the playoffs. Note that the existence of playoffs in professional sports leagues has two effects on teams. First, playoffs extend fan interest for the few teams who make the playoffs, raising their revenues, and also make for more attractive national television broadcast contracts, raising the revenues of all teams. Second, playoffs reduce the value of talent relative to leagues that crown the team with the highest winning percent as champion, because playoffs reduce the chance that the team with the best record wins the championship. This should reduce the investment by teams in talent, since it reduces the value of talent.

Note that playoffs are not ubiquitous in sports leagues. None of the domestic football leagues in Europe hold a postseason championship. Instead, the team with the most points in the season is crowned the league champion. Also, NCAA football in the US does not hold a postseason championship. Instead, a series of postseason "bowl games" are held. Holding postseason playoffs is a profit maximizing choice made by professional sports leagues in North America.

5.2.2   Joint Venture Functions

Joint venture functions consist of coordinated actions designed to increase the profits of all teams in a league. The easiest way to identify a joint venture function that it must involve multiple teams and be unrelated to making play happen. By undertaking joint venture functions, team owners act together to raise profits of all teams. In doing this, they must surrender part of their autonomy in order to make more money. Most joint venture functions are designed to increase the market power of teams. However, market power can be generated by means other than through joint venture functions.

Territory Definition and Protection

Leagues have been allowed (by government policy makers who have chosen not to apply anti-trust law to sports leagues) to grant exclusive territories to league members. Leagues divide up all of the area in the countries where they operate and assign specific areas to specific teams. These territorial agreements prohibit teams from moving into the territory already assigned to another team, creating monopoly power. For example, Jim Balsillie tried to buy the Phoenix Coyotes in 2009 and move them to Hamilton, Ontario. Hamilton was part of the territory of the Toronto Maple Leafs, and the league blocked Balsillie from buying the team. This is an example of territorial protection by a sports league.

Exclusive territories are defined and managed through *Franchise Agreements*. A franchise agreement is simply a contract between the league and each team owner that specifies exactly what it means to own a professional sports team. Franchise agreements specify the role of league, and what the owner must do. For example, franchise agreements specify that the team must participate in the regular and post season and spell out how much each team gets from national broadcast rights contracts. Exclusive territories are defined as part of the franchise agreement. Note that the territorial rules specified in franchise agreements has survived judicial review for decades and constitutes a core part of the implicit or explicit "anti-trust exemption" enjoyed by sports leagues. Without this exemption, there would be more freedom of entry into leagues.

Territorial agreements have important economic effects. They limit the number of teams that can play in any market and thus limit large markets to only one team in most cases. Why is there only one NHL team in Toronto (population more than 5.5 million)? Because the Leafs have exclusive territorial rights to Toronto. The metro area could probably support one or two additional NHL franchises.

Again, this represents a quantity restriction put in place by leagues to generate monopoly power and monopoly rents. Monopolists reduce output to maximize profits, and restricting the number of teams in a league is a key part of the development of monopoly power in sports leagues. However, leagues must carefully balance the restriction of the number of franchises against the possibility that if too many large markets are left open, it would invite the formation of a rival league. Table 5.1 shows that the NHL has increased the number of teams in the league over time. But this expansion was not enough to deter the formation of a rival league. The World Hockey Association formed in 1972, in part because the NHL had not expanded fast enough to fill all of the viable markets in North America that could support an NHL franchise. A number of WHL teams, including the Edmonton Oilers, were eventually merged into the NHL in 1979. As we will see in later chapters, the formation of rival leagues is bad for existing leagues because rival teams bid star players away from the existing league, driving up payroll costs, and also threaten the existence of existing leagues.

Expansion and Relocation

Sports leagues periodically expand, as can be seen from Table 5.1 which shows the NHL growing from 4 to 30 teams over the last 80 years. In addition, existing teams in sports leagues sometimes move to open markets. Why do leagues expand, and why do teams move? The answer is, of course, because it is profitable to expand and move, in some cases, and because leagues must deter the formation of rival leagues and the profitability of markets changes over time. The population of the US and Canada have grown steadily over time, which means that some formerly small cities expand to the point that they can support a professional sports team. In addition, migration and changes in the structure of the economy lead to regional differences in population and income that can change the relative profitability of cities as hosts to professional sports teams. This leads to expansion and relocation in professional sports leagues. Note that the promotion and regulation systems in place in European sports leagues ensures that teams will always exist in the most profitable cities, but North American leagues lack such a mechanism to allocate teams to cities.

To belabor the point, leagues never expand as much as they would if there was freedom of entry into these leagues. Sports leagues operate as monopolies and the exercise of monopoly power requires that some viable markets be left open. This provides the owners of individual teams with monopoly power that they use to extract subsidies from local governments, and to earn monopoly profits in their exclusive territories. League expansion and relocation is a joint venture activity, as it requires teams to cooperate to determine the number, and location of teams.

League Expansion refers to any increase in the number of teams in a league; franchise relocation refers to moving an existing team to a more profitable market. Expansion and relocation have both direct and indirect financial effects. The direct financial effects arise because league expansion affects the profits of all existing teams. When a league with N teams expands to add one additional team, all shared revenues are divided among $N + 1$ teams forever; expansion forces each existing owner to consider the effects of an additional permanent share of all common revenue streams in the league. In order to convince existing owners to agree to expansion, leagues charge new owners an *expansion fee* that gets divided among all existing owners, offsetting some of the lost revenue.

Table 5.2 shows the expansion fee charged for each of the NHL expansions in the past fifty years. Several features stand out on this table. First, expansion fees have risen considerably over this period. This reflects both an increase in the bargaining power of leagues and the increased importance of shared revenues. Second, notice that the merger of the WHL and NHL brought in relatively little in expansion fees (the same amount as was paid by the expansion franchises in the early 1970s, despite high inflation in the 1970s). This reflects the cost to the NHL of their failure to expand enough to deter rival league formation in the 1960s and 1970s. The NHL was in a weak bargaining position when the WHL succeeded, and the low expansion fees reflect this. Finally, note the increase in recent expansion fees. This suggests that the NHL thought that the new teams in the southern US would generate significant new revenues, as did the expansion team owners. How has this worked out?

Rival Leagues

The expansion decision raises the possibility of considerable strategic interaction among existing team owners and prospective expansion team owners. Most of these maximize the bargaining power of existing team owners in this process, leading to higher expansion fees. However, the specter of a rival league forming always exists in professional team sports, which gives some power to potential expansion team buyers, since failure to expand raises the probability of a successful rival league forming.

Table 5.2: NHL Expansion Fees

Season	Team	Fee	Record	Playoffs	Avg. Att.
'67-'68	California Seals	$2 mil	15-42-17	None	4,960
'67-'68	Los Angeles Kings	$2 mil	31-33-10	1st Rd.	8,031
'67-'68	Minnesota North Stars	$2 mil	27-32-15	2nd Rd.	11,861
'67-'68	Philadelphia Flyers	$2 mil	31-32-11	1st Rd.	9,625
'67-'68	Pittsburgh Penguins	$2 mil	27-34-13	None	7,407
'67-'68	St. Louis Blues	$2 mil	27-31-16	Finals	8,897
'70-'71	Buffalo Sabres	$6 mil	24-39-15	None	9,721
'70-'71	Vancouver Canucks	$6 mil	24-46-8	None	15,577
'72-'73	Atlanta Flames	$6 mil	25-38-15	None	12,515
'72-'73	New York Islanders	$6 mil	12-60-6	None	16,383
'74-'75	Kansas City Scouts	$6 mil	15-54-11	None	15,994
'74-'75	Washington Capitals	$6 mil	8-67-5	None	10,004
'79-'80	Edmonton Oilers	$6 mil	28-39-13	1st Rd.	15,200
'79-'80	Hartford Whalers	$6 mil	27-34-19	1st Rd.	14,570
'79-'80	Quebec Nordiques	$6 mil	25-44-11	None	10,742
'79-'80	Winnipeg Jets	$6 mil	20-49-11	None	13,193
'91-'92	San Jose Sharks	$50 mil	17-58-5	None	10,321
'92-'93	Ottawa Senators	$50 mil	10-70-4	None	10,035
'92-'93	Tampa Bay Lightning	$50 mil	23-54-7	None	10,013
'93-'94	Mighty Ducks of Anaheim	$50 mil	33-46-5	None	16,989
'93-'94	Florida Panthers	$50 mil	33-34-17	None	13,693
'98-'99	Nashville Predators	$80 mil	28-47-7	None	16,195
'99-'00	Atlanta Thrashers	$80 mil	14-61-7-4	None	17,206
'00-'01	Columbus Blue Jackets	$80 mil	28-39-9-6	None	17,457
'00-'01	Minnesota Wild	$80 mil	25-39-13-5	None	18,328

Table 5.3: Rival League Formation

League	Rival	Operated	Outcome
NL 1896	American Assn.	1883-91	Assimil.
	American Lg.	1901-02	Merged
MLB 1903	Federal League	1914	Buyout
	Continental Lg.	1961	Buyout
NHL 1917	WHA	1972-79	4 team mrg.
NFL 1922	AFL 1	1926	1 team mrg.
	AFL 2	1936	Partial mrg.
	AFL 3	1940	Bankrupt
	AAFC	1946	4 team mrg.
	AFL 4	1960	Merged
	WFL	1974-5	Bankrupt
	USFL	1983-5	Bankrupt
	XFL	2001	Bankrupt
	UFL	2009-12	Bankrupt
NBA 1949	ABL	1960-1	Bankrupt
	ABA	1967-1976	4 team mrg.

The possibility of a rival league forming has more impact on expansion than one might think. The formation of rival leagues takes place more often than you might think. It has happened relatively frequently in the past in all professional team sports in North America. Consider the history of rival league formation in North America over the past century, as summarized on Table 5.3. From the table, rival leagues formed at regular intervals in the history of sports leagues. Several factors affect the formation of rival leagues. First, for the conditions for a rival league to form to exist, some open markets must exist that are capable of supporting professional sports teams. Second, appropriate facilities must exist for teams in a rival league to play in. Third a rival league requires a minimum number of teams to get started. Play must take place in order for a rival league to form, and some minimum number of teams must exist for a viable rival league to form. This is an important barrier to formation.

Finally, in order for a rival league to form, the rival league must have a source of media revenues. The analysis of revenues in Chapter 1 shows how important media revenues are to sports leagues. Without a source of media revenues, no modern rival league is viable. Successful rival leagues have been able to bid star players away from existing teams; without access to significant media revenues, teams in rival leagues will not be able to acquire enough star players to compete with the existing league. On the other hand, the presence of a media contract cannot guarantee the success of a rival league - consider the example of the XFL in professional football. The current rival league in professional football in the US, the United Football League, has five teams located in large cities with no NFL franchises (Orlando, Florida, Hartford, Connecticut, Las Vegas, Nevada, Omaha, Nebraska, and Sacramento, California) and a television contract with Versus and the satellite channel HDNet. Note from Table 5.3 that relatively few rival leagues have formed since media revenues became a key source of revenues generated by professional sports leagues. This highlights the importance of media revenues in rival league formation.

League Level Negotiation

The final type of joint venture cooperation is league level negotiation. Sports leagues engage in a number of joint venture negotiation related activities that could be undertaken separately. What are these and why are they important? Leagues undertake three types of league level negotiations:

- *Broadcast Rights Negotiations*: Individual teams, or parts of leagues could negotiate with media companies to sell broadcast rights. This happens in NCAA football and basketball in the US, where individual conferences (and the University of Notre Dame) negotiate with networks for national broadcast rights. Why doesn't this take place in other settings? Because negotiating with media providers as a league increases market power, and drives up rights fees.

- *Negotiations with Players and Labor Relations*: Auto makers do not negotiate collectively with auto workers unions, but teams in sports leagues negotiate collectively with players unions. Why does this happen? Because collective negotiation with players unions increases leagues' market power in these negotiations. If teams negotiated separately with players unions, there would be less bargaining power for the league, and more bargaining power for the players. This is not true in other industries like the auto industry because the labor market in the auto industry is local, not national or international like in sport.

- *Negotiation with Host Cities*: Much more about this topic later, when we discuss the financing and economic impact of facilities in professional sports in Chapter 8.

5.3   A Model of League Behavior: The Two Team Model

This section develops a model of economic decisions made by sports teams, and then incorporates these decisions into a model of the behavior of a number of teams that form a sports league. The model developed in this chapter is not new. It is a generalized version of a number of economic models of team and league behavior in the sports economics literature. The "Readings and References" list at the end of the chapter contains a list of papers that contain detailed descriptions of the model built up in this chapter. Note that while this model superficially resembles the attendance model developed in Chapter 3, the model developed here has winning percent as the choice variable and includes interaction between teams in a league. The two models differ in important ways. Do not confuse them.

5.3.1   Teams

Sports leagues are composed of multiple teams. For simplicity, we will consider a league with just two teams. This assumption allows for a graphical solution to the problem of how winning percentages are determined in a league of profit maximizing teams.

We use the long run model of team decisions developed in Chapter 4. Consider two teams, X and Z that face the same marginal cost of talent p_1. The profit maximization problem for team X is to choose a winning percentage (W_{xi}) to maximize profits, given the team's market revenue potential A_{x1} and fixed costs F_{x1}

$$\max_{W_{xi}} \ \pi_x = R_{x1}(W_i, A_{x1}) - F_{x1} - p_1 W_{xi}. \tag{5.1}$$

The problem for team Z is to choose a winning percentage (W_{zi}) to maximize profits, given the team's market revenue potential A_{z1} and fixed costs F_{z1}

$$\max_{W_{zi}} \pi_z = R_{z1}(W_i, A_{z1}) - F_{z1} - p_1 W_{zi}. \tag{5.2}$$

Furthermore, assume that the two teams play in markets with different revenue potential. Assume that X plays in the smaller market and Z plays in the larger market, so $A_{x1} < A_{z1}$.

The Marginal Revenue Curve

A key to extending the model to a sports league with two teams is the derivation of an expression for the relationship between marginal revenue and winning percentage when the team is making profit maximizing decisions. Graphically, this relationship is depicted by a *marginal revenue curve*. The marginal revenue curve shows the increase in revenues attributable to all possible winning percentage that a team owner might choose.

Recall that marginal revenue at any W can be found from the slope of a line tangent to the revenue function at that point. Starting at the smallest W and increasing W (moving from left to right along the revenue curve) the tangent lines start out steep and get flatter as W increases until the maximum point is reached, where the tangent line has slope 0. That means that marginal revenue is decreasing as winning percentage increases.

Figure 5.1 shows the graphical derivation of a marginal revenue curve from a total revenue curve. The top panel shows the total revenue curve and the slope of lines tangent to this curve at various points, and the bottom panel shows the marginal revenue curve for this total revenue curve. At a low winning percentage, like W_1, the marginal revenue (MR_1) is relatively high because the slope os a line tangent to the total revenue curve at that point is steep. At a higher winning percentage, like W_2, the marginal revenue (MR_2) is lower because the slope of a line tangent to the total revenue curve is flatter.

There are three key points about the marginal revenue curves that emerge from a total revenue function like $R_i(W_i, A_1)$

1. Marginal revenue curves slope down. As a profit maximizing owner chooses higher winning percentages for his team, the amount by which total revenues increases in response to a unit change in winning percentage is lower.

2. The position of the marginal revenue curve depends on the "market revenue potential" parameter A. As A increases the marginal revenue curve shifts up and as A decreases the marginal revenue curve shifts down.

3. When $p_i = MR$, profits are maximized. But at any winning percentage where $p_i \neq MR$, profits are not maximized.

Figure 5.2 illustrates point two. The left panel of 5.2 shows a team with a relatively small market revenue potential, reflected by A_1. The right panel shows a team with a relatively large revenue potential, reflected by A_2. The lines tangent to the revenue curve on the left panel at W_1 and W_2 are flatter than the lines tangent to the revenue curve at W_1 and W_2 on the right panel. The marginal revenue curve for the team playing in the market with A_2 is higher than the marginal revenue curve for the team playing in the market with A_1.

Figure 5.1: Marginal Revenue Curve Derivation

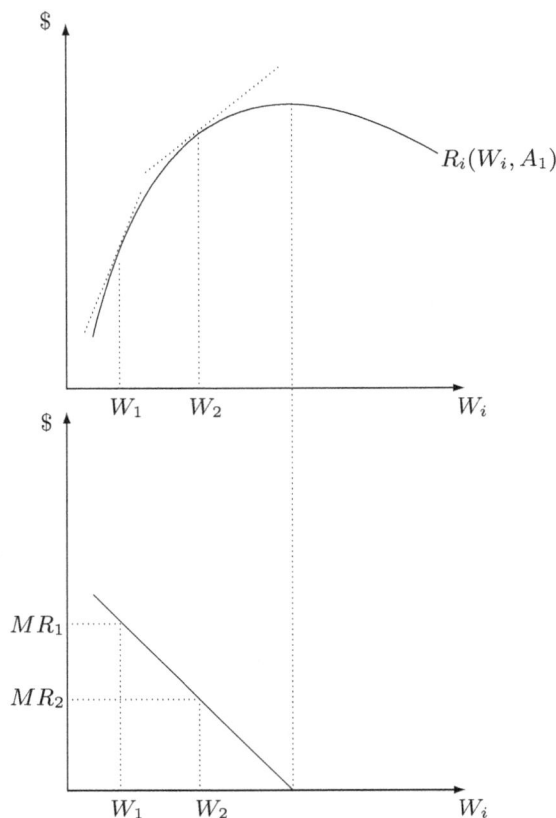

5.3.2   The League

Both teams play in the same league, so their games are all against each other. This means that each loss for Z is a win for X and each win for Z is a loss for X. The implication is that the sum of the winning percentages that each team chooses must be 1

$$W_{zi} + W_{xi} = \sum_{t=X,Z} W_{ti} = 1.$$

This constraint is called the adding up constraint on winning percentages.

In a sports league, the interesting question is, given two profit maximizing teams in a league, what is the equilibrium distribution winning percentage for each team, given that the adding up constraint must hold. The typical method of showing the outcome in the two team case is to graph the marginal revenue curve for both teams on the same graph. The graph showing the equilibrium outcome in a two team league has two vertical axes. The vertical axis on the left shows the marginal revenue and marginal cost for X, and Xs winning percentage increases from left to right. The left panel of Figure 5.3 shows Xs marginal revenue curve in this set up.

The vertical axis on the right shows the marginal revenue and marginal cost for Z, and Zs winning percentage increases from right to left. In other words, Z's winning percentage is read backward from Xs. The right panel on Figure 5.3 shows Xs marginal revenue curve in this set up.

Figure 5.4 shows the two marginal revenue curves on the same graph. Note that the MR curve for team Z has a larger intercept than the MR curve for team X. This means that Z can generate

Figure 5.2: Marginal Revenue Curves and A

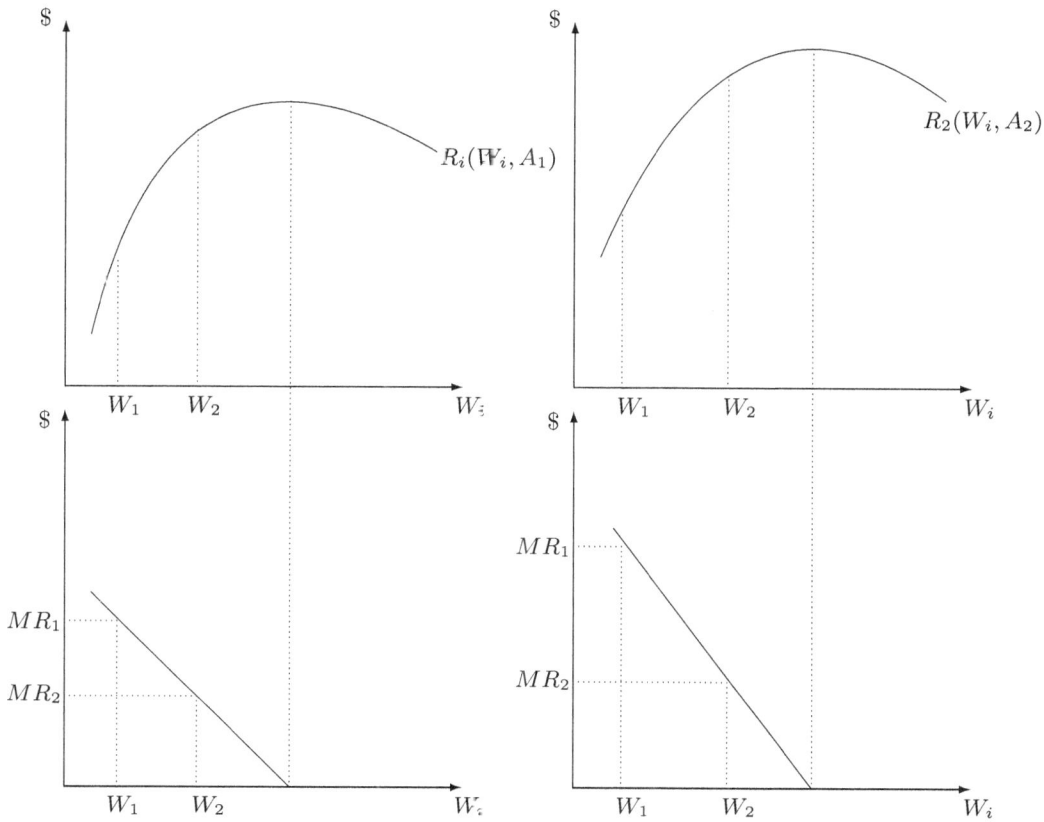

Figure 5.3: MR Curves

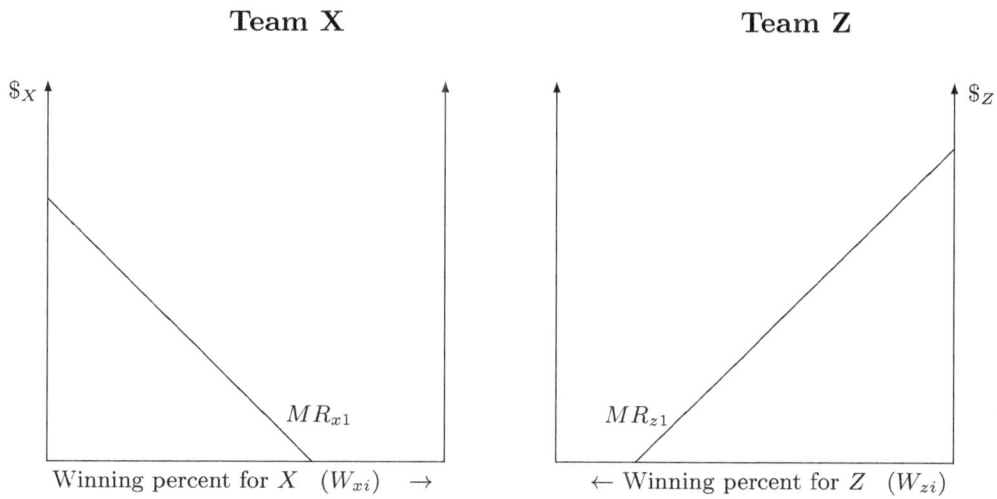

higher marginal revenue from any winning percentage than X can generate. This outcome stems from the higher revenue potential in team Zs market ($A_{z1} > A_{x1}$).

One important feature of this graph is that the adding up constraint has been imposed on the model by scaling the horizontal axis in this way. Starting at the bottom right hand corner of the graph, team Z wins no games and team X wins all the games. Moving right to left entails team Z winning games and team X losing games. Because the left-to-right scale for team X is the inverse of the right-to-left scale for team Z, any point represents an outcome where

$$W_x + W_z = 1.$$

Figure 5.4: MR Curves for Two Teams

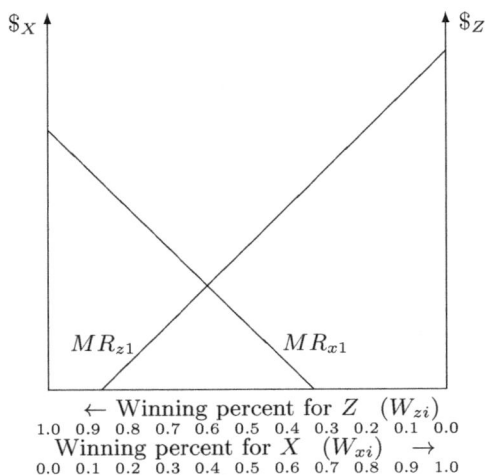

$$\leftarrow \text{ Winning percent for } Z \quad (W_{zi})$$

| 1.0 | 0.9 | 0.8 | 0.7 | 0.6 | 0.5 | 0.4 | 0.3 | 0.2 | 0.1 | 0.0 |

$$\text{Winning percent for } X \quad (W_{xi}) \quad \rightarrow$$

| 0.0 | 0.1 | 0.2 | 0.3 | 0.4 | 0.5 | 0.6 | 0.7 | 0.8 | 0.9 | 1.0 |

5.3.3 Equilibrium in the Two-team Model

Equilibrium in the model is found by placing both marginal revenue curves on the same graph. The point where the two marginal revenue curves cross, labeled E_1 on Figure 5.5, is the equilibrium point in the Two Team Model. At this point, team X maximizes profits by choosing a winning percentage of $W_x = 0.400$ and team Z maximizes profits by choosing a winning percentage of $W_z = 0.600$. Both teams have the same marginal revenue at this point, because E_1 is the point where the two MR curves cross. When team X has a winning percentage of $W_x = 0.400$, team X has a marginal revenue of MR_{E1}^X; this value is found from the marginal revenue curve for team X. When team Z has a winning percentage of $W_z = 0.600$, team Z has a marginal revenue of MR_{E1}^Z; this value is found from the marginal revenue curve for team Z.

The horizontal line running through point E_1 is also labeled p_1. This is the equilibrium marginal cost of an additional unit of winning percentage in the league, which is interpreted as the marginal cost of an additional unit of talent. Recall that this is the wage earned by players in the labor market. Because both teams maximize profits at E_1, the condition for profit maximization ($p_1 = MC = MR$) must hold, thus the horizontal line at p_1 identifies marginal costs (wages) in this graph and must run through the point where the two MR curves intersect. At equilibrium the marginal revenues for each team are equal, and both are equal to the marginal cost (wage) of hiring additional talent in the league.

Figure 5.5: League Equilibrium

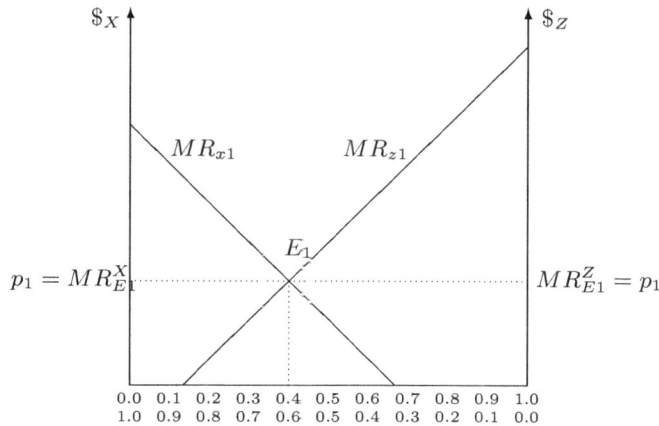

Also notice that at equilibrium point E_1 the league has a lack of competitive balance. To maximize profits in each season, team Z chooses a level of talent that leads to a 0.600 winning percentage and team X chooses a level of talent that leads to a 0.400 winning percentage. Team Z fields a winning team and team X fields a losing team. This disparity arises because of the different market revenue generation potentials for the two teams. This underscores an important prediction of the two-team model: as long as teams play in markets with different revenue generating potentials, the equilibrium outcome in the model features *competitive imbalance* in that team playing in markets with more revenue generating potential will field better teams than those playing in markets with lower revenue generating potential.

Figure 5.5 has a useful property. Think about the area of the rectangles formed by point E_1, the vertical axis, the origin, and the profit maximizing winning percentage for each team. In other words, for team X, the length of this rectangle is $W_X = 0.400$, because team X buys enough talent to field a team that plays 0.400 ball, and each of these units of talent costs p_1, the height of this rectangle. The area of this rectangle is $W_x \times p_1$, which is team X's total payroll. Similarly, team Z buys enough talent to field a team that plays 0.400 ball, which requires $W_Z = 0.600$ units of talent, which is the length of this rectangle. Each of these units of talent costs team Z p_1, the height of this rectangle. The area of this rectangle is $W_z \times p_1$, which is team Z's total payroll. The area of these two rectangles graphically depicts each team's payroll. In this case, team Z payroll is larger than team X's payroll, since $W_z \times p_1 > W_x \times p_1$.

Equilibrium is reached in the model by talent flowing from one team to the other. Consider an outcome to the right of point E_1 in Figure 5.5. For example, consider the outcome where $W_Z = 0.500 = W_X$ just to the right of E_1. If Z and X both field teams with enough talent to win half their games, the marginal revenue generated by team Z from a 1 unit increase in W, found from team Z's marginal revenue curve when $W_Z = 0.500$, is greater than MR_{E1}^Z. It's also greater than the marginal revenue that team X gets from one less unit of W at $W_X = 0.500$, $MR_{0.500}^X$, found from team X's marginal revenue curve. If there is free movement from one team to the other, through trades or free agency, then team Z will find it profitable to buy talent from team X, improving team Z on the field and making team X worse on the field. These trades will be profit maximizing for both teams, and will take place as long as there is a difference in marginal revenue. So any league at an outcome where $MR_Z \neq MR_X$ is not in equilibrium. The league is driven to the outcome where the two marginal revenue curves cross by player movements in the form of trades or free agent signings.

Equilibrium in a League with Identical Markets

Changing the relative size of A_{z1} and A_{x1} will lead to different levels of competitive balance in equilibrium in the league model. For example, consider the case where both teams in the league play in markets with identical revenue generating potential. In this case, the team X has a profit maximization problem

$$\max_{W_{xi}} \ \pi_x = R_{x1}(W_i, A_1) - F_{x1} - p_1 W_{xi}.$$

and team Z has a profit maximization problem

$$\max_{W_{zi}} \ \pi_z = R_{z1}(W_i, A_1) - F_{z1} - p_1 W_{zi}.$$

where $A_{x1} = A_{z1} = A_1$. From these equations, both teams clearly play in markets with the same revenue generation potential and face the same marginal costs of talent. Both teams also have the same fixed costs. In this case, the teams face identical revenue and cost functions. Graphically, their profit maximizing decisions are the same, as shown on Figure 5.6.

Figure 5.6: Teams with Identical A

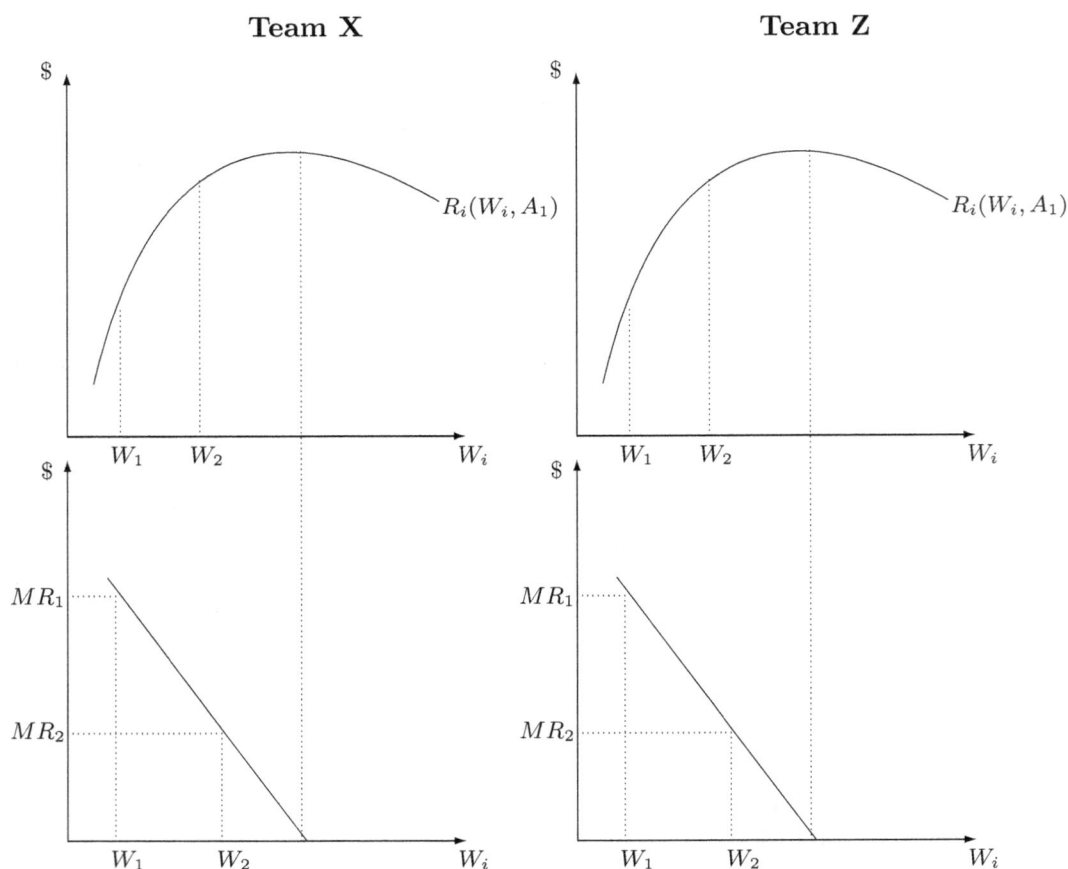

Under these conditions, the MR curves for the two teams will be identical. The league will have a different equilibrium outcome compared to the previous example where the teams played in markets with different revenue generating potentials and different As. The Figure 5.7 shows equilibrium in a league with teams playing in identical markets, at point E_2. In this league, both teams choose 0.500 as their profit maximizing winning percentage. In equilibrium, both teams choose an identical winning percentage, and the league has the maximum level of competitive balance possible. Both teams win exactly half the games played in the league.

In equilibrium in the two-team model, there is a clear relationship between differences in A and the equilibrium profit maximizing winning percentages chosen by the two teams. This relationship can be expressed

$$\frac{W_x}{W_z} = \omega \left(\frac{A_x}{A_z} \right).$$

where $\omega(1) = 1$. In other words, the larger the discrepancy between the market revenue potential for the two teams, the larger the difference in the equilibrium winning percentages, and the more the competitive imbalance in the league. According to this relationship, if $A_x = A_z$ (the teams play in markets with the same revenue generating potential), then $W_x = W_z$, and the league has competitive balance in equilibrium. But if $A_z > A_x$, then $W_z > W_x$ in equilibrium, and the league does not have competitive balance in equilibrium in equilibrium. To the extent that there are market disparities captured by A, the league will have problems with competitive balance in equilibrium. Note that the relationship between A_i and W_i above holds all other factors that might affect W, like marginal cost p and fixed cost F, constant.

Figure 5.7: League Equilibrium With Equal A

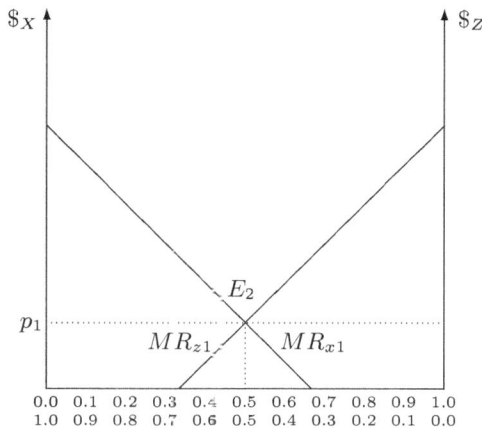

5.3.4 Remedies to Competitive Imbalance

To generalize the two-team model to a league with many teams, just interpret the two teams as representative of two groups of teams: teams playing in high revenue markets and teams playing in low revenue markets. The two-team model predicts that leagues with teams in markets with different revenue generating potentials will have a persistent group of winning teams (those playing in the high revenue markets) and a persistent group of losing teams (those playing in the low revenue markets). The teams playing in the low revenue markets will always field below average teams, and will always have losing records. They will win some of the game they play against other low revenue market teams, and lose most of the games they play against high revenue market teams. The league champion will always come out of the high revenue market teams. This sort of outcome is often called "competitive imbalance" and leagues frequently enact policies to try and address this imbalance. In Chapter 7 we will address economists attempts to quantify competitive balance and assess actual outcomes in professional sports leagues. As we will see, the evidence of persistent competitive imbalance in sports leagues is unsettled at best, and measuring competitive balance turns out to be a difficult task. However, leagues clearly claim that competitive imbalance is a problem, and have clearly put a number of policies in place that they claim are necessary to improve competitive balance. This section examines several of these policies in the context of the two team model.

Gate Revenue Sharing

One of the first solutions to the problem of competitive imbalance implemented was gate revenue sharing. Gate revenue sharing occurs when the home team and the visiting team in each game split a given fraction of the ticket revenues from each contest according to an agreed upon formula. Gate revenue sharing currently takes place in the NFL, NBA and NHL. In the NFL, the home team keeps 64% of designated gate revenues (excluding revenues from luxury boxes and premium seats) and the visiting team gets 36% of designated gate revenues. In the NBA, the home team keeps 95% and the visiting team gets 5%. The NHL revenue sharing is based on the characteristics of teams. In order to qualify for revenue sharing, an NHL team must be among the 15 clubs with the lowest revenues in the league, have a payroll below average, and play in a market with fewer than 2.5 million TV households. MLB shares all local revenues, including local media revenues. Under MLB revenue sharing, 20% of all local revenues are placed into a common pool and the proceeds from this pool are distributed equally to each team.

To analyze the effects of gate sharing, assume that the league consists of two teams, Team X and Team Z and Team Z plays in a large revenue potential market and Team X plays in a small revenue potential market. The initial equilibrium in the league is E_1 where Team Z wins most of the games and Team X loses most of the games. The league would be characterized by "competitive imbalance." Figure 5.8 shows the league equilibrium.

Figure 5.8: League Equilibrium with Gate Revenue Sharing

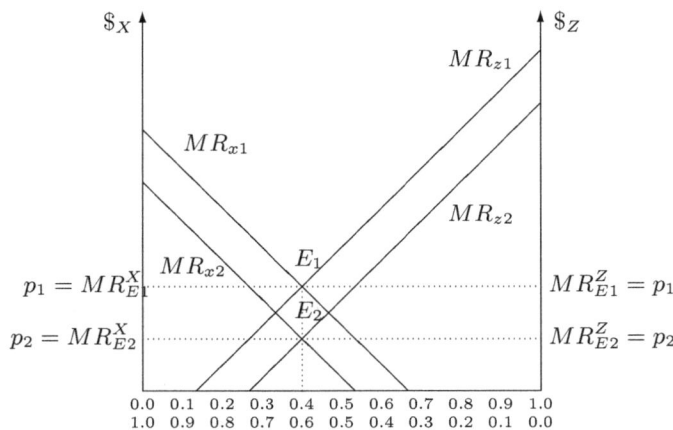

Suppose that the league enacts a gate revenue sharing policy to enhance competitive balance. The policy is that the home team in each game keeps a portion $0 \leq \alpha \leq 1$ of the gate revenues generated at each game and gives a share $(1 - \alpha)$ to the visiting team. Assume that each team plays the same number of home games in the regular season. Under this gate revenue sharing policy, the marginal revenue curve for each team is shifted down by $(1 - \alpha)$ for each team; the shift in the marginal revenue curves is proportional because the gate sharing is proportional to total revenues. The new marginal revenue curves for each team are MR_{z2} and MR_{x2} on Figure 5.8.

Since the marginal revenue curves shift down by the same proportion, the new equilibrium in the league, E_2 lies directly below the old equilibrium point, E_1. The revenue sharing policy has no effect on competitive balance in the league. Even after sharing gate revenues, the team in the high revenue generating market still wins a larger share of the games, and the team in the low revenue generating market wins a smaller share of the games. Also note that both teams are still maximizing their profits at E_2, although the total amount of profits earned by each team will change.

Although gate revenue sharing policy has no effect on competitive balance, it does have several important effects on both teams and on the league. First, the marginal revenue of a win for each team is reduced by revenue sharing. This can be seen immediately from the lower marginal revenue curves for each team. Second, since Team Z earns more revenues than Team X (look back at Figure 5.4 to see that this takes place), Team Z pays more to Team X at Team Zs home games than Team X pays to Team Z at Team Xs home games. The gate revenue sharing policy results in some of Team Zs revenues going to Team X in the form of a subsidy. Finally, since the marginal revenue from each additional win has decreased for each team, the marginal return to talent has also decreased. Because of this decrease, the teams have an incentive to invest in less playing talent, reducing the marginal cost of talent from p_1 to p_2 in equilibrium. In other words, the wage earned by all players in the league decreases, and total payrolls also decrease. The impact of gate revenue sharing is less wages to players.

Salary Caps

All of the North American professional sports leagues, with the exception of MLB, have "salary caps." The explicitly stated purpose of these league policies is to improve competitive balance in the leagues. However, the term "salary cap" does not really describe what is going on under these policies. A 'salary cap' does not limit the amount of money that can be paid to any player (although some exceptions exist.) The "salary cap" in place in North American professional sports leagues should be called a "revenue sharing payroll limit." These "salary caps" actually represent formal revenue sharing between team owners and players, and not limits on salaries. I will call these arrangements a "cap" but keep in mind that they do not generally impose limits on individual salaries.

A cap is set during the process of collective bargaining between leagues and players' unions in North American professional sports leagues. The outcome of collective bargaining is a Collective Bargaining Agreement (CBA) that specifies all of the conditions under which players interact economically with their teams. This process will be discussed fully in the chapter on sports labor markets. The important point for the determination of caps is that the CBA in place in each league contains a specific definition of revenues that will be used to determine the cap value. This is called Gross Revenue in the NFL, Business-Related Income in MLB, and Hockey Related Revenue in the NHL. In all cases, this is simply a specific, agreed upon definition of revenues that includes some types of revenues and excludes others. The definitions are detailed; the definition of Hockey Related Revenues takes more than 15 pages in the 2005 NHL CBA. Call this designated revenue

(DR).

A cap is simply defined as the minimum and maximum shares of designated cap revenues that can be used for payroll. Caps always contain both minimum and maximum percentages of designated cap revenue, so they are actually both a payroll ceiling and floor. The minimum and maximum shares and the definition of designated cap revenue are determined by negotiation between the players union and the league when the CBA is hammered out. A cap works as follows. The league CBA defines designated cap revenues, DR, the minimum share s_{min} and the maximum share, s_{max}. If the team has n teams, then the cap specifies that each team's payroll $payroll_i$ (for $i = 1, 2, \ldots, n$) must be in the range

$$\left(\frac{1}{n}\right) s_{min} \times DR \leq payroll_i \leq \left(\frac{1}{n}\right) s_{max} \times DR.$$

In 2002, a year covered under the NFL CBA currently in place, $s_{min} = 0.56$, $s_{max} = 0.63$, there were 32 teams in the league, and $DR = \$4,277,000,000$, so for the 2003 NFL season the cap values were

$$\left(\tfrac{1}{n}\right) s_{min} \times DR \leq payroll_i \leq \left(\tfrac{1}{n}\right) s_{max} \times DR$$
$$\left(\tfrac{1}{32}\right) 0.56 \times \$4,277,000,000 \leq payroll_i \leq \left(\tfrac{1}{32}\right) 0.63 \times \$4,277,000,000$$
$$\$74,847,500 \leq payroll_i \leq \$84,203,438.$$

NFL teams had to have a total payroll of anywhere between \$74 million and \$85 million in that season. Of course the CBA also defines exactly what is and is not counted as payroll for salary cap purposes.

Again, note that the cap does not actually limit the amount that can be paid to any player. It simply constrains total team payroll to lie between an upper and lower bound of designated cap revenues. Also, since caps are really a system of sharing revenues between teams and players, when CBAs are negotiated the players will push to get every last dollar of revenue generated by teams included in the definition of defined cap revenues while team owners will try to get some types of revenues excluded from designated cap revenues, as any excluded revenues will not have to be shared with players. In the same vein, the players will push for as large a s_{max} as possible and team owners will push for as small a s_{max} as possible.

To graphically analyze the effects of a cap in the two-team model, recall that the area of the rectangle formed by the equilibrium point, MR, W^* and the origin represents total revenue for each team. Assume that this shows designated cap revenue. A salary cap simply places some effective maximum value on the marginal cost of talent p that is below the equilibrium value of talent in a model with no cap. For example, on Figure 5.9, the equilibrium point is E_1, the marginal revenue for both teams is $MR_{E1}^X = MR_{E1}^Z$, the winning percent for Team X is W_{E1}^X the winning percent for Team Z is W_{E1}^Z, the equilibrium price of talent is p_1 and $W_{E1}^X < W_{E1}^Z$.

Total revenues for Team X are represented by the area of the rectangle $\overline{MR_{E1}^X E_1 W_{E1}^X 0}$. Total revenues for Team Z are represented by the area of the rectangle $\overline{MR_{E1}^Z E_1 W_{E1}^Z 0}$. The second vertical line on Figure 5.9 is drawn at $W^X = W^Z = 0.500$, which would presumably be the target for any cap. The effect of the cap in this model is to set an effective maximum marginal cost for talent, p_c which is below p_1.

Suppose that the cap is set such that the horizontal line drawn at p_c intersects Team Xs MR curve exactly where the horizontal like at $W^X = W^Z = 0.500$ intersects Team Xs MR curve, as shown on Figure 5.9. Now the total payroll for Team X is represented by the area of the rectangle $\overline{MR^X (0.500) p_c W_{0.500}^X 0}$. Total payroll for Team Z is represented by the area of the

Figure 5.9: A Salary Cap in the Two-team Model

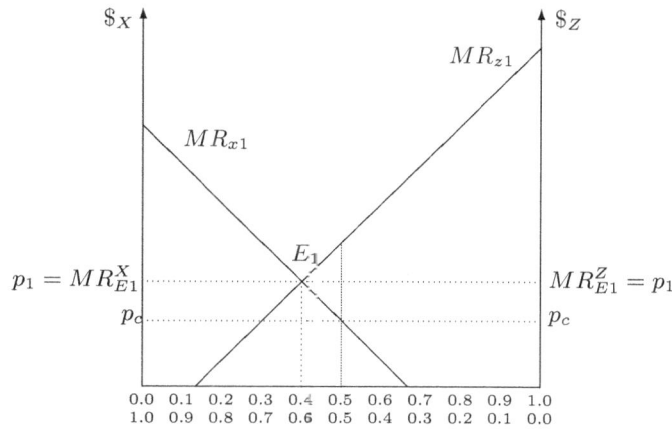

rectangle $\overline{MR^Z(0.500)p_cW^Z_{0.500}0}$, which has the same size. The cap has equalized the payrolls of each team. However, think about the economic incentives faced by each team under the cap. Team X is maximizing profits, as clearly $p_c = MR^X(0.500)$. By reducing the marginal cost of talent to p_c, the cap induces Team X to purchase more talent and field a better team. However, Team Z is not very happy with the cap. $MR^Z(0.500)$, the marginal revenue of fielding a team that wins half its games for Team Z can be found from the marginal revenue associated with Team Zs MR curve when the vertical line where $W^X = W^Z = 0.500$ hits Team Zs MR curve. For Team Z, the marginal revenue generated by a 0.500 team is much higher than the marginal cost of talent under the cap, p_c. Team Z wants to hire more talent and violate the cap. Put another way, the cap is not an equilibrium outcome in the two-team model.

In practice, salary caps are routinely violated in the NFL and NBA. Consider, for example, the 2003 NFL season. The cap minimum and maximum values are shown above. Table 5.4 shows the estimated NFl team payrolls from the 2003 season as reported in the USAToday NFL salary database. This estimate of team payrolls does not include the prorated portion of signing bonuses that are counted against the salary cap according to the NFLs rules, so the cap-based payrolls would be significantly higher. No matter what the actual cap-related payroll was for each team, it does not appear that the NFL cap was complied with by many NFL teams in 2003. Even based on these payroll estimates, the top six teams in terms of payroll were over the maximum cap value in 2003. Caps do not appear to be effective in the NFL. Similar outcomes have been reported for other seasons in the NFL and in the NBA. The reason is that profit maximizing teams have an incentive to violate salary caps any way possible, since the marginal revenue for talent exceeds the marginal cost of talent for many teams in sports leagues. If the league could effectively enforce the salary cap, then the imposition of a salary cap could lead to improvements in competitive balance in sports leagues. However, it appears that salary caps are difficult to enforce in practice. One thing is clear, salary caps to reduce the amount of total revenue that goes to players, and increased the amount of revenues that goes to team owners.

The MLB Luxury Tax

Instead of a cap, MLB currently uses a "luxury tax," which MLB calls a "competitive balance tax." This "tax" is based on specified salary thresholds spelled out in the CBA. Teams are free to spend

Table 5.4: Estimated NFL Payrolls, 2003

Team	Estimated Payroll
New Orleans Saints	$95,103,350
Tampa Bay Buccaneers	$88,084,700
Minnesota Vikings	$85,719,851
Cincinnati Bengals	$85,457,225
Atlanta Falcons	$84,861,253
Washington Redskins	$84,826,189
Seattle Seahawks	$84,227,732
Chicago Bears	$82,803,517
New England Patriots	$82,128,250
Dallas Cowboys	$81,042,307
Arizona Cardinals	$81,034,928
St. Louis Rams	$80,224,050
Jacksonville Jaguars	$78,735,117
New York Giants	$78,125,309
Detroit Lions	$77,662,097
Houston Texans	$77,591,518
Philadelphia Eagles	$77,436,900
Kansas City Chiefs	$77,394,073
Green Bay Packers	$77,230,121
Baltimore Ravens	$76,154,450
Tennessee Titans	$75,575,947
Carolina Panthers	$75,004,350
Indianapolis Colts	$74,998,224
Oakland Raiders	$74,904,848
Buffalo Bills	$73,299,382
San Diego Chargers	$73,230,536
New York Jets	$69,209,828
Miami Dolphins	$67,439,147
Denver Broncos	$64,826,919
Pittsburgh Steelers	$63,571,735
San Francisco 49ers	$60,519,309
Cleveland Browns	$53,849,750

Source: USAToday

whatever they want on payroll, but once the team's payroll passes the threshold value, the team must pay a progressively larger tax on additional payroll spending. In 2010 the threshold value was $170 million and the tax rate was 22.5%. This means that any MLB team that spent more than $170 million on team payroll in 2010 had to pay the league office 22.5% of their payroll as a tax. The tax increases to 30% for the second time a team exceeds the the threshold, and 40% for the third time. The MLB luxury tax penalizes teams differentially depending on how much talent they choose to purchase. This will affect competitive balance.

To graphically analyze the effect of the MLB luxury tax in the two-team model, think of the luxury tax as a way of reducing the marginal revenue of talent when the amount of talent purchased passes a certain value. Recall that in the two-team model, teams choose a profit maximizing winning percentage and then purchase the amount of talent needed to achieve that winning percentage at marginal cost p. The luxury tax means that each unit of talent purchased beyond the threshold value will have a lower marginal revenue, because 22.5% of each additional dollar of revenue generated by that talent will have to be paid to the league office. In the context of the two-team model, the tax threshold is not at a specific payroll level, but instead it is set at a specific winning percentage.

Suppose that the luxury tax threshold is set at a winning percent of $W = 0.500$ for each unit of talent purchased that increases a team's winning percentage above 0.500, the team must pay $t_l\%$ to the league office in tax. This reduces the marginal revenue of wins beyond 0.500 to $MR \times t_l$. On Figure 5.10, only Team Z is subject to the luxury tax. Team Z's MR curve to the left of $MR^Z(0.500)$ has a kink, and the new MR curve lies below the old MR curve, reflecting the lower MR under the luxury tax.

Figure 5.10: The MLB Luxury Tax in the Two-team Model

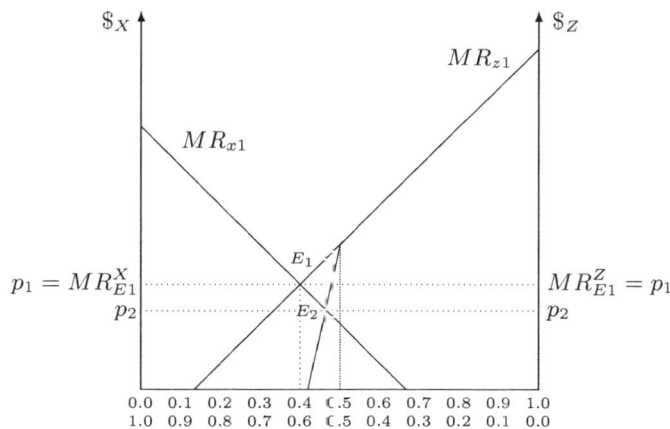

Point E_1 is no longer the equilibrium point in the two-team model. The new equilibrium point is E_2, which is found at the intersection between Team X's original MR curve and Team Z's new, lower MR curve. At the new equilibrium point, E_2, Team Z has a lower profit maximizing winning percent and Team X has a higher profit maximizing winning percent. Even though the luxury tax only gets paid by the team playing in the market with greater revenue generation potential, the tax affects both teams, because the tax affects the equilibrium marginal cost of talent in the league. Both teams have lower payrolls in equilibrium under the luxury tax. Note that the effect on the marginal cost of talent is to again lower p, which means that the wage paid to players again declines along with payroll. it is this decline in the marginal cost of talent induced by the luxury tax that gives Team X an incentive to acquire more talent and field a better team.

The Entry Draft

All professional sports leagues in North America operate an entry draft for new talent coming into the league. The terms of these entry drafts are, of course, dictated by the CBA in each league. The leagues claim that entry drafts are needed to maintain competitive balance in leagues, because without them, teams playing in markets with large revenue generation potential would buy up all the incoming talent, reducing competitive balance. The general format of entry drafts is the "reverse order" format, where teams with worse records in the previous season have earlier picks in the next draft. At one point in the past, all entry drafts operated by professional sports teams in North America were strict reverse order, in that the team with the worst record in the previous season had the first pick in the next entry draft, the team with the second worst record had the second pick, and so on. The NFL and MLB entry drafts still operate this way, but the NBA and NHL have gone to a "lottery" format where the order of finish in the previous season determines the relative probability that a team will get the first pick in the draft, but the actual allocation of the number one pick in the entry draft is determined by a random draw.

The idea behind reverse order entry drafts is appealing, in terms of its ability to enhance competitive balance. The worst team from the previous season gets first chance at the best player coming into the league, and thus the best chance at improving in the future. However, the implementation of entry drafts has been problematic, as entry drafts create disincentives for teams to win late in the season, and the remedies for this problem have sometimes been worse than the problem. Consider the entry draft formats used by the NBA.

NBA Entry Draft Formats The NBA has used more entry draft formats than any other North Americal professional sports league. The NBA began play in 1946 with 11 teams. In 1946, the NBA introduced a strict reverse-order amateur entry draft where the worst team received the first overall selection in the entry draft. Due to the newness of the league and, in an effect to increase individual teams' fan base, the NBA also included a territorial component in these early drafts. This territorial component allowed teams to exchange their first round selection for a player from their geographical region. The territorial draft continued until after the 1965-1966 NBA season when teams selected in traditional reverse order without any territorial picks.

Starting in 1966, a coin flip between the last place teams in each of the NBA's two conferences determined which team received the first overall pick. The draft order following the coin flip was in a strict reverse order format. This draft format remained in place until after the 1983-1984 season. In the early 1980's, the outcome of some NBA regular season games late in the season were called into question. Games late in the regular season involving teams already eliminated from playoff contention were viewed sceptically by some team owners and league executives because the eliminated teams appeared to intentionally lose games (or "tank") in order to receive a higher draft pick in the next year's entry draft. As a result, the NBA introduced an equal weighted draft lottery format for the 1985 NBA entry draft.

The equal weighted draft lottery was a format implemented by the NBA to combat the perception that teams were intentionally losing games late in the regular season. Under this format, instead of the worst team in each conference flipping a coin for the number one overall selection, all non-playoff teams had an equal probability of "winning the lottery" and receiving the number one overall pick in the next entry draft. This theoretically reduced the incentive for teams not making the playoffs to tank late in the regular season, since losing would not increase their chances at the next number one pick.

From the beginning, team executives questioned the purpose of the entry draft: was the intent to decrease the incentive for teams to tank or to increase league-wide competitive balance? When the NBA changed from the traditional reverse order draft tot he lottery draft, some teams pressured the league to return to the traditional reverse order format because the outcomes of the lottery did not appear to help very bad teams get better. For example, in the 1984-1985 draft, the Golden State Warriors had the worst overall record in the league. Under the strict reverse order format, Golden State would have picked no worse than second overall (first if they won the coin toss). However, under the equal probability lottery, the Warriors selected seventh overall. As a result, some team owners, as well as league executives, questioning the purpose of the draft lottery, and the fairness of the outcomes.

To balance between discouraging tanking and increasing competitive balance, the NBA implemented a weighted lottery draft format beginning with the 1990 NBA draft. The weighted draft lottery assigned probabilities of winning the draft lottery based upon the final regular season records of all non-playoff teams, with the worst team receiving the highest probability of winning the next number one pick. Like the equal weight lottery format, all non-playoff teams had a chance to receive the number one overall selection. However, moving from an equal probability lottery to a weighted probability lottery system brought back the incentive for teams to tank.

The general perception that teams had an incentive to tank, and in fact did tank late in the regular season did not disappear. Coaches, media, and team executives still believed that teams were tanking under the weighted lottery format. In addition, the league faced a publicity problem when the Orlando Magic won the 1993 NBA draft lottery for the second consecutive year. That year, the Orlando Magic had the lowest probability of capturing the first draft pick, as they barely missed out on the playoffs. After the draft, Commissioner David Stern said of the weighted probability draft format "Institutionally, we have a problem with it".

As a result, the NBA altered the weighted draft lottery format by increasing the probability that lower finishing teams would win the rights to the number one pick in the next draft. For example, the worst team in the league had a 25% chance of receiving the first overall selection compared to approximately 17% chance under the previous format. The adoption of the increased weight lottery format moved the NBA draft back closer to the traditional strict reverse order format. This entry draft format remains in place in the NBA.

Entry Draft Impacts The question of the relationship between entry drafts and competitive balance is empirical, and will be examined in Chapter 7. The two-team model cannot be used to analyze entry drafts from a theoretical perspective, because entry drafts affect the allocation of new talent across teams. However, entry drafts have several clear effects on sports leagues. First, entry drafts create monopsony power for teams. An entry draft assigns the rights of incoming players to specific teams, and these players cannot negotiate with other teams. A player can either negotiate with the team awarded his rights in the entry draft or sit out a year, losing a year of earnings. This greatly reduces the bargaining power that drafted players have, reducing their salary below what would be earned if all teams could bid for the rights to incoming players (the system that was in place before entry drafts). Second, entry drafts allocate new talent to teams playing in markets with lower revenue generation potential, who can in turn sell or trade these players to teams in markets with higher revenue generation potential. This generates a flow of revenues from high revenue teams to low revenue teams. The empirical evidence indicates that talent always moves to the market where it is valued the most - markets with higher revenue generation potential. The draft simply reduces the price paid to new talent and shifts some revenues from teams in high revenue markets to teams in low revenue markets.

5.4　Promotion and Relegation Leagues and Competitive Balance

Section 4.1.6 in Chapter 4 extended the long run model of team quality choice to the case of teams in open leagues with a promotion and relegation system. Equation 4.6 showed an expression for marginal revenues for a team in the top league of an open system with a promotion and relegation ladder. In the two team model developed here, a MR curve for each team was derived from the long-run model developed in Chapter 4, based on the locus of points where $R'_i = p_1$ for Team X and Team Z in a closed league. Equation 4.6

$$R'_1(W_i) + \frac{ar}{1+d}\left(R_1(W_1^e) - cW_1^e\right) + \frac{(1-ar)}{1+d}\left(R_2(W_2^e) - cW_2^e\right) = c.$$

can be used to define a similar line in an open league. Recall that d is a discount rate, ar is the probability that the team is not relegated to the lower division after the current season, and the e superscripts denote expected profits next season. Let $\pi_j^e = R_j(W_j^e) - cW_j^e$ for $j = 1, 2$ leagues where $j = 1$ is the top league and $j = 2$ is the bottom league. For simplicity, let $\pi_2^e = R_2(W_2^e) - cW_2^e = 0$. And recall that c is the marginal cost of talent, which is now p_1. The equation for marginal revenue becomes

$$R'_1(W_i) + \frac{ar}{1+d}\pi_1^e = p_1$$

which shows that in an open league profit maximizing teams in the top league have a marginal revenue curve that lies above the marginal revenue curve in a closed league, and the distance of the shift depends on d, ar and π_1^e, the expected profit earned by the team next year in the top league. Again, just like in Chapter 4, the presence of a promotion and relegation system makes teams increase team quality. However, there are still a limited number of wins to be had in the league.

Like the previous examples in this chapter, suppose that Team X plays in a relatively small market and Team Z plays in a relatively large market. In equilibrium, Team X earns lower profits than Team Z, implying that $\pi_{1x}^e < \pi_{1z}^e$. The marginal revenue curve for Team Z in an open league is farther above the marginal revenue curve for the closed league, since

$$R'_1(W_x) + \frac{ar}{1+d}\pi_{1x}^e < R'_1(W_x) + \frac{ar}{1+d}\pi_{1z}^e.$$

Figure 5.11 shows the comparison between the closed league outcomes (shown with a c subscript) and open league outcomes (shown with an o subscript). The closed league equilibrium is E_c where team X has marginal revenue curve MR_{xc} and Team Z has marginal revenue curve MR_{zc}. The equilibrium salary for players is p_c and the outcomes are $W_z = 0.6$ and $W_x = 0.4$. The closed league outcomes are not balanced; Team Z wins more games than Team X and both maximize profits.

Imposing a promotion and relegation system on the league shifts the marginal revenue curves up for both teams, and Team Zs curve shifts up by more, since Team Z is more profitable in the top league than Team X. At the new equilibrium in this open league, E_o lies to the left of the closed league equilibrium. Opening the league makes competitive balance worse compared to a closed league and increases salaries paid to players, since $p_o > p_c$. The intuition behind this result is that imposing a promotion and relegation system on the closed league creates incentives for both teams to increase the quality of the team beyond what would have been chosen in a closed league. The team in the more lucrative market, Team Z, faces larger incentives to increase team quality than the team in the less lucrative market, Team X, which leads Team Z to increase team quality by even more, reducing competitive balance. Salaries rise because the overall demand for talent in

Figure 5.11: Open vs Closed Leagues in Equilibrium

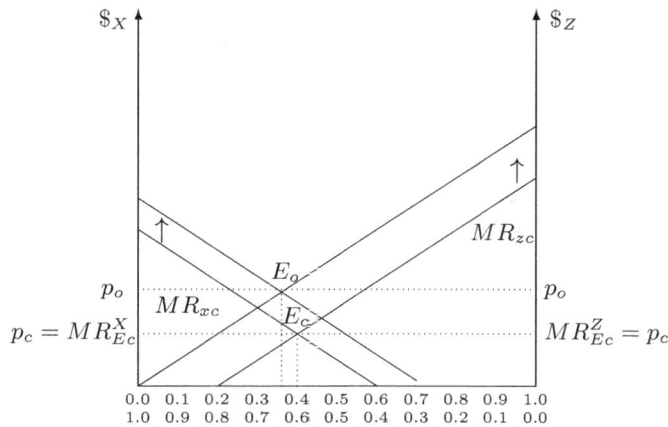

the league increases, raising salaries in the labor market. Note that this implicitly assumes that the labor supply curve for talent has a positive slope and is not horizontal.[1]

These changes roughly approximate league outcomes in open and closed leagues. Open leagues in Europe generally exhibit less competitive balance than closed leagues in North America. Professional football players in the top leagues in Europe like the EPL and La Liga earn relatively higher salaries than athletes in North American leagues, when roster sizes, roster limits, and salary caps are taken into account.

5.5 Summary

Leagues perform two important economic functions in professional team sports. They foster both single-entity cooperation and joint venture cooperation among teams. These activities help generate monopoly power for sports leagues, but they also generate a fundamental tension in sports leagues: profit maximization may not be compatible with competitive balance in sports leagues. The two-team model developed in this chapter illustrates the tradeoff between profits and wins at the league level, and highlights the importance of competitive balance in sports leagues. Although a number of policies aimed at improving competitive balance have been implemented in professional sports leagues, the effectiveness of these policies to improve competitive balance is unclear, and the primary effect of most of the policies appears to be to ensure that players receive lower wages and a smaller share of league revenues. Promotion and relegation systems increase competition among teams in leagues for talent, but appear to have a negative impact on competitive balance relative to closed leagues. Chapter 7 focuses on issues of measurement of competitive balance, assessment of the level of competitive balance in sports leagues, assessment of the effect of league policies on competitive balance, and the relationship between competitive balance and attendance in professional sports leagues.

---

[1]The slope of the labor supply curve, and the role it plays in this setting, are a matter of considerable debate in the literature. Szymanski (2004) examines this issue.

Readings and References

Eckard, W., (2006). Comment: Professional Team Sports Are Only a Game. *Journal of Sports Economics*, 7, 234-239.

El Hodiri, M. & Quirk, J. (1971) An Economic Model of a Professional Sports League. *Journal of Political Economy*, 79, 1302-1319.

Fort, R. & Quirk, J (1995). Cross-subsidization, Incentives, and Outcomes in Professional Team Sports. *Journal of Economic Literature*, 33, 1265-1299.

Fort, R. & Quirk, J (2004). Owner Objectives and Competitive Balance. *Journal of Sports Economics*, 5, 20-32.

Szymanski, S., (2004). Professional Team Sports Are Only a Game: The Walrasian Fixed-Supply Conjecture Model, Contest-Nash Equilibrium, and the Invariance Principle. *Journal of Sports Economics*, 5, 111-126.

Szymanski, S., (2004). Reply: Professional Team Sports Are Only a Game. *Journal of Sports Economics*, 7, 240-243.

Szymanski, S. & Kesenne, S. (2004). Competitive Balance and Gate Revenue Sharing in Professional Sports. *Journal of Industrial Economics*, 52, 165-177.

Vrooman, J. (1995). A General Theory of Professional Sports Leagues. *Southern Economic Journal*, 61, 971-990.

Vrooman, J. (1997). Franchise Free Agency in Professional Sports. *Southern Economic Journal*, 64, 191-219.

Review Questions

1. *True, False or Uncertain*: Suppose that the host city of Team A, a team in a two team sports league, imposes a 10% tax on the salaries of Team A's players. According to the two-team model of a sports league, this salary tax leads Team A to field a lower quality team.

2. *True, False or Uncertain*: In the English Premier League, the top professional soccer league in the UK, each of the 20 teams play the other teams in the league twice (home and away), for a 38 game regular season. This season schedule is an example of joint venture cooperation in a sports league.

3. *True, False or Uncertain*: Based on the two team model shown below, with two teams x and z and a league outcome at W_1, Team x can increase its profits by increasing the quality of the talent on the team.

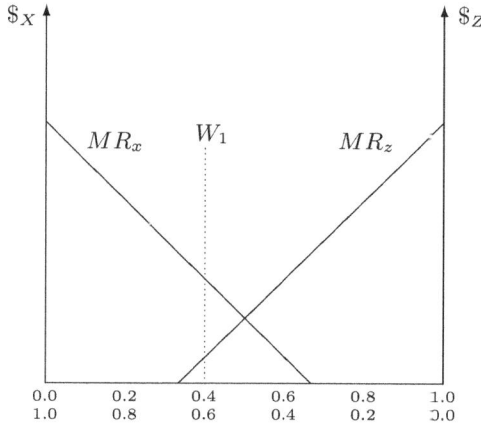

4. Consider a two team professional hockey league. The two teams, Manitoba (M) and Saskatchewan (S) each face the same marginal cost for buying talent (p_1), but M has higher fixed costs than S ($C_{FM} > C_{FS}$), so

$$C_M(W\%) = C_{FM} + p_1 W\%_M \qquad\qquad C_S(W\%) = C_{FS} + p_1 W\%_S.$$

Team S plays in a larger market than Team M, so

$$R_S(W\%, A_S) > R_M(W\%, A_M)$$

because $A_S > A_M$. The following questions examine the outcomes in this two team league.

(a) Discuss one reason why fixed costs could be higher for Team M.

(b) Using the two sets of axes below, show the cost line and revenue functions for each team. On your graph, clearly label the profit maximizing winning percentage that each team will choose [$W\%_M^*$ for Manitoba and $W\%_S^*$ for Saskatchewan].

Manitoba   **Saskatchewan**

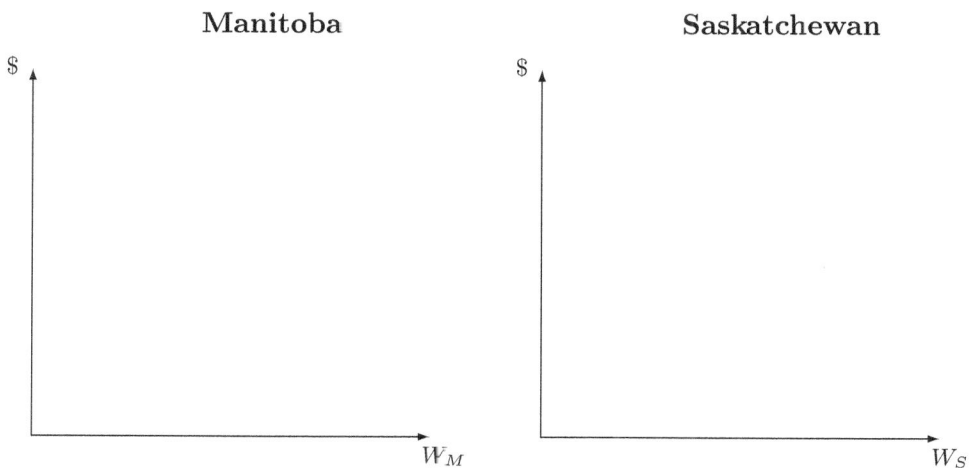

(c) Draw the marginal revenue curves from the graphs shown above on the axes below and label them MR_M and MR_S. Show the outcome of the league in terms of the profit maximizing winning percentage chosen by both teams in equilibrium.

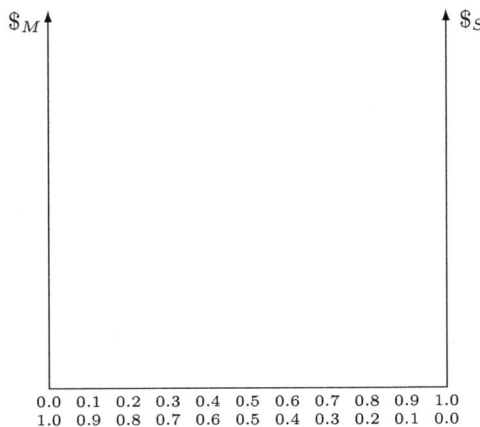

$\$_M$ $\$_S$

| 0.0 | 0.1 | 0.2 | 0.3 | 0.4 | 0.5 | 0.6 | 0.7 | 0.8 | 0.9 | 1.0 |
| 1.0 | 0.9 | 0.8 | 0.7 | 0.6 | 0.5 | 0.4 | 0.3 | 0.2 | 0.1 | 0.0 |

(d) Which team has the larger payroll? Explain your answer.

Chapter 6

Outcome Uncertainty and Consumer Choice

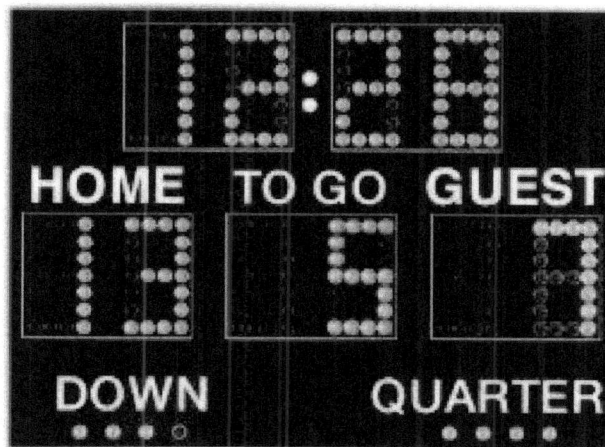

Chapter Objectives

- Understand the Uncertainty of Outcome Hypothesis and its role in sports economics

- Develop a consumer choice model of game attendance with reference-dependent preferences

- Understand the conditions under which the model generates predictions consistent with the UOH

- Understand loss aversion and its role in consumer choice

- Understand the implications of loss aversion for league design and competitive balance in sports leagues

6.1 The Uncertainty of Outcome Hypothesis

The uncertainty of outcome hypothesis (UOH) was a key proposition in the seminal sports economics paper by Simon Rottenberg (1956). Rottenberg (1956) remarked that the profits earned by teams in a sports league decline as competitive balance declines, an observation that has come to be called the "uncertainty of outcome hypothesis" or UOH in sports economics. Rottenberg (1956) provided a description of a demand function for live game attendance for a sports team: "Attendance at the games of any given team is a positive function of the size of the population of the territory in which the team has a monopoly right to play; the size and convenience of location of the ball park; and the average rank standing of the team during the in the competition of its league. It is a negative function of the goodness of leisure time substitutes for baseball in the area and of the dispersion of percentages of games won by the teams in the league. (page 246)" In a footnote he elaborates on the "rank standing" aspect of attendance, continuing: "That is to say the 'tighter' the competition, the larger the attendance. A pennant winning team that wins 80 percent of its games will attract fewer patrons than a pennant-winning team that wins 55 per cent of its games. (page 246, footnote 21)". Rottenberg (1956) went on to argue that if large market teams acquire more talent than small market teams, then "there will be wide variation among teams in the quality of play, contests will be come certain, and attendance will decline. (page 247)"

Another early sports economist, W.C. Neale, also mentioned the UOH in his 1964 paper "The Peculiar Economics of Professional Sports." Neale called this the "League Standing Effect." Neale's league standing effect referred to the idea that in order for fans to attend sporting events, listen to events on radio, or watch events on television, some uncertainty of outcome about the contest must exist. Neale (1964) pointed out "Of itself there is excitement in the daily changes in the standings or the daily changes in possibilities of changes in standings. The closer the standings, and within any range of standings the more frequently the standings change, the larger will be the gate receipts. (page 3)" Neale (1964) also discussed league championships and their effect on demand. Even at this early point in the literature, tension existed about the time frame over which the UOH operates. Rottenberg (1956) appears to have in mind uncertainty over the course of a season, while Neale (1964) appeared to have in mind individual games.

Interestingly, little research focused on how outcome uncertainty fits in a standard model of consumer decision making. Instead, research focused on developing models of team and league behavior that generated different levels of competitive balance, often reflected in the dispersion of winning percentages in leagues, depending on market characteristics. The archetypical "two team model' from Chapter 5 represents this line of research. But on the consumer choice side, it has simply been taken for granted that outcome uncertainty increases demand for live game attendance. This omission is curious, as fans exhibit considerable interest in the presence of dominant teams, or dynasties, in sports leagues, and fans also appear to enjoy the possibility of watching upsets, where stronger teams unexpectedly lose to weaker teams. Neither upsets or dynasties could occur in a completely balanced league where each team wins approximately half the games played in a season.

The UOH motivates research on competitive balance in sports leagues. According to the UOH, the more competitive balance in a sports league, the greater the uncertainty of outcome, and the greater fan demand for both attendance at games and radio and television broadcasts of live sporting events, increasing revenues earned by teams in the league. It is important to define uncertainty of outcome in terms of some specific temporal aspect of the competition that takes place in a sports league. Three forms of uncertainty of outcome have been identified in the literature

1. **Game or match uncertainty**: Exists when the winner of any particular game or match in a league cannot be easily predicted

2. **Seasonal uncertainty**: Exists when the rank standing of teams in the league at the end of the season cannot be easily predicted before the season begins

3. **Championship uncertainty**: Exists when the champion of the league cannot be predicted

before the season begins, in leagues with postseason play

This chapter focuses on the first type: outcome uncertainty at the game or match level.

Note that the UOH can be empirically tested. The UOH provides a clear prediction about the nature of the relationship between outcome uncertainty and attendance: when uncertainty of outcome is high, fan interest, and attendance, will be high. In order to empirically test the UOH, some measure of outcome uncertainty must be developed. Quantifiable measures of uncertainty of outcome include, at the game or match level, forecasting models based on previous team performance, outcomes from sports betting markets like point spreads and betting odds, and, for seasonal uncertainty, measures of competitive balance like the dispersion of winning percentages in the league. Despite the clear prediction and appealing nature of the UOH, evidence supporting the existence of the UOH is mixed. Studies that explain observed variation in game or match attendance using measures of outcome uncertainty find both positive and negative relationships between outcome uncertainty and attendance. Research that explains variation in attendance using betting odds or point spreads consistently finds that attendance is higher at games or matches where the home team is a clear favorite in the contest, and a substantial number report evidence that attendance is higher at games where an upset is possible, relative to games between evenly matched teams. This evidence comes from both European football matches and games in North American leagues.

In part, this mixed evidence may stem from difficulties measuring competitive balance. It can also be attributed to the fact that uncertainty of outcome exists at the game, season, and post-season level. Because competitive balance depends on a number of different facets of outcomes in sports leagues, any empirical analysis of the UOH depends heavily on the measure of outcome uncertainty used and the level of aggregation of the attendance data. Still, empirical research on outcome uncertainty suggests that the UOH may not adequately explain observed variation in attendance at professional sporting events. One reason may be that the UOH ignores important aspects of consumer decisions made under uncertainty.

Evidence from behavioral economics suggests that consumers exhibit "loss aversion" when making decisions under uncertainty; "loss aversion" refers to the idea that consumers value expected losses differently than expected gains. Based on outcomes in experimental settings, expected losses appear to weigh more heavily on the minds of consumers than expected gains. When applied to the sports setting, loss aversion suggests that fans of a team would prefer to see a game in which their team will almost certainly win to a game where their team stands a substantial chance of losing. This behavior differs significantly from the behavior underlying the UOH, which suggests that fans would prefer to see a game where their team has an equal chance of winning or losing.

6.2 A Consumer Choice Model of Outcome Uncertainty

At its core, the UOH posits that closer games, in other words games played between teams of relatively equal talent, provide more utility to consumers than games between teams with different levels of talent, other things equal; this increases consumer demand for games with uncertain outcomes. The decision to attend a sporting event involves the formation of expectations about the game by consumers. According to both Rottenberg (1956) and Neale (1964), consumers look at the schedule and standings when deciding to attend a game, and are more interested in games with a relatively uncertain outcome, other things equal. Any model of consumers' decisions to attend games must capture both the expectation of game outcomes and the effect of the relative quality of the teams playing in the game on the expected outcome, and, if the model is consistent with the UOH, utility should be higher for games with relatively uncertain outcomes and lower for games with relatively certain outcomes.

6.2.1   Reference-Dependent Utility

In models of *reference-dependent utility*, consumers derive utility from two separate events: utility generated by consuming a good or service (the standard utility from consumer theory) and utility that depends on a comparison of what they expect the consumption experience will be like before consuming the good or service relative to the actual experience of consuming the good or service. This second component of utility is called "gain-loss" utility. Consider the decision to attend a movie. According to reference-dependent utility models, the total utility derived from watching a movie depends both on the experience of sitting in the theater and on the quality of the movie relative to how good the movie was expected to be; if the movie was better than expected ("I was pleasantly surprised"), the consumer gets more total utility, but if the movie was worse than expected ("I thought it would be good, but it was terrible"), then the consumer gets less total utility. The key factor in reference-dependent utility models is the *reference point*, which captures the consumer's expectation about the good or service being consumed.

Suppose that the outcome of a game can be represented by a variable y that takes only two values: $y = 1$ indicates a win by the home team and $y = 0$ indicates a loss by the home team. Also, suppose that a consumer's reference point for a game is the expectation of the outcome of a game in terms of the probability that the home team will win the game, $E(y = 1) = p^r$. $E(\cdot)$ is the expected value of the variable y which indicates the game outcome and $0 \leq p^r \leq 1$ is the consumer's subjective probability that the home team will win the game. If a consumer thinks that the home team is very likely to win an upcoming game, because the home team has more talent than the visiting team, then p^r will be large, near 1; if a consumer thinks that the home team is unlikely to win an upcoming game, because the visiting team has more talent than the home team, then p^r will be small, near 0; in games with an uncertain outcome, p^r will be near 0.5. Again, p^r is the consumer's reference point for the game.

Attending a game that the home team wins ($y = 1$) generates both standard consumption utility from the game U^W and "gain-loss utility" from seeing a home team win ($y = 1$) conditional on the reference point p^r. Total utility from attending an expected home team win ($y = 1$), including both types of utility, is

$$U^W + \alpha(y - p^r) = U^W + \alpha(1 - p^r)$$

where $\alpha > 0$ reflects the marginal impact of a positive deviation from the reference point for the game.

To illustrate the nature of this utility function, consider an individual that attends two games and the home team wins both games. Suppose the expectation of a home win for the first game, the reference point for that game, is $p^r = 0.5$ and the reference point for the second game is $p^r = 0.8$. This fan expects that the home team will win the second game, but the outcome of the first game is expected to be a tossup. Total utility from attending the first game is

$$U_1 = u^W + \alpha(y - p^r) = u^W + \alpha(1 - 0.5) = u^W + 0.5\alpha.$$

Total utility from attending the second game is

$$U_2 = u^W + \alpha(y - p^r) = u^W + \alpha(1 - 0.8) = u^W + 0.2\alpha.$$

In other words, for the same outcome ($y = 1$), the individual gets more utility if the outcome is a bigger positive departure from the reference point. Note that for a home team win, the highest total utility from attending the game is $u^W + \alpha$, in which case an individual enjoys a home win

Figure 6.1: Utility, Outcomes and Reference Points

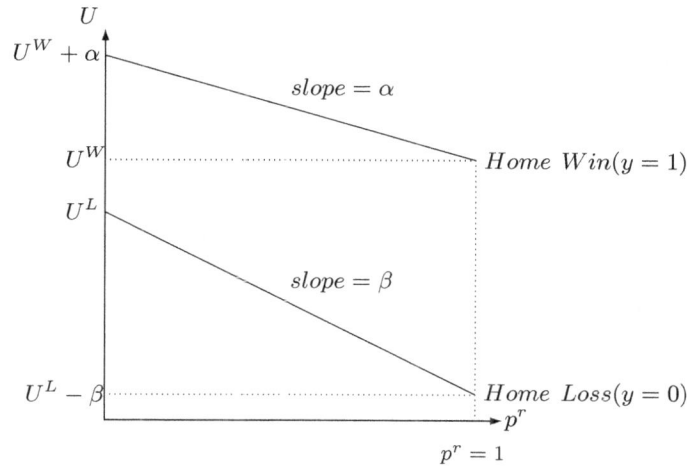

and the maximum enjoyment from the surprise that the home team wins when the fan believed that the home team had no chance to win ($p^r = 0$), and the lowest total utility is u^W, in which case an individual still enjoys a home win but gets no additional utility when the win was expected ($p^r = 1$).

Attending a game the home team loses ($y = 0$) also generates standard consumption utility from a home team loss U^L and "gain-loss utility" from experiencing a loss compared to the reference point p^r. The utility from attending a game that the home team loses ($y = 0$) is

$$U^L + \beta(y - p^r) = U^L + \beta(0 - p^r).$$

where $\beta > 0$ is the marginal effect of a negative deviation from the reference point on utility. Consider an individual who attended two games that home team lost. Again, suppose her reference point for a home win for the first game and the second game is 0.5 and 0.8 respectively, then her utility from watching the first game and the second game is $u^W - 0.5\beta$ and $u^W - 0.8\beta$. For the same outcome — a home loss ($y = 0$), this consumer gets more utility if the outcome is a smaller negative departure from the reference point, which is equivalent to a lower p^r.

For a game that the home team loses, the highest utility from attending the game is u^L, in which case an individual gets the intrinsic utility of a home loss and no additional utility loss because the loss is fully anticipated ($p^r = 0$). The lowest utility is $u^L - \beta$, in which case an individual gets the intrinsic utility of a home loss and also suffers from losing a game that the home team was expected to win for sure ($p^r = 1$).

Figure 6.1 summarizes the relationship between game outcomes, reference points, and total utility from attending a game. On Figure 6.1, total utility is graphed on the vertical axis and the reference point, the consumer's expectation of the game outcome, is shown on the horizontal axis. The top line reflects the utility generated by a home win and the bottom line the utility generated by a home loss. Assume that $U^W > U^L$, so the consumption utility generated by a home win exceeds the consumption utility generated by a home loss.

Again, the maximum total utility from a home win ($y = 1$) comes when the fan expects that the home team has no chance to win the game ($p^r = 0$), and the home team pulls off an epic upset. The leftmost point on the home win line represents this outcome, where the fan gets total utility of $U^W + \alpha$. Moving right along the home win line, total utility from a home win diminishes because the deviation of the game outcome ($y = 1$) from the reference point (p^r) declines. As fan expectation that the home team will win increases (p^r increases), total utility declines because the reference point is closer to the actual outcome. At the right end of the win line, the fan fully expects that the home team will win ($p^r = 1$) so a home team win generates total utility of U^W and no gain-loss utility.

Next, consider the utility generated by a home loss ($y = 0$). At the left end of the loss line, the home team loses ($y = 0$) and the loss was fully expected by the fan ($p^r = 0$). This outcome generates only consumption utility, U^L. At the right end of the loss line the home team loses ($y = 0$), but the fan completely expected a home team win ($p^r = 1$). This generates the smallest possible utility for the fan, $U^L - \beta$, because the consumption utility from attending the game, U^L, is reduced by the fact that a loss represents the maximum deviation from the reference point (the expectation of a certain win). Moving from left to right, utility is reduced because the reference point increases; the fan has an increasing expectation that the home team will win and experiences additional lost utility because the outcome differs more and more from her expectation.

Game outcomes cannot be known in advance - they are uncertain. Suppose that the consumer's reference point is equal to the objective probability that the home team will win a game $E(y) = p * 1 + (1 - p) * 0 = p = p^r$, which is also equal to the expected outcome of the game. In other words, consumers deciding whether or not to attend a game form a reference point equal to the objective probability that the home team will win the game. Under this assumption, the expected utility from attending a game is the objective probability that the home team wins (p) times the total utility from a home win plus the probability that the home team loses ($1 - p$) times the total utility from a loss

$$E[U] = p[U^W + \alpha(1 - p)] + (1 - p)[U^L + \beta(0 - p)]$$
$$E[U] = (\beta - \alpha)p^2 + [(U^W - U^L) - (\beta - \alpha)]p + U^L$$

$$(6.1)$$

The second line of Equation (6.1) represents the expected total utility a fan gets from from attending a game. Expected total utility is a quadratic function of the probability that the home team wins the game. This expected utility function incorporates game outcome uncertainty, in the form of the probability that the hope team wins the game, p, and also takes into account the utility gained by watching the home team win in an upset and the utility loss generated by watching the home team get upset when expected by fans to win. It incorporates both "gain-loss" utility and standard consumption utility.

6.2.2   The Consumer Choice Problem

Consumers choose to either attend or not attend a game; the choice is binary. Assume that an individual not attending a game gets utility v, which can be interpreted as the reservation utility from not attending a game; this can reflect the cost of attending the game and other factors like the weather. The consumer compares v to the expected utility generated by attending the game, which depends on the probability of a home team win (p), and attends the game if the expected utility exceeds the reservation utility. The decision rule used by consumers

Attend if $E[U] = (\beta - \alpha)p^2 + [(U^W - U^L) - (\beta - \alpha)]p + U^L \geq v$
Do not attend if $E[U] = (\beta - \alpha)p^2 + [(U^W - U^L) - (\beta - \alpha)]p + U^L < v$

distinguishes attendees from non-attendees based on a comparison of expected utility to reservation utility.

To understand consumer choices in this model, first consider a simple version of the model with no reference dependent preferences. Under this special case, $\alpha = \beta = 0$ and the expected utility function

$$E[U] = (U^W - U^L)p + U^L \tag{6.2}$$

is linear and increasing with the probability of a home team win p. In this case, expected utility increases monotonically with the subjective probability that the home team wins. The intercept of the linear expected utility curve is U^L and the slope of the expected utility line is $(U^W - U^L)$. Consumers only care about the team's wins, and deviations from expectations about wins and losses do not affect utility. Figure 6.2 shows the expected utility function in this case.

Figure 6.2: Insensitivity to Expectations, Expected Utility and Attendance

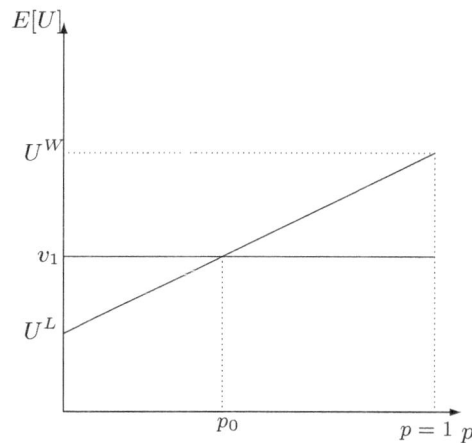

On Figure 6.2, consumer i has reservation utility v_1 which is how much utility consumer i gets if she does not attend the game. Consumer i attends a game so long as the probability of a home team win exceeds p_0, because for games where the probability that the home team wins is greater or equal to p_0, expected utility exceeds the reservation utility. Note that based on this expected utility function, total attendance at games should rise with the probability of a home team win, other things equal, because more people will have an expected utility greater than their reservation utility at games where p is large. Expected attendance could be calculated by graphing each consumer's reservation utility and adding up the number who would attend at each p. Also, note that this type of expected utility function is not consistent with the UOH. If consumers have this type of expected utility function, then they prefer to attend games with a specific and certain outcome: games that are likely to be won by the home team.

6.2.3 The UOH and Expected Utility

According to the UOH, demand is higher for games with relatively uncertain outcomes. In this model, games with an uncertain outcome have p near 0.5. If demand for games with uncertain outcomes is higher than demand for games with certain outcomes (games where p is near 0 or 1) expected utility should be higher when p is close to 0.5. The UOH is consistent with an expected utility function where the expected utility of games with p near 0.5 is greater than the expected

Figure 6.3: Expected Utility and the UOH

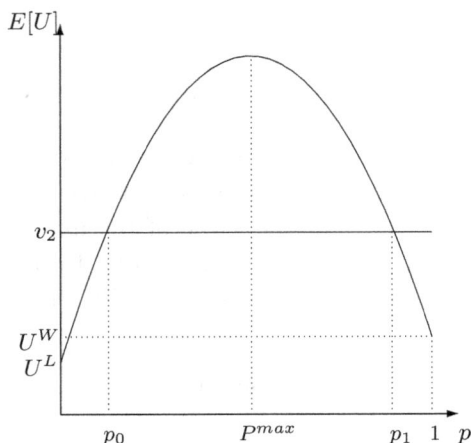

utility of games where p is large or p is small. Again, the expected utility function that includes reference-dependent preferences is

$$E[U] = (\beta - \alpha)p^2 + [(U^W - U^L) - (\beta - \alpha)]p + U^L$$

which is a quadratic function of p. The expected utility function will be concave in p (have a hill shape peaking at around $p = 0.5$) if $[(U^W - U^L) - (\beta - \alpha)] > 0$ and $(\beta - \alpha) < 0$. Recall that $U^W \geq U^L$, so the term $[(U^W - U^L) - (\beta - \alpha)]$ must be positive if $(\beta - \alpha)$ is negative, or if $\alpha > \beta$. α is the marginal utility of unexpected home wins and β is the marginal utility of unexpected home losses. The UOH is consistent with the case where the marginal utility generated by deviations of game outcomes from the reference point when the home team wins is greater than the marginal utility generated by deviations of game outcomes from the reference point when the home team loses. In other words, the UOH emerges from this model only when the marginal utility of unexpected home wins exceeds the marginal utility of unexpected home losses.

Figure 6.3 illustrates consumer decision making consistent with the UOH in this model. The expected utility function is concave in p and peaks at p^{max}. If reservation utility is v_2, a consumer will only attend a game if the probability that the home team wins is between p_0 and p_1. These games have a relatively uncertain outcome. Since v is different for different consumers, more people will have $E[U] > v_i$ when games have a relatively uncertain outcome, and attendance will be higher at these games.

Loss Aversion

The UOH emerges as a special case in the model, when $\alpha > \beta$. However, the case where $\alpha < \beta$ is also possible. If $\alpha < \beta$, the marginal utility from an unexpected loss (a loss that happens when consumers expect the home team to win), exceeds the marginal utility from an unexpected win (a win when consumers expect the home team to lose). *Loss aversion* is an important concept in behavioral economics. *Loss aversion* refers to the idea that consumers strongly prefer to avoid losses compared to experiencing gains. A large body of empirical evidence suggests that many consumers behave in a way consistent with loss aversion; for example, the *endowment effect*, where people value an object they possess own more than the identical object when they do not own it, is widespread. The idea of loss aversion was formalized by Tversky and Kahneman (1991). $\alpha < \beta$ in this model is consistent with fans's exhibiting loss aversion in terms of home team games.

If $\beta > \alpha$, then $(\beta - \alpha) > 0$ and the shape of the expected utility function depends on the sign of $[(U^W - U^L) - (\beta - \alpha)]$. If $[(U^W - U^L) - (\beta - \alpha)] < -2(\beta - \alpha)p$, the expected utility function is convex in p (U-shaped) and the UOH does not emerge as a prediction of the model; instead, games with relatively certain outcomes, where p is either large or small, generate more expected utility than games with uncertain outcomes. Figure 6.4 shows the expected utility function for loss averse consumers.

Figure 6.4: Loss Aversion and Expected Utility

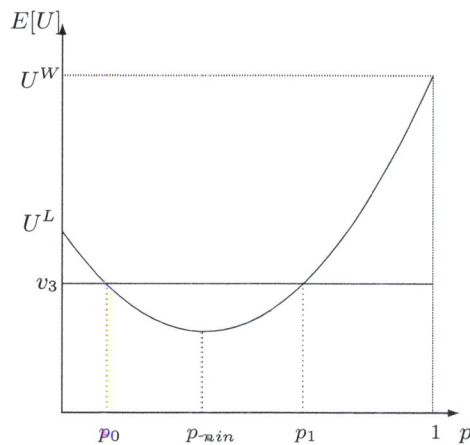

Under loss aversion, attendance at games with a relatively certain outcome, either an expected certain loss ($p = 0$) or an expected certain win ($p = 1$), generates higher expected utility than games with uncertain outcome. Consider the decisions by a fan with reservation utility v_3 on Figure 6.4. She gets more expected utility from either games with a relatively small p ($p < p_0$), that is games where the home team is not expected to win, or from games with a relatively large p ($p > p_1$) than from games with a relatively uncertain outcome. She likes to either see the home team win convincingly over a weaker opponent, or have a chance to see the home team upset a superior opponent, than seeing the team play a closely matched contest. The reason for this is loss aversion; if she expects the home team to win a close game, and the home team loses, her utility loss is large because of loss aversion.

In other words, this case of the model motivates observed interest among casual sports fans in seeing upsets. Clearly, strong fans of a team, in this context consumers with a low reservation utility, will attend games with either certain or uncertain outcomes. But among casual fans, in this context consumers with a relatively high reservation utility, the possibility of watching an upset often holds some allure. In the context of this model, an upset takes place when the home team is expected to lose the game (p is small) but the home team actually wins the game. This outcome generates a relatively large amount of gain-loss utility, since $\beta > 0$. The thrill of potentially seeing an upset explains the convexity of the expected utility function under loss aversion, in that the expected utility of seeing an upset when the home team is expected to lose outweighs the gain-loss utility of seeing a home team loss when the outcome of the game is relatively uncertain.

As was shown in Chapter 5, sports leagues claim to have devised many different policies like reverse-entry drafts and salary caps to make the competition in games closer; in the context of this model, leagues claim that they want to make p close to 0.5 for most games. However, loss averse fans will attend games in leagues with both dynasties (who always have large p for their games) and the chance of upsets (small ps); if fans are loss averse, then revenues could be higher in a league with both dynasties and the possibilities of upsets than they would be if most games were between evenly matched teams. The predictions of the two-team model show that (1) leagues with teams playing in markets with different revenue potential leads to competitive imbalance, since both teams maximize profits when the team in the more lucrative market wins more games than the team in the less lucrative market; and (2)league policies aimed at improving competitive balance actually have no effect on competitive balance but instead transfer revenues from players to teams. The presence of loss-averse fans who want to se both dynasties and upsets explains why leagues would not care much about improving competitive balance in a league with teams playing in more and less lucrative markets in terms of the marginal revenues from wins. Fans in the lucrative markets enjoy the presence of dynasties and fans of teams in less lucrative markets have the perennial hope of seeing their team upset the dynasty. Loss aversion and reference-dependent preferences suggests that David versus Goliath holds more fan interest than David versus Davie in an even match.

A large number of studies have attempted to estimate the relationship between the expected outcome of games or matches and attendance. These studies have used data from many different sports leagues; they often use data from betting markets to estimate the probability that the home team wins. No clear consensus has emerged from this literature; it contains evidence consistent with both the UOH and loss aversion, with a plurality of studies containing evidence consistent with loss aversion.

6.3   Summary

This chapter develops a consumer choice model of attending a sporting event. The model includes a "gain-loss" utility function and consumers who take expectations of game outcomes into account when deciding to attend a game. He model assumes that consumers compare their reservation utility to the expected utility from attending a game, which varies with their reference point, when deciding to attend. The model generates predictions consistent with the UOH as a special case, but if consumers have loss aversion, they may make different decisions, preferring to attend games expected to be certain wins or games where the home team has a chance to upset a stronger visiting team to games with uncertain outcomes. The UOH does not fully describe consumer demand for attendance.

The presence of loss averse consumers has important implications for league design and competitive balance. The two team model from Chapter 5 assumes that leagues maximize team profits by designing seasons where most games have uncertain outcomes. However, loss averse consumers would prefer to watch less balanced competitions with both dynasties and upsets by heavy underdogs. The presence of loss averse consumers calls into question the basic assumptions of the two-team model, and thus undermines the rationale for salary caps, revenue sharing, and entry drafts in leagues. Interestingly, the two team model predicts that these policies mainly serve to transfer money from players to owners, rather than to balance competition. perhaps leagues already understand the importance of loss averse consumers.

Readings and References

Benz, Men-Andri, Leif Brandes and Egon Franck, (2009). Do Soccer Associations Really Spend On A Good Thing? Empirical Evidence On Heterogeneity In The Consumer Response To Match Uncertainty Of Outcome, *Contemporary Economic Policy* 27(2), 216-235.

Coates, D., Humphreys, B. and Zhou, L., (2014). Reference-Dependent Preferences,Outcome Uncertainty, and Live Game Attendance, *Economic Inquiry*, 52(3): 959-973.

Neale, W. (1964). The Peculiar Economics of Professional Sports: A Contribution to the Theory of the Firm in Sporting Competition and Market Competition. *The Quarterly Journal of Economics*, 78(1): 1-14.

Rottenberg, S. (1956). The Baseball Players' Labor Market. *The Journal of Political Economy*, 64(3): 242-258.

Tversky, A. and Kahneman, D. (1991). Loss Aversion in Riskless Choice: A Reference-Dependent Model, *The Quarterly Journal of Economics*, 106(4): 1039-61.

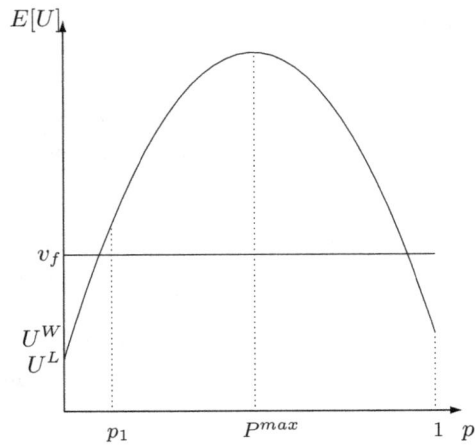

Review Questions

1. TFU: Based on the following graph, a fan with preferences as shown and reservation utility u_f would not attend a game at which the probability of the team winning the game was p_1.

2. TFU: Loss aversion implies that fans do not want to attend games in which the home team is expected to lose to the opponent.

Part III

Topics in Sports Economics

Chapter 7

Measuring and Analyzing Competitive Balance

Chapter Objectives

- Understand why measuring competitive balance is important

- Understand and interpret different measures of competitive balance

- Understand the strengths and weaknesses of different measures of competitive balance

- Understand how competitive balance has changed in MLB over time

- Understand the relationship between competitive balance and the uncertainty of outcome hypothesis

7.1 Why Research Competitive Balance

The two team model developed in Chapter 4 points out the importance of competitive balance in sports leagues, develops the idea that competitive imbalance may be a persistent feature of closed leagues like those that exist in North America, and provides a framework for analyzing policies that sports leagues have used in the past to improve competitive balance. But the existence of competitive imbalance in sports leagues is an empirical question, and in order to answer a questions "is there competitive imbalance in the NHL" requires the development of a measure of competitive balance that can be compared across time and across leagues. Sports economists have spent considerable time and effort developing measures of competitive balance and using these measures to analyze outcomes in sports leagues. Much of this competitive balance research focuses on testing the predictions that emerge from the two-team model of league behavior.

Sports economics also focuses on competitive balance because of the existence of a large amount of data on outcomes in professional sports leagues. Professional baseball has existed for more than 100 years, and the other three major professional sports leagues have existed for more than 60 years. This rich data provides an ideal environment for research on competitive balance, as outcomes are league readily measured and leagues have changed important institutional characteristics over time that can be interpreted as "natural experiments" that might be expected to change competitive balance. For example, the adoption of the designated hitter rule in the American League has been used as a natural experiment to see how rule changes affect competitive balance in a number of papers.

Finally, fans care about competitive balance passionately. Almost every sports fan on the continent has an pinion about the current level of competitive balance in his or her favorite sport, both compared to other leagues and compared to the past history of his or her favorite sport. Sports talk radio fixates on the level of competitive balance in professional sports leagues. Given these elements, competitive balance research holds considerable interest for sports economists and sports fans.

Measures of competitive balance can be grouped into two broad classifications: static measures and dynamic measures. Each is discussed in turn below.

7.2   Static Measures of Competitive Balance

Static measures of competitive balance are based on statistical measures of dispersion of winning percentages in sports leagues. Static measures were the first to emerge in the research literature, and these measures still constitute the "workhorse" methods of measuring competitive balance in sports leagues. They focus exclusively on measuring competitive balance within a single season in a sports league. The basic concept behind static measures of competitive balance is that in leagues with more competitive balance, winning percentages will be less dispersed and in leagues with less competitive balance winning percentages will be more dispersed.

Note: Calculating Winning Percentage   In sports leagues with no ties, winning percentage is simple to calculate. If w is the number of wins and l the number of losses, then winning percentage is

$$WPCT = \frac{w}{w+l}.$$

However, if ties are included in game outcomes, then winning percentage must be adjusted to reflect ties. There is no standard way to handle ties. Suppose that t is the number ot ties. Two approaches are

$$WPCT_{T1} = \frac{w}{w+l+t}$$

and

$$WPCT_{T2} = \frac{w+0.5t}{w+l+t}$$

which treats each tie as half a loss and half a win.

7.2.1   Standard Deviation of Winning Percentage

The standard deviation of winning percentage (SDWP) is the most common measure of competitive balance in sports leagues. It reflects the dispersion of winning percentages in a sports league. A standard deviation of zero indicates perfect competitive balance within a league. This will occur when each team in the league wins exactly fifty percent of its games in a season. The higher the SDWP, the worse the competitive balance is in a league. SDWP simply applies the usual formula for calculating the standard deviation of a variable to season winning percents in a sports league. Recall that the standard deviation of a variable is average of the squared deviation of each teams winning percentage from the league average winning percentage. If $WPCT_i$ is the winning percent of team i in a sports league with $i = 1, 2, \ldots, N$ teams, then the standard deviation of winning percentage for single season

$$\sigma_{W1} = \sqrt{\frac{\sum_{i=1}^{N}(WPCT_i - \overline{WPCT})^2}{N}}$$

where $\overline{WPCT}$ is the average winning percent in the league in that season. In leagues with a balanced schedule and no ties, $\overline{WPCT}$ must equal 0.500, and the denominator of the standard deviation is N. In leagues with unbalanced schedules or ties, $\overline{WPCT}$ must be estimated, and the denominator must use the degrees of freedom correction $N-1$ to calculate σ_{W1}. This distinction can have an important effect on calculating σ_{W1} if the number of teams in the league is small.

The relationship between SDWP and competitive balance is straightforward. Leagues with a higher SDWP have more variation in winning percentages around the mean and less competitive balance. Leagues with a lower SDWP have less variation in winning percentages around the mean and more competitive balance. Note that σ_{W1} declines with the number of games played in the league. This means that σ_{W1} will be lower in leagues with more games, like MLB, and higher in leagues like the NFL with fewer games.

The primary advantage of SDWP is simplicity. The SDWP measure of competitive balance provides a snapshot of the level of competitive balance in a league in each season.

SDWP can also be calculated over a number of seasons for a sports league. Consider a league with N teams over a period of T seasons. If $WPCT_{i,t}$ represents the winning percentage of team i, $i = 1, \ldots, N$ indexes teams in the league and $t = 1, \ldots, T$ indexes seasons, then the standard deviation of winning percentage for the league over T seasons is

$$\sigma_{W2} = \sqrt{\frac{\sum_{i=1}^{N}\sum_{t=1}^{T}(WPCT_{i,t} - \overline{WPCT})^2}{NT}}.$$

The interpretation of σ_{W2} is the same as σ_{W1}. Note that σ_{W2} is decreasing in the number of games played and in the number of teams in the league. While σ_{W1} is a reasonable measure of competitive balance in a single season, σ_{W2} has some shortcomings when applied over a number of seasons. In particular, the standard deviation of winning percentage can not capture changes in the relative standings of teams within a sports league over time.

7.2.2 The Idealized Standard Deviation

Since σ_{W2} depends on N and T it cannot be used to compare competitive balance across leagues, or competitive balance within leagues that have changed the number of games in the regular season over time. In order to compare competitive balance across leagues and within leagues that have changed the number of games in the regular season, sports economists use the idealized standard deviation of winning percentage (ISDWP) ratio. To find this ratio, we first need to standardize the variation in winning percentages to control for the number of games played. The standardization is based on an idealized standard deviation

$$\sigma_I = \frac{0.500}{\sqrt{G}}$$

Where G is the number of games played in the league. σ_I is the predicted variation in a league where each team has a 50% chance of winning each game played ($WPCT = 0.500$) corrected for the number of games played. The ISDWP ratio is simply the ratio of actual to ideal standard deviation of winning percentage

$$\sigma_{WI} = \frac{\sigma_{W2}}{\sigma_I}$$

This metric is sometimes called the Noll-Scully ratio in the literature, to recognize two sports economists, Gerald Scully and Roger Noll, who developed this measure at about the same time in the late 1970s. σ_{WI} is a standardized measure of competitive balance in that the actual variability of winning percentage is scaled or standardized by an idealized value. The closer the ratio is to 1, the more competitive balance in the league over that period. The farther the ratio is from 1, the less competitive balance in the league over that period.

σ_{WI} is a one-dimensional measure of competitive balance. Its power lies in the ability to compare one period's level of competitive balance to another period's level of competitive balance, controlling for the number of teams and games played. The idealized standard deviation of winning percentage ratio's main function is to compare competitive balance across professional sports leagues by correcting for differences in the number of regular season games ($\sqrt{G}$) in each professional sports league. This is important because professional sports leagues play different regular season schedules. For example, each team in Major League Baseball plays 162 games, the each team in the National Football League plays 16 games, and each team in the English Premier League plays 38 games. Since σ_{W2} would be lower in MLB than in the NFL even if the dispersion of winning percents was the same, σ_{W2} must be corrected to make a comparison.

7.2.3   Calculating Static Measures of Competitive Balance

In order to illustrate the calculation of different measures of competitive balance, consider the following simple example. Consider a simple sports league with five teams (A,B,C,D,E) that play each other once per season. The outcome of a single season is shown on Table 7.1. Team A won the league with a perfect 4-0 record, and team E finished in last place, winning no games.

Table 7.1: Won-Loss Records and σ_{W1}, Season 1

Team	W-L	$WPCT_{i,1}$	$(WPCT_{i,1} - 0.500)$	$(WPCT_{i,1} - 0.500)^2$
Team A	4-0	1.000	0.500	0.250
Team B	3-1	0.750	0.250	0.063
Team C	2-2	0.500	0.000	0.000
Team D	1-3	0.250	-0.250	0.063
Team E	0-4	0.000	-0.500	0.250
$\sum (WPCT_i - 0.500)^2 = 0.250 + 0.063 + 0.00 + 0.063 + 0.250 =$				0.625
$\frac{\sum (WPCT_i - 0.500)^2}{N} =$			$\frac{0.625}{5} =$	0.125
$\sigma_{W1} = \sqrt{\frac{\sum (WPCT_i - 0.500)^2}{N}} =$			$\sqrt{0.125} =$	0.354

In order to calculate σ_{W1}, the SDWP, the difference between the actual winning percentage and 0.500, and the square of this difference must be calculated for each team, the square of this difference must be calculated, and the squared differences summed. These calculations are shown on Table

7.1, in columns 4 (difference between actual and average) and 5 (squared difference). $\sigma_{W1} = 0.354$ for this season, a value that has little meaning without a comparator, another limitation of σ_{W1}. Table 7.2 shows the outcome of a second season in this simple sports league. In the second season, Teams A and B tied for first, and Teams D and E tied for last, and team C finished third. Again, the relevant calculations for finding σ_{W1} are shown on Table 7.2. In the second season, $\sigma_{W1} = 0.224$.

Table 7.2: Won-Loss Records and σ_{W1}. Season 2

Team	W-L	$WPCT_{i,1}$	$(WPCT_{i,1} - 0.500)$	$(WPCT_{i,1} - 0.500)^2$
Team A	3-1	0.750	0.250	0.063
Team B	3-1	0.750	0.250	0.063
Team C	2-2	0.500	0.000	0.000
Team D	1-3	0.250	-0.250	0.063
Team E	1-3	0.250	-0.250	0.063
$\sum (WPCT_{i,t} - 0.500)^2 = 0.063 + 0.063 + 0.00 + 0.063 + 0.063 =$				0.250
$\frac{\sum(WPCT_{i,t} - 0.500)^2}{N} =$			$\frac{0.250}{5} =$	0.050
$\sigma_{W1} = \sqrt{\frac{\sum(WPCT_{i,t} - 0.500)^2}{N}} =$			$\sqrt{0.050} =$	0.224

σ_{W1} can be used to compare the level of competitive balance in this league across these two seasons, since the same number of games were played in each season in the league. σ_{W1} is lower in the second season than in the first season, so the dispersion of winning percentages in season two was less dispersed than in the first season. This implies that the second season was more balanced than the first season in this league.

Note that the relative order of standings is the same in each season in this league. Team A finished is first, Team B tied for first or in second, and so on in each season. Static measures of competitive balance do not capture this feature of competitive balance. To illustrate this point, consider the records for teams in two hypothetical five team leagues shown on Table 7.3, which shows the won-loss record for each team in each of five seasons.

Each league has the same σ_{W2} over this five season period, 0.35. These two leagues have similar levels of competitive balance over this period, according to σ_{W2}. However, the relative standings over time in these two leagues are quite different. In League 1, the relative standings in each year are identical and Team A dominated the league, winning the championship in each season; there is no variation in relative standings over these five seasons in this league. League 2 has much more variation in relative standings over the period. Each of the five championships were won by a different team, and each team also finished last once over these five seasons. League 2 would appear to have more competitive balance over time than League 1 because of the turnover in relative standings. But σ_{W2} does not contain any information about changes in relative standings - it is simply a measure of dispersion of winning percentages in a league. Clearly, an alternative measure of competitive balance which could distinguish between these two cases would be a useful complement to the SDWP.

Note that teams in League 1 play 4 games and teams in League 2 play 8 games in each season. When comparing σ_{W2} across leagues, must adjust for the fact that this measure is sensitive to the number of games played by teams in the leagues. We can do this by calculating an ideal standard

Table 7.3: Won-Loss Records and Win % in Two Leagues

Team	League 1					Team	League 2				
	1	2	3	4	5		1	2	3	4	5
A	4-0	4-0	4-0	4-0	4-0	F	8-0	6-2	4-4	2-6	0-8
B	3-1	3-1	3-1	3-1	3-1	G	6-2	4-4	2-6	0-8	8-0
C	2-2	2-2	2-2	2-2	2-2	H	4-4	2-6	0-8	8-0	6-2
D	1-3	1-3	1-3	1-3	1-3	I	2-6	0-8	8-0	6-2	4-4
E	0-4	0-4	0-4	0-4	0-4	J	0-8	8-0	6-2	4-4	2-6
A	1.00	1.00	1.00	1.00	1.00	F	1.00	0.75	0.50	0.25	0.00
B	0.75	0.75	0.75	0.75	0.75	G	0.75	0.50	0.25	0.00	1.00
C	0.50	0.50	0.50	0.50	0.50	H	0.50	0.25	0.00	1.00	0.75
D	0.25	0.25	0.25	0.25	0.25	I	0.25	0.00	1.00	0.75	0.50
E	0.00	0.00	0.00	0.00	0.00	J	0.00	1.00	0.75	0.50	0.25

deviation for each league

$$\sigma_I = \frac{0.5}{\sqrt{G}}$$

where G is the number of games played by teams in the league. In this case, $\sigma_I = \frac{0.5}{\sqrt{4}} = 0.25$ for League 1 and $\sigma_I = \frac{0.5}{\sqrt{8}} = 0.177$ for League 2. Since the two leagues play a different number of games, σ_{WI} should be used to compare competitive balance in these two leagues, not σ_{W2}. In the simple example of two leagues shown on Table 7.3, $\sigma_{WI} = \frac{\sigma_{W2}}{\sigma_I} = \frac{0.35}{0.25} = 1.40$ for League 1. $\sigma_{WI} = \frac{\sigma_{W2}}{\sigma_I} = \frac{0.35}{0.177} = 1.98$ for League 2. σ_{W2} was just under 1.5 times its idealized value over this five season period, while σ_{W2} was almost twice its idealized value in League 2. Correcting for the number of games played, there was less competitive balance in League 2 than in League 1 over this period.

The importance of using σ_{WI} to measure competitive balance can be better illustrated with an example drawn from actual professional sports league outcomes, where season lengths have more variability. Table 7.2.3 shows the actual values of σ_{W1}, σ_I and σ_{WI} for the NFL, NBA and MLB in 2004. The idealized standard deviation ratio, σ_{WI}, can be calculated from either σ_{W2} as shown above, or from σ_{W1}, as shown here. Note the large differences between the value of σ_I across these three leagues. The larger is G, the smaller σ_{WI}. σ_{WI} for the NFL is more than four times σ_{WI} for MLB because of the difference in season length in these two leagues.

Based solely on σ_{W1}, would conclude that MLB had the most competitive balance in 2004, since σ_{W2} was much smaller in MLB than in the other leagues. But the longer baseball season makes a direct comparison of σ_{W1} inappropriate in this setting. Instead, after adjusting σ_{W1} with σ_I, competitive balance in baseball was almost 2.5 times the idealized value, while competitive balance in the NFL was just over 1.5 times its idealized value. Competitive balance in the NFL appears to have been better than in MLB, when the length of the season is accounted for.

Example: Competitive Balance in Baseball, Part 1

As a further example of the application of static measures of competitive balance, consider the standard deviation of winning percentages in MLB's American League East Division over the five

Table 7.4: σ_{W1}, σ_I and σ_{WI}, 2004

League	σ_{W1}	Games		σ_I	σ_{WI}
NFL	0.193	16	$\frac{0.5}{\sqrt{16}} =$	0.125	1.54
MLB	0.083	162	$\frac{0.5}{\sqrt{162}} =$	0.039	2.46
NBA	0.136	82	$\frac{0.5}{\sqrt{82}} =$	0.055	2.12

season period 2000-2004. Based on the values of σ_{W1}, what would you conclude happened to competitive balance in the AL East over this period? Although σ_{W1} increased in 2002, it generally decreased over the 5 season period, suggesting that competitive balance generally increased. The σ_{W1} value of 0.047 in 2005 was considerably lower than in any other season in this period, again suggesting a substantial deterioration in competitive balance as measured by the distribution of winning percentages. However, from the perspective of teams other than the New York Yankees, and especially from the perspective of the Tampa Bay Devil Rays, there was a lack of competitive balance in the division throughout the period. The Yankees won the division in each season, and the Rays finished in last place in each season. In fact, the relative ordering of the standings was identical in each season; the Yankees finished first, the Rex Sox second, the Blue Jays third, the Orioles fourth and the Devil Rays last in nearly every season. The only exception is 2004, when the Blue Jays finished last behind both the Orioles and Devil rays. Again, σ_{W1} and other standard deviation based measure of competitive balance are insensitive to relative standings, and do not reflect the unchanging relative standings in the Division over this period.

Table 7.5: Won-Loss Records and σ_{W1} AL East 2000-2004

Team	2004	2003	2002	2001	2000
New York Yankees	0.623	0.623	0.640	0.594	0.540
Boston Red Sox	0.605	0.586	0.574	0.509	0.525
Toronto Blue Jays	0.416	0.531	0.481	0.494	0.512
Baltimore Orioles	0.481	0.439	0.414	0.391	0.457
Tampa Bay Devil Rays	0.435	0.389	0.342	0.383	0.429
σ_{W1}	0.096	0.098	0.120	0.088	0.047

Interpreting σ_{W1}: The units of measure of σ_{W1} is the same as the underlying variable - winning percentage. MLB plays 162 games per season, so one win is $\frac{1}{162} = 0.006$ in $WPCT$. σ_{W1} values can be converted to wins by dividing by 0.006. In 2002, σ_{W1} was 0.120, and $\frac{.120}{0.006} = 20$ wins. The standard deviation of wins in the AL East in 2002 was plus or minus 20 wins. 66% of the teams wins were with plus or minus 20 wins of 80, or between 60 and 100 wins. That's a lot of variation.

7.3   Dynamic Measures of Competitive Balance

Sports economists noticed that relative standings could be an important component of competitive balance, and developed a number of alternative measures of competitive balance to address this limitation of the static measures discussed above. These alternative measures are called dynamic measures of competitive balance in the literature, because they capture changes in competitive balance over time.

7.3.1   The Variance Decomposition Measure

Eckard (1998) examined competitive balance in NCAA Division I football. In his paper, Eckard recognized one of the limitations of standard deviation of winning percentage based measures of competitive balance like σ_{W2} - the failure of static measures of competitive balance to address changes in the success of individual teams over time. He addressed this limitation by decomposing observed variation in winning percentage into two parts: the average of the variance in win percentage across teams at one point in time and the variance of win percentage over time. This approach captures both the interdependence between teams in a sports league and relative changes in standings over time in a league. Eckard's approach is to decompose σ_{W2}, making use of each team's average winning percentage over time

$$WPCT_N = \frac{\sum_{i=1}^{N}(WPCT_{i,t})}{T}.$$

where the N subscript refers to teams. This is simply the average winning percentage for a given team over the T seasons in the period. Adding and subtracting $WPCT_N$ to the equation for σ_{W2}

$$VAR_{wpct} = \frac{\sum_{i=1}^{N}\sum_{t=1}^{T}((WPCT_{i,t} - WPCT_N) + (WPCT_N - \overline{WPCT}))^2}{NT}$$

produces a variance expression that captures both the variability of each team's winning percentage over time (the first term) and the cumulative variability of winning percentages across all teams in the league over all years (the second term). With a bit of manipulation, this expression can be rearranged to show two additive terms that reflect the variance of individual team's winning percentage over time and the overall variance of winning percentage

$$VAR_{wpct} = VAR_{time} + VAR_{cum}$$

Applying the variance expression to the outcome in the simple sports leagues shown on Table 7.3 provides insight into the variance decomposition. The first term in the variance expression, $(WPCT_{i,t} - WPCT_N)$, is the deviation of the actual winning percentage for a team from the team's average winning percentage. This term corresponds to the VAR_{time} term in the linear variance decomposition. Consider Team A in League 1 on Table 7.3. $WPCT_N$ is team A's average winning percentage over 5 seasons. Team A went undefeated in each season, so ($WPCT_{i,t} = 1.00$ for each season, $T = 1, 2, \ldots, 5$ and $WPCT_N = 1.00$. Since Team A's average winning percentage is equal to the actual winning percentage in each season, $(WPCT_{i,t} - WPCT_N) = 0$ in each season. Team A has zero variation in winning percentage in each season. The same is true for Teams B, C, D and E. VAR_{time} is a measure of the average team-specific variation in winning percentage, so $VAR_{time} = 0$ in League 1.

The second term in the variance expression, $(WPCT_N - \overline{WPCT})$, is the deviation of the average winning percentage for each team from the league's average winning percentage. This term corresponds to the VAR_{cum} term in the linear variance decomposition. Consider Team F in League 2 on Table 7.3. $WPCT_N$ is team F's average winning percentage over 5 seasons. $WPCT_N = (1.00 + 0.75 + 0.50 + 0.25 + 0.00)/5 = 0.50$ for Team F. Clearly, $WPCT_N = 0.50$ for every team in League 2. Since each Team in League 2 plays every other team twice, $\overline{WPCT} = 0.500$ by definition. Since each team has the same average winning percentage over time in League 2, $(WPCT_N - \overline{WPCT}) = 0$ in the league. VAR_{cum} is a measure of the average league-specific variation in winning percentage, so $VAR_{cum} = 0$ in League 2.

7.3.2 The Competitive Balance Ratio

The example on Table 7.5 above shows a dimension of competitive balance, the variation in the relative standings of teams in a sports league over time, that σ_{W2} and σ_{WI} do not reflect. In Humphreys (2002), I developed a dynamic measure of competitive balance called the competitive balance ratio (CBR) that addressed this limitation. The CBR uses a similar approach as Eckard (1998) but the CBR expresses competitive balance as a single number that compares within-team and within-league variation in winning percentages. Variation in winning percentages in a sports league over seasons can be calculated in two different ways: using within-team variation in inning percentages, that capture team-specific variation over seasons, and within-league variation in winning percentages, that capture league-specific variation. The standard deviation of a team's winning percentage across seasons is one possible a measure of within-team variation

$$\sigma_{T,i} = \sqrt{\frac{\sum \left(WPCT_{i,t} - \overline{WPCT_i}\right)^2}{T}} \tag{7.1}$$

where $\overline{WPCT_i}$ is each team's average won-loss percentage over the T seasons. In this case, there will be a vector of $\sigma_{T,i}$s, one for each team in the league. The smaller the value of $\sigma_{T,i}$, the less the variation in team i's winning percentage over the seasons being analyzed. For the hypothetical leagues shown on Table 7.3, each team in League 1 has $\sigma_{T,i} = 0.0$ and each team in League 2 has $\sigma_{T,i} = 0.35$.

The within-season variation in won-loss percentages can be measured by the standard deviation of the won-loss percentage in each season across all teams in a league

$$\sigma_{N,t} = \sqrt{\frac{\sum (WPCT_{i,t} - 0.500)^2}{N}}. \tag{7.2}$$

In this case $\sigma_{N,t}$ is a vector with one value for each season being examined. For each year, $\sigma_{N,t}$ is identical to σ_L.

These two types of variation in winning percentage can be averaged to arrive at league-wide measures of each type of variation for any period. A measure of the average variation in teams' won-loss percentages can be found by averaging the $\sigma_{T,i}$s across teams in the league

$$\overline{\sigma}_T = \frac{\sum \sigma_{T,i}}{N}. \tag{7.3}$$

Similarly, the average variation in won-loss percentages in each season can be found by averaging the $\sigma_{N,t}$s across each season

$$\overline{\sigma}_N = \frac{\sum \sigma_{N,t}}{T}. \tag{7.4}$$

Note that if the same N teams play an identical number of games in each season, then $\overline{\sigma}_N$ will be equal to σ_{W1}. But league expansion, schedule adjustment, strikes, and postponed games that are not played reduce the periods over which this condition holds in professional sports leagues.

Using these two measures of average variation, the Competitive Balance Ratio (CBR) can be defined as

$$CBR = \frac{\overline{\sigma}_T}{\overline{\sigma}_N}. \tag{7.5}$$

Consider the values of these two statistics for the two hypothetical sports leagues shown on Table 7.3. $\sigma_{T,i}$ is zero for each team in League 1 and thus $\overline{\sigma}_T$ is zero for that league. Each team in that league finished in the same position in each season, so there is no time variation in winning percentages over those five seasons. The CBR is zero in League 1. Next consider Season 2. $\sigma_{N,i}$ is 0.395 for each team in League 2, so $\overline{\sigma}_N$ is 0.395 for that league. $\sigma_{T,i}$ is also equal to 0.395 for each team in League 2, so $\overline{\sigma}_T$ is also 0.395 for that league. The average variation in won-loss percentage over time for each team is the same as the average variation in won-loss percentage in each season in the league. The CBR, the ratio of the two, is equal to 1 in League 2.

The simple example of two five team leagues over a five year period above shows that some measures of competitive balance do not capture an important element of competitive balance: variation in relative standings over time. By construction, the Competitive Balance Ratio reflects both variation in relative standings and overall variation in winning percentage. The Competitive Balance Ratio scales the average time variation in won-loss percentage for teams in the league by the average variation in won-loss percentages across seasons; it indicates the relative magnitude of each type of variation across a number of seasons.

Expressing these two types of variation as a ratio has a number of appealing intuitive properties. First, unlike σ_{W2}, the CBR is easier to compare over different time periods because it does not have to be compared to an idealized value that depends on the number of games played in each season. In Major League Baseball, σ_I changes as the schedule expanded from 154 games to 162 games. This makes it difficult to compare the σ_L from the 1980s to that from the 1930s. Because it is a ratio, the CBR also has intuitively appealing upper and lower bounds of zero and one. This can be seen from the CBR for the two leagues shown on Table 7.3, which also illustrates the two bounding cases of the CBR. League 1 has no team-specific variation in won-loss percentage over these five seasons; each team in the league finishes in the same place in each season. The CBR for League 1 is zero. In league 2, the team-specific variation in won-loss percentage is equal to the within season variation over these five seasons; the CBR for League 2 is one. In a league with a CBR of 0.5 the team-specific variation is half the size of the within season variation over the period.

Because the denominator of the Competitive Balance Ratio is related to σ_{W2}, these two metrics are inversely related; the CBR reflects some of the same information as the standard deviation of winning percentage. However, the CBR is a useful complement to σ_{W2} because it also reflects the average amount of team-specific variation in won-loss percentage that will not be reflected in σ_{W2}.

Example: Between-Season Variation

Most dynamic measures of competitive balance make use of between-season variation in winning percentages for individual teams. Calculating between-season variation just applies the same calculation shown above on Table 7.5 for σ_{W1} to a single team. The difference is that any team's average $WPCT$ does not have to be 0.500 over any period, so the team's average winning percentage ($\overline{WPCT}$) for the period must be calculated for each team before calculating the standard deviation.

On Table 7.6, the final column shows the between-season variation in winning percentage, $\sigma_{i,T}$ for each team in the AL East.

Table 7.6: Team Specific Between-Season Variation

Team	2004	2003	2002	2001	2000	$\sigma_{i,T}$
New York Yankees	0.623	0.623	0.640	0.594	0.540	0.039
Boston Red Sox	0.605	0.586	0.574	0.509	0.525	0.041
Toronto Blue Jays	0.416	0.531	0.481	0.494	0.512	0.044
Baltimore Orioles	0.481	0.439	0.414	0.391	0.457	0.035
Tampa Bay Devil Rays	0.435	0.389	0.342	0.383	0.429	0.038
$\sigma_{w,i}$	0.096	0.098	0.120	0.088	0.047	

To calculate $\sigma_{i,T}$ for one team, say the Yankees, first calculate the Yankees' average $WPCT$ over the period

$$\overline{WPCT} = \frac{\sum WPCT_i}{T} = \frac{0.623 + 0.623 + 0.640 + 0.594 + 0.540}{5} = 0.604$$

Next, find the difference between the actual winning percentage, $WPCT$, and the average for that period, square it, and find the average of this value, then take the square root

$$\frac{\sum \left(WPCT_i - \overline{WPCT}\right)^2}{T-1} = 0.0016 \quad \Rightarrow \sqrt{0.0016} = 0.039$$

The sum of the squared deviations of actual team winning percentage from the team's average winning percentage is divided by $T-1$ because $\overline{WPCT}$ has to be estimated for each team. The $T-1$ includes a "degrees of freedom" correction. Notice that there is relatively little between-season variation in winning percentage in the AL East over this period. Each team had about the same winning percentage in each season over this period. In contrast to the small between-season variation in $WPCT$ in the AL East, consider the NL Central over the same period. Table 7.7 shows both the within-season variation in winning percentage, σ_{W1}, in the last row, and the between-season variation in winning percentage, $\sigma_{T,i}$, in the rightmost column. The $\sigma_{T,i}$ values are for the team listed in the second to last column.

Table 7.7: Standings, σ_{W1}, $\sigma_{i,T}$ 2000-2004 NL Central

2000		2001		2002		2003		2004		$\sigma_{T,i}$
0.586	Cards	0.574	Astros	0.599	Cards	0.543	Cubs	0.648	Cards	0.044
0.525	Reds	0.574	Cards	0.519	Astros	0.537	Astros	0.568	Astros	0.052
0.451	Brewers	0.543	Cubs	0.481	Reds	0.525	Cards	0.549	Cubs	0.075
0.444	Astros	0.420	Brewers	0.447	Pirates	0.463	Pirates	0.469	Reds	0.046
0.426	Pirates	0.407	Reds	0.414	Cubs	0.426	Reds	0.447	Pirates	0.031
0.401	Cubs	0.383	Pirates	0.346	Brewers	0.420	Brewers	0.416	Brewers	0.039
0.064		0.089		0.087		0.056		0.087		

The between-season variation is generally larger in the NL Central than in the AL East. There was more turnover in relative standings in the NL Central over the period than in the AL East. The CBR is just a ratio of variation measures. Average $\sigma_{W,t}$ over the five years ($\overline{\sigma}_N = (0.064 + 0.089 + 0.087 + 0.056 + 0.087)/5 = 0.078$). Average $\sigma_{T,i}$ over the five years ($\overline{\sigma}_N = (0.044 + 0.052 + 0.075 + 0.046 + 0.031 + 0.039)/6 = 0.048$). The CBR is just the ratio $\frac{\overline{\sigma}_T}{\overline{\sigma}_N}$ which is 0.62. Team-specific variation in winning percentage was about 60% of league-wide variation in winning percentage.

7.3.3 Markov Transition Probabilities

Markov Transition Probabilities capture variation in standings by teams within seasons. Hadley, Ciecka and Krautmann (2005) first showed how Markov transition probabilities could be used as measures of competitive balance in sports leagues. Markov Transitional Probabilities assume that what happens in the past helps determine what will happen in the future. This measure of competitive balance has some benefits. First, transitional probabilities track teams' performance from one season to the next season which static competitive balance measures fail to do. It also captures the cyclical aspect of performance professional sports teams. Under the assumption that teams maximize profits, the probabilities show how difficult it can be for a bad team to "jump the curve" and win after a long period of losing or how reluctant teams are to choose to hire the talent required to gain additional wins because of the effect of hiring additional talent on profits. A negative aspect to transitional probabilities is they do not take into account how close a winning team is to qualifying for the postseason. This might help more accurately predict a team's chances from one season to the next since not all losers are equal in a give season. A team that finishes two games away from making the playoffs is more likely to qualify for the postseason next season than a team that finishes at the bottom of the table, thirty games out of the playoffs.

At the heart of this measure of competitive balance is a Markov process. A Markov process is a state-dependent model in which outcomes at time $(t + 1)$ depend on the state at time t. The probability that a given team makes the transition from state a to state b, P_{ab}, is called the "transitional probability." State a and b are defined by the researcher, depending on the research question being examined. For example, state a could be when a team had a losing record at the end of the season and state b could be when a team had a winning record at the end of the season. Hadley, Ciecka and Krautmann (2005) defined state a as not making the playoffs at the end of the season and state b as making the playoffs. The transition probabilities are calculated by comparing end of season outcomes across two seasons.

For example, consider the AL East Standings from 2000 to 2001 from Table 7.5. In 2000-2004, the Yankees won the Division and went to the playoffs in each year. The Red Sox finished second in each year, but did not make it to the playoffs as the Wild Card team in 2000, 2001, or 2002; the Red Sox won the Wild Card and went to the playoffs in 2003 and 2004. There are four different transitional probabilities in a two-state Markov process: P_{aa}, the probability that last year's playoff team went to the playoffs this year; P_{ab}, the probability that last year's playoff team did not go to the playoffs this year; P_{ba}, the probability that a team that did not go to the playoffs last year went to the playoffs this year; and P_{bb}, the probability that a team that did not go to the playoffs last year did not go to the playoffs this year. On Table 7.5 there are five teams and four transition periods. The transitional probabilities for this five year period in thee AL East are

$$P_{aa} = \tfrac{5}{20} = 0.25$$

$$P_{ab} = \tfrac{0}{20} = 0.00$$

$$P_{bc} = \tfrac{1}{20} = 0.05$$

$$P_{bb} = \tfrac{14}{20} = 0.70.$$

Notice how small P_{ba} and P_{ab}, the transitional probabilities into and out of the playoffs, are over this period in the AL East. There was almost no turnover in the playoff positions in the division. Only one instance of a transition from not making the playoffs to making the playoffs happened: the Red Sox went from out of the playoffs in 2002 to the Wild Card team in 2003. The lack of change in relative standings in the AL East is reflected in the transitional probabilities in the Markov process.

7.4 Measures of Championship Distribution

7.4.1 The Gini Coefficient

Gini coefficients are another measure of win dispersion in a professional sports league. The Gini coefficient was developed by an Italian statistician, Corrado Gini in the early 20th century. The Gini coefficient is a measure of the inequality of the distribution of some outcome. A Gini coefficient of 0 indicates perfect equality of distribution and a Gini coefficient of 1 indicates complete inequality of distribution of an outcome. Gini coefficients are commonly used to measure inequality of the distribution of wealth or income in an economy, and has also been used in ecology and engineering. Gini coefficients are defined from a Lorenz Curve, which shows the distribution of a variable across a population.

Figure 7.1 shows an example of the distribution of a variable X across a population. Along the horizontal axis, the share of X accounted for by each individual in the population is shown, ordered from the individual with the lowest share of X to the individual with the highest share of X. Up the vertical axis, the cumulative distribution of X is shown. The 45° line, which has slope 1, represents perfect distribution. Along this line, 1% of X is distributed to each 1% of the population. The Lorenz Curve shows the actual distribution of X, and lies below the line of equality if the distribution of X is unequal. The farther below the line of equality, the more unequal the distribution of X across the population.

The Gini coefficient reflects the ratio of the area that lies below the line of equality and above the Lorenz Curve (area A on Figure 7.1) to the total area under the line of equality (area $A - B$ on Figure 7.1). So the Gini coefficient is

$$G = \frac{A}{A + B}$$

Gini coefficients are expressed as a number between 0 and 1 (and are sometimes expressed as a number between 0 and 100). If the Lorenz curve lies on the line of equality, the area of A is zero and the Gini coefficient is zero. There is perfect equality of distribution of X. If one individual has all of X, then the area of B, the area below the Lorenz Curve, is zero and $G = \frac{A}{A} = 1$.

Gini coefficients as a measure of competitive balance can easily be illustrated using shares of championships won in a sports league. Consider a simple league with 5 teams over a 10 season

Figure 7.1: The Lorenz Curve and Inequality of X

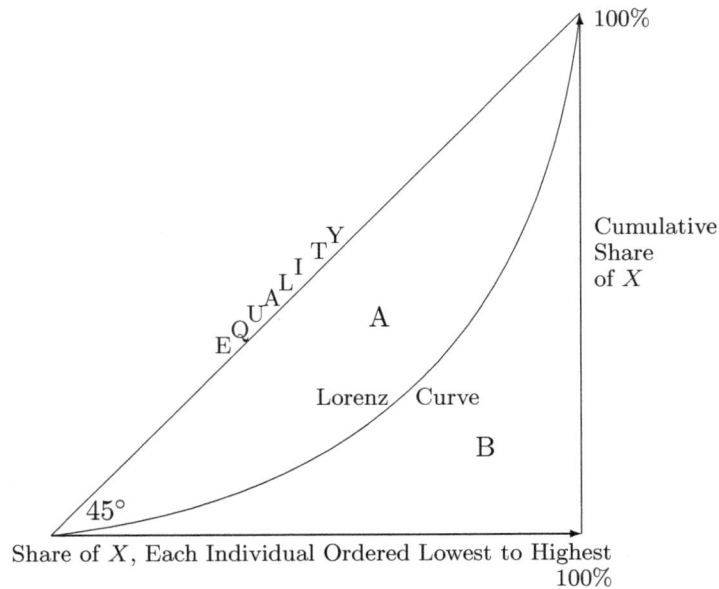

period. The distribution of championships won in this league is shown on Table 7.8. X represents championships, and there are 10 championships to be distributed int his league. Team A won 4 championships, Teams B and C each won two championships, and Teams D and E each won a single championship over this ten season period.

Table 7.8: Number of League Championships, 10 Season Period

Team	Championships	% of Seasons	% of Championships
Team A	4	20%	40%
Team B	2	20%	20%
Team C	2	20%	20%
Team D	1	20%	10%
Team E	1	20%	10%
Total	10	100%	100%

Figure 7.2 shows a Lorenz Curve for the distribution of championships in this league. The horizontal axis shows the fraction of the total championships won by each team in the league when the teams are ordered from the fewest championships to the most. Each team accounts for 20% of the team-seasons in the league. The first two teams graphed are Teams D and E. These two teams each account for 20% of the team-seasons, but each only won 10% of the championships. Next come Teams C and D. Again, each of thee teams accounts for 20% of the team-seasons in the league, and each won 20% of the championships. Finally, Team A accounts for 20$ of the team-seasons but 40% of the championships won.

Each dot on the graph represents the teams, ordered E,D,C,B,A from left to right. Connecting the dots would produce an estimate of the Lorenz Curve for the league. The area of A would

Figure 7.2: The Lorenz Curve for the League

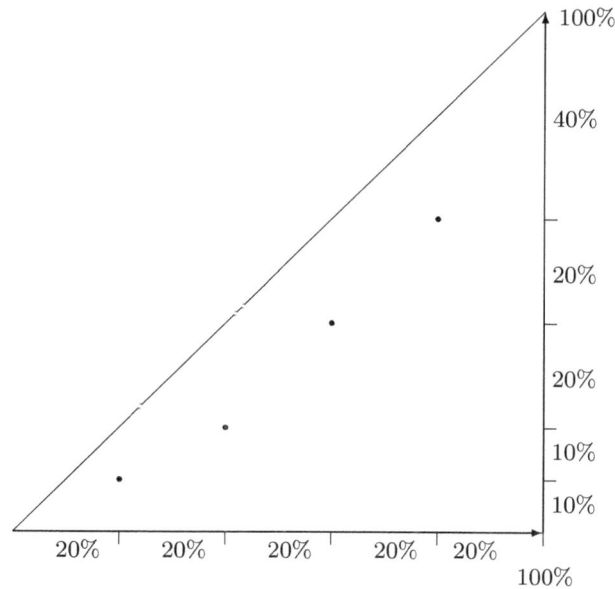

be relatively small compared to the area under the line of equality, so the Gini coefficient for this League would be small, suggesting relatively equal distribution of championships. However, Gini coefficients are difficult to calculate without an explicit function for the Lorenz Curve. If the Lorenz Curve can be represented as a function $Y = L(X)$, then the area of B can be found through integration and the Gini coefficient is simply

$$G = 1 - 2 \int_0^1 L(X)dX$$

However, writing down a function like $L(X)$ for the distribution of X is not simple. In some special cases, the Gini coefficient can be calculated. For example, for a population uniform on the values Y_i, $i = 1, 2, \ldots, N$ where i is indexed in non-decreasing order, so that $Y_i \leq Y_{i+1}$,, the Gini coefficient is

$$G = \frac{2 \sum i Y_i}{N \sum Y_i} - \frac{N+1}{N}$$

where $i = 1$ for Team E, $i = 2$ for Team D, $i = 3$ for Team C, $i = 4$ for Team B, and $i = 5$ for Team A. Y_i is the "% of Championships" column on Table 7.8. For the League shown on Table 7.8, the Gini coefficient is 0.28. Again, this is close to 0, indicating that the distribution of championships in the league was relatively evenly distributed over this period.

7.4.2 The Herfindahl-Hirschman Index

The Herfindahl-Hirschman Index (commonly known as HHI) is a concentration measure. The HHI is widely used in industrial organization to assess the amount of competition in a market. The most common use of the HHI in sports economics is for measuring the concentration of championships over a certain period in a sports league. However, the HHI can measure concentration of first place finishes within a division as well as the concentration of wins/points within a sports league. The HHI measure is simple to calculate: take the share of the outcome for each team (whether share is first place finishes, championships, wins, or points), square that number, and then sum the values across all teams to get the HHI. The higher the HHI, the higher the concentration of outcomes in the sample, and the less competitive balance in the league. In general, the HHI is

$$HHI = \sum_{i=1}^{N} s_i^2$$

where s_i is team i's share of the outcome and the league contains N teams. Shares of outcomes can be expressed two ways. If the shares are expressed as percents ($0 \le s_i \le 1$) then the HHI takes values from $1/N$ to 1. If the shares are expressed as whole numbers ($0 \le s_i \le 100$, meaning a percent share of 0.75 expressed as 75), then the HHI takes values up to $100^2 = 10,000$. The larger the HHI for a league, the less balance in that league.

A positive aspect of the HHI is its emphasis on the distribution of outcomes. In general, championships and first place finishes mean that a given team reaches post-season play. Postseason play, or playoffs, can benefit teams in two ways. First, the fans retain interest through the whole season as their team battles for a spot in the playoffs. The second benefit is playoffs can generate an unexpected league champion. This uncertainty benefits the fans of weaker teams throughout the league because once the playoffs begin. The HHI for championships in the league shown on Table 7.8 is

$$HHI = \sum_{i=1}^{N} s_i^2 = (0.4)^2 + (0.2)^2 + (0.2)^2 + (0.1)^2 + (0.1)^2 = 0.26.$$

The HHI lies between $1/N = 0.2$ and 1. 0.26 is relatively close to 0.2, again suggesting that the distribution of championships in this league was relatively equal over this ten season period.

Finally, both Gini coefficients and HHIs can be calculated for championships in these two leagues. For simplicity, assume that the team with the highest winning percentage is crowned the league "champion" in each season. Table 7.9 shows the championship shares in each league needed to calculate the Gini coefficient and HHI for these leagues. Both are simple to calculate.

Table 7.9: Won-Loss Records and Win % in Leagues

	League 1				League 2		
Team	Championships	% S	%C	Team	Championships	% S	%C
A	5	20%	100%	F	1	20%	20%
B	0	20%	0%	G	1	20%	20%
C	0	20%	0%	H	1	20%	20%
D	0	20%	0%	I	1	20%	20%
E	0	20%	0%	J	1	20%	20%

The Gini coefficient for League 1 is 1. Over this five season period all league championships were won by Team 1, and none by the other teams. The Gini coefficient for League 2 is 0. Each team won one championship over the five seasons, for a perfectly balanced distribution of championships. The Lorenz Curve lies on the line of perfect equality for this league. The HHIs also are at the extremes for these two leagues. For League 1

$$HHI = \sum_{i=1}^{N} s_i^2 = (1.00)^2 + (0.0)^2 + (0.0)^2 + (0.0)^2 + (0.0)^2 = 1.00.$$

the maximum value the HHI can take, indicating complete concentration of championships. For League 2

$$HHI = \sum_{i=1}^{N} s_i^2 = (0.2)^2 + (0.2)^2 + (0.2)^2 + (0.2)^2 + (0.2)^2 = 0.20.$$

Recall that the minimum value of the HHI is $1/N = 1/5 = 0.20$. In league 2, the HHI is as low as possible, indicating that the concentration of championships in League 2 is as low as possible. Both the Gini coefficient and the HHI for championships does a better job at reflecting changes in relative standings over time than the standard deviation based measures of competitive balance. However, these measures focus only on championships; they do not reflect changes in relative standings anywhere else except at the top if the league. in relatively large leagues, moving from the bottom half to the top half could be an important measure of competitive balance. Championship distributions will not reflect this sort of change in relative standings over time.

7.5 Example: MLB Competitive Balance

In order to illustrate the various measures of competitive balance discussed in this chapter, and to highlight their various strengths, weaknesses, and applications, this section analyzes competitive balance in MLB over the last 110 seasons using the competitive balance measures developed above.

7.5.1 Static Measures of Competitive Balance

Since there were many changes in MLB over this period, in terms of rules, number of teams, games in a season, length of the postseason, and other factors, I have broken MLB history into ten year periods beginning with the period 1900-1909. Dividing this period up into decades is somewhat arbitrary, but it provides one way of examining changes in the level of competitive balance over time. I consider the two leagues separately, because prior to the era of inter-league play, AL and NL teams faced each other only in the World Series.

The first measure of competitive balance developed is the standard deviation of winning percentage for a single season, σ_{W1}. Figure 7.3 plots σ_{W1} for the AL and NL over the 1900-2009 period.

Figure 7.3 shows a steady decline in σ_{W1} in both leagues over the period 1900-2009. Although quite a bit of season-to-season variability exists, this downward trend in σ_{W1} indicates that competitive balance improved in MLB over this period. In addition, σ_{W1} in the two leagues track each other relatively closely. No prolonged divergences exist between the two leagues. The large amount of season-to-season variation in σ_{W1} makes a direct visual comparison of the two leagues difficult, although a statistical comparison would be straightforward.

Table 7.10 shows two additional static measures of competitive balance, σ_{W2} and σ_{WI}, across decades in the two leagues. Note that in calculating the static measures of competitive balance shown on Table 7.10, I dropped expansion teams that played in 7 or fewer seasons in a decade from the calculations. This holds the composition of the leagues relatively constant in each of the decades, in terms of the composition of the leagues.

The length of the MLB season increased from 154 games to 162 games in 1961. Notice that σ_I is very similar across the two season lengths; the increase in the number of games was relatively small. σ_{W2} declines relatively steadily from the 1910s on in both leagues, with a few exceptions. This indicates that variation in winning percentages was declining in MLB over the past 100 years. Competitive balance, as measured by σ_{W2}, was better in the latter half of the 20th century than

Figure 7.3: AL and NL σ_{W1}, 1900-2009

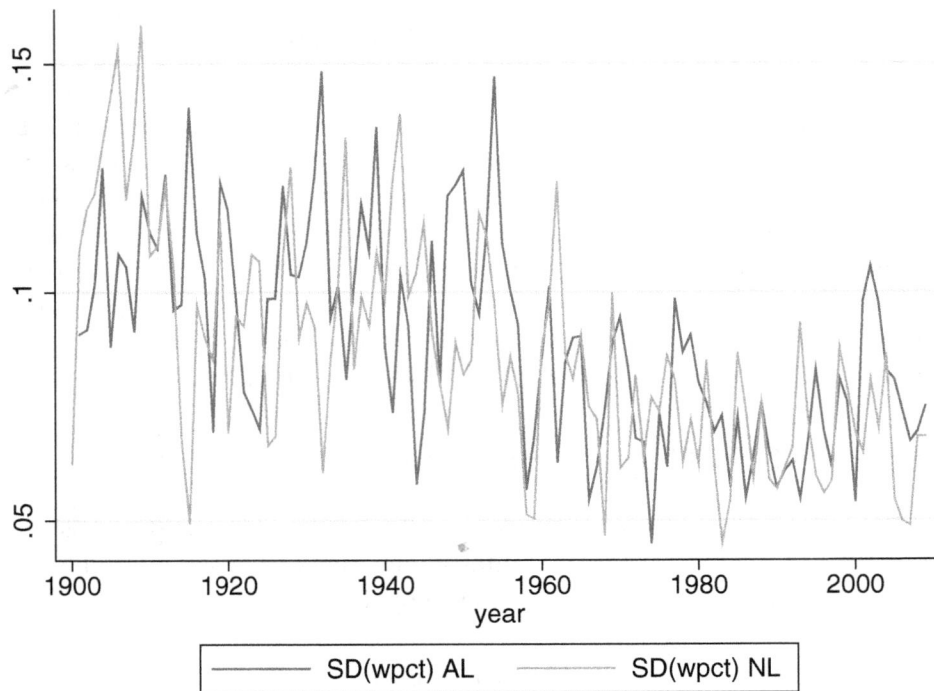

in the first half of the century. This downward trend in σ_{W2} mirrors the downward trend in σ_{W1} shown on Figure 7.3. A notable exceptions is the AL in the 2000s, when σ_{W2} increased from 0.066 in the 1990s to 0.079, roughly the same level of competitive balance as in the 1960s.

σ_{WI} also declined steadily over the period, which is to be expected since σ_{WI} is simply a transformation of σ_{W2}. Note that σ_{WI} is somewhat easier to interpret than σ_{W2}, as σ_{WI} is standardized by the ideal value, and this standardization makes the changes appear larger. From Table 7.10, competitive balance in the NL was almost three times the idealized value in the 1900s and declined to 60% to 70% above the idealized value by the end of the period. Competitive balance in the AL was about 2.5 times the idealized value in the 1900s and 1910s, and also declined to about 60% to 70% of the idealized value by the 1980s and 1990s before increasing to twice the idealized value in the 2000s. In general, the static measures of competitive balance suggest that competitive balance improved in MLB over time, with a slight decline in competitive balance after 2000. σ_{W1}, σ_{W2} and σ_{WI} all show a general pattern of decline over this 110 year period, indicating improvements in competitive balance. However, these static measures of competitive balance do not account for the distribution of championships or for changes in team's winning percentages over time.

Note that both σ_{W2} and σ_{WI} are random variables, since they are calculated from a sample of data. These random variables have a distribution, and in order to make a true statistical comparison between, say, the $\sigma_{W2,NL}$ value of 0.070 in the 1970s and 0.065 in the 1980s, the distribution of these random variables needs to be taken into account. While such statistical tests can be performed, they go beyond the scope of this chapter.

Table 7.10: Static CB Measures in MLB, 1900-2009

Decade	$\sigma_{W2,AL}$	$\sigma_{W2,NL}$	σ_I	$\sigma_{WI,AL}$	$\sigma_{WI,NL}$
1900	0.098	0.120	0.040	2.426	2.983
1910	0.104	0.092	0.040	2.587	2.282
1920	0.092	0.090	0.040	2.291	2.222
1930	0.108	0.091	0.040	2.669	2.268
1940	0.089	0.097	0.040	2.213	2.400
1950	0.098	0.081	0.040	2.437	2.006
1960	0.077	0.084	0.039	1.958	2.140
1970	0.076	0.070	0.039	1.943	1.780
1980	0.067	0.065	0.039	1.706	1.653
1990	0.066	0.069	0.039	1.676	1.748
2000	0.079	0.065	0.039	2.018	1.663

7.5.2 Dynamic Measures of Competitive Balance

A number of dynamic measures of competitive balance were discussed in Section 7.3 above. Dynamic measures of competitive balance must be calculated over a period of time, since they incorporate both between-season and within-season measures of competitive balance. In this example, past performance in MLB will be analyzed over ten year periods. This choice of time periods is arbitrary, but convenient for the purpose of analysis in this case.

Table 7.11 shows Markov transitional probabilities for the AL and NL over the period 1900-2009. In the example above, and in the Hadley, Ciecka and Krautmann (2005) paper, the two states analyzed were "in the playoffs" and "out of the playoffs." In Table 7.11, the two states are "winning record" and "non-winning record." That is, the transitional probabilities are for teams with a winning percent of more than 0.500 and teams with a winning percent of 0.500 or lower in a season. Again, there are 4 season-to-season transitional probabilities in this Markov state model:

P_{wl} Probability a team with a winning record in t has a non-winning record in $t+1$
P_{ww} Probability a team with a winning record in t has a winning record in $t+1$
P_{lw} Probability a team with a non-winning record in t has a winning record in $t+1$
P_{ll} Probability a team with a non-winning record in t has a non-winning record in $t+1$

P_{ww} measures persistence in winning records from season to season; it reflects the probability that a team with a winning record this season will continue to be successful in the following season. P_{ll} measures persistence in losing records; it reflects the probability that a team with a losing record will continue to be unsuccessful next season. The other two transitional probabilities are measures of changes in state. P_{wl} is a measure of switching from the unsuccessful state to the successful state; it reflects the probability that a losing team improves significantly in the following season. P_{lw} is a measure of switching from the successful state to the unsuccessful state; it reflects the probability that a successful team gets significantly worse in the next season. In leagues with little turnover in standings, P_{ww} and P_{ll} will be large and P_{lw} and P_{wl} will be small.

From Table 7.11, relatively little turnover takes place in MLB. The sum of P_{ww} and P_{ll} is always more than 0.5, and often exceeds 0.7. Most winning teams remain winning teams in the next season and most losing teams remain losing teams in the next season. It appears that P_{ww} declines over

Table 7.11: Markov Transition Probabilities from Winning to Losing in MLB, 1900-2009

Decade	American League				National League			
	P_{ww}	P_{ll}	P_{wl}	P_{lw}	P_{ww}	P_{ll}	P_{wl}	P_{lw}
1900	0.438	0.250	0.203	0.188	0.431	0.403	0.097	0.111
1910	0.350	0.300	0.175	0.175	0.338	0.363	0.150	0.150
1920	0.350	0.375	0.138	0.138	0.438	0.287	0.138	0.138
1930	0.412	0.375	0.100	0.112	0.425	0.313	0.125	0.138
1940	0.375	0.350	0.138	0.138	0.350	0.350	0.162	0.138
1950	0.425	0.375	0.112	0.087	0.325	0.438	0.112	0.125
1960	0.313	0.365	0.146	0.177	0.468	0.277	0.106	0.149
1970	0.379	0.347	0.121	0.153	0.342	0.375	0.150	0.133
1980	0.336	0.314	0.186	0.164	0.300	0.283	0.208	0.208
1990	0.288	0.360	0.180	0.173	0.259	0.326	0.207	0.207
2000	0.371	0.343	0.136	0.150	0.363	0.350	0.138	0.150

time in both leagues. The last decade with a value of P_{ww} over 0.4 was the 1950s in the AL and the 1960s in the NL. It also appears that P_{lw} increased in the NL over time. P_{lw} was larger than 0.150 only once in the first five decades in the NL, but exceeded 0.150 twice, and was equal to 0.150 or close to it, in two additional decades in out of the last six.

The other two dynamic measures of competitive balance are the CBR and the variance decomposition. These two measures of competitive balance address an important limitation of static competitive balance measures like σ_{W2} and σ_{WI} - their inability to reflect relative changes in standings over time. The general approach in both is to partition the variability in competitive balance into within-season and between-season components. Table 7.12 shows these two measures for the two leagues in MLB for decades over the period 1900-2009. Recall that the CBR is related to the variance decomposition, but expresses dynamic competitive balance as a single number, reflecting the amount of within-team variation in winning percentage relative to the within-season variation in winning percentage.

Relatively few patterns in the changes in competitive balance over time can be seen on Table 7.12. The CBR was relatively higher in the first two decades and in the last three decades in both leagues. This suggests that competitive balance first declined and then increased over this 110 year period. The CBR was higher in the NL than in the AL in the last three decades, indicating more competitive balance in the NL. The variance decomposition measures are difficult to interpret. The values are relatively small, as are the changes from year to year.

Note that the dynamic measures of competitive balance tell a different story about changes in competitive balance in MLB than the static measures. σ_{W1}, σ_{W2} and σ_{WI} generally declined, with the exception of the last decade. This decline in variation in winning percentage indicates that competitive balance was improving. However, the dynamic measures do not show a similar downward trend. Taken together, the two results suggest that winning percentages were more tightly bunched in MLB, but that relative turnover in standings did not change much.

Table 7.12: CBR and Variance Decomposition in MLB, 1900-2009

Decade	CBR_{AL}	CBR_{NL}	$var_{time,AL}$	$var_{time,NL}$	$var_{cum,AL}$	$var_{cum,NL}$
1900	0.763	0.710	0.012	0.016	0.016	0.025
1910	0.818	0.832	0.034	0.020	0.012	0.015
1920	0.760	0.568	0.016	0.015	0.004	0.016
1930	0.678	0.632	0.019	0.022	0.009	0.018
1940	0.711	0.689	0.008	0.015	0.008	0.019
1950	0.585	0.689	0.006	0.022	0.007	0.014
1960	0.750	0.657	0.008	0.010	0.013	0.015
1970	0.727	0.693	0.010	0.010	0.007	0.007
1980	0.859	0.918	0.008	0.006	0.010	0.008
1990	0.873	0.886	0.009	0.007	0.023	0.009
2000	0.698	0.811	0.011	0.011	0.007	0.007

7.5.3 Championship Distribution

Winning percentage does not tell the entire story about competitive balance in sports leagues. Team quality also depends on championships won, as well as postseason appearances. And the perceived level of competitive balance in a league also depends on the distribution of postseason appearances and championships. Two methods were discussed above for analyzing the distribution of championships and postseason appearances: the HHI and the Gini Coefficient. Both these measures reflect the distribution of championships, or postseason appearances, across teams in MLB. Table 7.13 shows the HHI for decades in MLB for Division winners, league winners, and World Series champions. Divisional play began in 1969. Before that, the regular season winners of the AL and NL played each other in the World Series. In 1994 the number of divisions expanded from 4 to 6. The World Series was not played in every year in the 1900s. No postseason play took place in 1994.

Note that these two measures of competitive balance have also been applied to winning percentages. Wins are also distributed across teams in sports leagues, and these measures can easily be applied to the distribution of wins.

Recall that the smaller the HHI, the more equal the distribution of championships and postseason appearances, and the larger the HHI, the more concentrated the distribution. The concentration of league championships, shown in the first two columns of Table 7.13, peaked in the 1950s in both leagues and declined thereafter. The concentration of league championships in the AL in mid-century can be attributed entirely to the New York Yankees, who won the AL fifteen times in eighteen years over the period 1947-1964. The 0.600 HHI for AL championships in the 1950s represents the Yankees winning the AL pennant in every year except 1954 and 1959, 8 of the 10 seasons in that decade. The NL had no such dynasty, and the HHI for league championships in the NL is generally lower. The HHI for World Series championships also peaks in the 1950s, when the Yankees won five World Series (1951, 1952, 1953, 1956, and 1958). With the exception of the mid-century Yankees dynasty, the HHI for World Series championships has been relatively low, suggesting relatively equal distribution of championships.

The Division Championship HHIs are generally higher than the LCS and Series HHIs. However, the number of teams in each division is smaller, so some concentration is to be expected. Also note

Table 7.13: LCS and World Series HHI, 1900-2009

| Decade | Won LCS | | Won WS | Won AL Division | | | Won NL Division | | |
	AL	NL		East	West	Central	East	West	Central
1900	0.259	0.300	0.222	—	—	—	—	—	—
1910	0.360	0.240	0.280	—	—	—	—	—	—
1920	0.420	0.260	0.180	—	—	—	—	—	—
1930	0.340	0.280	0.320	—	—	—	—	—	—
1940	0.320	0.280	0.280	—	—	—	—	—	—
1950	0.660	0.340	0.420	—	—	—	—	—	—
1960	0.300	0.220	0.160	—	—	—	—	—	—
1970	0.280	0.300	0.220	0.36	0.36	—	0.46	0.46	—
1980	0.140	0.200	0.120	0.17	0.26	—	0.22	0.26	—
1990	0.235	0.210	0.210	0.28	0.24	1.00	0.43	0.21	0.44
2000	0.240	0.140	0.140	0.66	0.42	0.38	0.46	0.26	0.46

that the three division set-up does not encompass the entire decade of the 1990s, which makes it difficult to compare to full decade measures of championship distribution.

7.6 Example: Competitive Balance, Drafts and Free Agency

This chapter introduces a number of measures of competitive balance. These measures of competitive balance can be used to compare league outcomes over time. In this section, the various measures of competitive balance are used to assess the effects of two policy changes, the imposition of an amateur entry draft in 1965 and the awarding of free agency to players with six years of major league experience in 1976. Since these two changes affect the distribution of talent across teams, they could have also changed competitive balance in the league. In order to assess the effect of the changes on competitive balance, the competitive balance measures developed in this chapter can be calculated over three periods (before the draft, between the draft and the beginning of free agency,a nd after free agency) and compared to determine if these changes had any effect on competitive balance.

7.6.1 The MLB Draft

The first MLB draft was held in 1965. Until then, new players entering the league were allowed to negotiate with any and all teams in the league for a contract prior to signing. After the draft was implemented, a player selected in the draft could only negotiate with the team that had drafted him. The purpose of the draft was to prevent teams playing in markets with a large revenue generation potential from signing al the top players coming into the league. The intent of the draft was to equally spread out incoming talent to promote competitive balance.

The first # 1 draft pick selected in the MLB draft was Rick Monday, an outfielder who played for Arizona State University. Monday was drafted first in the 1965 entry draft by the Kansas City Athletics (now the Oakland Athletics). Monday's debut took place on September 3 1966. Monday went on to play 19 seasons in MLB, retiring in 1984 at age 38. He had a 0.264/0.361/0.443/0.804

career ba/obp/slg/ops in 7162 plate appearances. He played for the Athletics, Cubs and Dodgers and was on the All-Star team in 1968 and 1978.

Clearly, the draft changed the allocation of players across teams in MLB. The two-team model developed in Chapter 4 predicts that unequal distribution of talent across teams leads to unequal outcomes in terms of winning percents. The imposition of the draft could potentially change competitive balance in the league.

7.6.2 Free Agency in MLB

From shortly after the beginning of professional baseball in North America until the mid 1970s, professional baseball players had no choice in the terms of their employment. All contracts between players and teams contained a clause, called *the Reserve Clause* that bound players to their team in perpetuity. This clause simply stated that the team reserved the right to renew every players' contract for the next year at the current salary or a higher salary. The Reserve Clause limited the movement of talent between teams to trades and the sale of contracts for cash. It also reduced salaries, because a team could pay a player any salary it wanted, and the player had no recourse except to accept the salary or not play professional baseball.

The Reserve Clause was under almost continuous legal attack by players. The first significant challenge came in the late 1960s when pitcher Curt Flood was traded from StLouis to Philadelphia nd challenged the trade by filing suit in 1970. The case went to the US Supreme Court, who in 1972 decided in favor of MLB. But the Reserve Clause was beginning to crumble. The Reserve Clause only lasted until 1975. In 1974, and arbitrator ruled that Oakland Athletics pitcher Jim "Catfish" Hunter was a free agent and could sign with any team at the end of the 1974 season because the A's owner, Charlie Finley had violated a clause in Hunter's contract by not making payments to Hunter's retirement fund. Hunter became a free agent and signed with the Yankees. The next season, two pitchers, Andy Messersmith and Dave McNally, who let their contracts expire at the end of the 1974 season played the 1975 season with no contract and sought arbitration when their teams invoked the Reserve Clause. The 1976 Collective Bargaining Agreement between the players and league allowed players to become free agents after 6 years of service; players with less than 6 years of major league service are still covered by the reserve clause. This change also altered the distribution of talent across teams in MLB, which could potentially change competitive balance.

7.6.3 Analysis of Competitive Balance

This analysis of competitive balance will focus on measuring competitive balance in three periods

1. The period from 1950 to 1964, the year before the draft began in MLB. Tis period begins in 1950, and not before, because of the integration of baseball that started in the mid 1940s. Black players began signing with MLB teams in 1947, but many teams were slow to sign black players. By 1950 most teams had integrated, and the big stars from the Negro Leagues were playing in MLB.

2. The period from 1965 to 1975. During this period, the draft was in place, but players had not gained free agency. Any changes in competitive balance in this period, compared to the earlier period, can be attributed to the draft and to other unmeasured factors. By assumption, the other factors will have a random effect on competitive balance, and the draft will have a systematic and detectible effect on competitive balance.

3. The period from 1976 to 1990. During this period, the draft and free agency were in place. The analysis stops at 1990 to avoid confusing the effects of free agency on competitive balance with the expansion and division re-alignment that took place later in the 1990s.

Figure 7.4 shows the basic level in each league in MLB over the three periods, as shown by σ_{W1} the measure of single season variation in winning percentage. The twi vertical red lines are drawn at 1964 and 1975, the two season when the specific changes took place in MLB. These two lines define the three periods of analysis in this example. In general, it appears that σ_{W1} declined throughout the three periods, suggesting that the imposition of the draft and the granting of free agency improved competitive balance. However, the other measures of competitive balance developed in Chapter 5 may tell a different story.

Figure 7.4: AL and NL σ_{W1} in Three Periods

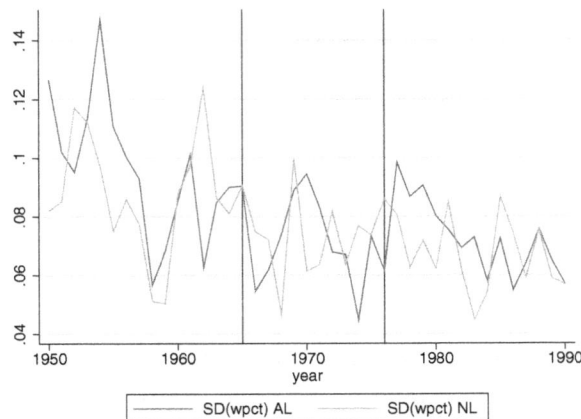

Table 7.14 shows the value of the two static measures of competitive balance, σ_{W2} and σ_{WI}, calculated over the three periods. σ_{W2} in the AL declined from 0.092 over the period 1950-1964 to 0.071 in the period 1965-1975. This suggests that competitive balance improved in the AL after the draft was instituted, in that the variation in winning percentage was lower in the period after the draft began than in the period before it was instituted. σ_{W2} in the NL also declined from 0.085 over the period 1950-1964 to 0.072 in the period 1965-1975. This also suggests that competitive balance improved in the AL after the draft was instituted. As would be expected, σ_{WI} also declined in both leagues after the draft began. The evidence on Table 7.14 suggests that the imposition of the draft in MLB in 1965 improved competitive balance in both leagues. Recall that he draft awards better incoming players to teams with worse players, and that under the reserve clause, those players were obligated to play for the team that drafted them forever. This mechanism for reallocating talent should improve competitive balance.

σ_{W2} and σ_{WI} in the AL were unchanged in the period 1976-1990 compared to in the period 1965-1975. The granting of free agency to players with more than six years of major league experience appears to have had no effect on the distribution of winning percentages in the AL. σ_{W2} and σ_{WI} in the NL both declined in the period 1976-1990 compared to in the period 1965-1975. σ_{W2} declined from 0.072 in the period 1965-1975 to 0.066 in the period 1976-1990. σ_{WI} also declined from 1.821 to 1.692.

Recall that these static measures of competitive balance do not reflect relative changes in standings over time. If the effect of either the draft or free agency on competitive balance affected

Table 7.14: σ_{W2} and σ_{WI} in MLB over Three Periods

Period	$\sigma_{W2,AL}$	$\sigma_{W2,NL}$	$\sigma_{WI,AL}$	$\sigma_{WI,NL}$
1950-1964	0.092	0.085	2.286	2.108
1965-1975	0.071	0.072	1.816	1.821
1976-1990	0.071	0.066	1.816	1.692

relative standings, then the static measures will not reflect these changes. Table 7.15 shows the dynamic measures of competitive balance in MLB for these three periods.

Table 7.15: Dynamic Measures of Competitive Balance in MLB over Three Periods

Period	American League				National League			
	P_{ww}	P_{ll}	P_{wl}	P_{lw}	P_{ww}	P_{ll}	P_{wl}	P_{lw}
1950-1964	0.407	0.398	0.110	0.119	0.448	0.371	0.112	0.112
1965-1975	0.328	0.344	0.164	0.164	0.369	0.328	0.148	0.156
1976-1990	0.359	0.320	0.160	0.160	0.300	0.311	0.194	0.194

Period	CBR_{AL}	CBR_{NL}	$var_{t,AL}$	$var_{c,AL}$	$var_{t,NL}$	$var_{c,NL}$
1950-1964	0.643	0.682	0.008	0.022	0.009	0.015
1965-1975	0.800	0.739	0.008	0.009	0.007	0.010
1976-1990	0.860	0.910	0.010	0.010	0.010	0.008

The top panel of Table 7.15 shows the Markov transition probabilities between the winning state (having a record over 0.500) and the not winning state (having a record of 0.500 or lower) for the three periods. In the American League, the probability of remaining in the winning state fell after the imposition of the draft, compared to before. Over the period 1950-1964, an AL team with a winning record in one season had a 40.4% chance of having a winning record in the next season; an AL team with a losing record in one season had a 39.8% chance of having a losing record in the next season. Over the period 1950-1964, an NL team with a winning record in one season had a 44.8% chance of having a winning record in the next season; an NL team with a losing record in one season had a 37.1% chance of having a losing record in the next season. After the draft began, the probability that an AL team with a winning record this season had a winning record next season dropped to 32.8%; the probability that an NL team with a winning record this season had a winning record next season dropped to 36.9%. There was more relative turnover after the draft was put in place in both leagues. Free agency had an ambiguous effect on the Markov transition probabilities. P_{ww} went up slightly in the AL over the period 1976-1990, compared to 1965-1975; P_{ww} declined from 36.9% to 30.0% in the NL over the period 1976-1990, compared to 1965-1975. These patterns suggest that the change in the distribution of talent in the AL was different from in the NL.

The bottom panel of Table 7.15 shows the CBR and variance decomposition measures for these three periods. The CBR and variance decomposition measures tell a similar story. The *CBR* went up in the AL and the NL after the draft began, indicating that the within-team variation in competitive balance increased relative to the between-team variation. The CBR also increased in both leagues after players were granted free agency, suggesting that competitive balance increased in the period 1976-1990 compared to the 1965-1974 period.

7.7   A League Done in by Competitive Imbalance

Professional sports leagues often claim that competitive balance must be preserved because the league's economic viability depends on it. The claim that a professional sports league might fold due to competitive imbalance might seem far-fetched. After all, the "big four" leagues all give the impression that they exhibit some degree of long run competitive imbalance and remain profitable and stable. However, a North American professional football league folded due to competitive imbalance within the lifetime of your grandparents. The All-American Football Conference (AAFC) was formed just after World War II as a rival league to the National Football League. The AAFC started play in 1946 with 7 teams, and at the time was regarded as a serious rival to the NFL (which was founded in 1920), as the AAFC attracted many of the best players of the era, operated an entry draft that competed with the NFL's draft and had teams in most major markets.

The AAFC was founded by Arch Ward, the sports editor of a major newspaper, the Chicago *Tribune*, in 1944. The fact that the league was founded by the sports editor of a major newspaper was not unlike having a national broadcast contract in the television era, as Ward ensured that the AAFC would have widespread media attention which generated demand for the league's product. Ward, a sports industry innovator, also invented the MLB All-Star game as a promotional event to increase demand. Wealthy individuals owned AAFC franchises, in many cases people who had unsuccessfully attempted to purchase NFL franchises in the past. The AAFC team owners were, on average, wealthier than the NFL owners at that time, which also gave the AAFC an advantage as a rival league. The first AAFC game, played between Cleveland and Miami on 6 September 1946, drew a then pro football record crowd of 60,000. The Miami Seahawks had two home games postponed by hurricanes, never drew any further substantial crowds, and were eliminated from the league after one season.

Table 7.16: All-American Football Conference

Team	1946	1947	1948	1949	Overall
Baltimore Colts		0.154	0.500	0.083	0.250
Brooklyn Dodgers	0.250	0.231	0.143		0.200
Brooklyn-New York Yankees				0.667	0.667
Buffalo Bisons/Bills	0.250	0.667	0.500	0.500	0.462
Chicago Rockets/Hornets	0.455	0.071	0.071	0.333	0.216
Cleveland Browns	0.857	0.923	1.000	0.900	0.929
Los Angeles Dons	0.583	0.500	0.500	0.333	0.481
Miami Seahawks	0.214				0.214
New York Yankees	0.769	0.846	0.429		0.643
San Francisco 49ers	0.643	0.667	0.857	0.750	0.722

The problem with the AAFC was that it had poor competitive balance. The Cleveland Browns, the same franchise that played in the NFL until moving to Baltimore in 1999, dominated the league, winning every league championship. Table 7.16 shows the league members and league outcomes for each of the four seasons that the AAFC was in operation. The Browns won nearly all their games in every season, and won all four AAFC championships. The other teams in the league were never competitive with the Browns. Total attendance in the 1948 season was almost 15% lower than total attendance in the 1947 season and game attendance fell throughout the 1949 season, as it became clear that the Browns would again dominate. Total league attendance for the 1949 season was 30% lower than in 948. The league folded after the 1949 season, and the Browns, the San Francisco 49ers, and the Baltimore Colts (interestingly **not** the same NFL franchise that moved from Baltimore to Indianapolis in 1984), were all accepted into the NFL in the 1950 season. The rest of the teams folded. Notably, the AAFC broke the color line before the NFL, and even before MLB integrated (Jackie Robinson played his first MLB game in 1947). The Browns had two black players on their opening day roster in 1946.

7.8 Summary

Competitive balance is an important outcome in professional sports leagues. Leagues clearly pay attention to the level of competitive balance balance, and often enact policies intended to promote competitive balance. Despite the importance of competitive balance, measuring and assessing competitive balance is difficult, and sports economists continue to struggle to develop a good measure of competitive balance.

All measures of competitive balance are based on measures of the distribution of wins or championships in sports leagues. Static measures of competitive balance, like σ_{W1}, σ_{W2} and σ_{WI}, reflect the distribution of wins in a sports league, but do not reflect relative changes in the standings of teams. Dynamic measures of competitive balance, like the CBR, the variance decomposition, and the Markov transitional probability, reflect relative changes in standings, but may not adequately capture the distribution of wins. Measures of championship distribution do not reflect the outcome of regular season games, the majority of games played in sports leagues.

Competitive balance changes over time in sports leagues. The two-team model from Chapter 5 predicts that competitive imbalance will exist in leagues where teams pay in markets with different revenue generation. The UOH provides a rationale for leagues to enact policies that enhance competitive balance, since increased in competitive balance should lead to greater profits.

Readings and References

Eckard, W. (1998). The NCAA Cartel and Competitive Balance in College Football. *Review of Industrial Organization*, 13(3): 347-369.

Fort, R. & Quirk, J (1995). Cross-subsidization, Incentives, and Outcomes in Professional Team Sports. *Journal of Economic Literature*, 33: 1265-1299.

Hadley, L., Ciecka, J. and A. Krautmann (2005). Competitive Balance in the Aftermath of the 1994 Players' Strike. *Journal of Sports Economics*, 6(4): 379-389.

Humphreys, B. (2002). Alternative Measures of Competitive Balance in Sports Leagues. *Journal of Sports Economics*, 3(2): 133-148.

Review Questions

1. Suppose that the standard deviation of winning percentage for a sports league over twenty seasons was as follows:

Period	σ_{W2}
Season 1-5	0.050
Season 6-10	0.085
Season 11-15	0.091
Season 16-20	0.095

Discuss how the level of competitive balance changed in the league over this period.

2. Now suppose that the Markov transition probabilities over this period from state S_w (team has a winning record) to state S_l (team has a non-winning record) were as follows:

Period	P_{ww}	P_{ll}	P_{wl}	P_{lw}
Season 1-5	0.40	0.40	0.10	0.10
Season 6-10	0.30	0.30	0.20	0.20
Season 11-15	0.25	0.25	0.25	0.25
Season 16-20	0.20	0.20	0.30	0.30

   (a) Based on these Markov transition probabilities, what happened to changes in relative standings in this league over the 20 season period shown?

   (b) How does this change your assessment of the level of competitive balance in this league from question #1? Explain your answer.

3. Fill in the table below and calculate σ_{W1}

	W-L	$WPCT_i$	$WPCT_i - \overline{WPCT}$	DEV^2
Team A	7-1			
Team B	6-2			
Team C	4-4			
Team D	3-5			
Team E	0-8			
	Average =		Sum =	

$\sigma_{W1} =$

4. Consider the following outcomes in a professional sports league

Period	σ_{WI}	CBR
Season 1-10	1.88	0.66
Season 11-19	1.85	0.75
Season 20-29	1.86	0.81

(a) Define σ_{WI} and explain how it measures competitive balance in a sports league

(b) Define the CBR and explain how it measures competitive balance in a sports league

(c) Discuss the level of competitive balance in this league based on σ_{WI}

(d) Discuss the level of competitive balance in this league based on the CBR

(e) Suppose that the league enacted a salary cap in season 30. What would you expect would happen to σ_{WI} and the CBR over the next ten seasons?

Chapter 8

Stadiums, Arenas, and Subsidies

Chapter Objectives

- Understand the amount of public subsidization of sport facility construction that has taken place in North America in the past

- Understand the problems with the claims about the economic impact of new sports facilities made by proponents of these subsidies

- Explain the difference between tangible and intangible economic impact

- Understand the existing evidence about the economic impact of professional sports on the economy

- Understand why government continues to subsidize the construction of sports facilities in North America

8.1 Introduction

A boom in new sports facility construction occurred in North America from the early 1990s until the mid 2000s. 53 new stadiums and arenas opened in North America in the 1990s, while only 78 new facilities opened in the previous forty years. In economic terms, a new stadium or arena represents a form of capital investment for profit maximizing professional sports teams Like all capital investment projects, the cost of building fiscal structures is large; new stadiums and arenas have large footprints and are often located downtown, further increasing the costs. Unlike capital investment projects undertaken by other profit maximizing firms, new sports facility construction projects tend to be heavily subsidized by local taxpayers. Taxpayers pay for about 75% of the cost of building a new stadium or arena in North America, despite the fact that the economic activities that take place inside these facilities benefit billionaire team owners and millionaire athletes.

Figure 8.1 shows the timing and cost of new stadium and arena openings over the period 1970-2010. On this figure, an **A** represents a new arena opening in that year and an **S** indicates a new stadium. Total construction costs are in millions of real 2010 dollars. The stadium and arena construction boom stands out on Figure 8.1. A number of new facilities opened in the mid

---

[1] Portions of this chapter draw from Dennis Coates and Brad R. Humphreys (2003), "Professional Sports Facilities, Franchises and Urban Economic Development," *Public Finance and Management*, vol. 3, no. 3, pp. 335-357 and Dennis Coates and Brad R. Humphreys (2000), "The Stadium Gambit and Local Economic Development," *Regulation*, vol. 23, no. 2, pp. 15-20.

1970s, including multi-purpose facilities like Three Rivers Stadium in Pittsburgh and Riverfront Stadium in Cincinnati. New facility openings thin out considerably in the 1980s and then increase dramatically in the early 1990s. This boom was accompanied by an increase in the inflation adjusted cost of new facilities; the average cost of a new facility opened in the 1990s was more than 25% larger than the cost of a new facility opened in the 1980s.

Figure 8.1: Total Facility Construction Cost, 2010 Dollars

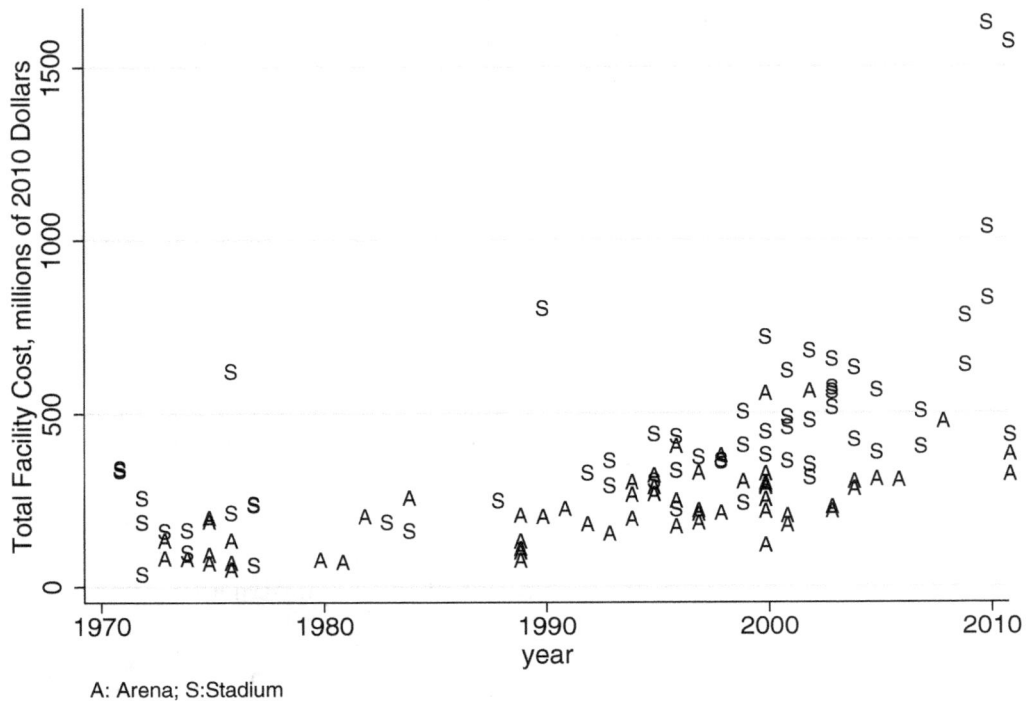

A: Arena; S:Stadium

The new facilities opened in the 1990s and 2000s cost more than those opened in the 1970s and 1980s. Figure 8.1 also shows a clear upward trend in total costs beginning in about 1990. Not only did facility cost increase in inflation adjusted terms during the boom, but total construction costs continued to spiral up. The three exceptionally expensive new stadiums at the upper right corner of Figure 8.1, home to the Dallas Cowboys (2009, $1.015 billion), New York Yankees (2009, $1.59 billion) and New York Giants/Jets (2010, $1.57 billion) are by far the most expensive stadiums ever built in North America. The two earlier outliers are SkyDome in Toronto, which cost $800 million when opened in 1990 ($440 million in current dollars), and the Louisiana SuperDome, which cost $620million when opened in 1976 ($163 million in current dollars).

New sports facility costs increased and taxpayers footed much of the bill. Figure 8.2 shows the share of total facility construction costs paid for by public funds over the period 1970-2010. At the left of this figure, teams pay all of the construction costs for new facilities; this occurs in about 10% of the cases. At the right of this figure, taxpayers pay all of the construction costs; this occurred in about 40% of the cases, and in another 15% of the cases taxpayers paid more than 80% of the construction costs. In a majority of the cases, taxpayers paid for more than half of the cost of building new sports facilities. Relatively few of the outcomes summarized in Figure 8.2 involved cost sharing, where both the team and local taxpayers equally share in paying for new sports facilities.

Figure 8.2: Public Share of Facility Construction Cost

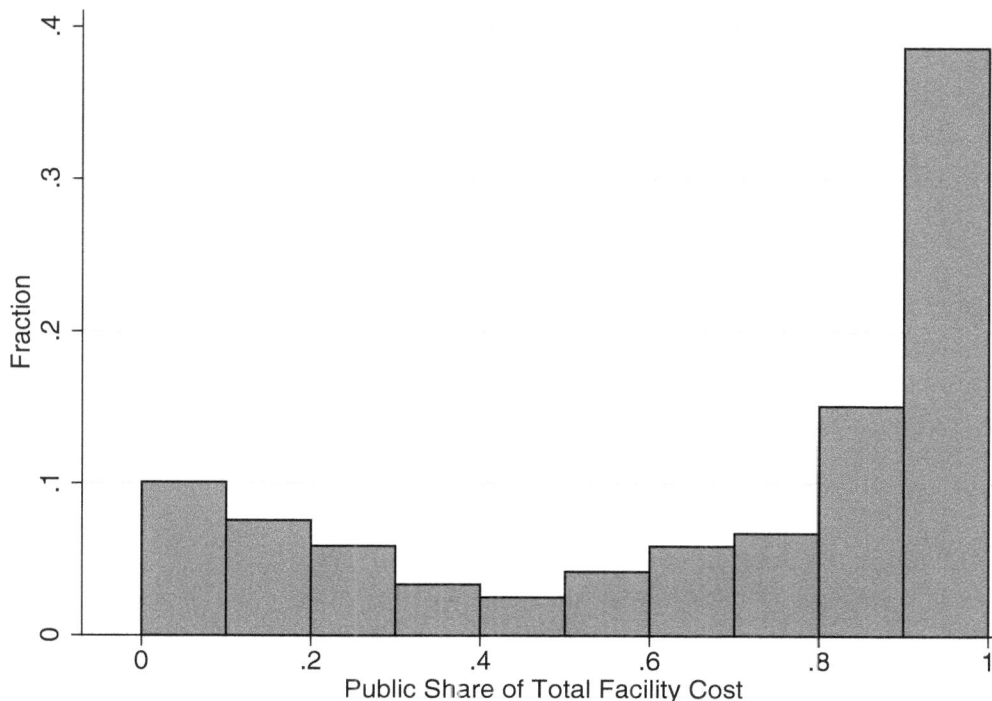

The fact that most new stadium and arena construction projects involve substantial public subsidization represents an interesting puzzle. Subsidies for new sports facilities arise from negotiation between teams and local government. Standard economic bargaining models like the Nash bargaining model predict that the likely outcome of any bargaining where both parties are fully informed is a 50-50 split. For example, if you and a friend bargain over who gets how much of a pizza, absent any significant distortions, the most likely outcome from that bargaining process is that you split it down the middle. Clearly, the standard 50-50 split from a Nash bargaining model does not reflect the outcome of bargaining between teams and local officials over construction costs for new sports facilities. Instead, teams win the vast majority of these negotiations, and local officials pay up with large subsidies.

Why does bargaining between teams and local officials over subsidies for new sports facility construction projects favor teams so heavily? A number of reasons can readily be identified. First, teams have important outside options in the bargaining process. As discussed in Chapter 5, league franchise agreements include territorial exclusivity and also keep new teams from forming in cities that are large enough to support a successful team. For example, no NFL team has played in Los Angeles since 1994, despite the fact that LA could clearly support one or more NFL teams. Other cities prematurely build arenas before attracting teams; Kansas City has an arena large enough to host an NBA or NHL team, but no team plays in that facility and the metro area would likely support a team.

These situations generate outside options for teams to exploit when negotiating with local officials over subsidies for new sports facility construction projects. Minnesota Vikings owner Ziggy Wilf threatened to move the Vikings to Los Angeles while negotiating over a subsidy for a new football stadium in Minneapolis and received a substantial subsidy from the State of Minnesota and the city of Minneapolis. Many other professional sports team owners have threatened to move in order to gain the upper hand in negotiations over subsidies for new facility construction projects.

Second, fans, and local decision makers have loss aversion when faced with the potential departure of the local team. As the reference-dependent preference model developed in Chapter 6 showed, loss aversion can have an important influence on economic decisions made by sports fans; local elected officials will make decisions that reflect the presence of this loss aversion. The endowment effect implies that fans will value the presence of a team more than they would if offered a chance to attract an expansion or relocated team that they had no experience with. Team owners clearly recognize that the presence of loss averse fans will allow them to extract even larger subsidies from local decision makers than they could get based only on their outside options.

Third, team owners, and other parties interested in new sports facilities like local construction companies, land developers, and media outlets – who generate additional viewers and readers by covering the local team – often claim that the presence of the team, and the construction of a new facility, will generate important tangible economic benefits in the local economy during the construction process, and far into the future. Additionally, subsidy proponents often claim that a new facility can be an important local economic development tool, generating a cornucopia of tangible economic benefits like new jobs, higher earnings, increased tax revenues, better and stronger teeth, and more attractive members of the opposite sex.

On the surface, sports facilities and franchises appear to be prime candidates for economic development projects. Unlike abstract economic development tools like tax credits or empowerment zones, sports facilities - stadiums, arenas, football pitches, etc. - are highly visible structures that attract large crowds of spectators on a regular basis. Sporting events are wildly popular throughout the world and widely understood and appreciated by residents of cities. In North America, new sports facilities are frequently touted as important drivers of economic growth and components of urban redevelopment initiatives.

However, a critical examination of the evidence about the economic impact of professional sports franchises, and the mechanisms for financing the construction of new sports facilities, reveals a different picture. In North America, sports franchises frequently use their monopoly power to extract rents from state and local government in the form of subsidies for the construction and operation of stadiums and arenas. A sports team owner will typically declare an existing facility unsuitable. The existing facility is too old, or too small, or lacks luxury boxes and premium seating to generate enough revenues to field a competitive team. The team owner reminds the government and business community that many other cities around North America would like to have a professional team, and many of those cities would be more than willing build a new facility if the team were to move there. Cities all over North America, desperate for a professional sports team, gear up to convince the team owner to move to their city. Often, the promise of a new facility and a sweetheart lease convinces the owner to stay, but some franchises move. For example, the SuperSonics of the NBA left Seattle in 2008 for Oklahoma City under exactly these circumstances. Regardless of whether the team stays or goes, taxpayers typically pay for a new facility, or renovations to an existing facility, as well as infrastructure upgrades like public transit access to make the new facility more attractive.

8.2 Trends in Stadium and Arena Financing

Public subsidies for stadium and arena construction increased significantly over time. Table 8.1 summarizes the construction of new professional sports facilities in the National Football League,

Table 8.1: NFL, NBA, MLB and NHL Stadium and Arena Construction, Real 2006 Dollars

All Facilities	1950s	1960s	1970s	1980s	1990s	2000s
Facilities Opened	10	27	27	14	53	36
Average Cost	43	148	237	195	258	428
Average Public Cost	29	90	194	116	152	248
Average Public Share of Costs	70%	79%	89%	65%	58%	63%
Stadiums						
Facilities Opened	6	13	16	4	22	27
Average Cost	48	137	328	320	298	475
Average Public Cost	31	114	260	149	233	268
Average Public Share of Costs	67%	87%	87%	46%	79%	59%
Arenas						
Facilities Opened	4	14	11	10	31	9
Average Cost	45	162	105	139	228	274
Average Public Cost	30	57	98	102	93	155
Average Public Share of Costs	67%	71%	91%	72%	43%	68%

National Basketball Association, Major League Baseball and the National Hockey League in North America over the past 60 years and the public subsidies that went to these construction projects. In the 1950s, 10 new facilities opened and the average public cost per facility was 29 million dollars expressed in 2006 dollars. In the 2000s, 36 new facilities opened and the average public cost per facility was $248 million.

Clearly, an enormous boom in publicly financed sports stadium construction took place in North America in the 1990s and 2000s. This boom is sometimes traced to the opening of Oriole Park at Camden Yards, the home of the Baltimore Orioles Major League Baseball (MLB) franchise, which opened in 1992. Unlike many of the new suburban sports facilities built earlier in distant suburbs, Oriole Park is located in Baltimore's Central Business District and figured prominently in the redevelopment plan for the downtown area of Baltimore. Oriole Park was widely praised on aesthetic and economic grounds and this model was soon widely copied by many other cities. The land acquisition and stadium construction costs for Oriole Park were almost entirely borne by taxpayers, another feature that was widely copied by other cities.

Table 8.1 contains information about the costs and extent of public subsidization for all of the new professional football, basketball, and baseball facilities opened in the United States in the past fifty years. This table shows the total costs of the new facility, including land acquisition costs, and the total amount of public money spent on these facilities in constant 2006 dollars. A number of additional facilities are already under construction or in the planning stages in North America. With a few notable exceptions, the majority of the financing from these new sports facilities came from public, not private, sources. Note that some of these facilities are home to both a professional basketball franchise in the National Basketball Association and a professional hockey franchise in the National Hockey League. There has also been a boom in the construction of new minor league professional baseball facilities over the past decade, but Table 8.1 does not include information on facilities that host minor league baseball, professional soccer, or other professional sports franchises in the US and Canada. From Table 8.1, on average, public financing accounted for between two thirds and three quarters of the cost of these new facility construction projects, and the average amount of public spending was $208 million.

The effective useful economic life of a sports facility appears to be roughly 30 years, a figure consistent with the average age of the stadiums replaced in the recent past in North America. There are currently 90 professional football, basketball and baseball franchises in North America and very few multi-purpose stadiums, suggesting an average of three facilities replaced a year in steady-state equilibrium. Some additional expansion or relocation is possible in all sports leagues. Many of the new sports facilities built in the past ten years contain features like extensive sections of premium seats and luxury boxes, swimming pools, restaurants, hotels, and theme-park like attractions that make sports facilities into entertainment centers. These features have the potential to generate revenues well above the familiar ticket, food, drink and parking revenue streams generated by sports facilities built ten or twenty years ago and could start a "stadium arms race" that would reduce the effective economic lifetime of sports facilities, leading to even more new facility construction in the future. Even without a decrease in the effective economic lifetime of sports facilities, there will continue to be a significant amount of sports facility construction in the future.

From the 1950s until 2010, 167 new stadiums and arenas were built, and $36.4 billion dollars was spent on facility construction in North America. $23.073 billion dollars in public subsidies were provided for the construction of these new sports facilities. On average, 71% of the cost of constructing these 167 new facilities came in the form of public subsidies.

During the time of increased public participation in sport facility construction, franchise values have also increased dramatically. In their book *Pay Dirt: The Business of Professional Team Sports*, James P. Quirk and Rodney D. Fort report that, for teams sold in the 1970s and sold again during the 1980s, franchise values rose at an annual rate of 12.5 percent in MLB, 12.3 percent in the NBA, and 11.5 percent in the NFL. For teams sold twice during the 1980s, the rates of increase were 23.5, 50.2, and 19.2 percent, respectively. The increase franchise values has shown no sign of slowing. For example, the expansion fees charged for new teams in the 1990s were large and increased rapidly. In 1992 the Colorado Rockies and Florida Marlins paid $95 million in expansion fees to join Major League Baseball. In 1997, the Arizona Diamondbacks and Tampa Bay Devil Rays paid $130 million. That was a 37 percent increase in five years, or about 7.4 percent per year. To (re-) join the NFL, the Cleveland Browns paid an expansion fee of $530 million in 1998; the newly awarded franchise in Houston agreed to a $700 million fee, a 32 percent increase in just one year. But the most extreme case of expansion price inflation occurred in the NBA. The expansion fee paid by the franchises in Minneapolis and Orlando in 1989 was $32.5 million; for Toronto and Vancouver, which joined the NBA in 1995, the fee was $ 125 million, a 285 percent increase in just six years, or an increase of 47 percent per year.

The owners of franchises in monopoly professional sports leagues have used the real or implied threat of moving to another city to persuade state and local officials and politicians to provide them with lavish new stadiums and arenas at little or no cost to the team owner. The owners appear to have profited handsomely, as suggested by the triple-digit increases in franchise values. In return, taxpayers receive nonpecuniary benefits in the form of increased civic pride and image, as well as other unmeasured consumption benefits associated with living in a city with professional sports teams.

In general, taxpayers are told that new teams, stadiums, and arenas create jobs and raise tax revenues and income in their city. The primary justification put forward for public subsidies for new sports facility construction projects is the tangible economic benefits that new facilities are forecast to generate in the local economy. The secondary justification is that new sports facilities can revitalize downtown neighborhoods, generating spillover benefits in the form of new retail establishments, bars, and restaurants and providing a vital urban core in cities. Both justifications are examined in detail below. The evidence does not support the claim that new sports facilities generate substantial tangible economic benefits.

8.3 Claimed Economic Benefits

The proponents of new sports facilities are quick to point out the forecasted tangible economic benefits that will be generated by a proposed new facility in a city. Cities across North America have struggled to attract or keep professional sports teams in recent years, and the idea that a team brings with it large economic benefits invariably arises in this process. Part of this process involves the commissioning of economic impact studies that purport to show just how much tangible economic benefit the city or region will realize. In the 1970s, proponents of the half-billion dollar Skydome in Toronto claimed that this new facility would generate $450 million in economic impact (in Canadian dollars) in the first year of operation and create some 17,000 new jobs in the greater Toronto area. In the 1990s, prospective NFL team owners in Jacksonville, Florida, claimed that a new NFL franchise would generate $340 million in new income in the city and create 3,000 new jobs. The Baltimore *Sun* reported in April 1999 that a new study supported tearing down the existing 36-year-old downtown Baltimore Arena and replacing it with a new $200 million dollar facility. This investment, the study claimed, would increase city tax revenues by $3.8 million and state tax revenues by $6.3 million. In addition, the new arena would reportedly generate up to $100 million in new income for the citizens of the city of Baltimore, despite the fact that it would have no "anchor" sports franchise in the NBA or NHL.

Contrast these forecasts with information from the 2007 edition of the *County and City Data Book*. In 2000, the State of Maryland collected $9.1 billion in taxes and the City of Baltimore collected $806 million. In Baltimore, the tax increase from the replacement arena would be, if the reported forecasts were correct, only about 0.47 % of 2000 city tax collections. For the state, the new tax collections represent less than one-tenth of one percent of 2000 tax collections. In 2000, personal income in the State of Maryland was $181 billion and $20 billion in Baltimore. Projected earnings from the new arena were about 0.15 percent of state personal income in 2000 and about 0.72 percent of Baltimore's total personal income in that year. Although the absolute numbers forecasted seem large and impressive, they are actually small compared to existing tax revenues and local economic activity, even if the proponents' estimates are accurate.

Such claims of tangible economic benefits are representative of others made across North America during the new stadium and arena construction boom of the 1990s and 2000s. The "evidence" supporting these claimed tangible economic benefits takes the form of economic impact studies carried out by consultants hired by the supporters of the construction projects. These economic impact reports are forecasts based on regional input-output models. They have a number of well-known flaws, and are seldom used in other settings.

8.3.1 Flaws in Impact Studies

Many reasons exist to doubt the accuracy of the forecasted tangible economic benefits claimed by economic impact studies justifying subsidies for new sports facility construction projects. Impact studies rely on input-output models of the local or regional economy in which the team and its new facility will operate; the estimates of new economic activity are prospective. Economic impact studies are economic forecasts that lack the usual context of economic forecasts like margins of error or confidence intervals. These studies ask the question: what will happen if a new facility appears in the local economy? The results of these studies reflect the desires of those who commission them, and advocates of new facility subsidies typically produce impact studies that find large tangible economic impacts, from building a new facility. Common problems with economic impact studies include . . .

Mythical Multipliers   The methodology used by economic impact studies has been criticized on a variety of grounds. All impact studies use multipliers to estimate the effect of each dollar spent directly on sports in the wider local economy. A multiplier greater than one means that each dollar spent in the new facility generated more than one dollar of additional economic activity in the surrounding economy. Many economic impact studies use multipliers of two, or larger, to forecast the economic impact of a new facility. Critics argue that, at best, the multipliers used in prospective impact studies overstate the contribution that professional sports make to an areas economy because they fail to differentiate between net and gross spending, the effects of taxes, and leakages of spending outside the area of economic impact. When computing the benefits of spending on a sports facility, the appropriate focus is on net benefits generated. That is, on benefits that would not have occurred in the absence of the new facility. Impact studies rarely focus on net benefits. One could think of this problem as a substitution effect. Specifically, because of the existence of new sport-related activities at the new facility, other types of local consumer spending declines as people substitute spending on movies, plays, and other entertainment activities for spending in and around the new sports facility. If the sports facility simply displaces dollar-for-dollar spending that would have occurred otherwise somewhere else in the city at some other time, then there are no net benefits generated by the new facility. This implies a multiplier of zero. To count spending on sport-related activities as new economic benefits overstates the economic impact of the new facility. A key issue for getting an accurate estimate of the benefits from a new sports facility is determining how much of the facility-related spending represents substitution away from entertainment spending that would have taken place even if a new facility was not built and how much of the facility-related spending is actually a net gain in local entertainment spending. Most impact studies assume that all spending in a new sports facility is new spending that would not have taken place absent the new facility.

A key related question to the size of substitution effects, and to the appropriate size of sports spending multipliers, is the size of the relevant geographic area impacted by the new facility. A stadium or arena will have more economic impact on a very narrowly defined impact area than on a large metropolitan or regional area. The reason for this is that the more narrowly the impact area is defined, the more of the spending at the sports facility and in nearby restaurants, bars, and hotels will come from outside the community. However, that spending will come largely at the expense of the home communities of the fans that travel to the facility from outside the impact area. The substitution effect for a broadly defined area is quite large, but for a narrowly defined geographic area it will be much smaller. In other words, new sports facilities can be viewed as a tool for redistributing income and other economic activity from the suburbs and outlying areas of a city to businesses located near the new facility. This is not new economic activity.

Omission of Opportunity Costs   Impact studies typically do not address alternative uses of public funds used to subsidize new sports facilities. Economics points out that all economic activity has opportunity costs – the cost of the most valuable forgone alternative. Politicians often seem to think that the means of financing a new sports facility generates free resources that have no alternative uses whatsoever. For example, when the state of Maryland discussed plans to lure the Cleveland Browns to Baltimore in the late 1990s, they made clear that part of the funding for the construction of a new football stadium for the team would come from the state lottery. In hearings on the issue, it was pointed out that lottery funds were essentially constant in recent years and that they were already dedicated, at least in part, to paying off the bonds issued to finance Oriole Park at Camden Yards, which was built in the early 1990s. If lottery funds did not grow over time, then to add the financing of the football stadium would require that the state dip into general tax revenues either to pay interest on the baseball stadium related bonds or to spend on the other public services supported out of lottery revenues like education. Alternatively, the state could choose to completely stop supporting other public. The Maryland senators dismissed this concern out of hand. Government funds have opportunity costs.

This issue is more than simply the existence of alternative uses for the public funds used to pay new sports facility construction. The fundamental issue is that a new sports facility is a public investment in real capital. The rules for sensible public capital investment apply to sport facility finance as much as they apply to public provision of highways, schools, and airports. Specifically, the key is comparing the return on the investment in the sports facility with the return on the same dollar invested in any alternative public use, including tax reduction. Efficient use of public resources requires that any given funds go to uses that provide the highest return per dollar. This, of course, makes estimation of the return on a new sports facility and other investments very important. But measurement of these returns is complicated by the fact that there are substantial services generated at a new sports facility and by sports franchises that do not pass through the marketplace, making them hard to value.

Unvalued Intangibles New sports facility subsidy advocates often raise the issue of civic pride and the image of cities when arguing for subsidies. According to this logic, only cities with professional sports teams are truly "world class." The gain in civic pride is, of course, very difficult to value. The benefits that accrue to individuals who never or rarely attend games at the stadium but who derive enjoyment from following the team in the newspaper or via the radio and television broadcasts are also difficult to measure. Such benefits are the result of an externality, a good or service provided by one individual or group that provides benefits to other individuals or groups and for which the latter provide no compensation to the former. The existence of these external benefits could justify some public participation in the provision of stadiums and sports franchises, although estimates of the value of these intangibles would help to clarify this issue. Evidence about the value of civic pride generated by professional sports is discussed below.

8.4   Evidence About Economic Impact

There are two categories of evidence about the economic impact of professional sports facilities on urban economic activity. One category includes the economic impact studies discussed above. Again, these impact studies are always prospective in nature - they forecast the future economic impact generated by a new publicly financed sports facility - and always conclude that there will be large positive tangible economic benefits to the local economy. Impact studies rely on the use of spending multipliers from regional input-output models to arrive at these large positive estimates of economic benefits. Referring to these studies, economist John Crompton said, "Too often, the motives of those commissioning an economic impact analysis appear to lead to adoption of procedures and underlying assumptions that bias the resultant analysis so the numbers support their advocacy position."

The second category of evidence about the economic impact of professional sports on urban economies comes from retrospective studies published in peer-reviewed academic journals. Most of these studies use econometric techniques to assess the effect that professional sports had on urban economies, in terms of changes in the average level of income per capita, average earnings of workers in various sectors of the local economy, and employment. We discuss these studies in more detail below. Some evaluations of the effects of stadiums and professional sports involve cost benefit analysis and others use contingent valuation techniques. The contingent valuation approach is discussed in more detail in the section on non-pecuniary benefits.

In contrast to the results claimed by prospective economic impact studies commissioned advocates of subsidies, the consensus in the academic literature clearly indicates that the overall sports environment in a city has no measurable effect on the level of real income in the local economy, on the growth rate of local income, or on local employment. Some research actually suggests that professional sports may be a drain on local economies rather than an engine of economic growth.

An example of a retrospective study that performed a full cost-benefit analysis is Rosentraub and Swindell (1991) who undertook a type of impact study analyzing the effects of relocation of a minor league baseball team to Fort Wayne, Indiana. The city of Fort Wayne was asked by owners of the Wausau Timbers, a minor league baseball team, to build the team a new stadium so that the owners could relocate the franchise to Fort Wayne. The ultimate decision of the city was to offer to loan the owners of the team $1.2 million dollars at 6.48% interest over 15 years to be used in the renovation of an existing stadium. The team was required to raise an additional $750,000 for this renovation. The city would pay for facility maintenance and the team would pay no rent for use of the facility. The owners could not find private sector support for the $750,000 so the team did not relocate. Rosentraub and Swindell (1991) concluded that Fort Wayne made the right decision in not funding the construction of a new stadium and that the loan "was the very most the city should have offered to the owners of the team."

Siegfried and Zimbalist (2000) surveyed the literature on retrospective studies of the economic impact of sports facilities and franchises. The literature published in peer-reviewed academic journals differs strikingly from the predictions in "economic impact studies." No retrospective econometric study found any evidence of positive economic impact from professional sports facilities or franchises on urban economies. While evidence exists suggesting that narrowly defined occupational groups, like workers employed in the sports industry (NAICS industy Code 79 - "Recreation and Amusements"), the construction of new sports facilities and attracting new professional sports teams did not raise income per capita or total employment in any US city over the period 1970-2000.

The difference between the impact studies commissioned by subsidy advocates and the academic literature is more than simply prospective versus retrospective methodology and the use of regional input-output models. Academic studies examined economic outcomes in a large number of metropolitan areas with professional sports teams over a long period of time and these econometric studies controlled for variation in other factors likely to affect economic activity and take a broadly defined view of the sports environment in a city. In other words, academic studies look specifically for evidence of some detectable the net impact of professional sports teams and facilities in a city on economic outcomes in cities. Coates and Humphreys (1999) attacked the issue of the effect of professional sports on local economies differently than earlier researchers. This study pooled data from each city hosting a professional football, baseball, or basketball team at any time over the period 1969 to 1996, a comprehensive group of cities with professional sports franchises during this period. The sample period contained many franchise moves and new stadium and arena construction projects that can be interpreted as "natural experiments" in these cities. Twenty-three percent of the metropolitan areas included in this sample attracted a new basketball franchise, 10 percent attracted a new football franchise, and 7 percent attracted a new baseball franchise; 2.5 percent built a new baseball stadium, 10 percent built a new football stadium, 10 percent built a new combined football and baseball stadium, and 21 percent built a new basketball arena during the sample period. The study used panel data econometric techniques to control for city and year specific heterogeneity in the unobservable factors that affect the level of income per capita and growth in income per capita in those cities. This study also introduced a broad array of variables to capture the entire spectrum of professional sport, and its effect on the local economic outcomes instead of a simple indicator variable for the presence of a sports team used in previous research. These included dummy variables for the entry or exit of teams within the past 10 years, indicator variables for construction of new stadiums and arenas within 10 years, the seating capacity of each facility in the city, and the presence of a team in each of the three major professional sports. The study found that , taken as a whole, the sports environment tended to reduce the per capita personal income in the city by a small but statistically significant amount.

Since it is not clear whether pro-stadium studies claim that a new sports facility will raise the level or the growth rate of income in a metropolitan area, Coates and Humphreys (1999) focused on identifying factors that affected both the level and growth of income per person in metropolitan areas. Although attracting a new football team or building a new basketball arena might have had some effect on real income per capita, and its growth rate, other factors certainly played an important role in the determination of these variables. The approach was to quantify the sports environment in each city, including the presence of sports franchises, franchise entry and departure, facility construction and renovation, the location of new stadiums and arenas, and the "novelty" effect of a new stadium or arena in professional football, basketball, and baseball. They estimated econometric models of the determination of the level and growth rate of income per capita in metropolitan areas and included the variables reflecting the sports environment. They took two different approaches to estimating these empirical models. First, taking advantage of the time-series cross-sectional nature of the data used, they controlled for unobservable city-specific factors that affect income or income growth, including trend growth, the decline of rust-belt cities and booms in sun-belt cities, and the effect of the business cycle. The use of city-specific effects, and these other control variables, means that they were able to make sure that the estimated effects of the sports environment variables were not contaminated with other historical or location-specific influences on the economic activity in the cities. Second, they used an event study approach to analyze the effect of professional sports on local economies. This event study method used the sports environment variables as a means of explaining why a particular city differs from the average city. This technique is widely used to examine the effects of changes in laws or regulations on the market value of firms in the finance and regulation literature. This approach can also be used to examine the impact of professional sports on local economies. In this approach, one regresses the level of income in each city on the average level of income across all the cities and a set of dummy variables reflecting changes in the sports environment. If the sports environment variables are statistically significant, the difference between that city and the average of all cities is not purely random but is a function of its different sports environment. The main drawback to this approach is that city-specific variables cannot be used.

Coates and Humphreys (2003) extended this research to examine the relationship between the presence of professional sports teams and earnings and employment in narrowly-defined occupational groups in US cities. This study found that earnings and employment in the SIC-code industry containing sports facilities and teams - SIC-code 79, "Amusements and Recreation Industries" - were higher but the earnings and employment in other important related sectors like Retail Trade, Hotels, and Eating and Drinking Establishments were lower after new sports facilities opened in US cities. The economic benefits from sports facilities and franchises appears to be concentrated in a small sector of the local economy and comes at the expense of economic activity in other sectors. The results in this second study support the idea that the economic activity associated with professional sports represents substitution in consumer spending on entertainment away from other activities like bars and restaurants and into spending in new sports facilities on tickets, parking and concessions.

Since these early studies, research has found that professional sports franchises and facilities have no effect on local sales tax revenues, that local economic activity does not change when professional sports leagues experience work stoppages, and that postseason appearances have no detectable effect on local economic activity. Taken together, this body of evidence indicates that the presence of a professional sports team and venue in a city has no net impact on economic activity in that city.

8.4.1 How Can Sports Subsidies Reduce or Have no Effect on Local Economic Activity?

If, as prospective team owners, developers, and politicians would have taxpayers believe, professional sports can be an important engine of economic growth, how can the estimates in in large literature on the economic impact of professional sports in scholarly journals be correct? How can the professional sports environment either have no impact on, or slightly reduce local economic activity? Potential answers to these questions fall into four broad categories.

- **Substitution in Public Spending** Public funds subsidize professional sports teams and the stadiums or arenas they play in. Public funds have alternative uses, such as maintaining local infrastructure; increasing the quality or provision of public health, safety, or education; and attracting new businesses to the area. The deterioration of local public capital or services over time could diminish the ability of the local economy to produce other non-sports-related goods and services, which in turn would reduce local income. For example, there may be fewer police on the streets, fewer firemen, less frequently repaired streets and highways, a weaker public education system, and so on, in cities that subsidize professional sports teams and venues. These reductions in the provision of publicly provided goods and services could result in lower productivity of workers and, therefore, lower income in a metropolitan area over time. No evidence exists that professional sports have a detectable positive impact on local government spending or tax revenues.

- **Substitution in Private Spending** Households face budget constraints; they must meet their unlimited wants with a limited amount of income. The arrival of a professional sports team in a city provides households with a new entertainment option. Households that attend games will spend less on other entertainment activities, things like going out to dinner in a local restaurant, bowling, or the movies. If the impact of each dollar spent on these forgone alternatives has a larger effect on the local economy than the impact of each dollar spent on professional sporting events, the local economy will contract and income will be reduced. Why would the impact of each dollar spent going to a professional basketball game be smaller than the impact of each dollar spent on bowling? This could easily occur if the revenue generated by the basketball team and arena, which in turn becomes the income made by the players and team owners, escapes the flow of transactions that make up the local economy to a greater extent than the income made by the owners and employees of the bowling alley or movie theater. In other words, household spending on sports - direct spending on tickets, licensed merchandise, etc. and indirect spending on food and drinks at or near a sports facility - is highly substitutable for other forms of entertainment spending like movie tickets, food and drinks in areas of the city far from the facility, bowling and the like. Professional sport does not induce residents to increase total spending by drawing on savings or borrowing against future earnings. Residents maintain their level of entertainment spending but alter the allocation of this spending toward sport-related spending and away from other close substitutes. Sports redirect spending by residents from one part of the local economy to another.

Economic impact analysis studies routinely ignore reductions in spending on other forms of entertainment due to substitution in private spending when they compute spending increases from the construction of a stadium or arena and the presence of a professional sports franchise. This systematically overstates the claimed economic benefits from new sports facilities and excludes any potential economic harm done to other businesses in the entertainment sector of the local economy.

Impact analysis studies also claim that a new sports facility will attract new visitors to a city, leading to additional economic benefits. Visitors attracted by a new sports facility may occupy hotel rooms and eat meals that would have been purchased by visitors who came to the city for other reasons, and the direct spending on sport made by these visitors would have gone to other entertainment establishments. Porter (1999) and Porter and Fletcher (2002) report little or no increase in hotel occupancy rates, retail sales, or airport traffic in cities that hosted Super Bowls and Olympic Games in the U.S. in the past ten years.

- **Compensating Differentials in Wages** Perhaps professional sports do not directly reduce the level of real per capita income in a metropolitan area. Instead, our results reflect a "compensating differentia" related to the presence of professional sports in some cities. Residents of cities with professional sports teams derive nonpecuniary benefits from the teams presence and, because of those nonpecuniary benefits, are willing to accept lower income in return for living in these cities, other things being equal. Just as wages are higher in jobs with more risk or requiring more skill, and lower in cities with desirable amenities like pleasant weather, good schools, and little pollution, wages may be lower in communities with professional sports franchises because citizens are willing to forego some income to have access to that amenity. This rationale implies that a recent college graduate might be willing to take a lower-paying job in a city with a professional sports franchise instead of a slightly higher-paying job in a city that has no professional sports franchises. The determining factor in the choice is whether the value of those nonpecuniary benefits is high enough. In other words, we may observe lower per capita income in cities with a professional baseball franchise because residents of those cities are willing to accept lower wages or salaries to have local access to a baseball franchise. A compensating wage differential does not entail any direct link between the sports facility and local economic activity. It does require sufficient in migration of individuals with strong preferences for access to professional sports and out migration of individuals without these preferences to produce a steady-state equilibrium with lower wages in cities with professional sports.

- **Negative Effects on Productivity** Productivity, broadly defined as the amount of output that a worker with a given amount of capital, experience, and education can produce, is an important determinant of income and explains much of the observed difference in per capita income across countries. The factors that affect the productivity of workers are notoriously difficult to pin down precisely, but small differences in productivity can lead to large differences in per capita income when those differences persist over time. Workers in cities with professional sports teams may spend more work time discussing the outcome of last nights game, organizing an office pool, or other similar activities than workers in cities without professional sports teams. These differences could, over a period of many years, lead to differences in income per capita.

The existence of professional sports could result in workers spending less time on the job working and more time on the job handicapping the upcoming game or discussing the outcome of the last game. This time is recorded as time at work, but output is lower, resulting in lower income. To date, little research has focused on the link between productivity and professional sports. Coates and Humphreys (2002) found that income per person was higher in the city that was home to the Super Bowl champion the previous season, Berument and Yucel (2005) found a positive relationship between the growth in industrial production and soccer wins in a city in Turkey, and Davis and End (2010) found a link between a wining NFL team in a city and higher real per capita income in that city, and interpret this as reflecting productivity gains generated by winning teams. These studies providing some evidence of a link between sports and the productivity or workers. However, they all suggest that successful teams generate local productivity gains; this effect implies that unsuccessful teams may generate productivity losses, harming the local economy. Since each season in a professional sports league is a zero sum outcome – half the teams have winning records and half the teams have losing records – any link between team success and productivity should have a zero impact on the overall economy, since the effect of winning on productivity in one city will be offset by the effect of losing in another city. If such a link exists, it cannot justify subsidies for new facility construction, since the economic benefits will only be realized if the team has a winning season every season.

- **Differences in Multipliers** In the context of regional input-output models, the multiplier for spending on sports in a city may be substantially smaller than the multiplier on other forms of entertainment spending. The majority of the revenues from professional sports go into salaries for players, managers, coaches, trainers, scouts and to income for the ownership. Most of these individuals, especially the more highly paid ones, do not live full time in the city where the games take place. Unlike the wages and salaries paid to employees of local restaurants, movie theaters, car dealerships, department stores, etc., the large salaries earned by players and coaches leak out of the local economy. Moreover, the spending and saving patterns of relatively highly paid players, with relatively short careers, differ from those of typical workers. Specifically, players save a larger portion - and spend a smaller portion - of their earnings than the typical worker because the wealthy tend to save more than the non-wealthy and because the high earnings of players are transitory and a substantial fraction will be saved until the years after their playing days are over. Siegfried and Zimbalist (2000) emphasize that the size of the multiplier on spending on professional sport depends on the location where the spending takes place. They claim that the size of the sports multiplier varies directly with the radius of a circle drawn around the stadium.

8.4.2   The Importance of Non-Pecuniary and Intangible Benefits

The evidence suggests that local economies receive no tangible positive economic benefits from the billions of dollars of public subsidies provided for the construction of new professional sports facilities in the past, and that professional sports may have a small but negative impact on local economies. What benefits have taxpayers received from these subsidies, and are they large enough to justify the costs?

A common justification for subsidizing professional sports is that there are substantial positive externalities from sports and that these would not be available without subsidies. For example, proponents of sports led development frequently refer to the "world class" status conferred on a city by the presence of professional sports franchises. It is also common to point out that citizens of a community may derive enjoyment from following the exploits of the local teams on television, the radio, or in the newspaper, but never attend a game. The difficulty is in measuring these benefits, whether from the world class city effect or the enjoyment of the fans, because these are not traded in a market where their value is determined.

Coates and Humphreys (1999) suggested that the negative impact on per capita personal income they find may be a measure of the value of the professional sports environment to the citizens. The reduced income is implicit compensation for the access to the sports environment of the city. The increase in per capita income associated with winning the Super Bowl that Coates and Humphreys (2002) found may measure the benefits of the world class city, as the victory swells the workers with pride and makes them happier and more productive.

Other research has used different methods to value the intangible benefits generated by professional sports. Johnson and Whitehead (2000) and Johnson, Groothius, and Whitehead (2002) used the contingent valuation approach to estimate the benefits of sports stadiums and sports franchises, respectively. In this approach, researchers ask individuals how much they would pay to avoid an undesirable event or to acquire a desirable one. For example, in Johnson, Groothius, and Whitehead (2002) people in Pittsburgh were told the local professional hockey team might leave town because their current arena is not adequate to generate sufficient revenues to put a quality team on the ice. The team was bankrupt at the time. They were then told that the city was considering buying the team to keep it in town and that doing so would require a tax increase of $X, where X is randomly assigned to the respondent and was either 1, 5, 10 or 25 dollars. Finally, the respondent was asked if he or she would be willing to pay $X each year in higher city taxes to keep the team in town. Respondents were then asked the most they would be willing to pay and presented with a card with dollar amounts listed for them to choose from. While the value of the intangible benefits generated by the team was substantial, the results of the study "suggests that the value of public goods generated by major league sports teams may not be large enough to justify the large public subsidies" (Johnson, et al., 2002).

Another method for valuing intangible economic benefits is to estimate the value of consumer surplus generated by some good or service. Recall from Chapter 3 that the area under a demand curve and above the equilibrium price in a market can be interpreted as the consumer surplus generated by the good or service; it is a measure of the difference between willingness to pay and actual expenditure, and represents the overall benefit that consumers get from the good or service. Alexander, Kern and Neill (2000) estimated the value of consumer surplus generated by live attendance at NFL, NBA, NHL and MLB games in 1996. They conclude that the consumer surplus generated by professional sports teams were between $8 and $25 million per year in 1996 dollars, or between $11 million and $35 million in 2010 dollars. While substantial, the study concludes that consumer surplus alone is not large enough to justify a subsidy large enough to build a modern professional sports facility.

Carlino and Coulson (2004) estimated hedonic regressions of the determinants of rents and wages in metropolitan areas to determine the extent to which these values are influenced by the presence of a team from the National Football League in the city. They assessed the value of the "public goods" a professional football team provides to the city and to compare that to the subsidies paid to the teams. In equilibrium, the value of public good benefits will be capitalized into rents and wages, with rents being higher and wages lower than they would be in an identical city without a football team. They report about a 8% boost in rents associated with an NFL team and a 2% reduction in wages. Based on these values, Carlino and Coulson concluded that the value of the public goods is substantially larger than the subsidies paid by cities and states to professional football teams.

The literature focused on measuring the non-pecuniary benefits of sports franchises and facilities shows considerable promise for explaining the persistence of subsides for professional sports facility construction. These papers apply novel empirical approaches to data not previously used in to study the economic impact of sports. The results are important in that wage models estimated with micro data imply large non-pecuniary consumption benefits when aggregated across the population of the typical metropolitan area.

As mentioned above, the presence of professional sports in a city, like good weather or access to a coast, may be viewed by workers as an amenity for which workers in those cities receive compensating wage differentials. This can be thought of as an intangible benefit. Under this assumption, the interpretation of the observed reduction in income per capita in cities with professional sports teams changes considerably. Rather than a drain on the local economy, firms in a city with professional sports teams can hire workers at a lower wage than firms in cities without professional sports teams, providing them with a comparative advantage in production. To determine whether sports facilities generate compensating wage differentials, researchers must turn to longitudinal or cross-sectional microeconomic data in order to control for the effects of individual characteristics like education and experience on wages. Some promising preliminary evidence supporting this theory has recently emerged. In particular, Coates and Humphreys (2011) and Carlino and Coulson (2004) both provide evidence of a compensating wage differential associated with the presence of professional sports teams in US cities, based on microeconomic data from the Current Population Survey.

The idea of compensating wage differentials linked to professional sports teams also hinges critically on the effect of access to sports on migration decisions. The existence of compensating wage differentials depends critically on a steady-state equilibrium where individuals sort themselves into cities based on the amenities and wages across these cities. To date, no research has examined the link between migration and sports, but this area is ripe for additional empirical analysis.

If a new facility does not generate tangible economic benefits, perhaps a new facility at least makes a team more competitive. After all, team owners frequently claim that a new publicly financed facility will help make the team more competitive. Unfortunately, empirical evidence does not support this claim. Quinn, Bursik, Borick and Raethz (2003) examined the winning percentage of NFL, NBA, MLB and NHL teams before and after they moved into new facilities over the past five decades in North America. After controlling for other factors that affect winning percentage, this study found that moving into a new facility had no effect on the winning percentage of NFL, NBA and NHL teams, and a small positive effect on winning percentages for MLB teams over the first seven years in a new stadium. The implication of these results is that the additional revenues generated by a new facility go into the pocket of the owner, and not to acquiring additional talent to improve the team's performance.

8.4.3   Voting on Sports Subsidies

Voters often decide on subsidies for professional sports facilities; some research analyzed these votes. The outcomes of referendums on new facility subsidies are not always positive: about half pass. Models of rational voting predict that voters weigh total expected costs of subsidizing a new facility against total expected benefits and vote for the subsidy if the benefits exceed the costs.

Agostini, Quigley and Smolensky (1997) developed statistical evidence, in the form of estimates from a regression model at the census tract level, relating the proportion of votes in favor of a subsidy for the construction of a new baseball stadium in San Francisco to a variety of characteristics of residents of these census tracts and concluded that higher income, better-educated voters were more likely to favor the subsidy. Males, counter-intuitively, were more likely to oppose the subsidy while Asians were more likely to favor it.

These regression models did not account for proximity to either the existing stadium or the proposed new stadium site. If a facility generates external benefits or costs, then some of these effects could depend on proximity. Coates and Humphreys (2006) analyzed a series of referendums in Brown County, Wisconsin, home of the Green Bay Packers, and in Harris County, Texas, home of the Houston Rockets. They matched voting precincts to census tracts and estimated regression models using data from these referendums controlling for characteristics of residents and proximity to the facilities.

In Green Bay, the first referendum focused on whether to increase the local sales tax rate with the proceeds earmarked for renovation of the existing football stadium. Subsequent referendums addressed the disposition of any remaining sales tax revenues after the stadium renovation was paid and whether or not the community should sell the right to name the stadium to reduce the cost. The evidence from Green Bay indicated that people living closest to the stadium supported the idea of raising the tax to refurbish the stadium, but people living farther from the stadium were not statistically more or less likely to support the subsidy.

In Harris County, Texas, referendums proposing new taxes on rental cars and hotel and motel stays were on the ballot in two successive years. In each case, the proceeds of the taxes would be used to pay for the construction of a new arena for the Houston Rockets. The first referendum included a surcharge on tickets to events at the arena; the second did not. The first referendum failed; the second passed.

Voting patterns in the Harris County referendums suggests two interesting ideas. First, people living in and around the existing arena and people living in and around the site of the proposed new arena were both more likely to vote in favor of the tax increase for new arena construction, suggesting that people with experience living near an arena did not find that experience to produce a net benefit. On the other hand, people in the vicinity of the proposed facility expected positive net benefits from living in close proximity to the venue. Second, because the two locations were close to one another, some precincts were "close" to both sites. People in these precincts tended to vote against the subsidy.

Coates and Humphreys (2006) concluded that living near an arena or stadium is a mixed blessing. Some people find the additional traffic, noise, garbage, crime, etc., generates costs high enough to offset whatever benefits they receive. Others, like people living near Lambeau Field in Green Bay, appear to find that living close to the stadium provides benefits that exceed the annoyance of game day traffic and other costs generated by football games in their neighborhood. The role played by the difference between 10 home football games a year in Green Bay and 41 or more home basketball games in Houston in these results is unclear.

8.4.4 Mega-Events

If local pro sports teams and facilities have no impact on the local economy, perhaps one time, short term, large attendance events like the Super Bowl, World Cup, or Olympic Games will spur growth and development in the local economy. Evidence on the net economic impact of mega-events issue is mixed. Hotchkiss, Moore, and Zobay (2003) analyzed economic performance in counties in Georgia before and after the 1996 Summer Olympic Games and found that, in those counties near to or hosting Olympic events, employment rose by 17% more than it did in non-Olympic counties. This research did not find any effects of hosting the Olympics on wages in those counties. Porter (1999) analyzed monthly commercial sales, hotel rates, and room occupancy data from three Florida counties that hosted 6 Super Bowls between 1979 and 1996 and concluded only one Super Bowl produced a small increase in commercial sales, two generated slight declines in commercial sales and three others had no detectable effects on hotel occupancy rates. Other research has found no evidence of tangible economic impact generated by the 1994 World Cup in the United States, the 2000 Summer Olympic Games in Sydney, Australia and the 2006 World Cup in Germany.

Coates and Humphreys (2002) analyzed the economic impact of hosting the Super Bowl and hosting postseason playoff games in baseball, basketball, and football in the US and found no statistically significant effect of any of these events on local income. Porter and Fletcher (2008) analyzed hotel occupancy, hotel room rates and traffic at local airports for the Olympic Games held in Atlanta in 1996and Salt Lake City in 2002. If the Olympic Games generate the economic development the proponents claim, measured perhaps by increased sales, then one should see that hotel occupancy rates increase and that arrivals at the local airports are larger than otherwise. This study found that hotel room rates increased dramatically in these cities during the Olympic Games, by 138% in Atlanta and 123% in Salt Lake City, but that occupancy rates and arrivals at the airports were essentially unchanged from the same period in non-Olympic years. Sales increased in Atlanta by $122.6 million, relative to a monthly average of $2.42 billion, but fell in Salt Lake City by $78.4 million. This also suggests that mega-events did not generate tangible economic benefits in the local or regional economy.

Unlike the literature on the economic impact of professional sports teams and facilities, there is some evidence that mega sporting events like the Super Bowl or the Olympic Games may have a beneficial effect on local economies. Employment may increase in the host communities, but wages do not appear to rise. However, this positive effect is offset by compelling evidence that these events also simply re-distribute spending to different parts of the urban economy. In addition, the evidence suggests that much of the inflow of tourists associated with hosting a mega event simply "crowds out" other tourists who would have traveled to the area if the mega-event did not take place. The fact that airport gate arrivals and hotel occupancy rates do not change much during mega-events indicates the presence of "displacement" in these cities. Cities that host mega-events tend to be tourist destinations in their own right. So holding the Super Bowl in Miami simply means that tourists traveling to Miami for the Super Bowl purchase plane tickets to Miami, rent hotel rooms in the city and buy meals and drinks in bars and restaurants that would have been purchased by other tourists who would have visited Miami if the Super Bowl were not held there that year. The evidence of positive economic benefits from mega sporting events should be considered weak at best.

8.5   An Assessment

Large cities all over North America periodically face the issue of how to pay for new or replacement sports facilities. The key issue is who will pay for the construction - the team or local taxpayers? For the past sixty years, taxpayers have funded the majority of the cost of constructing new sports facilities. In many cases, teams, and others who support subsidies for new sports facility construction, pointed to new tangible economic benefits as the primary justification for public subsidization of the construction of new sports facilities. A considerable body of research conducted over the past 30 years concludes that new professional sports facilities do not generate tangible economic benefits, despite these claims. Looking back at Table 8.1, one might charitably conclude that the reduction in subsidy rates in the 1980s and beyond, compared to the subsidy rates in the 1950s, '60s and '70s, indicates that public knowledge of the lack of evidence for the proposition that professional sports franchises generate tangible economic benefits has had some effect on these subsidies.

But Table 8.1 also shows that taxpayers still pay for more than half of the construction costs for new sports facilities, and the fraction increased in the 2000s. What factors explain the continued existence of public subsidies for the construction of new professional sports facilities? Several possible reasons exist:

Intangibles Matter   Although sports facilities do not generate net new economic benefits, they clearly generate a host of intangible benefits. The presence of a professional sports team in a city generates some consumer surplus each year. And although the estimated value of intangible benefits like "world class city status" and the sense of community generated by professional sports team in a city have a positive value, and the estimates of this value run into the tens of millions of dollars per year. Also, the evidence from studies of referendum voting on sports subsidies supports the idea that the intangible benefits generated by a sports team and facility are valuable. For example, the residents of Brown County, Wisconsin voted in favor of rasing their taxes by about $1,000 per household to finance the renovation of Lambeau Field. Adding up all these factors, and also including the effects of any compensating wage differential and the effect of a new facility on property values might produce a total value of intangible benefits large enough to justify the typical public subsidy that goes to the construction of a new professional sports facility in the 21st century.

Sport is a Public Good   Professional sports has many of the properties of a public good. Recall that public goods are non-rivalrous (my consumption of a public good does not affect your consumption of a public good) and non-excludable (the producer of a public good cannot exclude free riding by consumers). If we define the presence of a professional sports team in a city as the "product" produced by professional sports teams, then they are clearly a public good. Economic theory predicts that a true public good will be undersupplied by profit maximizing firms relative to the amount of the public good that society would prefer, and also suggests subsidization as one possible remedy for this under supply. However, if the product produced by a professional sports team is games, then the argument that professional sport is a public good becomes weaker. Owners can clearly exclude non-paying customers from a sports facility, and can even limit mediated access to the games (but not post-game coverage). So depending on the definition of "professional sport," subsidies could be justified on economic grounds in the absence of new tangible or intangible benefits.

Rational Actor Politics and Loss Aversion   The decision to subsidize a new professional sports facility often rests with elected officials, and even when the decision rests with the electorate, failed referendums do not always result in no subsidy (several referendums on public financing for the stadiums opened in the early 2000s in Pittsburgh were defeated at the ballot box, yet the facilities were still built with huge subsidies). Politicians do not always behave like rational economic actors, dispassionately calculating expected total economic costs and benefits and making decisions based on the pure calculus of cost-benefit analysis. And if they do, they may, like fans, exhibit loss aversion about the possible exit of the local team. Politicians have self-interested motivations. A considerable amount of political capital can be built up by keeping the local team in town by building them a new facility with public funds. Even the dimmest voter can look at a new arena and give credit to the mayor who got the facility built. In addition, no elected official wants to be remembers as "the guy who let Team X leave town" due to fan's loss aversion and affection for the local team. The personal cost of that reputation may be large enough to make any elected official agree to a new facility deal with a large subsidy and sweetheart lease. Finally, other powerful elites in a city may have a vested interest in keeping a professional sports team in town, contrary to taxpayers' best interests. Local newspapers and television stations benefit from having a professional team in the area, because coverage of the team sells papers and increases interest in radio and television coverage of the team and possibly games, increasing the profits earned by these businesses. Research has established that local television, radio, and print outlets are much more likely to provide favorable coverage of facility subsidies, and downplay the results of scholarly research disputing claimed economic benefits.

Teams Have Monopoly Power As a matter of public policy, governments in North America have extended implicit and explicit protection from anti-trust laws to professional sports leagues, and leagues enforce territorial exclusivity. Policy makers allow professional sports teams to operate as monopolies. Teams exploit this power in a number of ways. One is to restrict the number of teams in the league, which leaves cities that could support a team open. These open markets provide team owners with the ultimate threat in any negotiation with the local government over a subsidy for the construction of a new sports facility: build me a new facility, or I will move the team. These outside options increase teams' bargaining power. Teams move (ask NBA fans in Seattle, Vancouver and Charlotte), and even cherished local institutions like the New York Yankees are not above threatening to leave to extract a subsidy from the local government. The Yankees threatened to move to New Jersey (where the Jets and Giants already play) when their negotiations with the City of New York over a new stadium stalled. We have given leagues monopoly power, and teams regularly exercise this power by extracting huge subsidies from local governments for the construction of new facilities.

Readings and References

Agostini, Stephen J., John M. Quigley, and Eugene Smolensky. 1997. "Stickball in San Francisco," in Roger G. Noll and Andrew Zimbalist eds. *Sports, Jobs, and Taxes: The Economic Impact of Sports Teams and Stadiums*, Washington, D.C.: Brookings Institution Press. pp.385-426.

Alexander, Donald L., Kern, William, and Neill, Jon. 2000. "Valuing the Consumption Benefits from Professional Sports Franchises," *Journal of Urban Economics*, vol. 48, no. 2, pp. 321-337.

Berument, Hakan, and Eray M. Yucel. 2005. "Long Live Fenerbahce: Production Boosting Effects of Soccer in Turkey," *Journal of Economic Psychology*, Volume 26, Issue 6, Pages 842-861.

Carlino, Gerald and N. Edward Coulson. 2004. "Compensating differentials and the social benefits of the NFL." *Journal of Urban Economics*, Volume 56, Issue 1, pp. 25-50.

Coates, Dennis and Brad R. Humphreys. 1999. "The Growth Effects of Sports Franchises, Stadia and Arenas," *The Journal of Policy Analysis and Management*, vol. 18, no. 4, pp. 601-624.

Coates, Dennis and Brad R. Humphreys. 2002. "The Economic Impact of Postseason Play in Professional Sports." *Journal of Sports Economics*. 3(3): 291-299.

Coates, Dennis and Brad R. Humphreys, 2003. "The effect of professional sports on earnings and employment in the services and retail sectors in US cities," *Regional Science and Urban Economics*, vol. 33, pp. 175-198.

Coates, Dennis and Brad R. Humphreys. 2006. "Proximity Benefits and Voting on Stadium and Arena Subsidies, *Journal of Urban Economics*, vol. 59, no. 2, pp. 285-299.

Coates, Dennis and Brad R. Humphreys. 2011. "The Effect of Professional Sports on the Earnings of Individuals: Evidence from Microeconomic Data," *Applied Economics*, vol. 43, no. 29, pp. 4449-4459.

Davis, Michael and Christian End 2010. "A Winning Proposition: The Economic Impact Of Successful National Football League Franchises," Economic Inquiry, vol. 48, no. 1, pp. 39-50.

Hotchkiss, Julie L., Robert E. Moore and Stephanie M. Zobay, 2002, "Impact of the 1996 Summer Olympic Games on Employment and Wages in Georgia," *Southern Economic Journal*, vol. 69, no. 3, pp. 691-704.

Johnson, Bruce K. and John C. Whitehead. 2000. "Value of Public Goods from Sports Stadiums: The CVM Approach." *Contemporary Economic Policy*, 18(1): 48-58.

Johnson, Bruce K., Peter A. Groothuis, and John C. Whitehead. 2001. "The Value of Public Goods Generated by a Major League Sports Team: The CVM Approach." *Journal of Sports Economics*, 2(1): 6-21.

Porter, Phillip K. and Deborah K. Fletcher. 2008. "The Economic Impact of the Olympic Games: Ex Ante Predictions and Ex Post Reality," *Journal of Sport Management*, vol. 22, no. 4, pp. 470-496.

Quinn, Kevin G., Paul B. Bursik, Christopher P. Borick, and Lisa Raethz. 2003. "Do New Digs Mean more Wins? The Relationship between a New Venue and a Professional Sports Team's Competitive Success," *Journal of Sports Economics*, vol. 4 no. 3, pp. 167-182.

Rosentraub, Mark S. and David Swindell. 1991. "'Just Say No?' The Economic and Political Realities of a Small City's Investment in Minor League Baseball," *Economic Development Quarterly*, Vol. 5, No. 2, pp. 152-167.

Siegfried, John and Andrew Zimbalist, Summer 2000, "The Economics of Sports Facilities and Their Communities," *Journal of Economic Perspectives*, vol. 14, no. 3, pp. 95-114.

Review Questions

1. True, False or Uncertain: Professional sports can reduce income in a city because high ticket prices represent a drain on the local economy

2. True, False or Uncertain: Most professional sports teams in North America own their facility and paid for its construction

3. True, False or Uncertain: A new arena in downtown Edmonton will generate at least 1,000 new jobs in the local economy

4. Define consumer surplus and give an example of buyer's surplus generated by the Oilers in Edmonton. Explain how consumer surplus could justify subsidies to professional sports teams.

5. Define intangible economic benefits. Discuss one intangible benefit that will be generated by a new arena in downtown Edmonton.

Chapter 9

Sports Betting Markets

Chapter Objectives

- Understand the efficient market hypothesis, and how it applies to sports betting markets

- Understand the difference between weak form, semi-strong and strong form market efficiency

- Understand how economists look for evidence that betting markets are efficient

- Understand how bookmakers operate

- Understand the evidence that betting volume in sports betting markets is unbalanced and the implications of this observation

9.1   Overview of Sports Betting Markets

Betting on sporting events is a popular activity that is legal in many countries around the world. Evidence indicates that sports betting took place in ancient times. For example, the Circus Maximus in Rome was a horse racing track that seated 260,000 spectators who bet on the races that took place there. Estimates suggest that at least $30 billion is currently wagered on sports in the United States each year; in Canada, bets can be placed on sporting events at lottery outlets, through the *Sports Select* game. In the UK, private bookmakers have extensive operations. However, economists are not interested in sports betting because of the amount of dollars wagered, or because of the number of people around the world who enjoy betting on sporting events. Economists study sports betting because the economic activity that takes place in sports betting markets sheds considerable light on the economics of financial markets.

From an economic perspective, sports betting markets are simple financial markets, so analysis of betting markets can provide insight into the role of prices, risk taking, information, and other factors that affect financial markets. Although these factors are difficult to observe in financial markets, most are observable in sports betting markets. A bet resembles a financial asset like a stock or bond because both can be purchased at known price at some point in time, and both will generate some uncertain return in the future. In the case of a stock or bond, there are many possible outcomes that can be realized at many different points in time; in sports betting markets there are only two possible outcomes (the bet wins or the bet loses) that will be determined at a specific, near term, point in time - at the end of the game. Because the outcome of a bet on a sporting event is known at a specific point in time, economists have used sports betting markets as a laboratory for understanding how financial markets operate for some time.

9.2   The Efficient Market Hypothesis

The efficient market hypothesis, (EMH) is one of the cornerstones of modern financial economics. Developed by Eugene Fama at the University of Chicago in the early 1960s, the EMH asserts that financial markets are *informationally efficient* in that an investor cannot consistently earn returns in excess of the average market return (after adjusting for risk) given the information publicly available at the time a financial asset is purchased. In a nutshell, the EMH states that an investor cannot "beat the market" because the prices of financial assets like stocks reflect all relevant information available to investors. The "efficiency" refers to the fact that financial markets aggregate all relevant information that might affect the valuation of a financial asset. There are three versions of the EMH:

1. *Weak Form Market Efficiency*: Future returns cannot be predicted by past prices or past returns. Current prices fully reflect the information content of all prices and returns.

2. *Semi-strong Form Market Efficiency*: Future returns cannot be predicted by any past information that is publicly available. The current price fully reflects all currently available past public information

3. *Strong Form Market Efficiency*: Future returns cannot be predicted by any past information, including hidden, private, or insider information. The current price fully reflects all past information.

The existence of efficient markets is clearly an empirical question. Mixed evidence exists about the existence of weak form and semi-strong form market efficiency in many financial markets, but one reason for the lack of consensus may be related to problems quantifying relevant information and measuring payoffs.

Many of these problems can be mitigated in sports betting markets. As explained below, point spreads and odds can be interpreted as prices in sports betting markets. Applying the EMH to sports betting markets implies that it is impossible for bettors to earn excess returns by betting on sporting events, since the existing point spreads or odds should already reflect all relevant information. The application of the EMH to sports betting also implies that point spreads are efficient predictors of game outcomes, in that the median of the distribution of point spreads is equal to the median of the distribution of the difference in points scored in sports like basketball and football where point spread betting takes place.

9.3   Point Spread Betting

The most common form of betting on basketball and football (in North America) is point spread betting. Point spread betting was invented in the 1930s. The payoff in point spread betting depends on the difference in points scored by the two teams. Point spreads (PS) are traditionally reported as the number of points by which the home team is favored to beat the visiting team in the game, when the point spread is negative, and as the number of points by which the visiting team is expected to beat the home team, when the point spread is positive. For example, consider the following NBA playoff game from the 2008-2009 season

NBA Playoffs 28 April 2009	
Chicago Bulls at	
Boston Celtics	-7

In this example the point spread is $PS = -7$, so the Celtics, the home team in this game, must beat the Bulls, the visiting team, by more than 7 points for a bet on the Celtics to win. Let DP be the actual difference in points scored in a game, where $DP < 0$ if the home team won and $DP > 0$ if the home team lost. A bet on the home team wins if $|DP| > |PS|$, or $|DP - PS| > 0$. A bet on the visiting team wins if $|DP| < |PS|$, or $|DP - PS| < 0$. In the example above, the actual score of the game was Chicago 104, Boston, 106, so $DP = -2$. Bets on Boston lost and bets on Chicago won, even though Boston won the game. In the jargon of sports betting, the Celtics did not "cover" the point spread. In point spread betting, when $PS = DP$ the game is called a "push" and all bets are refunded. This is why point spreads are often in half point increments.

In point spread betting, bookmakers earn profits by charging a commission on losing bets. Sports bets operate on an "11 for 10 rule": bettors risk 11 units to win 10, so the commission, (or "vigorish" sometimes shortened to "vig") is 10%. In the above example, bettors who wagered $100 on the Celtics would have lost $110, while bettors who wagered $100 on the Bulls won $100. The bookmaker collects $110 from each bettor who bet $100 on the Celtics and pays $100 to each bettor who bet $100 on the Bulls. The commission, identified by the variable τ, again is 0.1.

The point spread can be interpreted as the price a bettor must pay for a claim to a given amount of money if a bet on the favored team pays off. Let p be the probability that a bet on the favored team pays off

$$p = Prob(DP - PS) > 0.$$

How much does it cost a bettor to win $1 by betting on the favored team? The price paid by the bettor is the amount wagered times the probability of losing the bet

$$price = \$(1 + \tau) \times (1 - p).$$

Since p falls as PS increases, the expected price of a wager on the favored team increases with PS. Thus the point spread can be interpreted as the price of a bet on the favored team. The application of the EMH to point spread betting implies that $p = 0.5$, in the case where bookmakers charge no commission. That is, in an informationally efficient market, point spreads would be set so that bets on the favored team would win in half the games played. However, the presence of a commission charged by bookmakers changes this prediction slightly. Again, let p represent the probability that a bet placed on the favored team wins, and τ be the commission or "vig" charged by bookmakers. The payoff on bets, in terms of odds, is 1 to $(1 + \tau)$. Informationally efficient markets mean an absence of profitable opportunities for bettors, which requires that the expected return on a bet on the favorite is no larger than the cost of that wager. In the presence of a commission of τ, the absence of profit opportunity on wagers requires that

$$\frac{1}{2 + \tau} \leq p \leq \frac{1 + \tau}{2 + \tau}$$

and if $\tau = 0.1$, this condition means that

$$0.476 \leq p \leq 0.524$$

so a bettor must win more than 52.4% of wagers made to earn a profit betting on sports under the "risk 11 to win 10" betting scheme used in point spread betting.

Table 9.1: NFL Betting Market Efficiency 2004-2009

	Games	Bets	Wins	Ties	Wins/Bets
All Games	1596	1552	747	44	0.481
Home Favorites	1116	1085	523	31	0.482
Home Underdogs	466	453	220	13	0.486
Favorite	1596	1581	755	44	0.476
	DP	PS	DP-PS	t-stat	
All Games	2.38(14.33)	2.70(5.62)	-0.23(13.10)	-0.705	
Home Favorites	5.52(13.78)	5.57(3.54)	-0.05(13.31)	-0.132	
Home Underdogs	-4.86(12.97)	-4.38(2.87)	-0.52(12.64)	-0.885	

9.3.1 Informational Efficiency

Recall that a bet on a sporting event can be interpreted as a simple financial asset. The EMH predicts that bettors cannot consistently make a profit by betting on sporting events. Given the 10% commission charged by sports bookmakers, this means that any betting strategy employed by a bettor should not yield a winning percentage greater than 52.4% or less than 47.6%. A simple way to understand the efficiency properties of sports betting markets is to examine how many bets of a given type would win over a long period of time.

Table 9.1 contains information on bets on NFL regular season games over the 2004 through 2009 seasons. There were 1569 NFL games played during these six seasons. bookmakers set a point spread on 1552 games. The results on Table 9.1 are based on the final "Las Vegas" point spread or "line" on NFL games when the betting period ended on each game. The "wins" column shows how many bets of a certain type paid off over this period. For the first row, the bet is: "always bet on the home team." In the NFL, a strategy of always betting on the home team would have resulted in 747 wins and 44 ties (where $DP = PS$). 747/1552 is 48.1%, so betting on the home team in every game would result in a bettor winning only 48.1% of the bets placed. Note that the figures shown on the first row of Table 9.1 also provides information on the bet: "always bet on the visiting team." The winning percentage for this strategy is $1 - p$ where p is the winning percentage on the strategy of always betting on the home team. The winning percentage for the strategy of always betting on the visiting team in each game over this period was $1 - 0.481 = 0.519$, or 51.9% of the games.

Notice that the winning percentage on the strategy "always bet on the home team" and "always bet on the visiting team" are both inside the range $0.476 \leq p \leq 0.524$, which means that after accounting for the 10% commission charged by sports books, neither strategy produced a positive profit for bettors over this six season period. Even though a bettor always wagering on the visitor in every game would have won more than 50% of 1552 bets placed, that bettor would not have made a positive profit because of the 10% commission paid on losing bets.

The fact that the winning percentage on these simple strategies did not earn a profit for bettors is evidence that sports betting markets are weak form efficient. The point spread on each game must reflect relevant information, at least in terms of publicly available information about the teams playing in each game. If the NFL betting market was not efficient, then a betting strategy like always betting on the home team would yield a positive profit for bettors – in other words excess returns.

Of course always betting on the home team is an extremely simple betting strategy, and it is possible that other more sophisticated strategies might yield positive profits. The second row on Table 9.1 evaluates the betting strategy "always bet on the home team when the home team is favored." There were 1085 games where the home team was favored in the NFL over these six seasons. Clearly, the home team is favored in a majority of NFL regular season games, reflecting the presence of the well-known "home advantage" in team sports. The difference between the number of games and the number of bets reflects the fact that sports books sometimes take the line "off" for some games, usually when there is some major injury or weather related factor. This argues against the existence of strong form efficiency in sports betting markets, since strong-form informational efficiency implies all bettors and bookmakers know about injuries and weather conditions. From the "wins" column on Table 9.1, always betting on the home team when the home team is favored over these six seasons would have resulted in 523 winning bets, a 48.2% winning percentage, and 31 "pushes." This was not a profitable betting strategy, nor was "always bet on the visiting team when the home team is favored."

The third row on Table 9.1 evaluates the betting strategy "always bet on the home team when the home team is an underdog." There were 466 games where the home team was the underdog in the NFL over these six seasons. The home team is rarely the underdog in NFL regular season games. From the "wins" column on Table 9.1, always betting on the home team when the home team was the underdog would have resulted in 220 winning bets, a 48.6% winning percentage, and 13 "pushes." Again, this was not a profitable strategy, nor was the strategy "always bet on the visiting ream when the home team was the underdog." The fourth row evaluates the betting strategy "always bet on the favored team." This also does not produce positive profits over the course of these six seasons.

None of these betting strategies produced a positive profit for bettors over a large number of games. Again, this is evidence that the NFL betting market is weak form efficient, in that point spreads reflect all relevant public information about the games. Although other strategies might produce a profit for bettors, there are a large number of papers in the sports betting literature that contain similar evidence based on more sophisticated betting strategies. For example, papers have examined strategies based on the size of the point spread, recent past performance of teams against the spread, and other sophisticated betting strategies. Very few of these strategies generate positive profits for bettors, and the ones that do typically examine only a single season and subsequent research shows that they did not produce positive profits in later seasons. The NFL betting market appears to be weak form efficient.

The bottom panel of Table 9.1 contains a different type of evidence of informational efficiency in NFL betting markets. Recall that the presence of market efficiency also implies that the point spread PS is an efficient predictor of the outcome of games, in terms of the difference in points DP in games. PS and DP are both random variables. The DP column on the bottom panel of Table 9.1 is the average difference in points in NFL games over these six seasons. From first row of the the bottom panel of Table 9.1, for the 1552 NFL games with point spreads over the six seasons examined, the average difference in points, defined as home team points minus visiting team points, was 2.38. On average, the home team won by just less than a field goal. The number in parentheses is the standard deviation, a measure of variability of the difference in points. The PS column on the bottom panel of Table 9.1 is the average point spread, defined as a positive number when the home team was favored and a negative number when the home team was the underdog, for the 1552 NFL games. The average home team was favored by 2.7 points in these NFL games. Again, the number in parentheses is the standard deviation, a measure of variability of the point spread. Notice that the point spread variable has a much lower standard deviation than the difference in points. There is much more variability in the distribution of the difference of points than in the distribution of point spreads in NFL betting.

The third column on the bottom panel of Table 9.1, headed $DP - PS$, shows the average difference between the difference in points and the point spread in NFL games. This new variable is very close to zero. The number in parentheses is the standard deviation, a measure of variability of the difference in these two variables. The final column is the value of the t-statistic on a test of the null hypothesis: $H_o : DP - PS = 0$. That is, the null hypothesis that there is no statistical difference between the difference in points scored in NFL games and the point spread on those games. The t-statistics are all very small, suggesting that there is no statistical difference between the difference in points scored and the point spread. This is a different test of efficiency of NFL betting markets. Weak form efficiency implies that prices in financial markets reflect all available public information. If point spreads, the price in this financial market, reflects all information, then the point spread should be quite close to the actual difference in points. This is clearly the case for all NFL games, as shown on The bottom panel of Table 9.1. It is also true for the subset of games where the home team was favored and where the home team was an underdog. The evidence on Table 9.1 suggests that NFL betting markets are highly efficient, in the weak form sense.

Table 9.2: NBA Betting Market Efficiency 2003-2008

	Games	Bets	Wins	Ties	Wins/Bets
All Games	8255	8073	4008	182	0.496
Home Favorites	5931	5795	2884	136	0.498
Home Underdogs	2267	2221	1093	46	0.492
Favorite	8255	8073	4012	182	0.497
	DP	PS	DP-PS	t-stat	
All Games	3.37(12.78)	3.44(5.87)	-0.06(11.49)	-0.499	
Home Favorites	6.09(12.07)	6.51(3.46)	-0.40(11.44)	-2.704	
Home Underdogs	-3.66(11.78)	-4.44(2.56)	0.78(11.56)	3.235	

Table 9.2 shows the same results of an analysis of point spreads and difference in points scored for regular season NBA games over the 2003-2004 season through the 2008-2009 season. Since there are more NBA regular season games, the sample size is much larger in this setting. There were more than 8,000 regular season games with point spreads set by sports bookmakers over this period. The bets analyzed on Table 9.2 are the same as those on Table 9.1. The first row examines bets on the home team, the second row examines bets on the home team when the home team is favored, the third examines bets on the home team when the home team is the underdog and the fourth bets on the favored team. Like in the NFL, home teams are, on average, favored in NBA games. Again, the evidence on the top panel of Table 9.2 indicates that none of the eight betting strategies examined (bet on home/bet on visitor, bet on home favorite/bet on road underdog, bet on home underdog/bet on road favorite, and bet on favorite/bet on underdog) produced positive profits over this period. All of the winning percentages on these bets lie in the $0.476 \leq p \leq 0.524$ unprofitable region. NBA betting markets also appear to be efficient, in that there is an absence of profit opportunities using these simple betting strategies. Again, analysis of more complicated strategies fails to uncover evidence of profitable betting strategies in the NBA.

From the bottom panel of Table 9.2, the average home team in the NBA was favored by 3.44 points and won by 3.37 points. Again, there is no evidence that the two variables DP and PD are different from each other on average, again supporting the idea that point spreads are good predictors of the difference in points on NBA games. Interestingly, it appears that for NBA games where the home team was the underdog, that $DP - PS \neq 0$. The t-statistic of 3.235 on the last row on Table 9.2 would reject the null that $H_o : DP - PS = 0$ at conventional significance levels, and indicates that point spreads were smaller than the difference in points in those 2221 NBA games when the home team was the underdog. However, this does not necessarily imply that there were profitable betting opportunities for bettors in these games, since the t-test on the null $H_o : DP - PS = 0$ does not take into account the commission charged by bookmakers. Again, the NBA betting market appears to be efficient.

What does this evidence imply about financial markets? Sports betting markets resemble financial markets in important ways, and sports betting markets appear to be weak form efficient. Financial markets operate in much the same way, only the opportunities to measure information and the lack of a clearly defined outcome in financial markets makes it difficult to test market efficiency. If sports betting markets are weak form efficient, then financial markets are likely weak form efficient as well. This implies that there is an absence of profit opportunities beyond the average market return in financial markets like stock markets. On clear implication for investors is that a diversified portfolio of stocks that reflects the average market return is a better investment than trying to pick individual stocks based on publicly available information, because in weak form efficient markets an investor cannot earn above average returns on individual stocks - the price of those stocks already reflects all existing public information.

9.4 Fixed Odds Betting

Point spread betting is not the only type of sports betting offered by bookmakers. One alternative to point spread betting is fixed odds betting. In North America, fixed odds betting is typically offered on hockey and baseball games. Throughout the world, fixed odds betting is offered on football matches, tennis matches, and many other sporting events.[1] In North America and the rest of the world, fixed odds betting is offered on horse racing. Odds betting on horse racing is often pari-mutual betting, where all dollars bet, less a commission or "take-out,"are pooled and returned to winning bettors. Fixed odds betting on sporting events is based on actual game or match outcomes, and not on point differences. This makes fixed odds betting more suited to games or matches with relatively low scores, like hockey, baseball and football. In fixed odds betting, bookmakers induce bettors to wager on weaker teams by offering a higher payoff to bets on the weaker team to win, and deter bettors from wagering on stronger teams by offering a lower payoff to bets on the stronger team.

9.4.1 Types of Fixed Odds

Unlike point spreads, fixed odds are expressed in different formats depending on the location and preferences of the bookmaker. There are three different formats for fixed odds.

- **Fractional odds:** Fractional odds are quoted by UK bookmakers and used in horse race betting world wide. Fractional odds are also referred to as British odds, UK odds or "traditional odds" in the UK. Fractional odds show the net total paid to the bettor on a winning bet relative to the amount wagered.

  For example, 4/1 fractional odds (read as "four-to-one" or sometimes "four-to-one against") mean that a bettor can make a $40 return on a $10 wager. 1/4 fractional odds (read as

---

[1]bookmakers in North America offer fixed odds betting on football and basketball games, called the "Moneyline" by Las Vegas bookmakers. This type of betting is not as popular as point spread betting on football and basketball.

"one-to-four") mean that a bettor can make $2.50 on a $10 wager. Winning bettors always receive the original wager back, so on a 4/1 fractional odds wager a winning bettor receives a total of $50 ($40 plus the original $10). Fractional odds of 1/1 are called even money or even odds.

- **Decimal odds**: Decimal odds are quoted by bookmakers in continental Europe, Australia, and Canada. Decimal odds are also referred to as European or continental odds. Decimal odds are equal to the fractional odds converted to decimal values plus one. The "plus one" accounts for the amount wagered, so decimal odds include the amount the bettor risks. For fractional odds (x/y), the decimal odds equivalent is (x/y)+1. Even (1/1) odds in decimal form are (1/1)+1=1+1=2. 4/1 fractional odds in decimal form are (4/1)+1=4+1=5. 1/4 fractional odds in decimal form are (1/4)+1=0.25+1=1.25

- **Moneyline odds**: Moneyline odds are quoted by US bookmakers and are often called American odds. Moneyline odds can be either negative or positive numbers and always contain a plus (+) or minus (-) sign. If the moneyline is positive, it shows home much will be won on a 100 unit bet. Even odds in moneyline form are shown as +100 or -100. Fractional odds of 4/1 would be quoted as +400. If the moneyline is negative, then it shows how much must be wagered to win 100 units. Fractional odds of 1/4 would be quoted as -400.

Fixed odds betting on football includes wages on the three possible match outcomes: a home team win, a draw, and a visiting team win. For example, consider the Manchester "Derby" match between Manchester City and Manchester United on 23 October 2011. The match was played at Old Trafford, the home of Manchester United. The UK bookmaker Ladbrokes listed the odds on this match as

English Premier League, 23 October 2011
Home Team: Manchester United   Visiting Team: Manchester City

Match Outcome	Decimal Odds
Home Win	2.1
Draw	3.3
Away Win	3.6

Man U was almost an even odds favorite in this match; Man City was a heavy underdog. Based on the Ladbroke's odds, $1 wagered on Man U to win would return $2.1 if Man U won the match. Manchester City won this match 1-6, the worst loss for Man U at Old Trafford since 1955. A $1 bet on Man City to win paid $3.60.

Bookmakers earn profits on fixed odds betting from overround. Suppose three bettors wager a given amount on the three outcomes of the Man U/Man City Derby to win $100. Bettor 1 wagers on Man U to win. Bettor 1 risks $47.60 to win $100 ($47.60 × 2.1 = 100$). Bettor 2 wagers on a draw and risks $30.30 to win $100 ($30.30 × 3.3 = 100$. Bettor 3 wagers on Man City to win and risks only $27.80 to win $100 ($27.80 × 3.6 = 100$). The bookmaker collects $47.60+$30.30+$27.80=$105.70, pays Bettor 3 $100, and keeps $5.70 in profit. Overround refers to the fact that the bookmaker collects more from bettors than is paid out to winners. Note that as long as the betting was balanced across these three outcomes, the bookmaker keeps $5.70 in profit no matter what the outcome of the match.

Fixed odds can be easily converted to estimates of the probability that an event occurs, and these probabilities are useful for understanding betting market outcomes and bookmaker behavior.

For decimal odds DO, the implied probability of an event e occurring is $p_{i,e} = 1/DO_e$. For the October 2011 Manchester Derby, the implied probability of a home win was $p_{h,e} = 47.6\%$, the implied probability of a draw was $p_{d,e} = 30.3\%$ and the implied probability of an away win was $p_{a,e} = 27.8\%$. However, those implied probabilities sum to more than one, since they reflect the overround charged by bookmakers. Implied event probabilities adjusted for over-round can easily be estimated by $p_{i,a} = 1/(DO_e * or)$ where or is the overround on the match. The adjusted implied win probabilities for the October 2011 Manchester Derby were a $p_{h,a} = 45\%$ probability of a home win, a $p_{d,e} = 28.7\%$ probability of a draw and a $p_{a,e} = 26.3\%$ probability of an away win.

9.4.2 Informational Efficiency

A simple test of weak form efficiency in fixed odds betting markets can be performed by comparing the average implied probability of each outcome (home win, draw, away win) with the actual fraction of matches with these outcomes. If the implied probability of a home win based on betting odds is equal to the actual probability of a home win, then the betting market outcomes are consistent with weak form efficiency. Table 9.3 shows the results of this simple test for matches in the top domestic professional football leagues in England, Spain, France, Germany, Italy and Portugal over four seasons (2008-2009 through 2011-2012). HW% is the fraction of matches won by the home team and $p_{h,a}$ is the average implied probability of a home win based on the posted betting odds at Ladbrokes Ltd. accounting for the actual overround in each match. D% is the fraction of matches that ended in a draw, and AW% is the fraction of matches won by the visiting team. *t-stat* is the absolute value of the t-statistic for the null hypothesis that the actual fraction of outcomes equals the predicted probability of the event. When the t-statistic is greater than about 2, there is evidence that the means of the two random variables are statistically different from one another.

Table 9.3: Football Betting Market Efficiency 2008-2011

League	Matches	HW%	$p_{h,a}$	t-stat	D%	$p_{d,a}$	t-stat	AW%	$p_{a,a}$	t-stat
England	2280	0.478	0.449	3.01	0.267	0.256	1.60	0.255	0.295	4.69
Spain	2280	0.504	0.455	5.08	0.225	0.257	3.61	0.270	0.288	2.09
France	2280	0.439	0.443	0.38	0.297	0.284	1.34	0.263	0.272	1.02
Germany	1836	0.450	0.450	0.06	0.243	0.260	1.64	0.307	0.291	1.51
Italy	2270	0.491	0.450	4.07	0.255	0.277	2.41	0.254	0.272	2.15
Portugal	1440	0.433	0.438	0.04	0.275	0.263	0.99	0.292	0.299	0.64

Table 9.3 contains mixed evidence supporting weak form efficiency in this fixed odds betting market. The actual percentages for the three match outcomes are not equal to the implied percentages in the English Premier League, La Liga, and Serie A. For example, over this period, home teams in the EPL won 47.8% of their matches while the Ladbroke's betting odds implied that home teams would win only about 44.9% of matches; visiting teams won about 25.5% of matches played while the betting odds predicted that visiting teams would win 29.5% of matches played. In the other three leagues, the Bundesliga, Ligue 1 and the Primeira Liga in Portugal, the actual match outcomes compared to the betting odds based implied probabilities support weak form efficiency, since the actual outcomes are not statistically different from the predicted outcomes based on the betting odds. However, these tests are not strong evidence against weak form efficiency. Just because the home team won 47.8 percent of the EPL matches played over this period and the betting odds implied that bookmakers only predicted that the home team would win 44.9 percent

of the matches played does not mean that bettors were able to exploit this difference to earn excess returns by betting on the home teams. The presence of overround in this market means that the bookmaker effectively charges a commission on losing bets in this market; a stronger test of efficiency would account for this commission when assessing the efficiency of the market.

9.5 Bookmaker Behavior

The idea that bookmakers set point spreads to balance the volume of bets on each side of a game is ubiquitous in the research literature on point spread betting in sports. Nearly every paper published in this area over the past 30 years includes a discussion of an implicit model of sports book behavior that includes this feature. For example, Woodland and Woodland (1991) wrote in the *Journal of Political Economy*

> "In most situations, the bookie has no desire to participate as an active gambler. Rather, he establishes an odds or spread line to balance the wagers so that his commission is independent of the final outcome of the contest. For the equilibrium spread line, this is equivalent to equalizing the total amount of money wagered on each team. For the odds or "money" line, the equilibrium weighting is proportional to the odds that are offered. This eliminates all risk for the bookie. (pages 638-639.)"

The model implicit in such statements, the "balanced book" model, seems to generate clear predictions. The model predicts that, if we could observe the dollar value of bets on different sides of games, the dollar value wagered would be relatively balanced on either side, so the sports book has an incentive to make sure this outcome occurs; the "balanced book" model also predicts that observed changes in point spreads should be explained by imbalances in betting volume, as the model posits point spreads as the mechanism sports books use to balance betting that has become unbalanced as orders are taken in the market. This model has considerable support in the empirical literature. However, this support takes the form of a large number of tests confirming that point spreads are generally optimal predictors of actual score differences in games in many different settings.

Some recent research has emerged challenging the validity of the "balanced book" model. Levitt (2004) documented the outcome of a season long prediction contest for National Football League (NFL) games. While this contest did not resemble sports betting markets in many respects, the contest generated detailed information about participant's decisions and clearly revealed that the volume of bets was not balanced on a majority of the games that were picked by contestants. Levitt (2004) also developed a theoretical framework to explain the observed imbalances in betting on NFL games in this contest, and used this framework to show how a sports book would "shade" the point spread to take advantage of uninformed participants in the betting market. Paul and Weinbach (2007) analyze detailed betting volume data from an on-line sports book, sportsbook.com, and found evidence of unbalanced volume on bets placed on NFL games in the 2006 season. Paul and Weinbach (2008) found evidence of unbalanced betting volumes on National Basketball Association (NBA) games in the 2004 - 2006 seasons. The evidence in these papers suggests that the "balanced book" model may not describe actual outcomes in sports betting markets, and that a relationship exists between unbalanced bet volume and point spread shading in sports betting markets.

9.6 A Model of Bookmaker Behavior

While the behavior of bookmakers has been widely discussed in the literature, few have bothered to write down a formal model. Two notable exceptions exist. Levitt (2004) developed a framework for interpreting the results from a contest that involved picking winning NFL teams against the spread in the 2001 season. 285 handicappers participated in the contest. The choice variable in this framework was the probability that a team won the game, which does not closely resemble sports book behavior, since a sports book can only set a point spread and take bets that are made at this point spread.

To motivate the model of sports book behavior, first consider the simple case where a sports book accepts wagers on a single game played by two teams, Team 1 and Team 2. Let H represent the total amount of dollars wagered on this game, f_1 the fraction of dollars wagered on Team 1, and $f_2 = (1 - f_1)$ the fraction of dollars wagered on Team 2. H can simply be normalized to one

$$H = f_1 + f_2 = f_1 + (1 - f_1) = 1$$

which allows the analysis to be carried out in terms of units bet or fractions bet on either team. Sports books operate by charging a fee or commission on losing bets only. Let v be the commission or "vig" charged on losing bets. Since each game has only two possible outcomes, the unconditional net gain or loss (R) on each game is

$$
\begin{aligned}
\text{Bets on Team 1 Win} \quad & R = f_2(1 + v) - f_1 \\
\text{Bets on Team 2 Win} \quad & R = f_1(1 + v) - f_2.
\end{aligned}
\tag{9.1}
$$

If Team 1 wins, then the sports book keeps all money wagered on Team 2, plus the commission, and pays off those bets placed on Team 1. If Team 2 wins, then the sports book keeps all money wagered on Team 1 plus the commission and pays off bets placed on Team 2. The amount of profit or loss on a game depends on the amount that is wagered on each team. The gain or loss on a game can be expressed in terms of the fraction bet on Team 1 by substitution

$$
\begin{aligned}
\text{Bets on Team 1 Win} \quad R &= f_2(1 + v) - f_1 \\
&= (1 - f_1)(1 + v) - f_1 \\
&= 1 - f_1 + v - f_1 v - f_1 \\
&= 1 - 2f_1 - f_1 v + v \\
\text{Bets on Team 2 win} \quad R &= f_1(1 + v) - f_2 \\
&= f_1(1 + v) - (1 - f_1) \\
&= f_1 + f_1 v - 1 + f_1 \\
&= 2f_1 + f_1 v - 1
\end{aligned}
\tag{9.2}
$$

Note that no matter which bets win, the bookmaker's profits increase with the commission. If bets on Team 1 win, then gains on this game fall as the fraction of the bets on Team 1 increase; if bets on Team 2 win, then gains on this game rise as the fraction of the bets on Team 1 increases.

A break even condition on bets taken on this game can be derived from equation (9.2) by setting the profit equation equal to zero and solving

$$
\begin{aligned}
\text{Bets on Team 1 Win} \quad & R = 1 - 2f_1 - f_1 v + v = 0 \\
& 1 - 2f_1 - f_1 v + v = 0 \\
& 2f_1 + f_1 v = 1 + v \\
& f_1(2 + v) = 1 + v \\
& f_1 = \frac{1+v}{2+v}
\end{aligned}
\tag{9.3}
$$

$$
\begin{aligned}
\text{Bets on Team 2 Win} \quad & R = 2f_1 + f_1 v - 1 = 0 \\
& 2f_1 + f_1 v = 1 \\
& f_1 = \frac{1}{2+v}.
\end{aligned}
$$

Note that $\frac{1}{2+v} < \frac{1+v}{2+v}$. These two terms constitute upper and lower bounds for profitability of a bet from the perspective of the sports book, no matter what the outcome of the game. So long as $\frac{1}{2+v} < f_1 < \frac{1+v}{2+v}$ the sports book makes a profit on bets on this game. These two expressions can be used to calculate of the fraction of bets that must be won by any betting strategy to earn a profit for the bettor. If $v = 0.1$, then $\frac{1}{2+v} = 0.476$ and $\frac{1+v}{2+v} = 0.524$, implying that so long as the fraction of the bets on Team 1 is between these two bounds, the sports book makes a profit on the bet no matter what the outcome of the bet. The sports book might be able to make larger profits than this, conditional on the outcome, bettors expectations, or other factors, but this profit is unconditional.

Finally, as v increases, the bounds on the certain profit condition expands. By equating the expressions for the profit earned under each outcome in (9.2), when $v = 0.5$ the same profits are earned for either outcome for any value of f_1. From (9.3), $v = 0.5$ corresponds to unconditional profit bounds of $0.40 < f_1 < 0.6$. Put another way, if the sports book could charge a commission of 50%, that sports book would make a certain profit on bets on the game no matter what outcome, so long as the fraction of the bets on one team was between 40% and 60% of the total.

9.6.1   A "Balanced Book"

The break even condition can be used to illustrate the "balanced book" outcome. In the context of this simple model, a "balanced book" refers to the case where a sports book sets the point spread on a game to balance the volume of betting on either side of the bet, so that $f_1 = f_2 = f = 0.5$. Under the balanced book condition, profits are

$$
\begin{aligned}
\text{Bets on Team 1 Win} \quad & R = f(1+v) - f = fv = \frac{v}{2} \\
\text{Bets on Team 2 Win} \quad & R = f(1+v) - f = fv = \frac{v}{2}
\end{aligned}
\tag{9.4}
$$

proportionate to the commission charged v no matter what the outcome of the wagers turns out to be. This outcome involves no risk on the part of the sports book; if the volume of bets on each team is equal, the sports book earns a profit proportional to the commission charged no matter what the outcome. This result motivates much of the empirical research on point spread betting in sports. Most research on point spread betting assumes that point spreads are set to achieve this outcome. However, an expanded model highlights some of the problems with this approach.

9.6.2   Outcome Uncertainty

Levitt (2004) developed an expanded expression for the expected profit of a sports book that included a term for the probability that a bet on a given team wins, an extension to the unconditional analysis above. In Levitt's (2004) model, the probability that a bet on Team 1 wins was assumed to be the choice variable for the bookmaker, and this probability can be manipulated by changing the point spread. An alternative approach to modeling bookmaker behavior is to formulate the model in terms of the probability that a bet on a given team wins. In particular, suppose that the probability that a bet placed on Team 1 wins is π_1 and the probability that a bet on Team 2 wins is $\pi_2 = (1 - \pi_1)$. In this case, the expected profit earned by the bookmaker is

$$E[R] = [(1 - \pi_1)f_1 + (1 - \pi_2)f_2](1 + v) - (\pi_1 f_1 + \pi_2 f_2). \tag{9.5}$$

The first term on the right hand side of Equation (9.5) is the fraction of betting action the bookmaker keeps on losing bets. The second term is how much of the betting action the sports book pays out on winning bets. This can be written in terms of Team 1 outcomes by substituting $\pi_2 = 1 - \pi_1$ and $f_2 = 1 - f_1$. This expression, when written in terms of π_1 and f_1 can be simplified to

$$E[R] = (2 + v)[f_1 + \pi_1 - 2\pi_1 f_1] - 1. \tag{9.6}$$

For simplicity, assume that Team 1 is the favored team. In this expanded function, the expected return on any bet depends on both the amount bet on Team 1, the "vig" and the probability that Team 1 wins the game. Levitt (2004) assumed that the probability that a bet on team 1 wins, π_1, is the choice variable for the sports book, and derived an expression for the return maximizing probability. However, sports books do not directly control this probability. Sports books set a point spread and take bets at this point spread. The probability that a bet on Team 1 wins depends on the point spread, the relative strengths of the two teams, and random events that take place before and during the game. Assume that a relationship exists between the fraction of the money bet on Team 1 and the probability that a bet on Team 1 wins, and that sports books affect the fraction of bets on team 1 by setting the point spread. Formally,

$$\pi_1 = \sigma f_1 \tag{9.7}$$

This relationship can be motivated by interpreting π_1 as the objective probability that a bet on Team 1 wins and f_1 as bettors' subjective probability that a bet on Team 1 will win. f_1 depends on bettors' preferences and expectations, the relative strengths of the two teams, random events, and the point spread set by sports books. Sports books can affect f_1 by changing the point spread, and empirical evidence exists that f_1 increases with point spreads (Paul and Weinbach, 2007). π_1 depends on only the point spread, the relative strengths of the two teams, and random events that take place during the course of the game. σ captures the effect of bettors' expectations and preferences. If $\sigma = 1$, then $\pi_1 = f_1$ and bettors subjective expectation that that a bet on Team 1 will win is equal to the objective expectation. If $\sigma \neq 1$, then bettors expectations and preferences will distort their subjective expectation that a bet on Team 1 will win. There are a number of reasons to think that $\sigma \neq 1$. Models of the utility of gambling predict that bettors do not take into account the financial implications of a gamble, but instead derive utility from the act of gambling. Bettors who place bets on Team 1 for utility maximizing reasons may not take into account factors like the relative strengths of the two teams, or the point spread. These bettors would bet on Team 1 because they are fans of the team, they like the team's colors, or perhaps because Team 1 was the favored team, and they derive enjoyment from betting on and rooting for the favored team. Also, bettors who use heuristics to make decisions about gambling, like those described by Tversky and Kahneman (1973), rather than calculations based on "fundamentals" like team strength and past performance, might also exhibit biased decisions, leading their subjective probability that a bet on Team 1 will win to differ from the objective probability that this bet would win. If $\sigma > 1$, then $\pi_1 > f_1$ bettors subjective probability that a bet on Team 1 will win exceeds the objective probability; if $\sigma > 1$, then $\pi_1 > f_1$ bettors subjective probability that a bet on Team 1 will win is lower than the objective probability.

Substituting equation (9.7) into the expression for the expected return to the sports book on each bet, Equation (9.6), gives an expression for expected returns on a bet in terms of the choice variable, f_1, the fraction of money bet on team 1

$$E[R] = (2 + v)[f_1 + \sigma f_1 - 2\sigma f_1 \cdot f_1] - 1. \tag{9.8}$$

According to this function, the expected return on bets first rises and then falls with f_1. Taking the derivative of this expression with respect to changes in f_1, setting equal to zero, and solving for f_1 gives an expression for the fraction of bets on Team 1 that maximizes the expected return on a bet

$$f_1^* = \frac{1 + \sigma}{4\sigma}. \tag{9.9}$$

This expression defines the fraction of bets on Team 1 that the sports book should target to maximize the expected return on bets taken on a game. Clearly, a balanced book only maximizes expected returns if bettors are "unbiased" in that $\sigma = 1$. However, if $\sigma \neq 1$, and biased bettors exist in the pool of bettors, then a balanced book does not maximize expected returns for the sports book. The sports book manipulates the point spread to take advantage of the biased bettors in the market and increase expected returns above what they would expect to earn by balancing the volume of bets on either side of each game.

In the economics of gambling literature, this incentive to move point spreads away from the level that equalizes betting has been attributed to the presence of heterogeneous bettors in the market. Consider a betting market with both informed and uninformed bettors. The uninformed bettors are insensitive to the point spread and bet on a given team for reasons like loyalty or non-monetary motivations. Levitt (2004) showed that participants in the betting contest he analyzed tended to bet on the favored team, suggesting that they placed bets based on the point spread only, not on "fundamentals" like relative team strengths. Informed bettors make decisions based on the point spread, and their expectation of the actual outcome of the game. Uninformed bettors will bet on their preferred team at any point spread, while informed bettors will bet either side of a game, depending on the point spread. In this case, bookmakers can increase their profits by changing the point spread in a way to decrease the probability that bets placed by uninformed bettors win. Levitt (2004) showed that the probability that a bets placed on the favored team had a less than 50% chance of winning in the betting contest he analyzed, and interpreted this as evidence that sports books shade point spreads. Neither Levitt's (2004) model or this model explicitly consider how bettors make decisions, limiting both models' ability to explore this point.

This model of the expected returns to sports books shows that the "balanced book" model frequently discussed in the literature maximizes the expected returns earned by sports books only when all of the bettors in the market have an unbiased subjective probability that a bet on one of the teams in the game will win. When some biased bettors place bets on a game, and their subjective probability that a bet on the favored team will win does not equal the objective probability that a bet on the favored team wins, a sports book can make higher expected returns by accepting more bets on one side of the game, and shading the point spread to take advantage of these biased, or uninformed bettors. Previous research assumed that a balanced book was a relatively easy outcome for sports books to generate, or at least that sports books attempted to attract an equal volume of bets on either side of a proposition. Expanding a commonly used model of sports book behavior to the case where the probability that a bet on the favored team depends on the fraction of bets made on that team, and the sports book can manipulate this fraction by setting the point spread, and bettors switch their bets to the other team in response to changes in the point spread, generates

Table 9.4: Summary Statistics, NFL Betting 2005-2007

| | 2005 | | 2006 | | 2007 | | 2008 | |
Variable	Mean	SD	Mean	SD	Mean	SD	Mean	SD
Score Difference	3.78	14.0	0.85	14.4	2.86	15.4	2.56	15.3
Opening Point Spread	2.51	5.6	2.77	5.6	2.46	6.8	2.70	6.1
Closing Point Spread	2.70	6.1	2.80	5.9	2.42	6.7	2.67	6.13
Home team bet win %	0.49		0.47		0.50		0.44	
Favored team bet win %	0.55		0.42		0.51		0.49	
Fraction of bets on favorite	61.60	13.2	60.33	14.4	62.34	12.3	61.5	12.8
Games	256		256		256		256	

a prediction that expected returns may not be maximized when the book is balanced. The next section examines the relationship between point spreads, betting volume, and actual gains and losses in the market for point spread bets on NFL games to assess how often the volume of betting is equal on either side of propositions in this market.

9.7 Evidence

Much of the previous research on point spread betting focused on examining the efficiency of point spread betting markets. Because point spreads and game outcomes were readily available, but betting volumes were not, researchers assumed that the point spread was set in a way to equalize the volume of betting on either side of a game, and focused attention on the ability of point spreads to predict game outcomes. Recently, economists have gained access to betting volume data from point spread betting markets and have begun to examine point spreads and betting volumes. The model presented above demonstrates the conditions under which an unbalanced book, an outcome where the the volume of bets is not equally distributed, can still generate the largest expected return for the sports book. This section uses a data set that contains information on actual bet volumes from four on-line sports books to see if evidence supporting the predictions of the model exists.

Recently, data on betting volumes have become available, primarily from on-line sports books. The data come from Sports Insights, a firm with agreements to obtain betting volume data from four large on-line sports books: BetUS, Carib Sports, Sportbet, and Sportsbook.com. The data files that Sports Insights makes available include the opening and closing point spreads, the actual score of the game, and the percentage of bets reported on each side of a proposition for all regular season games played in the National Football League (NFL) in the 2005 - 2008 seasons. The data collected by Sports Insights represents an average across the four participating sports books. The betting volume is not available for all sports books and is not available for each game played over the course of the season. In addition, the total dollars bet on each game is not known. Table 9.4 shows summary statistics for key variables.

The NFL regular season runs from September until early January each year. A number of "pre-season" games are played in August and early September, but these games do not count toward the league championship. The data analyzed here include both pre-season and regular season games. Most NFL regular season games are played on Sunday afternoon and evening. In addition to Sunday games, one (and occasionally two) games are played on Monday night, and some other games are played on Thursdays and Saturdays later in the season. Each team plays 16 regular season games spread over 17 weeks. A small number of teams with the best records during the regular season advance to the postseason knock-out tournament that culminates in the Super Bowl. Betting on NFL games takes place on a rigorous schedule. Sports books issue an opening point spread on each game early in the week for the entire slate of games scheduled to take place over the next week. The opening line is made public on Sunday evening or Monday morning. Throughout the week, information about the status of injured players is made public, and the sports books observe the order flow in the market. Point spreads are changed on some games, either in response to new information about players or weather conditions, or in response to observed betting volumes on the games. The final point spread is the point spread that is posted immediately prior to the start of each game, when betting ends.

The first row on Table 9.4 is the average actual score difference, expressed as home team score minus visiting team score, for all NFL games in the data set in each season. The second two rows are the average opening and closing point spread set by the four on-line sports books on each game in each of the three seasons. Note that the actual score difference exhibits considerably more variation than either of the point spreads. Similar patterns exist in data on betting on National Basketball Association (NBA) games. On average, the point spread changed by roughly one point from the opening line to the closing line in all three seasons. However, in a significant number of games, 28% of them, the point spread did not change over the course of the week. The next two rows show the win percentage of bets placed on the home team and the favored team in each game. The overall average winning percentage for bets on the home team (0.48) and bets on the favored team (0.49) are less than 0.50, suggesting that sports books may shade the point spread against these bets. However, these winning percentages show considerable variation across seasons, indicating the presence of an important random component in these outcomes. Note that two of these season average winning percentages, betting on home teams in 2008, and betting on favorites in 2005, have average winning percentages outside the absence of profit bounds (0.476, 0.524) described above.

The last row reveals some interesting information about betting volumes. The data set contains information on the volume of bets placed on either side of the propositions for each game. This fraction will not be equal to the fraction of money bet on each side when the average value of the bets on the two sides are different. However, anecdotal evidence suggests that the volume of bets on each side is equal to the volume of money bet on each side. Clearly, the volume of bets on either side are not balanced very often in these data. The average fraction of bets are not equal to 50% in any season, and the standard deviations are relatively large, indicating substantial variation in the volume of bets. Bettors like to bet on favorites in the NFL. In each season, more than 60% of the bets placed were on the favored team. Again, the fact that a majority of the bets were placed on the favorite, and the win percentage of bets on the favorite was less than 50% suggests shading of the point spread by bookmakers, potentially to take advantage of uninformed bettors.

9.7.1 Distribution of Betting Volume

The disparity in the volume of bets placed on either side of games revealed on Table 9.4 does not fit with the typical "balanced book" model described in the literature. The volume of bets made is skewed toward favorites, the team that is expected to win the game, in all four NFL seasons. A closer look at the data on the fraction of bets made on either side of propositions shows a large number of games with unbalanced betting. The large standard deviations on the bet volume data shown on Table 9.4 suggest that the betting volume on individual games might be quite different from a balanced book.

Table 9.5: Distribution of Bet Volume and Dollars Bet

Variable	2005	2006	2007	2008
Average % of bets on favorite	61.6	60.3	62.3	61.5
Median % of bets on favorite	63.0	62.5	64.0	63.5
Skewness	-0.36	-0.52	-0.54	-0.51
Kurtosis	2.31	2.48	3.24	2.82
% of games where $47.6 \leq$ % of bets on favorite ≤ 52.4	7.8	10.5	6.6	7.8
% of games where % of bets on favorite > 60.0	59.0	60.0	64.1	62.9
% of games where % of bets on favorite > 75.0	21.4	19.4	14.1	13.3

Table 9.5 takes a closer look at the distribution of betting volume data across individual games. From the break even condition, equation (9.3), if the fraction of bets on the favored team falls between 47.6% and 52.4%, then the sports book makes a profit on the betting no matter which team wins the game. If the fraction of bets on the favored team falls outside this range, the then the sports book takes a position on the game, and can either gain more or lose more, depending on the outcome of the game. From Table 9.5, the distribution of the bets placed on the favored team is quite skewed. Sports books consistently take positions on games, and these positions are mostly on the underdog. The fifth row on Table 9.5 shows the percent of games in which the observed fraction of bets on the favorite fell inside the certain profit range in the 2005-2007 NFL seasons. In more than 90% of the games in these three NFL seasons, the observed fraction of bets on the favorite fell outside the certain profit range. In other words, the four on-line sports books represented in this data set took a position, on average, on 9 out of 10 NFL games that they took bets on. Either these books were exceptionally bad at setting point spreads to to equalize betting on either side of the game, or achieving a balanced book was not the goal of sports books taking bets on NFL games.

Figure 9.1 shows the distribution of the fraction of bets on the favored team in each game in each season. The red vertical lines on Figure 9.1 show the boundaries of the certain profit region. Figure 9.1 shows a large amount of variation in the fraction of bets on the favorite. Again, Figure 9.1 indicates that sports books took large positions on games, and that a majority of bettors prefer to bet on the favored team.

The distribution of the bets on the favored team in point spread betting on the NFL falls well outside the certain profit range for almost all games, indicating that sports books take positions on games frequently. Most previous research has assumed that sports books attempt to set point spreads to balance the volume of bets on either side of the game. If this were the case, we would expect to see many more instances of the betting volume falling in the certain profit range. Previous research also indicates that point spreads are unbiased and minimum variance estimators of actual game outcomes. One reason for the unbalanced book outcomes observed above could be that point spreads were not efficient during these three seasons for some reason.

9.7.2 Market Efficiency Tests

One important characteristic used to evaluate sports betting markets is the efficiency of the market. Efficiency in sports betting markets is typically defined as the absence of profit making opportunities; that is, in efficient sports betting markets bettors are unable to make positive profits in

Figure 9.1: Distribution of Fraction of Bets on Favored Team

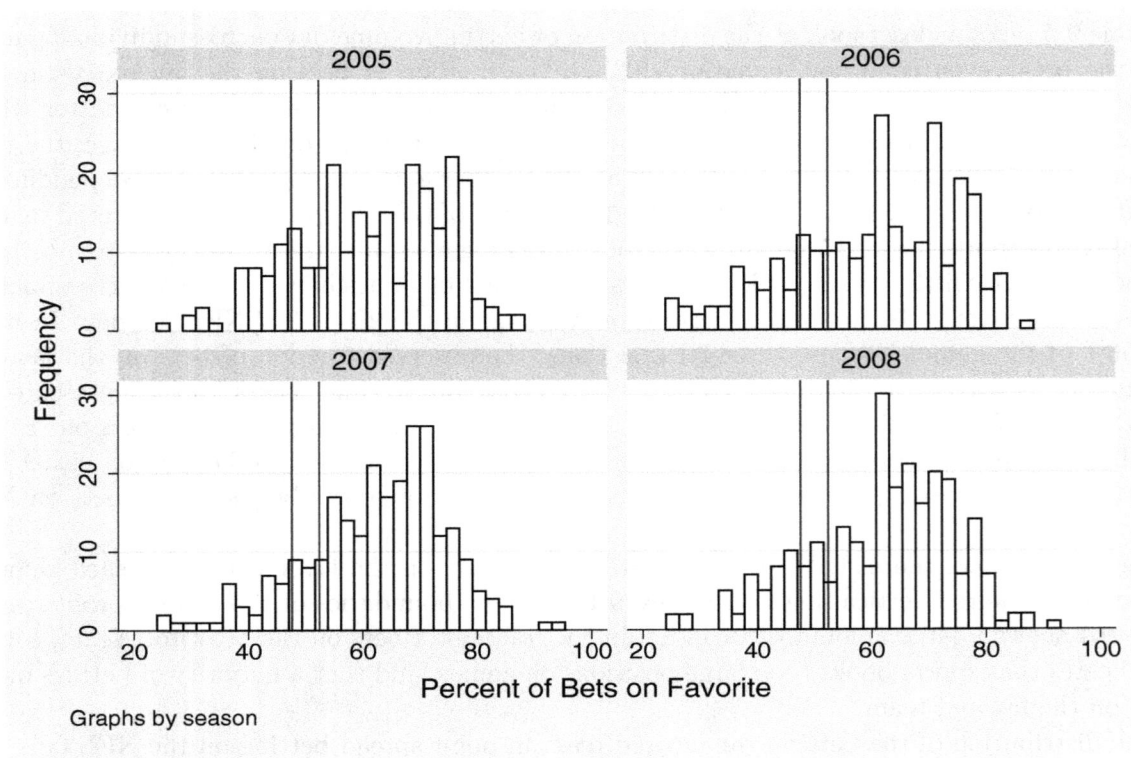

Graphs by season

Table 9.6: Market Efficiency Tests

	2005	2006	2007	2008
Intercept	0.636	-1.58	0.186	-0.155
P-Value	0.472	0.096	0.837	0.871
Opening Point Spread	1.254	0.879	1.090	1.003
P-Value	0.001	0.001	0.001	0.001
R^2	0.231	0.116	0.228	0.162
Observations	256	256	256	256
F-stat, $\alpha = 0$, $\beta = 1$	2.81	2.78	0.37	0.01
P-value	0.062	0.058	0.689	0.986
Intercept	0.531	-1.50	0.137	-0.219
P-Value	0.545	0.112	0.878	0.818
Latest Point Spread	1.202	0.838	1.126	1.039
P-Value	0.001	0.001	0.001	0.001
R^2	0.243	0.118	0.242	0.173
Observations	256	256	256	256
F-stat, $\alpha = 0$, $\beta = 1$	2.06	3.28	0.65	0.05
P-value	0.129	0.039	0.524	0.954

the long run. Given the unbalanced betting volume described above, testing for efficiency in this setting seems to be warranted, in order to exclude the possibility that the unbalanced bet volumes reflect the presence of inefficiencies in this market. Sauer (1998) showed that efficiency in sports betting markets implies that, given symmetry of the distribution of point score differences, the point spread set by sports books on a game is an unbiased, minimum variance estimator of the difference in points scored in the game. In practical terms, tests of efficiency in sports betting markets are based on a regression model

$$DP_i = \alpha + \beta PS_i + e_i \qquad (9.10)$$

where DP_i is the difference in points scored by the two teams involved in game i, PS_i is the point spread set by sports books on game i, and e_i is an unobservable random variable assumed to be distributed with mean zero and constant variance that captures all other factors that affect the difference in points scored. In this regression model, tests of efficiency are based on the joint hypothesis test based on the null

$$H_o : \alpha = 0 \text{ and } \beta = 1.$$

By convention, the points scored variable is expressed as visitor's points scored minus home team's points scored, and the point spread is expressed as negative numbers when the home team is favored and positive numbers when the home team is the underdog. The distribution of the points scored variable is relatively symmetric, the mean is -2.42 and the median is 3, so regression based efficiency tests appear to be appropriate in this case. The opening and closing lines are observed in this data set, and bets can be placed at either, so efficiency tests can be performed for both the opening line and the closing line.

Table 9.6 shows the results of estimating equation 9.10 using data from the 2005, 2006, 2007 and 2008 seasons separately. The key statistics on this table are the F-statistics on the test of the joint hypothesis that the intercept is equal to zero and the slope parameter is equal to one. This is the conventional test of betting market efficiency; if the null is accepted, then the point spread is an unbiased minimum variance estimate of the difference in points scored. This rejection implies the absence of profit opportunities for bettors in this market. This null hypothesis is accepted at conventional significance levels for all seasons for both the opening point spread and the closing point spread. Only tests based on the closing line in the 2006 season shows weak evidence that point spreads may not be a good predictor of game outcomes. Pooling data across seasons also led to a rejection of the null hypothesis. Both the opening line and closing line are good predictors of the actual point score in NFL games in these four seasons, despite the imbalanced bet volumes. This result is consistent with other tests of efficiency in NFL point spread betting markets found in the literature.

9.7.3   Losses, Gains, and Profits

One way to test the predictions of the model of sports book behavior developed in this chapter is to analyze the actual returns earned by sports books, given the observed point spreads, game outcomes, and distribution of bets on either side in this market. Available data contains enough information to conduct financial simulations of the profitability of sports books but not to calculate the exact profits earned by sports books for three reasons. First, data from specific sports books are lacking. The betting volume data available are averages across four different on-line sports books. If there is a significant amount of heterogeneity in point spread, bets taken, and the volume of bets on each side of a game across these sports books, then the average data will not reflect this heterogeneity. Second, I do not have access to data on the timing of individual bets. Only the opening line and the closing line on each game and the final volume of bets on each side is known. Because the point spread changes, by an average of about 1 point, in about 75% of the games, the exact amount of money wagered on each side at each point spread that was available during the week that bets could be placed on games cannot be known. This is important because point spread bets pay off based on the point spread that was posted at the time the bet was made, not based on the last point spread posted. Third, the total amount of money wagered on each game is not known; only information on the fraction of bets placed on either team in each game is available. Because of these limitations, simulations can be used to estimate the gains, losses, and profits earned by sports books on point spread bets in NFL games taken over these three seasons.

The simulations are straightforward. For each game, a simulation compares the opening and final point spread on the game to the actual game outcome to determine which side of the bet won, and which side lost. The winning bets enter the simulations as losses, since bookmakers must pay the bettors who made these bets. The losing bets enter the simulations as gains, plus the 10% commission charged on losing bets. That means for each $100 wagered on a losing bet, the sports book collects $110 from the bettor. In addition, assume that the the average size of bets on the favorite is equal to the average size of bets on the underdog. Under this assumption, the fraction of bets made on each side is equal to the fraction of dollars bet on each side. Using the fraction of bets placed on each side on each game, the gains and losses on each game can be calculated, and summed over the entire season.

The simulations also assume an equal number of dollars was bet on each game in the season. For simplicity, assume that 100 total "units" were bet on each game. While this assumption probably does not match reality – the total amount bet on games may vary depending on the teams involved – it is a convenient baseline for comparing the simulation results. Table 9.7 shows selected summary

Table 9.7: Average Loss, Gain, and Returns 2005-2008 Seasons

	2005 Season		2006 Season		2007 Season		2008 Season	
	100 Units bet, all bets at opening spread							
	Mean	SD	Mean	SD	Mean	SD	Mean	SD
Loss	-50.1	17.7	-48.4	17.6	-50.3	17.5	-49.4	17.1
Gain	54.8	19.4	56.6	19.4	54.6	19.3	55.6	18.8
Return	4.7	37.2	8.4	37.0	4.2	36.8	6.2	36.0
	100 units bet, all bets at closing spread							
Loss	-50.6	17.7	-48.7	17.6	-50.0	17.5	-49.7	17.1
Gain	54.3	19.4	56.4	19.4	55.0	19.3	55.3	18.8
Return	3.7	37.2	7.7	37.1	5.0	36.8	5.5	36.0
Games	245		249		251		250	

statistics for the simulations. The top panel assumes that all bets are made at the opening point spread; the bottom panel assumes that all bets are made at the final point spread. The actual distribution of the timing of bets lies somewhere between these two points, unless the line does not change over the course of the week.

Several interesting features emerge from the simulations. First, despite the lack of a balanced book for nearly all the games, the sports books make a positive return on average, and over the course of the season, no matter which point spread is used. Because of the assumption that 100 units are bet on each game, averages reported on the "Return" row can be interpreted as the percent return on all bets taken. So, for example, in the 2005 season the average return on all bets taken, assuming that they were made at the latest point spread, was 3.7, or 3.7%. Second, notice that the average return varies quite a bit over the three seasons simulated. The results of these simulations indicate that, no matter what the reason for moving point spreads, the effect of these changes appears to increase the returns earned by sports books on bets. Also, note that the variability of losses is smaller than the variability of gains in the simulations, and that the variability of profits is largest of all. Operating a sports book is a risky business, because profits are highly variable. The minimum and maximum values on Table 9.7 underscore just how risky operating a sports book can be. Assuming that all bets are made at the latest point spread, the largest loss in each of the four seasons was between 64% and 73% of the average bet volume on each game.

How do these returns compare to what would have been earned if the book was balanced on all games and an equal number of dollars were wagered on each side? In point spread betting, each bettor must risk $11 to win $10. Consider the simple case where only two bettors wager on a game, and each bettor wagers $110 to win $100 on each team. The sports book collects $220 from the two bettors and the betting is balanced. The losing bettor loses $110, and the winning bettor gets her $110 wager back, plus $100. The sports book keeps $10. The book's return is 10/220=4.55%.

From Table 9.7, the simulated rate of return exceeds 4.55% in three of the four seasons examined. By setting point spreads in a way to produce an unbalanced book on 9 of 10 games played, bookmakers earned a rate of return higher than the certain return in the 2006, 2007 and 2008 seasons, and a lower return in the 2005 season for the simulation, based on the closing point spread. In the 2005 season, the return at the opening point spread, 4.7%, exceeds the certain rate of return from operating a balanced book.

Note that no clear pattern in the size of returns exists for the opening and latest point spread. In three seasons, returns are higher at the opening point spread, and in one season returns are higher at the latest point spread. Again, no information exists on the timing of bets during the week leading up to NFL games, and this analysis can only conclude that the actual return to bookmakers lies between these two point spreads.

Also note that the average return was lowest in the 2005 season. Recall, from Table 9.4, that on average, more than 60% of the bet volume was on favored teams, and that 55% of the bets on favored teams paid off in the 2005 season. In the other three seasons bets on favored teams paid off much less frequently. The lower simulated returns earned by sports books in the 2005 season are consistent with this observed higher winning percentage on the bet favored by sports bettors.

Insufficient data exist to estimate the variance of returns, so it is unclear how likely a sports book is to earn a return in excess of the certain return of 4.55% by taking positions on games in the long run. The simulations suggest that it is possible, and likely, for sports books to earn returns larger than the certain return generated by a balanced book by operating an unbalanced book. Levitt (2004) raised the possibility that unbalanced bet volumes arise because of the presence of uninformed bettors in the betting market, and that sports books systematically "shade" point spreads to take advantage of these uninformed bettors. The simulation results indicate that sports books earn larger returns by operating an unbalanced book.

9.8   Summary

Sports betting markets appear to be efficient. Bettors on sporting events cannot earn profits using simple betting strategies, because point spreads incorporate all relevant public information. This has implications for financial markets, since sports betting markets function like other financial markets yet have observable prices, outcomes and payoffs. If sports betting markets are weak form efficient, then financial markets should also be weak form efficient.

Despite the clear efficiency of sports betting markets, the behavior of sports bookmakers appears to be more complex than standard economic theory predicts. Efficiency implies that point spreads are efficient predictors of game outcomes, and a significant amount of evidence supporting efficiency exists, so sports books must be very good at setting point spreads. Standard economic theory, in the form of the balanced book model, predicts that a sports bookmaker could earn a certain return by setting point spreads in a way to balance the volume of betting on either side of games. Despite the efficiency of point spreads, and the seeming simplicity of the balanced book model, sports bookmakers routinely set point spreads in a way that induces imbalanced betting volume on games. In addition, sports bookmakers appear to make larger profits by accepting imbalanced betting volume on games than they would have earned with a balanced book.

The presence of unbalanced betting volume on sporting events, coupled with the clear efficiency of point spreads, implies an interesting outcome in sports betting markets. Sports books appear to be able to set point spreads in a way to efficiently predict game outcomes and still earn a profit from the presence of unbalanced betting by gamblers. On the face of it, this appears to be a difficult trick to pull off. bookmakers must both set point spreads in a way that they efficiently predict game outcomes and selectively shade point spreads so that, on average, bettors on the "popular" side of bets (the side with the largest volume of bets placed) lose more than they win. Two possible explanations exist for this outcome. One is that sports bookmakers are better forecasters of game outcomes than sports bettor. They are right on average, and the public is wrong on average, and bets the wrong side in large numbers. The second is that sports bookmakers understand the betting patterns of their customers very well. They know exactly which games will be bet on heavily by casual bettors who like to bet on favored popular teams at any point spread, and selectively alter the point spread on on these games in a way that will make it less likely that the large number of bets on the "popular" side will win. This could be a relatively small number of games involving popular teams like the Dallas Cowboys or Indianapolis Colts.

Readings and References

Levitt, S. D. (2004). Why are gambling markets organized so differently from financial markets? *The Economic Journal*, 114, 223-246.

Paul, R. J. & Weinbach, A. P. (2005). Bettor misperceptions in the NBA, *Journal of Sports Economics*, 6(4), 390-400.

Paul, R. J. & Weinbach, A. P. (2007). Does Sportsbook.com set point spreads to maximize profits? Tests of the Levitt model of sportsbook behavior. *Journal of Prediction Markets*, 1(3), 209-218.

Paul, R. J. & Weinbach, A. P. (2008). Price setting in the NBA gambling market: Tests of the Levitt model of sportsbook behavior. *International Journal of Sports Finance*, 3(3), 2-18.

Sauer, R. D. (1998). The economics of wagering markets. *Journal of Economic Literature*, 36(4), 2021-2064.

Tversky, A. and D. Kahneman (1974) Judgment under uncertainty: Heuristics and biases, *Science*, New Series, 185(4157), 1124-1131.

Review Questions

1. Define the "balanced book" model of sports book behavior. Provide one reason why betting volume might be unbalanced on professional sporting events.

2. Define weak form efficiency in financial markets. Discuss one type of evidence that weak form efficiency exists in sports betting markets.

3. According to the model developed in this chapter, the expected returned earned by a sports book is

$$E[R] = [(1 - \pi_1)f_1 + (1 - \pi_2)f_2](1 + v) - (\pi_1 f_1 + \pi_2 f_2).$$

   Explain in words what the two terms on the right hand side of this equation mean.

4. True, False or Uncertain: Since bettors cannot earn profits on simple betting strategies like "always bet on the favored team" sports betting markets are inefficient.

Chapter 10

Pay and Performance in Professional Sports

Chapter Objectives

- Understand how marginal revenue product theory can be used to explain outcomes in sports labor markets

- Understand how human capital affects earnings of professional athletes

- Understand the principal-agent relationship that exists between teams and players, the incentives present in this setting, and the problems inherent in agreeing to compensation before observing the effort of players

- Understand how professional athletes respond to incentives in labor markets

10.1 Introduction

Sports labor markets are inherently interesting. The salaries earned by professional athletes are public knowledge and much larger than most people earn. Unlike other professions, the contribution of each professional team athlete to total team output is easily observable and quantifiable. Sports fans can compare the salaries of players on the local team to other players and to their own expectations about how much these players *should* be earning. These factors make sports labor markets interesting to fans. In addition, sports labor markets are interesting to economists. Models of firms' behavior make specific predictions about the relationship between compensation and inputs to production. In sports labor markets, unlike other labor markets, compensation, inputs and output are all easily observed, making sports labor markets an ideal laboratory for testing the predictions of economic models.

Table 10.1 shows some basic summary statistics about salaries earned by professional team sports athletes in North America in the 2008 and 2011 seasons. These salary data come from the *USA Today* salary database. On average, NBA players earn the highest salaries, at just over $4.6 million per year and NFL players earn the lowest salaries, at just under $2 million per year. The medians in the leagues are much lower than the average, indicating that there is a great deal of skewness in the distribution of salaries in these leagues. The skew takes the form of a long right tail, where a few players earn salaries much higher than average. The final columns show the highest paid player in each league in 2011-2012, and his salary. These reveal the extent of the skew in the

Table 10.1: Professional Sports Salaries

Sport	Average 2008	Median 2008	Highest Paid Player 2011	Salary
NBA	4,658,460	2,900,000	Kobe Bryant (Lakers)	27,849,149
MLB	3,131,041	1,000,000	Alex Rodriguez (Yankees)	29,000,000
NHL	2,135,201	1,250,000	Shea Weber (Predators)	14,000,000
NFL	1,947,402	931,680	Drew Brees (Saints)	20,000,000

distribution of salaries in professional sports leagues. The highest paid player in each league earns an annual salary many times the average salary in the league.

This chapter applies economic models of labor market outcomes to professional sports. The chapter develops a model to explain why professional athletes earn the salaries they do, and why salaries differ across sports and across players. The outcomes generated in sports labor markets provide interesting information about the predictions of economic models, and the models provide insight into observed outcomes.

10.2 Characteristics of Professional Sports Labor Markets

Before presenting the standard model of labor market outcomes, it is important to point out that labor markets in professional team sports have several unique characteristics not found in other labor markets. These features include entry drafts, the presence of the *reserve clause* in employment contracts, limited free agency and roster size limitations. The NFL, NBA and NHL also have salary caps in place that can affect labor market outcomes, although these restrictions limit total payroll, and not individual salaries. Salary caps were discussed in Chapter 5.

Potential employees in most labor markets are free to apply for a position with any firm in the industry they choose to work in, contingent on meeting the minimum requirements for jobs in that industry. This is also the case for new players seeking employment with professional football teams in Europe. But new entrants to professional sports leagues in North America generally enter the league through an *entry draft*. Entry drafts assign incoming players to specific teams through a structured process. Entry drafts in North America are held every year and are *reverse order*, meaning that the team with the worst record in the previous season has the first selection from the pool of incoming players, the team with the second worst record has the second selection, and so on. The entry draft creates monopsony power for teams, since it assigns the rights to negotiate and sign a player to a single team. A drafted player can either sign a contract with the team that selects him in the entry draft or not play professionally.

Entry drafts are a mechanism to prevent teams from competing to sign new players. The alternative to an entry draft is an open market where teams compete for new players by offering them salary and other compensation. An open market for incoming players would result in much higher salaries paid to new incoming players.

The first entry draft in North America was held in 1936 by the National Football League in Philadelphia, Pennsylvania. 81 college players were selected. The first pick of this first entry draft was Jay Berwanger, who played at the University of Chicago and won the first Heisman Trophy. Berwanger was selected as the #1 pick by the Philadelphia Eagles, but they did not want to meet his salary demands ($1,000 per game, or about $16,000 per game in 2013 dollars) and traded his rights to the Chicago Bears. Berwanger requested $15,000 from the Bears, who offered him only \$13.500. He turned them down and took a job at a rubber factory. Berwanger never played professional football. The next North American league to hold an entry draft was the NBA, which first held an entry draft in 1947. The NHL held its first entry draft in 1963, and MLB held its first entry draft in 1965.

The *reserve clause* is one of the oldest labor market characteristics in professional sport. It refers to actual language in the standard employment contract between players and teams. The reserve clause simply states that upon expiration of the contract signed by the player, the player's rights were retained by the team to which the player was signed. This language effectively gives teams the rights to employ specific players forever. A reserve clause was added to the standard professional baseball contract beginning in 1879, just three years after the formation of the National League, the first professional sports league in North America. The reserve clause allowed teams to unilaterally set salaries paid to players, since they only had the option to play at the contract price or quit playing. The reserve clause was in effect in professional sports leagues until 1976 when MLB players gained free agency after six years of major league service. Free agency came to other sports leagues shortly after. A free agent's contract does not contain the reserve clause.

All professional sports leagues in North America limit the number of players that any team can have under contract at any point in time, a *roster limit*. The roster limit in the NFL is 53 players; 13 in the NBA, 23 in the NHL. In MLB, a team can have 25 players on the active roster at any time, and a limit of 40 players who can be employed under a major league contract. Only these 40 players are eligible to appear on the 25 man active roster. Roster limits are designed to enhance competitive balance in sports leagues, by prohibiting a small number of teams from stockpiling talent. Professional football teams in Europe do not face roster limits.

10.3 Economic Models of Labor Markets

The economic model of labor markets explicitly reflects the behavior of the sellers of labor (workers) and the buyers of labor (firms) and also shows the determination of the price of labor (the wage) set in the market and the quantity of labor services bought and sold. This model is simply a tool for understanding how labor markets work. Once you understand how to apply the economic model of a market to the determination of salaries in professional sports, you can apply the model to a number of other situations in order to gain insight into economic behavior.

The following sections discuss the behavior of workers and firms in labor markets. After specifying how workers and firms behave, the interaction of workers and firms in a labor market are examined, and the determination of the equilibrium wage in the market is explained.

10.3.1 Labor Supply

Individual workers supply labor to labor markets. Individuals decide whether or not to take part in a labor market (called the *labor force participation decision*), and if they decide to participate, how much labor to supply. The "how much" question is usually framed in terms of hours per week in labor markets. The labor decision depends on the preferences of the individual for work and for *leisure* – defined here as not working – and how much the individual will earn when working. The decision to work is complex, and depends on many factors. In the context of the economic model of labor markets, the most important factor influencing an individual's decision to work, and how much to work, is the wage.

Generally, as the wage rises, individuals supply more units of labor, other things equal. In other words, holding everything that affects individual's decisions to work but the wage constant, as the wage rises people will supply more labor to the labor market. This prediction is based on an optimizing model of individual behavior, the familiar "consumer choice" model of microeconomics.

In the labor market model, individual's decisions about how much to work at any wage are summarized by a *labor supply curve*.

Labor Supply Curve: Shows the amount of labor an individual is willing to supply to the labor market at every wage, holding constant other factors that affect the labor supply decision like preferences and income.

A labor supply curve simply reflects individual's choices about how much to work based on the return to work – the wage – while holding other factors that affect the decision to work constant. It shows how labor supply decisions change as the wage changes.

Figure 10.1: A Labor Supply Curve

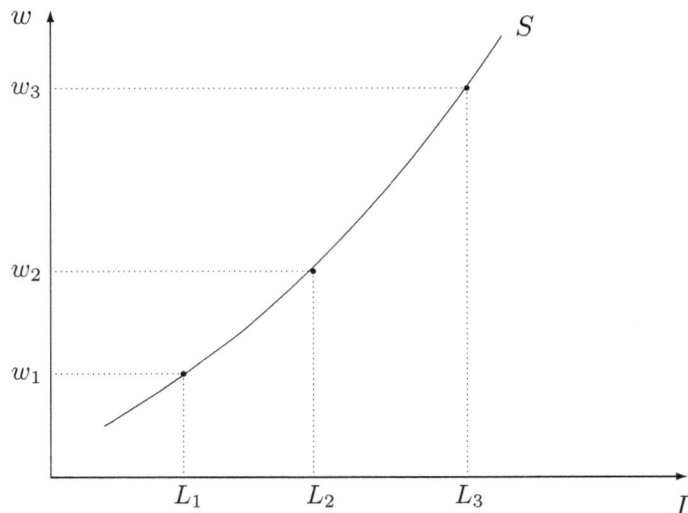

The implication of the prediction that more labor is supplied as the wage rises is that an individual's labor supply curve slopes up. Figure 10.1 shows a labor supply curve for an individual. The wage w is graphed on the vertical axis and the amount of labor supplied L is graphed on the horizontal axis on this figure. At low wages like w_1, little labor is supplied to the labor market. As the wage rises to w_2, labor supply increases to L_2; at a high wage like w_3, a lot of labor (L_3) is supplied to the labor market.

10.3.2 Individual and Market Labor Supply Curves

Suppose that many individuals supply labor to a labor market. Figure 10.1 shows the decision of one individual, but how can the decisions of many individuals be depicted? It is easy to combine individual labor supply curves to get a "market" labor supply curve that reflects the labor supply decisions made by all the individuals who participate in a labor market, using "horizontal aggregation" (this is just jargon for "adding things up horizontally.")

Figure 10.2 shows how horizontal aggregation can be used to derive a market labor supply curve from individual labor supply curves. Suppose that three individuals [Anne (A), Betty (B), and Cathy (C)] participate in a labor market. Figure 10.2 shows the labor supply curves for each

Figure 10.2: Horizontal Aggregation

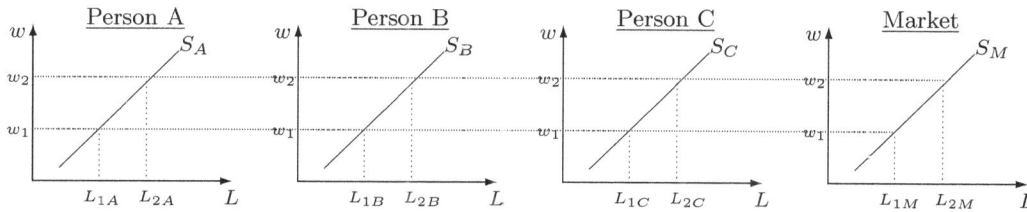

of the participants. At each wage, w_1 and w_2 for example, the individual labor supply curves show how much labor each participant will supply at each wage. Anne supplies L_{1A} at wage w_1 and L_{2A} at wage w_2; Betty supplies L_{1B} at wage w_1 and L_{2B} at wage w_2; Cathy supplies L_{1C} at wage w_1 and L_{2C} at wage w_2. The right panel shows the market labor supply curve S_M. The Ls are found by adding up each individual's labor supply at each wage. So at wage w_1, the market labor supply L_{1M} is just the sum of the three participant's labor supply $L_{1M} = L_{1A} + L_{1B} + L_{1C}$. At wage w_2, the market labor supply L_{2M} is just the sum of the three participant's labor supply $L_{2M} = L_{2A} + L_{2B} + L_{2C}$. The important point is that the shape of the market labor supply curve – upward sloping – remains the same as the slope of each individual labor supply curve.

10.3.3 Using Labor Supply Curves

Labor supply curves are a useful concept for analyzing the workings of labor markets. One important distinction is the difference between moving along a given labor supply curve (called a change in the quantity of labor supplied) and a shift in the entire labor supply curve (called a change in supply). Figure 10.3 shows these two different changes in a labor supply curve.

Figure 10.3: Using Labor Supply Curves

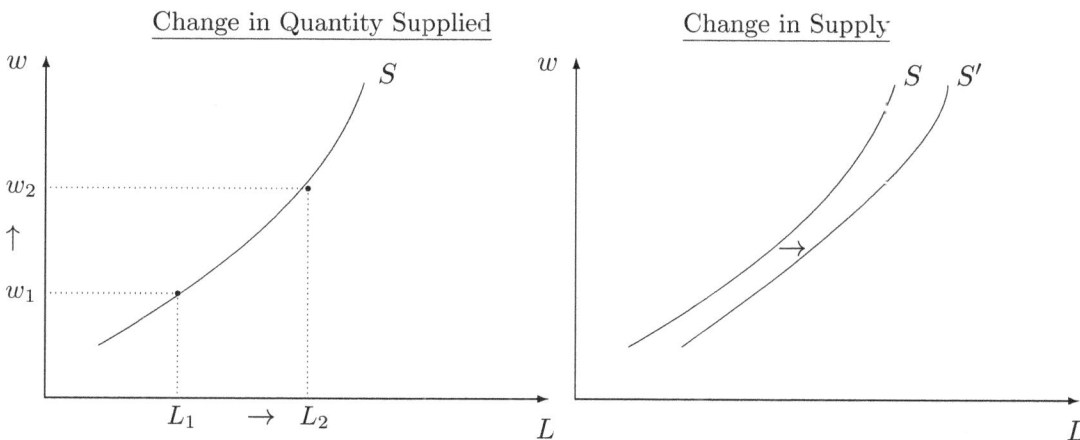

On the left panel of Figure 10.3, the wage increases from w_1 to w_2, inducing the existing participants in the labor market to increase labor supply from L_1 to L_2, an *increase in the quantity of labor supplied*. Higher wages induce the existing workers in the labor market to work more. On the right panel of Figure 10.3, a change in some factor independent of the wage leads more people to work at any given wage. This change could be, for example, an increase in the number of participants in the labor market.

Figure 10.4: An Individual and a Market Labor Supply Curve

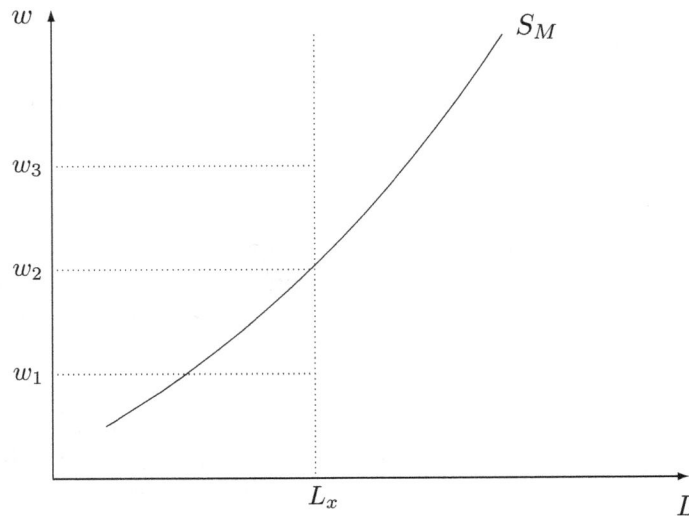

Economists sometimes interpret market labor supply curves as showing the wage at which a number of individuals are willing to work when sorted from the lowest wage to the highest wage (recall that the decision to work is called the *labor force participation decision*.) Under this interpretation, each point on a labor supply curve shows the optimal labor supply behavior of an individual, with the labor market decisions for individuals willing to work at relatively low wages grouped on the left of the graph and the labor market decisions for individuals willing to work at relatively high wages grouped on the right of the graph.

Figure 10.4 illustrates the interpretation of a labor supply curve as a summary of the labor market participation decisions of a large number of individuals. One individual, individual x, is identified on Figure 10.4, as point L_x on the labor supply curve. The vertical line above L_x shows the wage at which this person is willing to work. From Figure 10.4, this individual is willing to work at any wage greater than or equal to w_2. For example, this individual would be willing to work at a higher wage like $w_3 > w_2$. However, for any wage below w_2, for example w_1, the individual is not willing to work and will supply no labor to the labor market. At wages below w_2, the individual's opportunity costs and non-labor market opportunities provide this individual with more utility than working at a wage as low as w_1. This person will choose to exit the labor force – not work and not actively look for work, but instead pursue non-work activities like watching television – because these activities make this person better off than going to a job and earning w_1.

10.4   Labor Supply in Sports Labor Markets

The preceding general discussion of labor supply curves applies to a generic labor market with homogenous participants who have some discretion over the number of hours or days that they work in any given period of time. The positive slope of an individual's labor supply curve reflects the idea that, for a high enough wage, individuals would be willing to increase their labor supply - work overtime or take second jobs at night or on the weekend.

Sports labor markets have a number of features that differ from this generic labor supply model. At first blush, it might appear that labor supply curves in the sports labor market should be horizontal lines - perfectly elastic - because many people would be willing to take jobs as professional athletes at wages much lower than the prevailing wages in most professional sports occupations. However, this reasoning does not control for variation in ability, and a correctly defined labor supply curve holds the level of ability of the participants constant.

Participation in professional athletics – sport played at the highest possible level – requires relatively rare physical abilities like exceptional strength, endurance, foot speed, hand-eye coordination, height, and other abilities that are not present in a large portion of the population. Participation at the highest level also requires years of intensive training, practice and coaching. There is also a great deal of uncertainty of outcome in sports labor markets that discourages participation in professional sports at the highest level. Athletic potential becomes apparent at a young age, and requires early specialization by participants. But only a small number of gifted young athletes will play professional sports, because of injury, diminished desire, lack of access to high-quality coaching, or other factors. Also, the specialization required to develop into a professional athlete has large opportunity costs, as the time devoted to practice and conditioning could be devoted to the accumulation of human capital (education) with a much less uncertain payoff, or to work in some other occupation. These factors reduce the pool of participants in professionals sport labor markets, and shift the market labor supply curve to the left.

For a group of athletes with similar ability and training, the market labor supply curve will still have a positive slope. Participation in sports has opportunity costs for every individual. At low wage rates, this opportunity costs may exceed the wage, causing some individuals to drop out of the sports labor market. For example, noted Stanford University sports economist Roger Noll was a talented basketball player as an undergraduate at Cal Tech. He was named a small college all-American in his senior season and after graduation he was drafted by a team in the now-defunct American Basketball Association (ABA). However, Noll had been accepted into the PhD program in economics at Harvard, and the value of his graduate stipend at Harvard exceeded the salary he was offered to play in the ABA, and he chose to enter graduate school rather than play professional basketball.[1] At the other end of the labor supply curve, at higher the wage, it is less likely that the participant's opportunity cost will exceed the wage, and the more individuals with sufficient ability and training participating in the sports labor market; the market labor supply curve in sports labor markets should still slope up.

In North America the supply of participants in professional sports leagues comes from the existing participants, from minor league "farm teams," international tours in sports like golf, and from colleges and universities (and to a lesser extent from secondary schools in sports like professional basketball and soccer). Professional sports leagues have instituted a number of mechanisms - reverse entry drafts, minimum age requirements, rookie salary caps, etc. – that have a large effect on the job market opportunities available to new entrants in these labor markets. These restrictions have a large effect on wages and employment of new participants in professional sports labor markets; they are complex enough to warrant a more complete treatment than is possible here.[2] This chapter focuses only on the determination of wages in labor markets with few restrictions.

---

[1]This story was related to me by Professor Noll at a conference in 2003.

[2]Interested readers can consult Sherwin Rosen and Allen Sanderson (2001) "Labour Markets in Professional Sports," *The Economic Journal*, vol. 111, pp. F47-F68, and the references in that paper for a full examination of labor supply restrictions in professional sports labor markets.

10.5   Labor Demand

Firms purchase labor services in labor markets. In the context of professional sports, teams demand labor in the form of sports talent, coaches, trainers, and front office personnel; here we focus only on team's demand for players. Teams hire labor in order to produce output and maximize the profits generated by selling this output. Profit (π) is the difference between total revenues (R) and total costs (C)

$$\pi = R - C.$$

Sports teams earn revenues from ticket sales, signage in stadiums, concessions, parking, television and radio broadcast rights, licensed merchandize sales, and other sources. Teams' costs include salaries for players, coaches, and administrative personnel, travel, scouting, and other areas. Teams produce output from inputs. Inputs to production include labor (variable inputs) and capital (fixed inputs) like stadiums, offices, and practice facilities. According to the economic theory of production, firms must purchase more inputs to produce more output and earn more revenue. This theory predicts that firms purchase inputs until the contribution of the last unit of an input to revenues is equal to the cost of purchasing that unit of input. The contribution of each unit of an input to revenues is called **Marginal Revenue Product (MRP)** and the cost of purchasing a unit of an input is called **Marginal Cost (MC)**. Formally, firms purchase inputs until $MRP = MC$.

In this context, teams hire sports talent in order to produce wins. The teams then sell these wins to spectators and media outlets to generate revenues. The marginal cost of an additional player is that players wage or salary. To maximize profits, sports teams are willing to pay players a salary equal to their MRP, each player's individual contribution to team revenues.

Formally, let $WPCT$ represent wins produced by a sports team, expressed as winning percentage. In this case, the MRP of any individual player can be expressed as a function of wins

$$MRP(WPCT) = MP(WPCT) \times MR(WPCT)$$

$MP(WPCT)$ is the marginal product of the player - the number of additional wins that can be attributed directly to the player. $MR(WPCT)$ is marginal revenue, the additional revenue that the team can generate from the additional wins the player creates. $MP(WPCT)$ depends on the on-field performance of the player. $MR(WPCT)$ depends on characteristics of the market the team plays in and the marketing skill and effort of the team. The contribution of any player to total team revenues, MRP, depends on both the marginal product of the player, $[MP(WPCT)]$, and the marginal revenue from each additional win $[MR(WPCT)]$.

10.5.1   MRP and the Labor Demand Curve

Suppose that a 0.500 baseball team (a team with an 81-81 record in the previous season, so $WPCT = 0.500$) considers signing an additional star player through free agency. This additional star player will increase the number of wins that the team is able to produce, given the current production of wins $WPCT$. The additional wins generated by this star player is captured by $[MP(WPCT)]$. The additional wins will allow the team to earn more revenues by drawing more fans to the park, selling more concessions and licensed merchandise, etc. and this additional revenue is reflected in $[MR(WPCT)]$. The product of these two factors, MRP captures an individual player's contribution to revenues earned by the team. Economic theory predicts that the team will be willing to sign this star free agent player as long as the salary he will sign for is less than or equal to the MRP he generates.

Sports teams will continue to hire players so long as each player's salary is less than or equal to his MRP. This decision process can be summarized graphically by a labor demand curve.

Labor Demand Curve: Shows the amount of labor an individual firm is willing to purchase in the labor market at every wage, holding constant other factors that affect the labor demand decision like the price of output and the production technology.

In sports leagues, as in most other settings, marginal revenue (MR) declines as on-field success ($WPCT$) increases. The additional revenues generated when a team improves from 81-81 to 82-80, is greater than the additional revenues generated when a team improves from 100-61 to 101-60, other things equal. This implies that MRP falls as $WPCT$ rises, and the labor demand curve slopes down.

Figure 10.5: A Labor Demand Curve

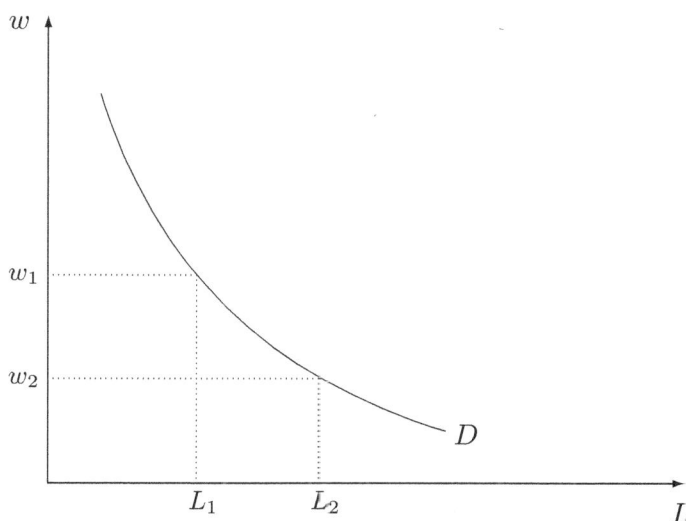

Figure 10.5 shows a labor demand curve for a profit maximizing sports team. The wage paid to players, w, is graphed on the vertical axis and labor inputs, L, are graphed on the horizontal axis. The labor demand curve shows how much sports talent the team will purchase in labor markets at every wage. Based on the wins produced, and the revenues generated by these wins, a sports team is willing to pay w_1 for L_1 units of sports talent. When the amount of sports talent hired increases to L_2, the team is only willing to pay w_2, because even though the increase in sports talent leads to more wins for the team, the additional (or marginal) revenues generated from these additional wins decreases.

As was the case for labor supply curves, the labor demand curve can also be thought of a reflecting the MRP of all of the players on a MLB team's roster when ordered from highest to lowest. At the left end of the labor demand curve are the star players on the team. These players have high $MP(WPCT)$ and earn high salaries. At the right end of the labor demand curve are utility infielders, fourth outfielders, and long relievers who pitch mop-up duty. These players have relatively low $MP(WPCT)$ and earn low salaries.

10.5.2   MRP and Labor Demand: An Example

A team's labor demand curve shows the MRP for each additional player that the team hires. For example, suppose that a team who finished 86-76 ($WPCT = 0.530$) last year is thinking about signing outfielder Jones (J). Based on his previous performance, the team believes that J has $MRP = \$5,000,000$, that is

$$MRP_J = MP(WPCT)_J \times MR(WPCT)_J = \$5,000,000$$

The marginal contribution of outfielder Jones (J) to the team's wins times the marginal revenue generated by those wins is worth \$5,000,000 to the team. Figure 10.6 shows outfielder J on the team's labor demand curve. Jones is player L_J on the vertical axis, and going up to the labor demand curve above this point, and reading over to the horizontal axis gives Js MRP as \$5,000,000. Also, remember that this \$5,000,000 MRP is composed of both Js contribution to team wins [$MP(WPCT)_J$] and the additional revenue that these additional wins earn the team [$MR(WPCT)_J$].

Figure 10.6: Player J on a Labor Demand Curve

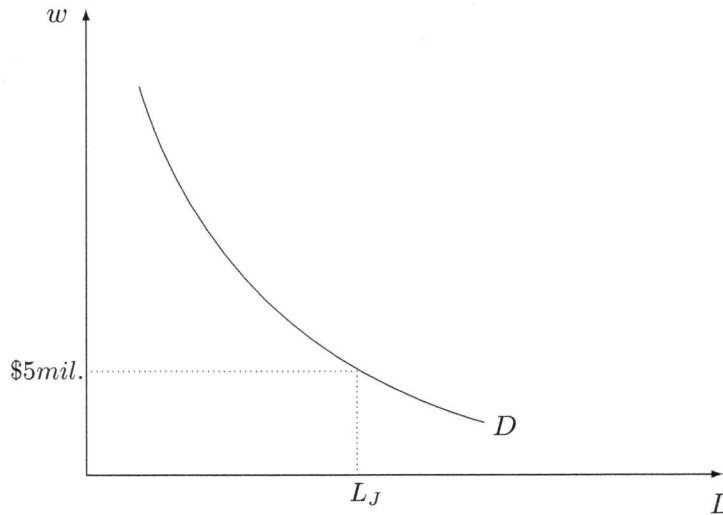

Now suppose that free agent outfielder J asks the team for a one year \$6,000,000 contract. Should the team accept J's offer? It depends on the relationship between the team's expected MRP for the player. Again, recall that the relationship between a players wage and his MRP is

$$MRP = MP(WPCT) \times MR(WPCT)$$

and profit maximizing teams will compare a players expected MRP and his cost, or wage. In this case

$$MRP_J = MP(WPCT)_J \times MR(WPCT)_J = \$5,000,000 < \$6,000,000 = w_J$$

so it does not make sense for the team to sign J for \$6,000,00 per season, because the team believes that adding J to the roster will only produce an additional \$5,000,000 in revenues. The team would expect to lose \$1,000,000 if J was signed. This decision can be shown on a graph of the team's labor demand curve, shown on Figure 10.7. J's expected MRP is again found from the labor demand curve. J's salary demand of \$6,000,000 is the horizontal line above J's MRP. Since this line lies above the team's labor demand curve above L_J, it is not profit maximizing for the team to sign J at this salary.

Figure 10.7: Player J's Salary demand and MRP

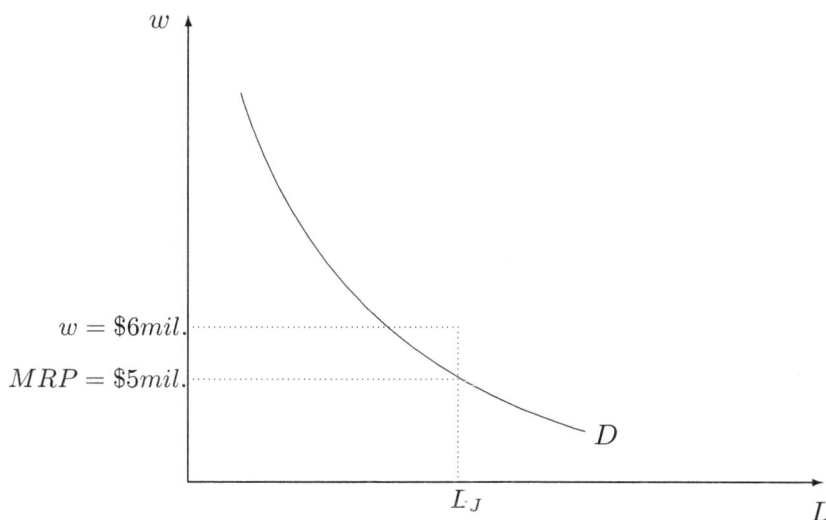

10.5.3 The Estimation of MRP in Practice

Gerald Scully, in his seminal 1974 article "Pay and Performance in Major League Baseball" in the *American Economic Review*, devised a way to estimate a players MRP from actual player's statistics and team revenue data. Scully's idea was that a player's individual statistics map into wins for his team, and teams sell wins to fans, in the form of tickets and media rights, to earn revenues. Scully assumed that players add value to teams in observable ways: position players generate offense and pitchers get outs and prevent the opposing team from scoring. He ignored the effects of the defensive contributions by position players. Scully estimated the value of hitting and pitching to a team, holding everything else constant, using multiple regression models in a two-step procedure. The first step was to estimate marginal product based on a production function for wins, much like the one used in Chapter 4. The production function assumed that teams produce wins $W\%$ using player inputs (T) and non-player inputs (I)

$$W\% = F(T, I) \tag{10.1}$$

where the non-player inputs include managers, coaches, capital and "nebulous inputs such as team spirit." In his two step procedure, Scully first estimated the relationship between team slugging percentage, TSA_t and team winning percentage, $W\%_t$ and the relationship between team strikeout to walk ratio, TSW_t using a regression model and data from the 1968 and 1969 MLB seasons. Rather than use player-specific data, Scully used team-specific data to estimate the marginal product of one additional point of slugging percentage or strikeout-to-walk ratio and one additional win percentage point. The regression model also controlled for other factors that affect marginal product like where the team finished in the final standings and the league the team played in. The key regression results reported by Scully

$$W\%_t \;=\; 37.24 \;+\; 0.92 \;\; TSA_t \;+\; 0.90 \;\; TSW_t$$
$$\quad\quad (0.39) \quad\quad (4.37) \quad\quad\quad (5.92)$$

indicate that both slugging percentage and strikeout-to-walk ratio had important effects on team winning percentage. In this equation the top number is the regression parameter estimate on that variable and the bottom number is the t-statistic for a two-tailed test of the null hypothesis that the parameter estimate is equal to zero. The results show that each additional one point increase in team slugging percentage led to a 0.92 increase in winning percentage points, other factors held equal; also each additional one hundredth point increase in the team strikeout-to-walk ratio increased team winning percentage by 0.90 points other things equal. The slugging percentage is a performance measure for position players and the strikeout-to-walk ratio a performance measure for pitchers. The t-statistics are large, indicating that the parameter estimates are statistically different from zero. 0.92 is an estimate of the marginal product of an additional outcome that contributes to slugging percentage (total bases divided by at bats) and 0.90 is an estimate of the marginal product of an additional outcome that contributes to strikeout-to-walk ratio (one additional strikeout or one fewer walk). Note that Scully used performance metrics, slugging percentage and strikeout-to-walk ratio, currently in vogue among MLB performance analysts long before they became popular, and eschewed the common performance measures used at that time like batting average and earned run average.

Note that the winning percentage points used by Scully can easily be converted to wins. Each win adds 6.2 winning percentage points in MLB, since

$$81 \; wins = \frac{81}{162} = 0.5000W\% \; and \; 82 \; wins = \frac{82}{162} = 0.5062W\%.$$

The second step in Scully's procedure was to estimate the marginal revenue of an additional win for a MLB team. Again, he used a regression model to estimate MR. This regression model had team revenue $Revenue_t$ as the dependent variable and team winning percentage, $W\%_t$, and market characteristics as explanatory variables. Again using data from the 1968 and 1969 seasons, Scully estimated the MR of a win and the MR of other factors using a linear regression model

$$Revenue_t \;=\; -1,735,890 \;+\; 10,330 \;\; w\%_t \;+\; 494,585 \;\; SMSA_t$$
$$\quad\quad (1.69) \quad\quad\quad (6.64) \quad\quad\quad\quad (4.61)$$

where $SMSA_t$ is the population in the metropolitan area that the team played in millions. Scully's MR estimates indicate that each one point increase in winning percentage increased revenues by $10,330. Since each additional win increases winning percentage by 6.2 points, the marginal revenue generated by additional win was $10,330 \times 6.2 = \$64,046$. This is $402,182$ in 2010 dollars. Each additional million persons in a team's market generated about $500,000 in additional revenues, which is worth $3,138,000 in 2010 dollars. The regression model contained other explanatory variables.

Scully's two-step procedure generated estimates of the marginal product of increases in slugging percentage and increases in the strikeout-to-walk ratio, performance measures for hitters and pitchers. These MP estimates show how individual player performance contributes to wins by the team. It also generated estimates of the marginal revenue of an additional win. Taken together, Scully's estimates can be used to generate estimates of the MRP of players, based on their performance, in terms of slugging percentage for hitters and strikeout-to-walk ratio for pitchers. For example, each additional point in slugging percentage increased winning percentage by 0.92. So the MRP estimate for hitters is

$$MRP\ Hitters = 0.92 \times \$10,330 = \$9,504\ per\ point\ TSA.$$

This can easily be updated to current value. \$10,330 in 1968 is worth \$64,840 in 2010. So the current MRP of a point of team slugging average is

$$MRP\ Hitters = 0.92 \times \$64,840 = \$59,652\ per\ point\ TSA.$$

Similarly, for pitchers, Scully estimated that each additional hundredth of a point increase in strikeout-to-walk ratio increased winning percentage by 0.09. So the MRP estimate for pitchers is

$$MRP\ Pitchers = 0.90 \times \$10,330 = \$9,297\ per\ \frac{1}{100}\ point\ TSW.$$

In 2010 dollars

$$MRP\ Pitchers = 0.90 \times \$64,840 = \$58,356\ per\ \frac{1}{100}\ point\ TSW.$$

As Scully pointed out, converting these MRP estimates to salaries requires making assumptions about how individual player performance affects team averages for slugging percentage and strikeout-to-walk ratios. Scully assumed that individual performance has no externalities (so adding a player has no effect on the performance of teammates – this effectively assumes that individual player performance can be added to get team performance). Most MLB rosters have 10 pitchers and 15 position players, and 8 of those pitchers will contribute regularly as starters or relievers, and 12 of the position players will play regularly as starters or relievers (the other pitchers and position players represent seldom used reserved players or players rotating up and back from the minor leagues). If a team has 8 regularly contributing pitchers, an average pitcher with a strikeout-to-walk ratio of 2.0 will contribute about $1/8 \times 2.0 = 0.25$ to team strikeout-to-walk ratio. If a team has 12 regularly contributing position players, the average hitter with a slugging percentage of 340 will contribute $1/12 \times 340 = 28.3$ to team slugging average.

These figures can be used to generate estimates of the MRP of players of different ability, in terms of their average slugging percentage or strikeout-to-walk ratio over a season. Table 10.2 shows the MRP estimates for hitters and pitchers in Scully's paper and the estimates converted to 2010 dollars for different levels of performance, based on Scully's assumptions about the contributions of individual players to team average slugging percentage and strikeout-to-walk ratio.

From Table 10.2, in 1968 and today, even mediocre players generate substantial MRP. The average slugging percentage in 2008 among regular MLB players was 426, so the average hitter generated \$2.1 million in marginal revenue product. Even bad pitchers, with strikeout-to-walk ratios of 1.6 (the league average in 2008 was 2.3) generated MRP estimates in 2010 in excess of \$1 million. Of course this exercise assumes that the factors determining MR and MP in MLB in 1968 are the same as the factors in place in 2010. Nonetheless, these estimates provide some information about salaries and MRP, and give an indication of why salaries in MLB are relatively high: because the players generate significant MRP.

Table 10.2: MRP Estimates, 1968 and 2010

	Hitters			Pitchers	
$\overline{SA}$	MRP_{68}	MRP_{10}	$\overline{SW}$	MRP_{68}	MRP_{10}
270	213,840	1,342,170	1.6	185,940	1,167,120
290	229,680	1,441,590	1.8	209,183	1,313,010
310	245,520	1,541,010	2.0	232,425	1,458,900
330	261,360	1,640,430	2.2	255,668	1,604,790
350	277,200	1,739,850	2.4	278,910	1,750,680
370	293,040	1,839,270	2.6	302,153	1,896,570
390	308,880	1,938,690	2.8	325,395	2,042,460
410	324,720	2,038,110	3.0	348,638	2,188,350
430	340,560	2,137,530	3.2	371,880	2,334,240
450	356,400	2,236,950	3.4	395,123	2,480,130
470	372,240	2,336,370	3.6	418,365	2,626,020
490	388,080	2,435,790	—	—	—
510	403,920	2,535,210	—	—	—
530	419,760	2,634,630	—	—	—
550	435,600	2,734,050	—	—	—
570	451,440	2,833,470	—	—	—

MRP and Experience

Marginal product is not constant over a player's career. Some of the factors that affect a player's MRP – health and injuries, for example – are random and unpredictable and lead to random year-to-year fluctuations in performance. But some of the factors that affect a player's MRP are relatively stable and predictable. Empirical analysis of career performance of many athletes shows that a player's year-to-year performance, and thus his MRP, rises over the course of a career until a peak year and then declines until retirement. Wages reflect player's MRP, so we should see a similar pattern in earnings over the careers of professional athletes.

Economists call the relationship between experience (or sometimes age, which is closely correlated with experience) and wages the *experience earnings profile*. Earnings and experience data from many other occupations shows a similar pattern of wages rising over the beginning of worker's careers and then falling until retirement. Economic theory attributes this "hump shaped" experience-earnings profile to the acquisition and depreciation of *human capital*. Human capital is a generic term for education, experience, and accumulated wisdom gained through formal schooling and on-the-job training.

Figure 10.8 shows a representative age-earnings profile for a worker. The idea is that MP starts off low, and then increases with experience as the player reaches peak performance years and then begins to decline. Since earnings depend on MRP and MRP depends on MP, this leads to a predictable increasing and then decreasing pattern in lifetime earnings of workers, including athletes. Economists call this the age-earnings relationship, and represent it with an age-earnings profile. Age-earnings profiles graph time, in terms of the player's age or experience, on the horizontal axis and MRP, which is equal to the players salary, on the vertical axis. Age-earnings profiles have a humped shape, reflecting MP that rises at first and then falls over a career. Coaches and Managers have similar MPs, age-earnings profiles, and MRP, which is why they earn high salaries later in their careers.

Figure 10.8: An Age-earnings Profile

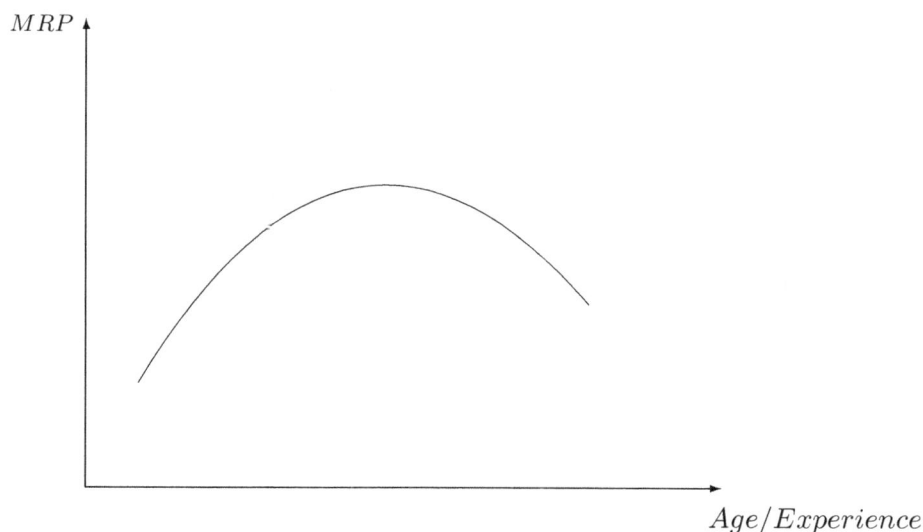

Athletes' experience-earnings profiles look like the experience earnings profiles of other workers – rising from the beginning of work to a peak and then falling until retirement, suggesting that athletes, like other workers, are able to gain important experience and knowledge over the course of their careers that lead to increases in their marginal product. Human capital, like physical capital, also tends to wear out, or depreciate, over time. In the case of athletes, the natural aging of the human body leads to physiological changes that reduce athlete's productivity - slower speed and reaction times, increased susceptibility to injury, deterioration of eyesight, and other factors.

As an example of the experience-earnings profile of an athlete, consider the following data on the career performance and earnings of Greg Maddux, a long-time starting pitcher in Major League Baseball. Maddux made his major league debut 3 September 1986 for the Chicago Cubs. Notice the relationship between Maddux's age and performance and the relationship between his age and earnings. His age and salary started relatively low in the late 1980s, increased and then declined toward the end of his career. The relationship between his age and performance - measured by ERA – are similar. His season ERAs started out high, fell, then rose. These relationships reflect the familiar patterns discussed above. His earnings changed systematically with his experience. Economic theory explains these changes with Maddux's acquisition of human capital. Over the early part of his career, Maddux was accumulating human capital through on-the-job training. He was learning how to be an ace starting pitcher. As he aged, his human capital began to depreciate, and his productivity declined.

Also note the major salary jump in his fifth year, when Maddux became eligible for limited free agency. This is a common feature of the age-earnings profiles of athletes in Major League Baseball, and the following section on salary arbitration examines this feature in detail. Also note that, like many estimates of the relationship between earnings and experience from other occupations, his earnings peaked after his performance. Maddux's salary peaked in 2003 and his ERA was lowest in 1994-1995; his maximum pay lagged his maximum performance, another common feature of the age-earnings relationship.

Table 10.3: Experience-Earnings Profile, Greg Maddux

Year	Age	W	ERA	Team	Salary
2004	38	16	4.02	Chicago Cubs	$6,000,000
2003	37	16	3.96	Atlanta Braves	$14,750,000
2002	36	16	2.62	Atlanta Braves	$13,100,000
2001	35	17	3.05	Atlanta Braves	$12,500,000
2000	34	19	3.00	Atlanta Braves	$10,500,000
1999	33	19	3.57	Atlanta Braves	$10,600,000
1998	32	18	2.22	Atlanta Braves	$9,600,000
1997	31	19	2.20	Atlanta Braves	$6,500,000
1996	30	15	2.72	Atlanta Braves	$6,500,000
1995	29	19	1.63	Atlanta Braves	$5,500,000
1994	28	16	1.56	Atlanta Braves	$4,000,000
1993	27	20	2.36	Atlanta Braves	$5,500,000
1992	26	20	2.18	Chicago Cubs	$4,200,000
1991	25	15	3.35	Chicago Cubs	$2,400,000
1990	24	15	3.46	Chicago Cubs	$437,500
1989	23	19	2.95	Chicago Cubs	$275,000
1988	22	18	3.18	Chicago Cubs	$82,500
1987	21	6	5.61	Chicago Cubs	$62,500

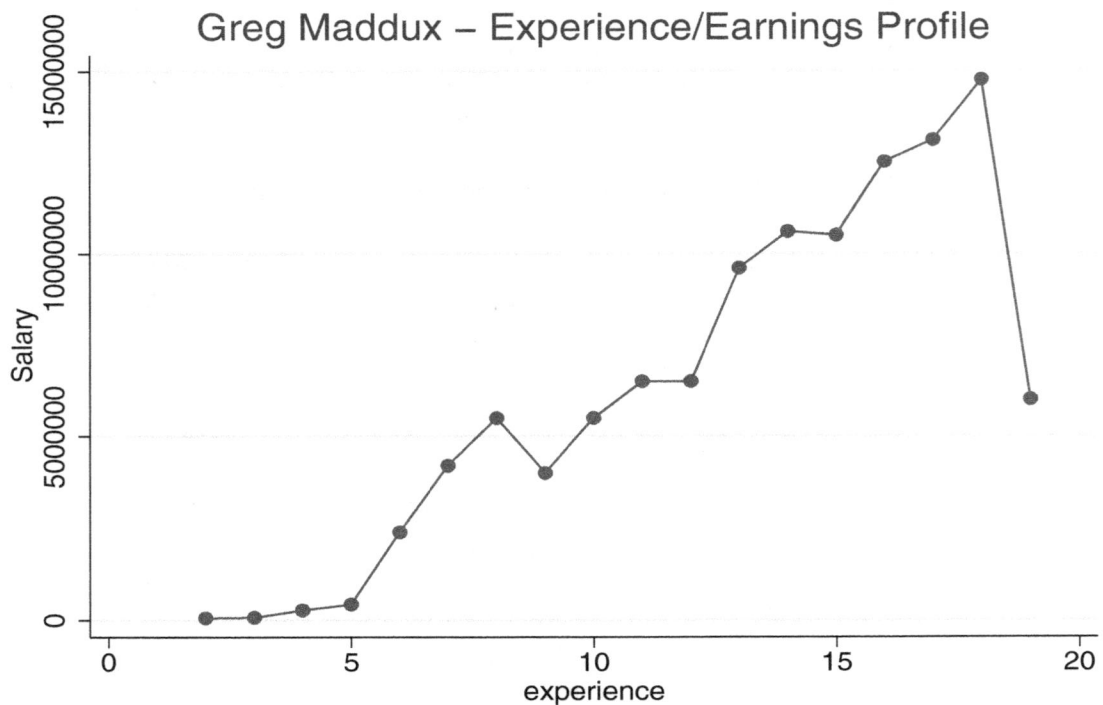

Greg Maddux – Experience/Earnings Profile

10.5.4 MRP and Position

The MRP explanation for observed earnings in professional sports can explain a number of observed patterns in the compensation of professional athletes. For example, the contribution to wins of players in different positions on a sports team differs systematically. The marginal product of the quarterback on a football team differs from the marginal product of a defensive lineman. This difference in MP should also lead to differences in the MRP of a player, and to systematic differences in earnings. Table 10.4 shows the average salary by position for a number of different positions on professional sports teams in 2003.

From Table 10.4, the average salary for different positions shows some clear differences. In MLB, much of the variation across positions has to do with offensive production and with sorting by age. Designated hitters earn the highest salaries, probably because designated hitters tend to be older players who can no longer play a defensive position. Their hither salary reflects both more experience on average and greater offensive production. First and third basemen also earn relatively high salaries, while catchers and second basemen earn relatively low salaries. The MRP approach explains the difference between the salaries of corner infielders (first and third) relative to middle infielders (short and second base) based on a difference in the average MP of players at these positions. In the NFL, quarterbacks clearly earn higher salaries than players at other positions, reflecting their higher MP. In the NBA, centers and players who play at either center and forward (C-F, primarily center) or forward and center (F-C, primarily at forward) earn higher salaries. In the NHL, there is not much difference in the salaries of players at different positions, withe the exception of left wingers, who earn lower salaries and presumably have lower MP. All of these averages do not control for age and experience, which affect salaries. If players move from position to position as the age, as happens in MLB, this can also systematically affect earnings.

10.5.5 MRP and Uncertainty

The economic theory of the determination of wages in labor markets explained so far provides insight into observed behavior in sports labor markets. It also omits several factors that play an important role in these markets. One important omitted factor so far is uncertainty about player's future performance. When determining the appropriate salary to offer a player, the team must – explicitly or implicitly – make a forecast of how the player will perform. As any sports fan knows all too well, player performance varies from season to season. The performance of both position players and pitchers in MLB varies quite a bit from season to season, making prediction of future performance an uncertain exercise. Some variation in player performance can be due to health and injuries, which are inherently unpredictable. Because performance affects a players marginal product $[MP(WPCT)]$, a major component of player's contributions to team revenues is, to some extent, difficult to predict with any precision. There is uncertainty about future performance.

Salaries are set in advance of performance in professional sports leagues. While many contracts contain incentive clauses that provide additional compensation to players who achieve certain milestones like selection to the All-Star team or winning awards, all contracts specify some base salary that the player receives no matter how well or poorly he performs. Because salaries are determined before the season begins, any sports season will feature a number of "busts" – high paid players performing well below their previous standards of performance – and "bargains" – low paid players having unexpectedly good seasons. These "busts" and "bargains" tend to offset each other over the course of a season and over the entire league, but this might not take place within any given team, leading to significant variation in a team's year to year performance and profitability.

It is also possible that team owners make systematic mistakes when forecasting player's future

Table 10.4: Professional Sports Salaries by Position, 2008 Season

Position	MLB	NBA	NFL	NHL
Catcher	2,160,425	—	—	—
Designated Hitter	8,819,003	—	—	—
First Baseman	4,551,346	—	—	—
Outfielder	3,715,254	—	—	—
Pitcher	2,709,819	—	—	—
Second Baseman	2,337,463	—	—	—
Shortstop	3,208,449	—	—	—
Third Baseman	4,672,867	—	—	—
C	—	4,425,995	—	—
C-F	—	6,415,333	—	—
F-C	—	5,756,639	—	—
F	—	4,703,313	—	—
G	—	4,481,940	—	—
G-F	—	3,889,282	—	—
F-G	—	3,638,316	—	—
CB	—	—	2,062,616	—
DE	—	—	2,410,453	—
DT	—	—	1,932,796	—
LB	—	—	1,631,388	—
OL	—	—	1,986,121	—
P/K	—	—	1,155,398	—
QB	—	—	3,474,812	—
RB	—	—	1,674,002	—
S	—	—	1,493,597	—
TE	—	—	1,482,797	—
WR	—	—	2,108,588	—
C	—	—	—	2,139,854
D	—	—	—	2,245,089
LW	—	—	—	2,205,036
RW	—	—	—	1,844,332
G	—	—	—	2,188,110

performance. For example, an eternally optimistic owner might systematically over value the future performance of free agent players, leading that owner to systematically offer these players a salary that exceeds the players actual MRP. In the short run, these owners could operate teams; but in the long run, teams run by such owners would consistently perform poorly on the field and financially and eventually these owners would be forced to sell their teams. Also, to the extent that teams make systematic mistakes when forecasting the MRP of players, it may be possible for some teams to exploit these forecast errors. This is the point made by Michael Lewis in his recent book about the Oakland Athletics, *Moneyball* (2004).

10.6 Labor Market Outcomes

10.6.1 Equilibrium in the Talent Market

MRP explains observed earnings in professional sports adequately. Athletes and coaches earn high salaries because they have high MRPs. As long as competition for coaches and players is brisk (there are multiple bidders for the services of a player or manager), team owners will have to pay players and coaches salaries near their MRPs. This is an equilibrium outcome in sports labor markets. We can graphically depict this equilibrium outcome in two equivalent ways.

The first way to characterize equilibrium outcomes in labor markets uses the equilibrium in the two-team league model from Chapter 5. Recall that in equilibrium in the two-team model, MRP is equal to MC, which is the market price of a unit of labor. The market price of a unit of labor is the salary earned by all athletes in that model, shown as w^* on Figure 10.9. Recall that in this model, all talent is homogenous, and all athletes have the same marginal product. But marginal revenue declines as winning percentage increases, leading to a downward sloping marginal revenue curve.

Figure 10.9: Equilibrium in the Two-team Model and Salaries

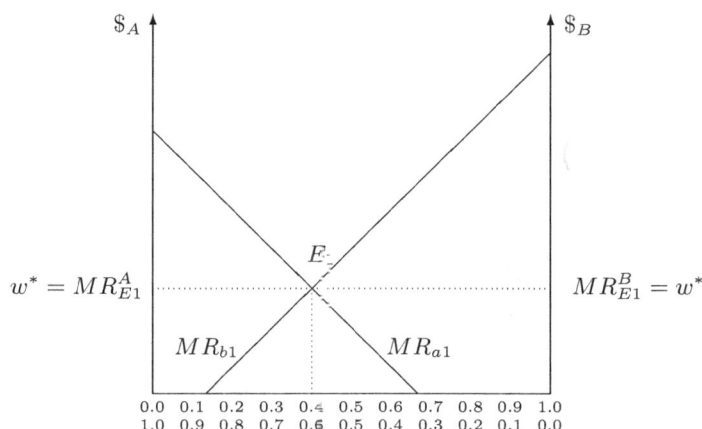

The second way to motivate this outcome is using the labor supply and demand model developed above. Suppliers and demanders of labor interact in labor markets. Suppliers and demanders negotiate in these markets, and in those cases where they agree, the labor market matches workers who are willing to work for a certain wage with firms who are willing to pay that wage in exchange for labor inputs. The wage is the mechanism that matches buyers and sellers in this market.

The interaction between buyers and sellers in labor markets can be seen when the labor supply and labor demand curves are combined to show the decisions made by both types of participants in the labor market. Figure 10.10 shows the operation of a labor market in terms of the economic decisions made by both workers and firms. In this figure, w^* is the equilibrium wage – the wage at which workers are willing to supply labor to the market and firms are willing to hire workers.

Figure 10.10: Labor Market Equilibrium

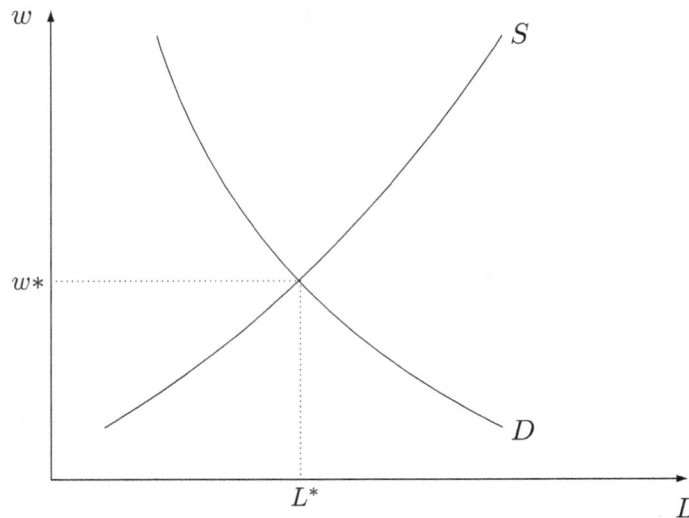

At wages above $w*$ labor supply exceeds labor demand - more individuals are willing to work than firms are willing to hire. At wages below $w*$ labor demand exceeds labor supply - firms are willing to hire many workers, but few workers are willing to work at this relatively low wage. At wage $w*$ the number of workers that firms want to hire is exactly equal to the number of individuals who are willing to work. Labor supply is exactly equal to labor demand.

Economists find it useful to think about the conditions under which the prevailing wage in a labor market will be driven to $w*$ and labor supply equals labor demand. This outcome is called *equilibrium* in the labor market. One set of conditions where this happens is when all workers and firms are identical, there are many workers and firms in the market all of whom are free to enter and leave the market at will, and all the participants have perfect information about wages, abilities and working conditions. Under these conditions, all workers will be paid the equilibrium wage $w*$. A market where these conditions exist is called a *perfectly competitive market*. These conditions are not often replicated in actual labor markets, but they represent a useful benchmark against which actual labor market conditions and outcomes can be compared.

One key hallmark of a perfectly competitive labor market is that workers are free to sell their labor to the highest bidder, and there is complete information about the ability of players. Sports talent markets with free agency – for example the market for MLB players with more than six years of experience – are relatively competitive.

Economists characterize markets by their degree of competitiveness. In competitive labor markets players should get paid a salary close to or equal to their MRP. Thus a competitive labor market is one where $w = MRP$. In terms of the labor market equilibrium shown on Figure 10.10, at the equilibrium wage w^* firm's value of worker L^*, the MRP found from the labor demand curve, is exactly equal to the wage earned by L^*; an outcome characteristic of a perfectly competitive market.

10.6.2 Assessing the Model: Outcomes in Labor Markets

The MRP explanation for the determination of salaries provides insight into variation in salaries earned by professional athletes. The model predicts that players earn a wage equal to their marginal revenue product, and that players with similar abilities and characteristics should earn similar salaries. The model also identifies a number of factors that affect salaries. For example, consider the performance measures and salaries for the two NHL players shown on Table 10.5. Evgeni Nabokov and Roberto Luongo both played the same position, goalie, and started their professional careers at the same time. Nabokov is a bit older than Luongo, and Luongo is a bit bigger then Nabokov. Age and physical characteristics affect salaries, so these factors are not held constant in this comparison, but their experience, playing time, and position are comparable. Nabokov was drafted much later than Luongo, which could indicate that Luongo has higher ability than Nabokov; however, Nabokov was drafted from Kazakhstan, and his low draft position could also reflect a lack of information about his actual ability because he played in Kazakhstan.

Note that Nabokov was a free agent after the 2009-2010 NHL season. When little interest in signing him appeared in the NHL, he signed a contract with SKA St. Petersburg of the Kontinental Hockey League in Russia for a reported $24 million dollars over 6 years, which is the basis for the $4 million dollar contract reported on Table 10.5. He played only 22 games and the contract was terminated by mutual consent on 10 December 2010. Nabokov returned to North America and signed a one year contract with the NY Islanders in 2011.

The performance and salary information on Table 10.5 show several interesting features that support the predictions of the MRP model of salary determination. For example, the salaries of both players increase over the period shown on the table, consistent with the idea that human capital is an important determinant of earnings, and increases in the early years of an athletes career. One important feature revealed on Table 10.5 is that over the period 2006-2010 Luongo earned about $1 million to $1.5 million more per season than Nabokov; in percentage terms, Luongo earned about 25% more than Nabokov. Why would two starting goalies with similar experience and physical characteristics earn such different salaries?

Recall the the model predicts that salary should equal marginal revenue product. That is, profit maximizing firms produce wins, W, players are inputs to production and their individual contribution to the production of wins can be captured by their marginal product, $MP(W)$, and teams earn revenues based on the number of wins they produce and the marginal revenue of an additional win is $MR(W)$. Under these conditions, and if there are no other institutional factors like the reserve clause affecting salaries, then a players salary, S, should equal his marginal revenue product

$$S = MRP(W) = MP(W) \times MR(W).$$

Let L subscripts on variables identify Roberto Luongo and N subscripts identify Evgeni Nabokov. From Table 10.5, $S_L > S_N$ over the four season period 2006-2007 through 2009-2010; Luongo earned more than Nabokov over this period. The model identifies several specific factors that can explain this observed difference in salary. These factors fall into two broad categories:

1. $S_L > S_N$ because $MP(W)_L > MP(W)_N$, Luongo has a higher marginal product than Nabokov. That is the contribution of Luongo to wins produced by the Canucks was greater than the contribution of Nabokov to wins by the Sharks. Note that we cannot simply look at the records of the two teams, because the model predicts that the *marginal* contribution of each player affects earnings, not the total team production. The model identifies a number of factors that affect the marginal product of individual players. These include: underlying skill

Table 10.5: Roberto Luongo vs. Evgeni Nabokov

Evgeni Nabokov, Goalie
Born Jul 25 1975 Kamenogorsk, Kazakhstan; Height 6.00, Weight 200, Shoots L
Selected by San Jose Sharks Round 9 #219 overall 1994 NHL Entry Draft

Season	Team	GP	Min	GA	SO	GAA	W	L	T	Svs	Salary
2000-01	San Jose Sharks	66	3700	135	6	2.19	32	21	7	1582	$500,000
2001-02	San Jose Sharks	67	3901	149	7	2.29	37	24	5	1818	$575,000
2002-03	San Jose Sharks	55	3227	146	3	2.71	19	28	8	1415	$3,525,000
2003-04	San Jose Sharks	59	3455	127	9	2.21	31	19	8	1483	$3,625,000
2005-06	San Jose Sharks	45	2575	133	1	3.10	16	19	7	1027	$3,363,000
2006-07	San Jose Sharks	50	2778	106	7	2.29	25	16	4	1121	$5,000,000
2007-08	San Jose Sharks	77	4561	163	6	2.14	46	21	8	1639	$5,000,000
2008-09	San Jose Sharks	62	3686	150	7	2.44	41	12	8	1513	$5,500,000
2009-10	San Jose Sharks	71	4194	170	3	2.43	44	16	10	1998	$6,000,000
2010-11	St. Petersburg KHL	22	1230	62	2	3.02	8	8	5	492	$4,000,000
2011-12	NY Islanders	42	2378	101	2	2.55	19	18	3	1071	$570,000

Roberto Luongo, Goalie
Born Apr 4 1979 Montreal, Que; Height 6.03, Weight 205, Shoots L
Selected by New York Islanders Round 1 #4 overall 1997 NHL Entry Draft

Season	Team	GP	Min	GA	SO	GAA	W	L	T	Svs	Salary
2000-01	Florida Panthers	47	2628	107	5	2.44	12	24	7	1333	$925,000
2001-02	Florida Panthers	58	3030	140	4	2.77	16	33	4	1653	$907,500
2002-03	Florida Panthers	65	3627	164	6	2.71	20	34	7	1847	$1,600,000
2003-04	Florida Panthers	73	4251	172	7	2.43	25	33	14	2303	$1,900,000
2005-06	Florida Panthers	75	4305	213	4	2.97	35	30	9	2275	$3,200,000
2006-07	Vancouver Canucks	76	4490	171	5	2.28	47	22	6	1998	$6,000,000
2007-08	Vancouver Canucks	73	4233	168	6	2.38	35	29	9	1861	$6,500,000
2008-09	Vancouver Canucks	54	3181	124	9	2.34	33	13	7	1418	$7,000,000
2009-10	Vancouver Canucks	68	3899	167	4	2.57	40	22	4	1748	$7,500,000
2010-11	Vancouver Canucks	60	3590	126	4	2.11	38	15	7	1627	$10,000,000
2011-12	Vancouver Canucks	55	3126	127	5	2.41	31	14	8	1450	$6,716,000

GP: Games Played; Min: Minutes played; GA: Goals against; GAA: Goals Against Average
Svs: saves; SO: shutouts; W: wins; L: Losses; T: Ties.

or ability, age, experience, athletic "intelligence," health, conditioning, the relative quality of teammates, tactical or strategic decisions made by team coaches, and other factors. An examination of the performance statistics of the two players might reveal differences in marginal productivity. One indicator of differences in ability is the draft position of the two players. When drafting players, teams assess potential draftees, and select the players with the most expected future ability. Draft order should contain information about relative ability, and the higher a player is selected in the draft, the more ability and higher marginal productivity of the player. Comparisons across drafts can be difficult, as the composition of the player pool can change from year to year, but draft order should still contain information about unobservable ability. Luongo was the fourth player selected in the 1997 draft. Nabokov was the 219th player selected in the 1994 draft. This is a large difference in draft position, and may indicate that Luongo has more ability, and thus a higher marginal product than Nabokov.

2. $S_L > S_N$ because $MR(W)_V > MR(W)_{SJ}$, the Canucks have a higher marginal revenue from each additional win than the Sharks. Note that the V subscript refers to the Canucks and the SJ subscript to the Sharks. Team specific subscripts are needed, because the team sells wins to fans to earn revenues, not the players. The models of team decision making developed earlier in the book identify a number of factors that affect the marginal revenue of a win. These include population and income per capita in the market, the presence of other professional sports teams, the price of substitutes, and fans' preferences.

10.7 Compensation Contracts in Professional Sports

The MRP approach to analyzing the pay-performance relationship in professional sports assumes that a player's underlying marginal product is not under the players control. Players are assumed to have a specific level of productivity, and, absent market imperfections, teams observe this productivity and the conditions in the output market (captured by marginal revenue) and compensate players accordingly. While this set-up can explain a number of empirical regularities in the observed pay-performance relationship in sport, it does not capture several important features of the relationship. First, the contribution of individual players to the production of wins depends on both the player's ability and the effort put forth by the player. While ability may not change, or may change slowly as human capital changes over a career, effort is quite variable and under the control of the player. Most economic models of effort also assume that effort is costly to the employee and rising at the margin. Providing additional effort generates increasing costs. This makes employees reluctant to provide effort. The provision of effort is variable and subject to increasing cost. Labor economists call the sub-optimal provision of effort by employees "shirking."

Ability clearly differs across athletes. Teams, and sports leagues, go to great lengths to try and assess the ability of players before signing them to a contract, or drafting them in the entry draft. Professional teams watch film of amateur players in action, send scouts to observe them in person, conduct closely observed workouts or tryouts, and hold mass tryouts like the NFL Combine where amateur players can be observed individually and in groups. This activity suggests that information asymmetries exist in this setting; teams have difficulty determining the actual ability of prospective players.

Second, a professional sports team and a player must agree to a level of compensation before the team observes how much effort the player will provide, and potentially before the team can observe the true ability of the player. Even a one year contract specifies how much a player will be paid over the course of a season, and is signed before the player's effort level is observed. Multi-year contracts are also common in professional sports, and under these contracts a level of compensation is specified years in advance of the point at which effort will be observed. This timing can lead to problems for the team, because of the possibility that low ability player will be mistaken for a high ability player, or that a player will provide less effort than anticipated when signed to a contract.

Third, monitoring of employees is costly for firms. In many settings it can be relatively easy for an employee to reduce effort supplied on the job without attracting the attention of the employer. In professional sports, this type of behavior can take a number of forms. Modern professional athletes must work continually to stay in top shape to perform at the highest possible level. This includes year-round conditioning and study of a team's tactical approach (studying play books, interacting with coaches and other players, etc.). Also, professional teams use complex in-game tactics designed to maximize on-field success and these tactics require significant preparation and repetitive practice to successfully execute. These tactics also require players to adjust their actions during the course of a game and the game conditions change and in response to the opponent's actions. Monitoring where a player is at on the field and where the player is going at any point in the game, relative to where the player is supposed to be at and is supposed to be going based on the specific tactic determined by the coaching staff at that point in the game may be impossible for the team. Watching a game differs significantly from monitoring a player, since fans cannot easily discern what a player was supposed to do at any point in the game.

Fourth, players may be risk averse. Injuries are common in professional sport; an athlete's career can end or be seriously disrupted in the blink of an eye due to injury. The provision of effort may increase risk, and players may be unwilling to provide increasing levels of effort because they are unwilling to accept the additional risk that comes with the provision of additional effort.

These problems are widespread in labor markets, and are not limited to professional sports. The interests of workers (high salaries and relatively low provision of effort to reduce costs) are often different from the interests of firms (high provision of effort and low salaries to maximize profits). In general, firms attempt to solve these problems by providing workers with formal incentives in the form of compensation schemes specified in employment contracts in order to induce the employee to behave in the way the firm wants, typically to provide enough effort even though effort is costly and monitoring difficult.

One common feature of sports labor contracts is performance bonuses. For example, in the NFL in 2009, the last year that detailed contract data are available, the *USAToday* reported salary information for 1,856 NFL players. The average base salary in this sample was \$1,157,990. 78% of these players had a contract with a performance bonus of some sort, and the average value of the performance bonus paid to NFL players was \$324,072, roughly 28% of the average base salary. In the NFL, base salary is paid to a player who remains on the roster for the entire season, no matter how many games are played or how well or poorly the player performs and performance bonuses are paid based on in-season outcomes, implying that teams want to provide players with some incentives during the season. The next section develops a model to motivate this compensation scheme.

10.7.1   A Principal-Agent Model of Compensation Contracts

Consider a contract between a team (the principal) and an athlete (the agent) that the team uses to influence the behavior of the athlete. A player can take some action, $a \geq 0$, which can be thought of as effort. a is not easily observed by the team, but the team wants the player to take this action in order to win games and maximize profits. This action could be characterized as "doing what the coach wants the player to do when the coach tells the player to do it" in this context. The player is risk averse and cares only about wages w and the action a, which is costly to undertake. The cost of action to a player is

$$c(a) = \frac{c}{2}a^2$$

where c is the marginal cost of the player providing an additional unit of athletic action. The player's utility function is

$$V = v(a) = -e^{-r\left(w - \frac{c}{2}a^2\right)}$$

where $r \geq 0$ is a parameter that captures the player's risk aversion. The larger is r the more risk averse the player. r is called a constant absolute risk aversion parameter in this context, and

$$\frac{-v''(a)}{v'(a)} = r.$$

The player has reservation utility U^* which is simply the utility the player gets from his best option outside professional sport. The player chooses a to maximize utility given his wages.

The team is risk neutral. Although the team cannot directly observe a, it can observe a signal related to a. This observed signal is

$$y = a + \alpha + \varepsilon_y$$

where α is the player's ability and ε_y is a random variable distributed normally with mean zero and variance σ_y^2. ε_y represents random factors that keep the team from perfectly observing a, and σ_y^2 is the measurement error associated with the observable signal y. In a sports context, observing the signal y and not a player's action a means that the coaching staff can observe the outcome of a specific set of tactical decisions used in a game, but not the actual activity that the player puts into executing this set of tactical coaching decisions. Ability, α, is observable and known to both the team and the athlete. The higher player ability, the larger the observable signal y.

The team maximizes profit, which is expected output minus wage costs: $\pi = a + \alpha - w$.[3] This assumption implies that the output of the team is the player's ability plus the expected actions supplied by the player. It abstracts from pricing and marginal revenue effects.

Given the player's utility function and team's objectives, and normally distributed random components, it can be shown that the optimal compensation contract offered by teams to players takes a linear form in this context

$$w = \beta_0 + \beta_y y$$

where β_0 is "base" salary that does not depend on performance and β_y is a performance bonus per unit of observable signal. In this linear compensation contract, compensation is a function of two additive components. β_y is called "piece-work" compensation in the contracting literature, since it is pay per unit of some observable output by the worker. The role of the base salary β_0 in this contract is to get the player to join the team, which depends on the reservation utility. The base salary must be at least as large as the player's reservation utility, or the player will not sign the contract. The performance bonus is designed to induce the player to supply the amount of action desired by the team to maximize profits. Given this contract, profit is

$$\pi = a + \alpha - w = a + \alpha - (\beta_0 + \beta_y(a + \alpha + \varepsilon_y)) = (1 - \beta_y)a + (1 - \beta_y)\alpha - \beta_0 - \beta_y\varepsilon_y.$$

---

[3]Note profit depends on expected output. Actual output is $a + \alpha + \varepsilon_y$ and $E[a + \alpha + \varepsilon_y] = a + \alpha$ since $E[\varepsilon_y] = 0$.

Substituting the definition of output and wages into the utility function yields

$$V = -e^{-r\left(\beta_0 + \beta_y(a + \alpha + \varepsilon_y) - \frac{c}{2}a^2\right)}$$

Given the optimal linear contract, the optimal level of action provided by the player is

$$a^* = \frac{\beta_y}{c}.$$

The largest action level a team can induce a player to supply is $\frac{1}{c}$, which only takes place when $\beta_y = 1$. However, in this case the team earns zero profits, since it means that $w = a + \alpha$. The team can only induce the player to provide maximum action by offering to pay the player the total revenues earned by the team. This outcome happens in real world labor contracting agreements. For example, the owner of taxicabs must come to a compensation agreement with drivers. The effort and revenues generated by a taxi are difficult for cab owners to monitor, since the cabs are on the road and compensation based on sharing metered fares can be manipulated by the driver accepting fares off meter. Most compensation contracts for taxis involve the owner receiving a flat fee from the driver and the driver keeping all revenues generated in the cab.

Instead, in this setting it is possible to show that the largest performance bonus a profit maximizing team will offer is

$$\beta_y^* = \frac{1}{1 + rc\sigma_y^2} \leq 1.$$

This expression for the optimal incentive provided by teams to players, in terms of compensation per unit of observable signal, has clear intuition. If players are risk neutral ($r = 0$), $\beta_y^* = 1$ and $a^* = \frac{1}{c}$, so players provide maximum action. One reason teams cannot induce players to provide maximal action is because players are risk averse. Another is the noise in inferring the player's effort (a) based on the observable signal (y). This noise is captured by σ_y^2. When $\sigma_y^2 = 0$, there is no measurement error in the signal and variation in y reflects variation in a. In this case, $\beta_y^* = 1$ and players provide maximum effort; as $\sigma_y^2 = 0$ a gets farther from a^*.

This expression for performance bonus size highlights an important feature in the labor contracting literature: a tradeoff exists between player's risk aversion and incentives to provide additional effort. Risk averse workers do not respond as strongly to incentives as risk neutral workers. This tradeoff is reflected in the inverse relationship between r and β_y^**.

10.7.2 Implications of Compensation Contracts

This principal-agent contracting model has several other important implications for the relationship between performance and pay in professional sport. First, the fact that the optimal contract in this setting implies that compensation should depend on both effort (a) and ability (α), leads to the *Informativeness Principal* which says that any measure of worker performance that reveals information about worker effort (a) should be included in the compensation contract. Contracts in professional sports contain a wide variety of performance bonuses. many of these bonuses depend on general achievement, like making all-star teams, and not specific events like the number of home runs hit or the number of points scored. The informativeness principal applies to sport, but not completely. The reason for this is that athletic performance is a complex activity that involves many different contributions, and not all contributions contribute to winning. For example, consider a performance bonus based on the number of home runs a player hits in a season. A player facing this sort of incentive might attempt to hit home runs in every batting situation, even when, for example, the current situation required a sacrifice fly instead of a home run.

A second important implication of this model is that *relative performance evaluation* matters more than absolute performance evaluation. The measurement error inherent in the observation of employee effort makes it difficult for the firm to sort out the effects of worker effort (a) from the noise component (σ_y^2). However, in the case where employees working in similar positions are subject to correlated random noise, then comparing the performance of these employees can provide information about their effort. Consider two sales workers selling the same product in a setting where both of these sales persons are subject to market wide random variation in demand. The number of units of the good sold by each are both subject to the same demand shocks, going up and down by the same proportion in response to market wide variation. So the relative performance of each reveals information about the effort provided by both.

A third important implication is that selection effects of contracts are important in this context. Suppose that the firm cannot observe worker ability (α) but workers know their true ability. In this case, high ability workers (those with large αs) will want contracts with large β_y, because the return to effort is higher under these contacts. To see this, consider two workers, Worker 1 and Worker 2. Worker 1 has higher ability than Worker 2, so $\alpha_1 > \alpha_2$. The firm only observes $y = \alpha + a$, so for any level of observed signal y, Worker 1 has to supply less effort to achieve a signal equal to Worker 2's. Worker 1 will prefer a larger performance bonus than Worker 2. Relative performance evaluation policies enhance this effect.

In professional sport, it is often the case that the team observes only the outcome of the collective effort of all players, and can only imperfectly observe the effort of individuals. The outcome of an individual offensive play in a football game depends on the actions of all the offensive players. The case where individual effort cannot be easily observed and output depends on the actions of many workers is called "team production" in the compensation contract literature. The key aspect of team production is the classic free-riding moral hazard problem. If the contribution of individual players to team success cannot be easily monitored by the coaching staff, then each individual player has an incentive to provide less effort, as his reduced effort means lower effort cost without lowering his earnings proportionately. In other words, under team production, each individual member of a team has an incentive to free-ride on the effort of other team members.

Professional sports teams clearly face potential free-riding problems associated with team production. A number of solutions to this problem have been explored. The most common solution to free-riding in team production is profit sharing. Under profit sharing, the compensation contract features terms where each member of a team receives an equal share of the profits generated by the team.

Profit sharing is not common in professional sports, except in the allocation of money from playoff appearances. Consider, for example, the allocation of postseason bonuses in Major League Baseball. Postseason appearances are not typically covered as part of the standard contract signed by each MLB player. Instead, playoff appearances are compensated through the use of a playoff pool, which is 60% of the gate revenues from each postseason game for the minimum number of games played in each level of the postseason (the Wild Card game, the first three games of each five game Division Series, and the first four games of the seven game League Championship and World Series). Each player receives a share of the revenue pool for compensation, an example of profit sharing. Note that the compensation pool is based on the minimum number of games, and not the actual number of games played to remove any incentive for players to extend the length of a series just to earn additional compensation. Consider a team up 3-0 in a best-of-seven playoff series. The team up three games would have a strong incentive to lose game four if the compensation pool was based on the gate revenues for each playoff game, since an additional playoff game could potentially increase the compensation pool by 20%.

Also, note that the free riding problem under team production also implies selection problems when ability is unobservable. Workers with less ability will want to work in a team environment, since their lower ability can earn a higher return in that environment, where other workers can make up for their lower ability with an increased provision of effort.

Finally, the optimal compensation contract developed above is linear; given the utility function and presence of risk aversion, teams offer players a base salary plus performance money that rises uniformly with player actions. This linear property is a function of the properties of the utility function assumed. In may other contexts, the optimal contracts are non-linear functions of the signal observed by firms. This is consistent with observed compensation contracts in professional sport. Many of the performance bonuses are non-linear: players get a specified amount of money for making the all-star team or league MVP, and zero otherwise. Such contracts are non-linear in player performance.

10.8 Summary

Professional athletes in team sports earn large salaries. Economic theory predicts that players earn these large salaries because profit maximizing firms pay workers a wage equal to marginal revenue produce, and professional athletes have a high MRP. In addition, professional athletes have relatively rare abilities which also commands a premium in the labor market.

In general, the pay-performance relationship in professional sport bears out the standard predictions of the economic theory of labor markets. Empirical research suggests that athletes in the absence of market imperfections like the Reserve Clause generally earn a salary equal to their estimated MRP. Human capital has an important effect on earnings, and the age-earnings profile of professional athletes follows the standard hump-shape generated by the accumulation and eventual depreciation of human capital.

Although the standard model of labor markets predicts that workers earn a salary equal to their marginal revenue product, most player contracts in professional sports leagues include both a base salary and some performance related compensation. Teams and players must agree on a compensation scheme before the team observes the ability and effort put forth by players. This leads to standard principal-agent problems like moral hazard and shirking. The principal-agent model of compensation contracts developed in this chapter highlight the problems that arise when teams and players contact for compensation before ability and action are observed, and when action is costly to players, as well as solutions to these problems. The contracts observed in professional sports are consistent with the predictions of principal-agent models of compensation contracts. The presence of many performance bonuses in professional sports contracts suggest that teams realize that they must offer players incentives to provide more effort. However, little empirical research has been done on this relationship in sports economics to date. One reason for this lack of evidence is that the selection effects are very difficult to separate from the incentive effects.

Readings and References

Lewis, M. (2003) *Moneyball: The Art of Winning an Unfair Game*, W.W. Norton and Co.: New York, NY.

Prendergast, C. (1999) "The provision of incentives in firms," *Journal of Economic Literature*, 37(1):7-63.

Scully, G, (1974) "Pay and Performance in Major League Baseball," *American Economic Review*, 64(6): 915-930.

Rosen, S. and A. Sanderson (2001) "Labour Markets in Professional Sports," *The Economic Journal*, 111(5): F47-F68.

Review Questions

1. True, False or Uncertain: Prior to the introduction of free agency in MLB, most players were paid a salary equal to their marginal revenue product. (*10 points, 10 minutes*)

2. The table below shows performance statistics for two NHL players for the 2000-2001 and 2001-2002 seasons. Age and experience are in years. Salaries are in US dollars. Jarome Iginla grew up in St. Albert; Peter Bondra grew up in the USSR. The following questions pertain to these two players.

Player	Position	Season	Team	Salary	Games	Points	Age	Experience
Jarome Iginla	RW	2000	Flames	1,700,000	77	71	23	6
Jarome Iginla	RW	2001	Flames	1,700,000	82	96	24	7
Peter Bondra	RW	2000	Capitals	3,775,000	82	81	32	11
Peter Bondra	RW	2001	Capitals	4,500,000	77	70	33	12

   (a) Briefly explain the economic model of the determination of salaries discussed in this chapter.

   (b) Based on this model, what factors contributed to the observed difference between the salary earned by Iginla and Bondra in these two seasons.

   (c) Explain the experience-earnings relationship in labor market. Explain how the experience-earnings relationship applies to the case of the Iginla-Bondra salary comparison.

Chapter 11

The Economics of Individual Sports

Chapter Objectives

- Understand why sports contests often use non-linear prize structures

- Understand the relationship between the incentives generated by prize structures and effort supplied by participants in contests

- Understand the predictions made by tournament theory, and how this applies to sports and other settings

- Understand the evidence supporting the predictions of tournament theory

11.1 Introduction: Contests

The 117th Boston Marathon was run in April 2013. In addition to a mass-participation sporting event, this race attracted a field of top men's and women's marathon runners from around the world. The race attracted elite runners by offering prizes for the fastest times in the field; the total prize purse for the race was $806,000. Table 11.1 shows the distribution of prizes awarded to different runners by gender and age. In addition to these prizes, the race offered to pay a $50,000 bonus to any male runner breaking the men's World Record Marathon time of 2:03:02 or any female runner breaking the women's World Record Marathon time of 2:15:25, and a bonus of $25,000 for any runner breaking a course record time. The "Masters" class contains runners age 40 and up; smaller bonuses were offered to Master's class runners as well.

Note the highly "non-linear" prize structure. The farther down in the standings a runner finished, the smaller the prize, and the smaller the gap between prizes. The second place prize is 50% of the first place prize, the third place prize is 53% of the second prize, and the fourth place prize is 62% of the third place prize.

Ethiopian Lelisa Desisa won the Men's competition in 2 hours 10 minutes and 22 seconds. Second place finisher Micah Kogo of Kenya finished just 5 seconds behind Desisa, and third place finisher Gebregziabher Gebremariam of Ethiopia finished only one second behind Kogo. Look at the difference in winnings for these three runners. 5 seconds made the difference between a $150,000 and a $75,000 payoff for Kogo, and six seconds the difference between $150,000 and $40,000 for Gebremariam.

Why did the organizers of the Boston Marathon offer this prize distribution? Why did they offer prizes at all? Economists call individual sporting events like road races, golf tournaments, tennis

Table 11.1: 2013 Boston Marathon Prize Structure

Class Place	Men Open Prize	Women Open Prize	Men Masters Prize	Women Masters Prize
1	$150,000	$150,000	$10,000	$10,000
2	$75,000	$75,000	$5,000	$5,000
3	$40,000	$40,000	$2,500	$2,500
4	$25,000	$25,000	$1,500	$1,500
5	$15,000	$15,000	$1,000	$1,000
6	$12,000	$12,000	——	——
7	$9,000	$9,000	——	——
8	$7,400	$7,400	——	——
9	$5,700	$5,700	——	——
10	$4,200	$4,200	——	——
11	$2,600	$2,600	——	——
12	$2,100	$2,100	——	——
⋮	⋮	⋮	⋮	⋮
15	$1,500	$1,500	——	——

tournaments, and other individual sporting competitions *rank order tournaments*, because the rank order of finish, and not the actual difference in times or scores, determines where competitors finish in the contest. The fact that the fourth place finisher was nearly a minute behind third place finisher Gebremariam made no difference in the final standings.

Almost all rank order tournaments in professional sport have non-linear prize structures. Similar competitions in other areas of the labor force, like in corporations, exhibit similar payoff structures. Economists studying the salary structure of large corporations noticed that the top employee, the CEO, typically earns much more than the second ranking employee. Working for a corporation can be viewed as a contest where many employees vie for the position of CEO but only one "wins" the top prize and gets the large payoff.

Corporations and race organizers face a similar design problem. They want to design a compensation system that provides an incentive for the best people to join the competition (or take a job in the corporation) and for all participants (or employees) to provide maximum effort in the contest. The organizers of the Boston Marathon are interested in putting on an exciting race, where the best marathon runners in the world compete, and all competitors run as fast as possible over the course of the race; this type of race will be of interest to fans, sponsors, and media outlets, and generate maximum profits for the race organizers. This chapter explores the relationship between incentives, in the form of prizes, and effort in contests like the Boston Marathon, the United States Open Golf Tournament, and the contest to become the next CEO of Amazon.

11.2   Tournament Theory and Contest Design

Consider the problem facing the organizer of a sporting contest or tournament. This contest could be a foot race, bicycle race, car race, or swimming contest. The organizer is a profit maximizer who can be thought of as the owner of the venue where the event will be held. The organizer generates revenues through the sale of tickets, concessions, broadcast rights, and other economic activities related to the staging of the event. The organizer assumes that the number of spectators will depend on the quality of the athletes that enter the event and the effort put forth by entrants. The higher the quality of the entrants and the more collective effort put forth, the greater fan interest, and the larger the revenues earned by the organizer.[1]

The organizer wants to design a contest that will attract the highest quality participants and elicit maximum effort on the part of the participants, as this will maximize the revenues earned. The organizer provides incentives to participants in the form of prizes awarded in a predetermined way. This is an economic decision involving incentives on the part of the contest organizer and entry and effort decisions on the part of athletes.

11.2.1 A Two-Person Contest

Consider a simple contest with only two participants, Al (a) and Bob (b). Al and Bob will compete for two prizes; the winner of the contest gets W_1 and the loser gets W_2 where $W_1 > W_2$. Note that this is not the only possible prize structure; a single prize W could be offered instead of two prizes, resulting in a winner-take-all contest. We seldom observe winner-take-all contests in sport, so they will not be discussed here, but the analysis and predictions are similar. Alan and Bob compete by supplying effort, e. Think of effort as running faster, or jumping higher, in the contest. Most individual sporting events involve contestants supplying effort in some form. Al and Bob choose effort levels e_a and e_b.

Effort is costly to supply. Running or swimming faster eventually becomes painful; economists call this increasing pain the "cost" of Al and Bob supplying effort. Some might argue that elite athletes supply maximum effort in every contest they enter. But effort could also include time and attention put into training that takes place over weeks or months and maximum effort could be difficult to maintain over this time period. In addition, marathons last hours, golf tournaments four days, and Grand Slam tennis tournaments several weeks; athletes are unlikely to be able to supply maximum effort throughout this long a period of time. Assume that the marginal cost of supplying effort increases. A cost function reflects the cost of supplying any level of effort for both contestants ($i = a, b$)

$$C_i = C(e_i)$$

and a simple cost function with increasing marginal cost of effort is

$$C_i = \frac{c}{2}e_i^2 \tag{11.1}$$

The marginal cost of effort can be found by differentiation: $C'(e_i) = ce_i$ for Equation (11.1). ce_i is the marginal cost of effort and this marginal cost increases with e. Graphically, this is a simple quadratic function running through the origin. The slope of a line tangent to the effort cost function at any effort level is the marginal cost of effort. Note that based on 11.1, the slope of these tangent lines increase moving left to right along the effort cost curve.

The outcome of this contest is uncertain. The relationship between the amount of effort supplied by each contestant and the the probability that a contestant wins the first prize W_1 is called a *contest success function* or CSF. Assume a simple contest success function

$$P_i = \rho e_i$$

---

[1]The standard reference for tournament theory is Lazear and Rosen (1981). Rosen (1988) is a good non-technical discussion of these models.

Figure 11.1: Effort Return and Cost Functions

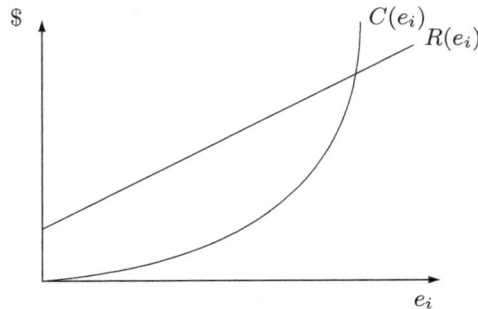

where P is the probability that contestant i wins the first prize and ρ is the return to effort, in terms of the increased probability of winning the contest for each additional unit of effort supplied by the contestant. Effort can be defined as the percent of total possible effort supplied ($0 < e < 1$) to limit success probabilities to the (0,1) interval. If P_i is the probability of winning the first prize and there are two contestants, then the probability of winning the second prize is $(1 - P_i)$, and the expected return to the contestant is

$$R_i = R(e_i) = W_1 P_i + W_2 (1 - P_i)$$

Substituting the CSF into this equation for the return to effort gives

$$R_i = R(e_i) = W_1 \rho e_i + W_2 (1 - \rho e_i)$$

which shows how the expected return changes as each contestant supplies more effort. The expected return is increasing in effort, as can be seen on Figure 11.1. As effort increases, the probability that the contestant wins the first prize increases, which increases expected return. Note that the return function is a linear relationship and can be rearranged into standard slope-intercept form

$$R(e_i) = \rho(W_1 - W_2)e_i + W_2$$

where W_2 is the intercept and $\rho(W_1 - W_2)$ is the slope of this linear expected return function. The slope of the expected return function is also the marginal return to increasing effort by one unit; $R'(e_i) = \rho(W_1 - W_2)$.

The optimum effort supplied by each contestant is found at the point where effort generates the maximum net return. That is the level of effort where the vertical distance between the effort return line and the effort cost curve is largest. This vertical distance is maximized when the marginal return to effort is equal to the marginal cost of effort. Graphically, this involves shifting the effort return down until it is tangent to the effort cost curve and finding the effort level beneath this point.

Algebraically, the optimum level of effort can be found by setting marginal revenue equal to marginal cost and solving for effort

$$MR = R'(e_i) = \rho(W_1 - W_2) = ce_i = C'(e_i) = MC$$

the optimal effort level of effort supplied by the contestants is

$$e_i^* = \frac{\rho(W_1 - W_2)}{c}. \tag{11.2}$$

Note that this expression has intuitive appeal. The optimal level of effort increases with the marginal return to effort ρ, and decreases with the marginal cost of effort c. Also, the optimal level of effort supplied increases with the spread of the prizes $(W_1 - W_2)$. This explains why contest organizers like the organizers of the Boston Marathon, the US Open, and other individual sports contests, adopt non-linear prize structures with a large drop off between the first and second prize: this prize structure induces additional effort supply from all contestants. However, contest organizers cannot make the prize spread too large, because reducing the value of the second prize, W_2, reduces optimal effort.

If we assume that Al and Bob are identical, in that they both have the same marginal return to effort, ρ and marginal cost of effort, c, then Al and Bob both supply the same amount of effort in the contest. While this makes determining the winner of the contest difficult, it is straightforward to add a random aspect to the contest which will determine the winner even when equal effort is supplied by the contestants. The next section adds a random component to the contest. If Al and Bob have different ρ and c, then the contestant with the largest ρ, or smallest c supplies more effort and wins the contest.

Next, consider the problem faced by the contest organizer. A contest organizer takes the actions of the participants as given, in terms of the optimum effort that will be supplied by the participants, and sets a prize structure that maximizes total effort. In this simple model, we assume that the contest organizer only cares about the total effort supplied by all contestants. It would be easy to change the model to include that assumption that total effort has some monetary return to the contest organizer, in terms of ticket sales or media broadcast rights, but this would not alter the predictions that emerge from the model.

The contest organizer maximizes profits, which is defined as the difference between the total effort supplied by contestants and the total prize pool paid out to winners. Again, assuming identical abilities, Al and Bob supply the same amount of effort in this contest, $e_a^* = e_b^* = e$, so total effort supplied is $e^* + e^* = 2e^*$. The total prize pool is $W_1 + W_2$, so total profit earned by the organizer is $2e - (W_1 + W_2)$. This is usually written as

$$MAX \quad e - \left(\frac{(W_1 + W_2)}{2} \right) \tag{11.3}$$

where the second term is the *average* prize, since this reflects what a contestant could expect to win. The contest organizer chooses W_1 and W_2. However, the contest organizer also faces an additional constraint. The prize pool offered must be large enough to attract contestants to enter the contest. This is important because effort is costly to participants, and they will not enter a contest that has an expected prize that is not large enough to cover this cost. Formally, this constraint, called the *participation constraint* is

$$\left(\frac{(W_1 + W_2)}{2} \right) = C(e)$$

where $C(e)$ is the effort cost function faced by participants. Substituting the participation constraint into the profit maximization problem solved by the contest organizer, Equation (11.3) gives a profit function for the contest organizer of $e - C(e)$. Since the contest organizer chooses W_1 and W_2 and takes the decisions of the participants as given, the contest organizer's decision can be better seen by substituting the equation for the optimum effort by participants, Equation (11.2) and the effort cost function, Equation (11.1) into this profit function. This gives a profit function for the organizer

Figure 11.2: Contest Organizer's Profit Function

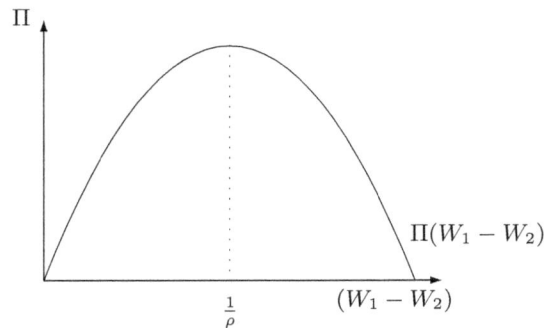

expressed only in terms of W_1, W_2 and parameters. The contest organizer chooses W_1 and W_2 to maximize profits

$$\Pi = \frac{\rho}{c}(W_1 - W_2) - \frac{c}{2}\left[\frac{\rho}{c}(W_1 - W_2)\right]^2 .$$

Note that this is a quadratic function of the prize spread $(W_1 - W_2)$. As the prize spread increases, profits initially increase as the effort supplied by contestants increase. However, the marginal cost of also increases, and the this requires the organizer to increase the second prize by more in order to satisfy the participant constraint and get participants to enter. This eventually reduces profits. Figure 11.2 graphically depicts the contest organizer's profit function.

The profit maximizing prize spread can be found from the profit function using calculus. Taking the derivative of the profit function with respect to $W_1 - W_2$, setting equal to zero and solving yields a solution: $W_1 - W_2 = \frac{1}{\rho}$. The profit maximizing prize spread is proportional to the inverse of the return to effort, ρ. As the return to effort gets smaller, the profit maximizing prize spread gets larger. Put another way, the profit maximizing first prize is the second prize plus a mark-up that depends on the marginal return to effort, $(W_1 = W_2 + \frac{1}{\rho})$, and the smaller the return to effort, the larger the markup.

11.2.2   Random Factors in Contests

Now suppose we observe the combination of the actual effort that Alan and Bob exert in the contest and some random performance component that represents luck, or factors beyond Al and Bob's control, like the weather. Many contests involve both planned effort and luck or other unpredictable aspects. Let ϵ represent this random component of performance. In the contest, we actually observe y, the sum of effort and luck, for each participant. For Al, we observe

$$y_a = e_a + \epsilon_a$$

and for Bob we observe

$$y_b = e_b + \epsilon_b.$$

and the participants only control e_i as before. The presence of random factors affecting outcomes changes the relationship between effort and success. Both Al and Bob are subject to random "shocks" in the form of realizations of random variables ϵ_a and ϵ_b that affect the observed outcomes, y_i. The probability that Al wins the contest is now

$$P = Prob(e_a + \epsilon_a > e_b + \epsilon_b) = Prob(e_a - e_b > \epsilon_a - \epsilon_b).$$

This probability depends on both the effort supplied by Al and Bob and the distribution of the random variables ϵ_a and ϵ_b. We can define a probability function $G(e_a - e_b)$ that reflects the probability that $e_a - e_b$ is greater than $\epsilon_a - \epsilon_b$. That is, the probability that the difference in the effort supplied by Al and Bob is greater than the luck experienced by Al and Bob. This function captures the effect of luck on the contest outcome and depends on the distribution of the random variables ϵ_a and ϵ_b. Given this new component of the contest, the optimal effort supplied becomes

$$e_i^* = g(e_a - e_b)\frac{\rho(W_1 - W_2)}{c}. \tag{11.4}$$

where $g(e_a - e_b)$ is the probability density function for the probability distribution function $G(e_a - e_b)$. $g(e_a - e_b)$ reflects the importance of luck in the contest, and as luck becomes more important in determining the outcome, $g(e_a - e_b)$ gets larger. Clearly, the presence of luck in contests leads to increased optimal effort supplied by contestants, which explains why contest organizers may intentionally introduce features in their contests that increase the importance of luck, for example mass starts or holding contests in conditions where weather plays a role in the outcome. We can now determine the winner of the contest even when equal effort is supplied, based on the realizations of ϵ_a and ϵ_b. If $\epsilon_a > \epsilon_b$, then Al wins the contest.

11.2.3 Contests with Multiple Participants

The simple contest analyzed above has only two participants, which makes it easy to analyze graphically. However, most actual contests in sport have more than two participants. Szymanski (2003) analyzed the economics of contests with many participants. In these models, the outcomes depend on the effort supplied by contestants, as in the models above, but the contest success function takes a different, expanded form

$$p_i = \frac{e_i^\gamma}{\sum_{j=1}^n e_j^\gamma}$$

where p_i is the probability that contestant i wins the contest, e is contestant effort and γ is a measure of the discriminatory power of the contest success function. As γ gets larger, the CSF is able to distinguish among smaller and smaller differences in contestant effort. As γ gets smaller, the CSF cannot easily distinguish between levels of effort. Contests based solely on time, or height jumped, would have large γ while contests based on judging, like figure skating, or partially on judging, like ski jumping or slopeside skiing, have small γ.

The optimum effort supply for a contest with a first prize W_1 and second prize W_2 and with this sort of contest success function is

$$e_i^* = \frac{\gamma(W_1 - W_2)(n - 1)}{n^2}$$

where n is the number of participants. This is quite similar to the expressions described above for optimum effort, except that this optimal effort equation equation predicts that the larger the number of participants in the contest, the less effort supplied by each participant. The more participants, the lower the likelihood that any participant wins the contest, and the less effort supplied. This explains why most sports contests limit the number of participants in some way; examples include the cut line in golf, minimum qualifying times in foot races, and the use of qualifying heats in many athletic contests. Letting more participants in the contest reduces total effort, reducing the profits earned by the organizers.

11.3   Evidence on Tournament Theory

The contest models described above have clear predictions about prizes and outcomes: larger prize spreads induce more effort on the part of participants, contests with a high degree of discriminatory power induce more effort, and more participants in a contest leads to lower participant effort. There is another important aspect of tournament theory, called the *sorting effect*. Most athletes have different abilities. Larger prize pools attract better athletes to enter contests or tournaments, since the return to winning is larger in these contests. Thus contests with larger total prize pools should have better performance. Given these clear predictions, and the availability of data on tournament prize structures and outcomes, a large number of studies have analyzed the outcomes of athletic contests for evidence of tournament effects.

Empirical tests of tournament theory typically analyze variation in an outcome variable related to effort as the dependent variable in a regression model, and use explanatory variables that reflect the total prize pool or the spread in prizes to capture the strength of the tournament incentives, and other factors that might affect effort like weather and other factors that might exogenously affect contestants, as explanatory variables to explain observed variation in effort.

In the first test of tournament theory using sports data, Ehrenberg and Bognano (*Journal of Political Economy*, 1990) analyzed the outcomes of Professional Golfers' Association (PGA) tour events in the 1984 season. The effort variable was total strokes by each participant in each tournament. Ehrenberg and Bognano observed that the prize structure was identical for all PGA events in their sample, but the value of the total prize pool differed; because of this, Ehrenberg and Bognano used only the total prize pool as an explanatory variable to proxy for the tournament incentives present in these contests. Ehrenberg and Bognano found that increasing the total size of the prize pool by $100,000 decreased average scores in a PGA tour event by about 1.1 strokes per round played. This is interpreted as evidence of tournament incentives affecting effort in these contests.

A number of additional empirical tests of tournament theory have been carried out in many different settings involving individual sports. These studies use different measures of effort: time in foot races and alpine skiing events, average speed in NASCAR races, games won in tennis matches, etc. In general, these effort measures are observed for every participant in the contest. These studies also use different measures of the spread in the prize distribution in these contests, including interquartile range, standard deviations of prizes offered, and Gini coefficients; many simply use the total prize pool, like Ehrenberg and Bognano.

Figure 11.3 summarizes the results of a number of tests of tournament theory. In this figure, the relationship between the prize spread or total prize pool and effort has been converted to an elasticity. The values on the vertical axis show the increase in effort, in percent, associated with a 1% increase in the prize pool or prize spread in these sports. The horizontal axis shows the year that the data come from; in the case where multiple seasons of data were analyzed, the value on the vertical axis is the last year of data in the sample.

Empirical tests of tournament theory assume that the observed outcomes for each participant reflect optimal effort supply. Recall that the optimal effort function from the model developed above predicts that the optimal effort supplied depends on the prize spread (or total prize pool), and other factors like the extent that luck plays in determining the winner, the ability of the CSF to discriminate among effort levels, and the number of participants. Wile the elasticity should be positive, the size of the elasticity of effort with respect to changes in tournament incentives will vary with these other factors, and may also be affected by econometric problems like omitted variables.

The elasticities shown on Figure 11.3 are positive and statistically different from zero, providing strong evidence supporting the predictions of tournament theory. Athletes in these contests apepar

Figure 11.3: Effort Elasticity Estimates

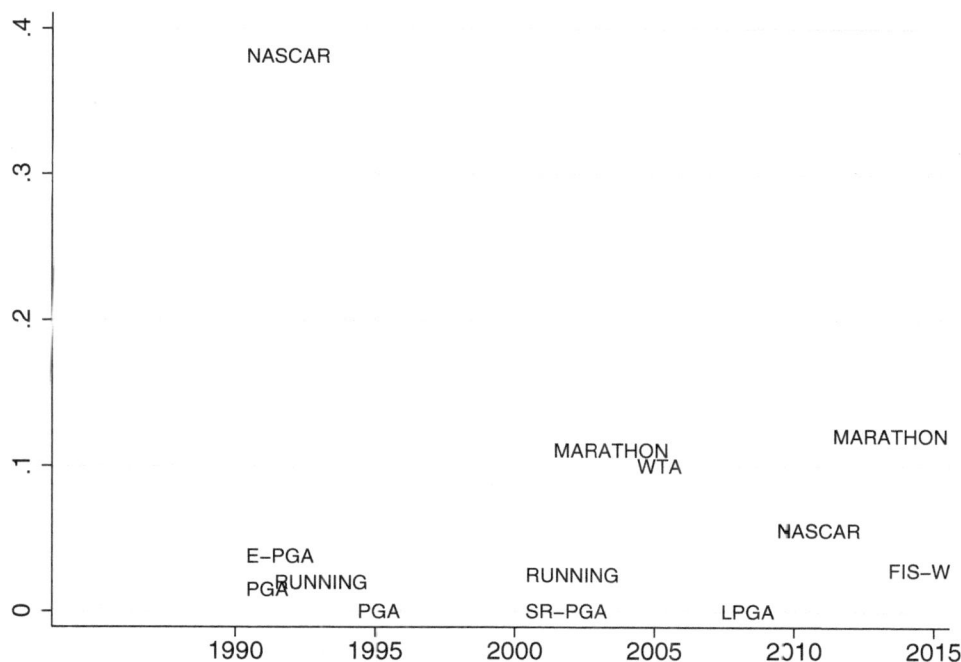

to increase effort in response to increases in the prize spread or prize pool. However, many of the effort elasticities are quite small. For example, the effort elasticities in the various golf tournaments are generally very small, on the order of 0.02, but statistically different from zero, suggesting that the effort response to changes in the prize spread or prize pool in these events is quite small. This could reflect the fact that course conditions and the nature of the game prohibit players from shooting very low scores relative to par. The effort elasticities from the two studies analyzing running contests, and the women's alpine skiing study (FIS-W), are also relatively low. The evidence from running events (foot races) comes from a very heterogenous sample of races at different distances and includes races with relatively small prize pools that may not attract high quality runners; this may limit the ability of participants to increase effort to the same extent as elite runners. The FIS event, women's downhill, is a relatively short duration, high-speed race, and the high risk of crashing in this race may also limit the effort response by driving up the cost of effort. The estimated effort elasticity for marathon races, tennis, and NASCAR, are all much higher, which may reflect the ability of marathon runners, tennis players, and NASCAR drivers to more easily increase their effort.

The differences in the effort elasticities for the two NASCAR studies differs substantially. This difference can be explained by the different proxies for effort used in the two studies. In the early NASCAR study with a very high estimated effort elasticity, the effort variable was constructed based on the rank order finish in each race and the winning time, a rather crude approximation of actual times. In the later study with lower estimated effort elasticity, the effort variable is the average speed of participants in each race.

Summary

Athletic contests like the Boston Marathon and the US Open often have highly non-linear rank-order payoffs to winners. In these contests, a small difference in effort can lead to large differences in winnings; putts on the last few holes of the final round in golf's "major" tournaments can lead to changes in winnings of hundreds of thousands of dollars for players at the top of the leader board. This chapter develops a model, called tournament theory or contest theory by economists, to explain why we observe these type of payoff structures in athletic events, and to illustrate how these incentives affect effort put forth by participants. This model assumes that providing effort is costly, and the cost rises at the margin; it also assumes that contest outcomes are uncertain. In this model, profit maximizing contest organizers realize that the supply of effort is costly, and design prize structures to induce participants to provide maximum effort, and to enter the contest.

The predictions of this model have significant empirical support. A large number of studies analyzing the relationship between effort supplied in foot races, golf tournaments, car racing, and other individual sports find that effort increases with the prize structure and total prize pool, suggesting that participants in athletic contests respond to these tournament incentives. This model also has applications outside sport. For example, human resource departments in large corporations often use concepts from tournament theory when designing the compensation structure in corporations. In this sense, corporate employees provide effort (work long hours) in an attempt to climb the corporate ladder and win the grand prize of a multi-million dollar CEO salary.

Readings and References

Ehrenberg, Ronald G and Bognanno, Michael L, (1990). Do Tournaments Have Incentive Effects?, *Journal of Political Economy*, 98(6), 1307-1324.

Lazear, Edward P and Rosen, Sherwin, (1981). Rank-Order Tournaments as Optimum Labor Contracts, *Journal of Political Economy*, 89(5), 841-864.

Rosen, Sherwin. (1988). Promotions, elections and other contests. *Journal of Institutional and Theoretical Economics*, 144(1), 73-90.

Szymanski, S., (2003). The Economic Design of Sporting Contests. *Journal of Economic Literature*, 41(4), 1137-1187.